Coolies and Cane

Coolies and Cane

Race, Labor, and Sugar in
the Age of Emancipation

Moon-Ho Jung

The Johns Hopkins University Press
Baltimore

© 2006 The Johns Hopkins University Press
All rights reserved. Published 2006
Printed in the United States of America on acid-free paper
9 8 7 6 5 4 3 2 1

The Johns Hopkins University Press
2715 North Charles Street
Baltimore, Maryland 21218-4363
www.press.jhu.edu

Library of Congress Cataloging-in-Publication Data

Jung, Moon-Ho, 1969–
   Coolies and cane : race, labor, and sugar in the age of emancipation /
Moon-Ho Jung.
       p.   cm.
   Includes bibliographical references and index.
   ISBN 0-8018-8281-8 (hardcover : alk. paper)
       1. Asian Americans—History. 2. Reconstruction (U.S. history,
1865–1877)—Louisiana. 3. Chinese Americans—Louisiana—Social
conditions—19th century. 4. Immigrants—Louisiana—Social conditions—19th century. 5. Agricultural laborers—Louisiana—Social conditions—19th century. 6. Alien labor, Chinese—Louisiana—History—
19th century. 7. Sugar growing— Social aspects—Louisiana—History—
19th century. 8. Louisiana—Race relations. 9. Louisiana—Social
conditions—19th century. 10. Louisiana—Economic conditions—19th
century. I. Title.
   E184.A75J86 2006
   305.895'10763'09034—dc22   2005014175

A catalog record for this book is available from the British Library.

To Tefi and

To the Memory of Louisiana's Working Peoples

Contents

Acknowledgments

I could not have finished this project without the generous support of numerous institutions. Fellowships and travel grants from Cornell University and an Albert J. Beveridge Grant from the American Historical Association helped me complete my dissertation, the book's foundation. The University of Washington has nurtured the transformation of an unwieldy dissertation into this hopefully less unwieldy book. I thank the Walter Chapin Simpson Center for the Humanities and the Harry Bridges Center for Labor Studies for granting me the time and funds to complete my research and to reconstruct my ideas. A timely grant from the Howard and Frances Keller Endowed Fund in History was instrumental in procuring visual images.

Librarians and archivists were most responsive to my innumerable inquiries and requests. My greatest debt is to the folks at the Hill Memorial Library, Louisiana State University, who made my prolonged residence at the corner table productive and enjoyable. I thank the knowledgeable staffs at Hill, the Historic New Orleans Collection, Tulane University, the University of North Carolina, Duke University, the National Archives, the National Archives–Southwest Region, and the New-York Historical Society for their courtesy and efficiency. Cornell University's interlibrary department tracked down resources on Louisiana with amazing speed and precision.

The Johns Hopkins University Press has been a wonderful introduction to scholarly publication. I am grateful to Bob Brugger for his early and sustained support of my project and to Melody Herr and Amy Zezula for their attention to detail. Julia Ridley Smith is a superb copyeditor.

I learned to think critically and engage politically—that is, I woke up and grew up—at Cornell University. I still recall my undergraduate courses with James Turner and Margaret Washington, who opened my eyes to the power of scholarship and teaching. They remain my role models. Robert L. Harris Jr. and Locksley Edmondson, members of my dissertation committee, asked challenging questions and offered encouraging advice. Gary Y. Okihiro, my mentor and ally, saw what I was working on long before I did. I will always remember and appreciate his steadfast support of my work and resolute commitment to Asian American Studies.

Friends and colleagues generously heard and read multiple incarnations of this book. Judy Wu and Leslie Alexander organized an enthusiastic audience at Ohio State University that reinvigorated the project. The History Research Group at the University of Washington wrestled with a trial run of the introduction. Lisa Lowe, Jodi Melamed, Ed Rhoads, Leti Volpp, Alys Weinbaum, fellows at the Simpson Center for the Humanities, and especially Chandan Reddy shared critical insights on individual chapters. K. Scott Wong and an anonymous reader provided helpful suggestions on an early draft of the whole thing. Moon-Kie Jung, Tefi Lamson, Mary Ting Yi Lui, Gary Okihiro, and Nikhil Pal Singh read the book's penultimate draft and sharpened my thoughts and words for the ultimate draft.

Although I spent far too much time alone at my desk, I fortunately did not write this book in isolation. Over the past decade, Mary Lui has moved months ahead of me through life's major turns, from the general exams and dissertation to the first book and baby. I am all the better for her counsel and friendship at every turn. My collaboration with kindred colleagues, particularly David Kamitsuka and Pablo Mitchell at Oberlin College and Chandan Reddy and Nikhil Singh at the University of Washington, makes our intellectual and political pursuits meaningful (and fun). Teaching U.S. and Asian American history has been vital to my own learning. I thank the students in my courses at Cornell, Oberlin, and the University of Washington for reminding me everyday what is at stake.

My family has been a constant source of support and inspiration. I do not know a world without the unconditional love of my grandma Soon-Ok Kwon, parents Minja Ahn and Woo-Hyun Jung, and brother Moon-Kie Jung. They shaped my sense of right and wrong, the driving force behind my work. The Lamsons humored my maniacal work habits and laughed at my caustic jokes, even those aimed at them. They spend holidays with me anyway. Mac, my sweet old gray cat, has been an ideal writing companion all these years. Tefi Lamson knows this book better than anybody should. Her demands for clarity drove me nuts on many occasions, but our conversations always defined and refined my ideas. The book's dedication is a small attempt to express my deepest appreciation of our true partnership. Our daughter Mina arrived in time to see the last pages of this book written and to hear this most important acknowledgment. Mina makes Appa very happy.

Coolies and Cane

Introduction

Tye Kim Orr's circuitous migration to the United States in 1867 had little to do with the California Gold Rush or the building of the transcontinental railroad, the signal events that usually mark the beginnings of Asian American history. An ethnic Chinese born and raised in the British colony of Straits Settlements in Southeast Asia (the present nation-states of Malaysia and Singapore), Orr probably had no idea how much his life would be affected by events on the other side of the world. Or perhaps he did. Like colonized peoples across Asia and the Americas, he acquired worldly desires and visions, a consequence of and a response to Europe's expansion. The British Empire had shaped his early experiences, including a formal education in a school run by the London Missionary Society, and would continue to guide his life choices. By the time Confederate general Pierre G. T. Beauregard ordered the first shots of the U.S. Civil War in 1861, Orr had settled with his wife and children in Singapore. He worked as a government land surveyor and, in his spare time, as a Christian lay preacher. But, as military battles engulfed South Carolina, Louisiana, and other states, Orr made up his mind to leave the comforts of the Straits Settlements for the metropole. Apparently moved to spread the gospel, he sailed alone to London in 1864, the first leg of a remarkable journey that would carry him to the battle-torn Louisiana countryside within four years.[1]

Orr was an extraordinarily articulate man with a knack for attaining funds and positions. In London, he successfully lobbied influential missionary leaders to fund his trip to work among Chinese residents in British Guiana. When Orr landed in the colonial capital of Georgetown in July 1864, he must have seen scores of South Asian and Chinese workers—so-called coolies—awaiting their assignment to sugar plantations. Recruited as indentured laborers since 1838, Asian migrants had come to form an integral part of postemancipation life in British Guiana. Orr's mission was to serve the needs of the Chinese contingent, then numbering nearly ten thousand. Upon his arrival, he immediately organized a Chinese Christian congregation in Georgetown and frequently visited laborers on nearby sugar estates. He found that misery and frustration prevailed among the local Chinese. To his "surprise," Orr informed the colonial government in January 1865, "his people were not as prosperous here as those who had been an equal time in other countries" and "a large proportion of the immigrants are in consequence dissatisfied with their condition and prospects, and are contemplating emigration at the end of their indentures."[2]

Despite these discouraging signs, the first year of Orr's mission exceeded all expectations. He petitioned the government for a land grant to establish a permanent settlement for the Chinese within the colony to allay "their discontent" and "determination to go elsewhere" and to convert them to Christianity. Aided by his personal rapport with the colonial governor, Orr's petition resulted in the founding of Hopetown Settlement in February 1865. During its first year, Hopetown attracted 170 Chinese residents and operated a thriving business in charcoal production. Orr personally supervised every aspect of the enterprise, from the clearing of the land to the sale of charcoal in Georgetown. "Disheartened by no failure, and daunted by no difficulties," the local press acclaimed, he completed work that "would have killed a man of ordinary constitution." In the summer of 1866, Orr was appointed the official missionary to Chinese residents, a government post that earned him a steady income. He then conceived a more ambitious plan, asking the governor to expand the settlement by subsidizing direct migrations from China to Hopetown, an idea that surely would have generated stiff local opposition. British Guiana's sugar-planting elite—who already feared that Hopetown would encourage Chinese workers to abandon their plantations—had no inclination to allow the public funding of Asian migrations for purposes other than indentured plantation labor.[3]

Before Orr's proposal received a public hearing, the missionary's standing in British Guiana plummeted. Several Chinese residents accused him of embezzlement and extortion, charges that Orr's accounting records seemed to corroborate. To make matters worse, his love affair with a "colored" woman in Georgetown, now pregnant with their child, generated "scandalous tales" throughout the colony. Amid charges of hypocrisy and immorality, the disgraced missionary fled British Guiana in July 1867, three years after his arrival. Orr first went to Trinidad, another British colony, and then to Cuba, where he may have worked as an overseer on a sugar plantation. He did not remain there long. Orr joined other Chinese passengers on a ship bound for Louisiana, where planters and merchants eagerly awaited their arrival. A New Orleans newspaper soon announced that "a dozen fullblooded Coolies" had arrived from Cuba, under contract to work in Louisiana.[4] Orr may have found Louisiana's landscape strangely familiar, its rivers, bayous, and sugarcane estates perhaps reminding him of his recent sojourn in British Guiana. Louisiana's sugar planters likewise exhibited a strong demand for coolies that he would exploit in due course. In the meantime, he needed to earn a living.

Unlike the dozen workers he traveled with, Orr himself was not a plantation laborer under contract. His educational and religious background combined with his experienced dealings with government officials opened up other opportunities in postemancipation Louisiana. Orr managed to secure a teaching position in a school established and supervised by the Freedmen's Bureau. The local bureau agent who hired him reported that the "new School . . . taught by Mr. O Tyekim 'a chinaman' is indeed worthy the efforts he is making, he is well qualified to teach." The new teacher, he noted, "speaks & writes the English language fluently, labors hard, and takes great pride in the work." Orr's school, unlike the other bureau schools nearby, included "white" and "colored" students. Orr himself was classified sometimes as "colored" and other times as "white" in bureau documents.[5] Scarcely three years after the Civil War, a Chinese man was teaching black and white students in a Freedmen's Bureau school. Orr would switch professions again in 1869, becoming a leading promoter of coolie labor, and would eventually make his way back to Asia to recruit laborers on behalf of Louisiana sugar planters.

Behind what may appear to be the singular globetrotting adventure of an exceptional individual lay commercial and migration routes that carried conceptions of race and labor, along with shiploads of sugar, across the world during Orr's lifetime. It is not surprising that he and his fellow travelers found themselves in New Orleans. Long before the nineteenth century, Louisiana's leading port city was a place where ideas, peoples, and material goods converged, driven by the currents of Spanish and French mercantile capitalism. Filipino sailors, for example, established perhaps the oldest Asian American settlement in St. Bernard Parish, possibly as early as the 1760s. Impressed to work on trade vessels, these "Manilamen" jumped ship to find refuge from the brutality of Spanish colonialism within what was then, like the Philippines, a Spanish colony.[6] The passing of Louisiana back to France and then to the United States did not break its global ties, particularly as sugar and slavery took root. Louisianians in particular, and Americans in general, kept a close eye on the Caribbean, where British West Indian and Cuban planters began hiring Asian workers in the 1830s and 1840s to ease and to delay the end of slavery without interrupting production. Situating the sugar-producing region of Louisiana within the wider universe that sugar made, this book tells the story of how another wave of Asian migrants came to call New Orleans and its surrounding parishes home in the nineteenth century.[7]

What I originally envisioned as a study of plantation workers in Louisiana has also become a broader inquiry into the historical origins and transmutations of coolies in American culture. In source after source, I came across coolies. They were everywhere, in planters' personal letters, abolitionist and proslavery periodicals, government reports, political speeches, and travel accounts. But who or what were coolies? It is a question that very few scholars of Asian American history have contemplated, beyond the now nearly universal claim that Asian immigrants in the United States were *not* coolies. Coolies, it is generally presumed, were Asians coerced into migrating to and working in the Caribbean.[8] The habitual assertion of this false binary—coolies versus immigrants—not only reifies coolies and American exceptionalism but ironically reproduces the logic and rhetoric of nineteenth-century debates on whether Asians in the United States were, in fact, coolies. No one, in the United States or the Caribbean, was really a coolie, but Asian workers were surely racialized as coolies across the world, including in the United States. Orr's traveling companions from Cuba did not remake themselves from coolies into immigrants once they landed in New Orleans. They remained coolies, and full-blooded ones at that.

Coolies were never a people or a legal category. Rather, coolies were a conglomeration of racial imaginings that emerged worldwide in the era of slave emancipation, a product of the imaginers rather than the imagined. To get at the roots of coolies, I propose, we must relocate the origins of American notions of Asian labor from the gold mines of California to the sugar plantations of the Caribbean and Louisiana. While the mass entry of Chinese migrants into California beginning in the 1840s and 1850s may have alarmed American transplants on the West Coast, the greater transport of coolies to the Caribbean and its possible extension to the U.S. South had profound and lasting effects on the historical formations of race and nation in the nineteenth century. The problem of coolies in the British West Indies, Cuba, and eventually Louisiana was inextricably bound to questions of global sugar production under the reign of chattel slavery and in the emerging order of free trade and free labor. This book is about the local, national, and transnational forces that made and remade coolies in American culture, and about how they came to embody the hopes, fears, and contradictions of emancipation. It contends that their evolving definitions and ultimate ambiguities—a slippery and disruptive creation between and beyond slavery and freedom, black and white—rendered coolies pivotal in the reconstruction of racial and national boundaries and hierarchies in the age of emancipation.

This book begins with the emergence of coolies in American culture in the antebellum era. Chapter 1 explains how reports from the British West Indies and Cuba transmitted contradictory images of coolies, as an industrious labor force to hasten slavery's demise and an inferior race brutally exploited by American merchants and Caribbean planters. The former view, reproducing British and Spanish justifications of their migrant labor systems, quickly lost credibility as the political discourse shifted to the China-Cuba coolie trade. Dominated by U.S. shipping firms and attended by mass rebellions, violent repression, and high mortality rates, the coolie trade came to epitomize the cruelty of coerced labor, perhaps, at least symbolically, more than chattel slavery itself. The antebellum equation of coolies with enslaved plantation labor in the Caribbean drove Republican officials to prohibit American participation in the coolie trade during the Civil War. The 1862 federal law, I argue, established the racial logic that would lead to the exclusion of Chinese laborers from the United States two decades later. Developments in the Caribbean led Americans to equate coolies with slaves in the age of emancipation, enabling anti-Asian forces to present

Chinese exclusion as an antislavery, pro-immigrant measure. As much as the Page Law (1875) and the Chinese Exclusion Act (1882) heralded a new era of immigration restrictions in U.S. history, they also marked the culmination of nineteenth-century slave-trade prohibitions.

Emancipation spread across the Americas gradually but fiercely, beginning in Saint Domingue and concluding in Brazil nearly a century later, and generated a multitude of social and political questions. Chapter 2 turns to Louisiana, the preeminent sugar-producing region in the antebellum United States, and its history of slavery, sugar production, and emancipation. The tumult of the Civil War and emancipation—driven by a mass slave uprising (as in Haiti) and contained by a government-supervised program of supervised plantation labor (as in the British West Indies)—set the stage for postbellum calls for coolie labor in a state with extensive cultural, commercial, and political connections to the Caribbean. But there was a cultural and legal hurdle that aspiring recruiters, many of them former advocates of slavery, had to overcome in the 1860s and 1870s. If coolies were enslaved laborers, would their arrival signal a revival of the slave trade and slavery in violation of federal laws and, after the Thirteenth Amendment's ratification, the U.S. Constitution? The British West Indies afforded an unexpected answer. As antislavery sympathizers looked to British tropical colonies to justify Union wartime policies on slavery and plantation labor, they recast coolies as immigrants. The successful government oversight of British emancipation and Asian "immigration," they hoped, foreshadowed a peaceful and gradual transition to free labor in the United States.

Coolies, at the same time, continued to defy simple categorizations. In a nation struggling to define slavery and freedom, coolies seemed to fall under neither yet both; they were viewed as a natural advancement from chattel slavery and a means to maintain slavery's worst features. Coolies confused the boundary between slavery and freedom, between black and white, causing the mass demand for Asian migrant laborers as well as appeals for their exclusion in the postbellum United States. The Civil War, as discussed in chapter 3, transformed coolies into a domestic political issue, no longer simply a matter of American merchants misbehaving on the high seas. Once emancipation finally became a reality in the United States, Louisianians with ties to the Caribbean wasted no time in promoting and recruiting coolies from Cuba, actions that attracted the interest of sugar planters and the suspicion of federal officials. The possible extension of the coolie trade to New Orleans galvanized Republicans into participating in the impossible task of ascertaining if Asian migrants in Louisiana were really coolies. Meanwhile, contrary to the racial images that preceded their arrival, Chinese migrant workers struck for freedom in Cuba and in Louisiana; their struggles, I argue, eventually closed off Cuba as a site of American coolie recruitment. Louisiana recruiters, in turn, shifted their sights to China and California, both made accessible by the steam engine's reach across the seas and over land.

Chinese migrants began arriving in the United States, including Louisiana, as chapter 4 explains, in an era of intense turmoil, marked by significant steps toward a multiracial democracy and strides toward a greater accumulation of capital at a national and global level. Within the major social crises of the 1860s—battles over the legal, political, and social standing of slaves, masters, blacks, and whites in the United States—coolies represented a vexing anomaly whose contested status would reconstruct American identities after emancipation. Where would coolies fit in a race-obsessed society that no longer bound blacks to enslaved labor or allowed racial barriers to citizenship rights? In response to federal disapproval of coolie schemes, would-be traders quickly refashioned themselves as promoters of "voluntary immigrants" and attributed "white" traits to Asian migrant laborers, who, they now claimed, deserved a chance to join the "nation of immigrants." Although federal officials extended Chinese migrants the provisional legal status of immigrants, they refused to disentangle race and citizenship in matters of naturalization. A dozen years before passing the Chinese Exclusion Act, the U.S. Congress denied Asian migrants the right to become naturalized citizens, in the process defining immigrants as white and European against the perils posed by coolies. Louisiana planters, meanwhile, continued to feel marginalized in an industrializing world, unable to control sugar or labor markets abroad and at home, making their dreams of coolies too precious to give up.

Coolie labor, as championed by leading planters, was supposed to resurrect the sugar industry to its antebellum glory, but, as I argue in chapter 5, opposition to this movement provided a means to protest growing class divisions among whites. If racial imaginings of coolies disrupted the boundary between slavery and freedom, they also seemed to dissolve the racial divide between "colored" and "white." The coolie question provoked ideological rifts in Louisiana, where white supremacy seemed threatened as never before, particularly with African American men voting in elections and electing Republicans. Decrying the slaveocracy of yesteryear, self-appointed representatives of Louisiana's white workers and farmers demanded the partition of sugar plantations into small farms operated by native-born and immigrant whites and insisted on the exclusion of coolies, who, like slaves, they claimed, would enrich only the rich. Symptomatic of the expansion, consolidation, and capitalization of the sugar industry worldwide and America's eager embrace of cheaper sugar from the Pacific and the Caribbean, only a small elite of the planter class had the resources to expand their landholdings, modernize their mills, and experiment with migrant labor. The postbellum movement for white immigrants and *against* Asian coolies, I contend, evolved from the racist antislavery arguments before the war and represented a critique of the emerging industrial capitalist order.[9] The contrasting visions and class divisions among whites were ultimately resolved through common but variegated reassertions of white supremacy—namely, political violence ("redemption") and a central factory system that masked tenant cane farming as independent agrarianism.

While imagined coolies existed in the minds of sugar planters, political officials, and others, thousands of real human beings cast as coolies actually arrived, lived, and worked in Louisiana. Chapter 6 concludes this study by surveying the migration and work patterns that arose as a result of and in opposition to cultural representations. As much as the dominant racial ideology, rife with contradictions, determined and affected the real life opportunities available to Louisiana's working peoples, it never encompassed all aspects of social relations in Louisiana, nor did it go unchallenged. Within these challenges lay the reasons behind the instability of race and its persistent reinscription in American history. Chinese and African American laborers did not fight one another for planters' good graces but engaged in multifaceted struggles against plantation owners that defined the relations of sugarcane production in the age of emancipation. Louisiana planters, in the end, never found the cheap, submissive, and stable labor force they desperately searched for. On a broad level, their labor problems, mostly couched and understood in racial terms, as historian Edward D. Beechert has noted, existed and persisted in every sugar plantation society.[10] This was true in the Caribbean, where planters complained continually of labor shortages. These "problems" and "shortages" were clear reflections of workers' struggles and aspirations. Chinese migrants' struggles, I argue, paradoxically made them increasingly invisible in Louisiana, allowing coolies to emerge again as a foreign threat to American interests. Cries against coolie competition in Hawai'i, Cuba, and elsewhere on behalf of American workers and sugar reverberated against the backdrop of an expanding U.S. empire in the Pacific and the Caribbean.

In the transition from enslaved to free labor and from old dreams of Jeffersonian agrarianism to realities of industrial capitalism, the imagined coolie profoundly shaped American racial, class, and national identities. The racialization of Asian workers as coolies vis-à-vis the Caribbean and the South—either as a conduit toward freedom or a throwback to slavery—served to upset and recreate social and cultural dualisms at the heart of race (black and white), class (enslaved and free), and nation (alien and citizen, domestic and foreign) in the United States. The impetus to extirpate slavery in the South, whether rooted in abolitionist zeal or racist animus, gave birth to the foundational logic that would lead to the eventual exclusion of Asian laborers. The construction of coolies, moreover, formed a crucial ingredient in redefining blackness and whiteness—and Americanness—when equality under the law (Reconstruction) and wage labor (industrialization) seemed to erode their meanings. The portrayal of Asian "dependence" and "servility" had the dual effect of reifying white "independence" and quelling black "insolence." In such ways, locating, defining, and outlawing coolies, at home and abroad, became an endless and indispensable exercise that resolved and reproduced the contradictory aims—racial exclusion and legal inclusion, enslavement and emancipation, parochial nationalism and unbridled imperialism—of a nation deeply rooted in race, slavery, and empire.

The movements of capital, ideas, and peoples that I explore in this book map a history that makes Orr's personal journey comprehensible and, indeed, logical. Tracing the origins of Asian American history compels us to interrogate the naturalized borders of the United States, to draw historical connections barely visible amid recycled narratives of universal inclusion and liberal progress. Long before Asian migrants landed in the United States, as historian Gary Y. Okihiro reminds us, Europeans and Americans had begun accumulating capital by seizing distant lands, displacing indigenous peoples, and opening up commercial and labor markets—in Louisiana, California, Hawai'i, China, Africa, and beyond. These violent developments eventually led to new systems of migrant labor that brought Asians, those imagined to be coolies, side by side with blacks on sugar plantations on both sides of the Gulf of Mexico. Asian American history therefore cannot focus solely on transpacific voyages, beginning in Gold Rush California and traversing eastward.[11] As Orr's life reveals, it must take into account European colonization of Asia and the Americas, planters' demands for labor in the Caribbean and Louisiana, and workers' struggles within and against systems of migrant labor. For these reasons, this book suggests the need to frame Asian American history as a story of labor migrations and struggles—

shaped by American conceptions of coolies as a global migrant labor force and not a people worthy of equal rights and opportunities—rather than of immigration and assimilation. What follows is a history of labor migrations and struggles in Louisiana, a phase of a global history of coolies and cane in the age of emancipation.

A Note on Coolies and Race

Earlier drafts of this book always had quotes around *coolies* to convey the unstable and imagined character of that racial designation. Initially upon the advice of my editors, I agreed to dispense with the endless sea of quotation marks. But there is a broader reason behind my decision. As Matthew Frye Jacobson notes, the selective punctuation of some racial categories can have the ironic effect of reifying others, such as whites and blacks.[12] With or without the quotation marks, this book aspires to reveal the historical formation of race, its social constructedness, and its very real, material consequences.

CHAPTER ONE

Outlawing Coolies

A vote for Chinese exclusion would mean a vote against slavery, against "cooly importation," a California senator warned in 1882. "An adverse vote now is to commission under the broad seal of the United States, all the speculators in human labor, all the importers of human muscle, all the traffickers in human flesh, to ply their infamous trade without impediment under the protection of the American flag, and empty the teeming, seething slave pens of China upon the soil of California!" The other senator from California added that those who had been "so clamorous against what was known as African slavery" had a moral obligation to vote for Chinese exclusion, "when we all know that they are used as slaves by those who bring them to this country, that their labor is for the benefit of those who practically own them." A "coolie," or "cooly," it seemed, was a slave, pure and simple. Rep. Horace F. Page (California) elaborated on the same point, branding the "Chinese cooly contract system" and polygamy the "twin relic[s] of the barbarism of slavery." The United States was "the home of the down-trodden and the oppressed," he declared, but "not the home for millions of cooly slaves and serfs who come here under a contract for a term of years to labor, and who neither enjoy nor practice any of our religious characteristics."[1]

Some of their colleagues demanded clarification. If the bill aimed to exclude coolies, why did it target Chinese laborers wholesale? New England Republicans, in particular, challenged the conflation of coolies and laborers. "All coolies are laborers," inquired a Massachusetts representative, "but are all Chinese laborers coolies?" Somewhat flustered, Page claimed that they were synonymous in China and California, where Chinatowns overflowed with "coolies and women of a class that I would not care to mention in this presence." His reply failed to sway the bill's detractors, who assailed its indiscriminate prohibition of Chinese immigration. With the Civil War and Reconstruction fresh in everyone's memory, Senator George F. Hoar of Massachusetts vowed never to "consent to a denial by the United States of the right of every man who desires to improve his condition by honest labor—his labor being no man's property but his own—to go anywhere on the face of the earth that he pleases." There were limits to "honest labor" though. Echoing a sentiment common among the dissenting minority, Hoar called for more exacting words that would strike only at the "evil" associated with "the coming of these people from China, especially the importation of coolies." "It is not importation, but immigration; it is not importation, but the free coming; it is not the slave, or the apprentice, or the prostitute, or the leper, or the thief," he argued, "but the laborer at whom this legislation strikes its blow."[2]

These congressional debates remind us in plain terms of the extent to which slavery continued to define American culture and politics after emancipation. The language of abolition infused the proceedings on Chinese exclusion, with no legislator challenging the federal government's legal or moral authority to forbid coolies from entering the reunited, free nation. Indeed, by the 1880s, alongside the prostitute,[3] there was no more potent symbol of chattel slavery's enduring legacy than the coolie, a racialized and racializing figure that anti-Chinese (and putatively pro-Chinese) lawmakers condemned. A stand against coolies was a stand for America, for freedom. There was no disagreement on that point. The legal exclusion of Chinese laborers in 1882 and the subsequent barrage of anti-Asian laws reflected and exploited this consensus in American culture and politics: coolies fell outside the legitimate borders of the United States.

This consensus took root in the decades before the Civil War and the abolition of slavery, a result not so much of anti-Chinese rancor in California but of

U.S. imperial ambitions in Asia and the Caribbean and broader struggles to demarcate the legal boundary between slavery and freedom. A year before Abraham Lincoln delivered the Emancipation Proclamation on January 1, 1863, he emblematized this consensus by signing into law a bill designed to divorce coolies from America, a little known legislation that reveals the complex origins of U.S. immigration restrictions. While marking the origination of the modern immigration system, Chinese exclusion also signified the culmination of preceding debates over the slave trade and slavery, debates that had turned the attention of proslavery and antislavery Americans not only to Africa and the South but also to Asia and the Caribbean. There, conspicuously and tenuously at the border between slavery and freedom, they discovered coolies, upon whom they projected their manifold desires. Ambiguously and then unfailingly linked with slavery and the Caribbean in American culture, coolies would eventually make possible the passage of the nation's first restrictions on immigration under the banner of "freedom" and "immigration." The legal and cultural impulse to prohibit coolies, at home and abroad, also enabled the U.S. nation-state to proclaim itself as "free" and to deepen and defend its imperial presence in Asia and the Americas. The historical association of coolies with slavery, in turn, would fundamentally shape postemancipation battles over Asian migrations to the United States.

Coolies and Freedom

The word *coolie* was largely a product of European expansion into Asia and the Americas, embodying the contradictory imperial imperatives of enslavement and emancipation. Of Tamil, Chinese, or other origin, *coolie* was initially popularized in the sixteenth century by Portuguese sailors and merchants across Asia and later was adopted by fellow European traders on the high seas and in port cities. By the eighteenth century, *coolie* had assumed a transcontinental definition of an Indian or Chinese laborer hired locally or shipped abroad. The word took on a new significance in the nineteenth century, as the beginnings of abolition remade coolies into indentured laborers in high demand across the world, particularly in the tropical colonies of the Caribbean. Emerging out of struggles over British emancipation and Cuban slavery in particular, *coolies* and *coolieism*—defined as "the importation of coolies as labourers into foreign countries" by the late nineteenth century—came to denote the systematic shipment and employment of Asian laborers on sugar plantations formerly worked by enslaved Africans.[4] It was during this era of emancipation and Asian migration that the term *cooly* entered the mainstream of American culture, symbolized literally by its relocation from the appendix to the main body of Noah Webster's American dictionary in 1848.[5]

By then, like the word, the idea of importing coolies as indentured laborers to combat the uncertainties of emancipation circulated widely around the world. Even before the permanent end to slavery in the British Empire in 1838, sugar planters from the French colony of Bourbon and the British colony of Mauritius, both islands in the Indian Ocean, had begun transporting South Asian workers to their plantations. These initiatives inspired John Gladstone to inquire into the feasibility of procuring a hundred "coolies" for at least five years of labor on his sugar estates in British Guiana. Doubting that black "apprentices"—the status forced upon former slaves for six years in 1834—would work much longer, Gladstone contended that planters had "to endeavor to provide a portion of other labourers whom we might use as a set-off, and when the time for it comes, make us, as far as possible, independent of our negro population." Coolies were his solution. A British firm foresaw no difficulty in extending its business from Mauritius to the West Indies, "the natives being perfectly ignorant of the place they go to or the length of voyage they are undertaking." In May 1838, five months before apprenticeship came to a premature end, 396 South Asian workers arrived in British Guiana, launching a stream of migrant labor that flowed until World War I.[6]

What happened to the "Gladstone coolies," as they came to be known, exposed a contradiction inherent in coolieism that would bedevil and befuddle planters and government officials in the Americas for decades. Did the recruitment and employment of coolies represent a relic of slavery or a harbinger of freedom? Early reports decidedly indicated the former. Upon the complaints registered by the British Anti-Slavery Society, British Guiana authorities established a commission to investigate conditions on the six plantations to which the "Gladstone coolies" had been allotted. Witnesses testified that overseers brutally flogged and extorted money from laborers under their supervision. By the end of their contracts in 1843, a quarter of the migrants had died and the vast majority of the survivors elected to return to India. Only sixty remained in British Guiana. Undaunted, the colony's sugar planters proceeded with plans to expand the experiment but met resistance in India and London. The Indian governor-general prohibited further emigration at the end of 1838, a policy that the secretary for the colonies refused to amend in February 1840. "I am not prepared to encounter the responsibility of a measure which may lead to a dreadful loss of life on the one hand," explained Lord John Russell, "or, on the other, to a new system of slavery."[7]

British Guiana's freedpeople, in the meantime, recognized all too well what freedom ought to mean. Gladstone's prognostication of impending labor trouble materialized immediately after emancipation. Dissatisfied with prevailing wage rates and working conditions, women and children began withdrawing their labor, particularly at critical stages of sugar production. Planters responded with a series of wage controls and labor codes, the severest of which they devised in December 1841. British Guiana's plantation laborers rejected the new social order and in 1842 organized their first mass strike, which lasted three months. Their employers felt compelled to retract the labor code and to extend a moderate wage increase but, at the same time, redoubled their efforts to secure an alternative labor force.[8] They were not alone. Planters across the British West Indies recruited laborers from all over the world in the decades following emancipation, from one another's colonies as well as from Asia, Portugal (particularly the Atlantic isles of Madeira, Cape Verde, and the Azores), the United States, and Africa. Perhaps the resort to "liberated" Africans—those who had been rescued from slave smugglers—bore the closest connection between the slave trade and postemancipation migrations. Their liberation from bondage consisted of being pressured to indenture themselves to labor in the West Indies. Officials in London again feared embarrassing comparisons to the slave trade in the age of emancipation.[9]

Far from facing recalcitrant opposition, West Indian planters soon found a sympathetic hearing in London. They could have their migrant laborers as long as the state regulated all phases of recruitment, transportation, and employment. Applied to African "immigrants" and then to Asian coolies in the 1840s, state intervention was championed in British political circles as the guarantor of freedom. For a time, despite persistent protests and investigations, the employment of coolies appeared to signal a departure from the evils of the slave trade, from coercion and servitude. It seemed to represent the hallmarks of freedom, sanctified by voluntary contracts, legal rights, and public subsidies and enforced by the imperial and colonial state apparatus. In practice, however, the system placed a preponderance of power in the hands of planters and their allies, to the detriment of indentured workers who faced criminal prosecution for violating civil contracts. State enforcement on behalf of employers—along with rampant extralegal practices like kidnapping, deception, and corporal punishment—more often than not eclipsed state protection of workers. These contradictions

This woodcut of a plantation manager's house in British Guiana by "a clever Chinese immigrant" conveys "the grievances likely to arise under the Coolie system." Groups of South Asian and Chinese migrant workers sit bound, supplying their blood to the manager and his family up above and the plantation owners in Britain.

From Edward Jenkins, *The Coolie: His Rights and Wrongs* (New York: George Routledge and Sons, 1871), 8.

notwithstanding, London and the colonial regimes in India and the West Indies worked together, albeit contentiously at times, to institute the mass migration of laborers bound to five-year indentures as a mainstay of postemancipation life by the 1860s. Coolieism became inextricably linked with emancipation, but not even the highest aspirations of numerous inquiry commissions and reform measures could erase its roots in slavery and "apprenticeship."[10]

Meanwhile, Cuba, the Caribbean's premier sugar-producing colony in the nineteenth century, magnified the contradictions presented by British West Indian coolieism. Sugar planters there demanded laborers in numbers and conditions that the illicit transatlantic slave trade—prohibited in Anglo-Spanish treaties in 1817 and 1835 and in Spanish law in 1845—could no longer supply by the 1840s, at least not without deep political and economic costs. Following the British example, a Spanish merchant engaged in the slave trade suggested the procurement of Chinese laborers in 1846, four decades before slavery would be abolished in Cuba. Within a year, his firm had made arrangements for two shiploads of workers bound to eight-year contracts with wages fixed at four pesos per month. This experiment initiated and defined a migrant labor system that Cuban planters found indispensable over the next two decades, especially as their recruiting forays in Africa, Mexico, the Canary Islands, and elsewhere failed to yield the results they had hoped for. Ultimately, almost 125,000 Chinese laborers landed in Cuba between 1847 and 1874 to work under conditions approximating slavery, unbeknownst to them and despite legal distinctions and safeguards. Enslaved and indentured labor flourished side by side in Cuba, casting chattel slavery's dark shadow over the "free" aspects of coolieism.[11] British authorities, in response, laid claim to moral superiority through state intervention, in Africa and India as well as in China, whence 17,904 laborers arrived in the British West Indies under conditions similar to the larger system involving close to half a million South Asian migrants.[12]

These developments on the other side of the Gulf of Mexico immediately captured the notice of Americans engaged in their own struggles over slavery. As in British denunciations of the Gladstone experiment, abolitionists wasted no time in vilifying coolie labor as a new variant of slavery. New England periodicals related to readers in the 1840s that coolies in the British West Indies were "in a state of nudity and hardly any of them decently clothed" and "suffering from severe sickness," with many complaining vociferously and running away. The plight of the early coolies was so miserable that "their belief is, that they are slaves" and "the negroes appear sincerely to pity them." Trinidad's officials received and distributed coolies like slaves "in pure Baltimore or Cuban style," *Littell's Living Age* reported, while "coolies, half naked, scabby, famishing, helpless from ignorance, and overrun with vermin, infest the highways" of British Guiana. Coolies faced a cycle of coercion in that colony, where "the authorities have hounded on them . . . drive[n] them into the lock-up house, (surely an illegal act,) and the planters cry out for permission to conclude contracts of indenture, that is, with beguiled strangers, who cannot comprehend the signification thereof." William Lloyd Garrison's *Liberator* hoped that "the abolitionists of Great Britain will succeed in their efforts to break up entirely a system that produces so much cruelty and misery."[13]

Within a few years though, Caribbean planters' and European officials' propaganda campaigns had their desired effect on American reports, many of which began touting coolie labor as a means to expedite and effect emancipation. Chinese emigration heralded a new era across the world, exclaimed an advocate of Chinese labor, that would benefit "both the Chinaman and the Negro, if you can at once relieve the hunger of the former and preserve the freedom of the latter." Four years of Chinese migrants residing in Cuba had proved them to be "laborious, robust—almost as much so as the best Africans—more intelligent, and sufficiently docile, under good management." Similar results prevailed in British Guiana and Hawai'i, but would "prejudice or a mistaken philanthropy" prevent a migration beneficial to all parties? Chinese dispersion across the globe and American expansion across the Pacific and Asia would proceed apace, he concluded. "Instead of the labor-market of the new empires of Oceanica being supplied, like that of Eastern America, by means of violence, and with the captive savages of Negroland, it will be voluntarily occupied by the free and industrious outpourings of China."[14]

Coolies were cheap, industrious, and free, other reports concurred, characteristics especially suited to tropical production across the world. Planters on Mauritius now "fully appreciated" the "importance of free labor," a writer exclaimed, as "an equal amount of work" could be extracted from "a less number of hands" at "lower rates of wages" than previously. Coolies, he stated, were "an intelligent race" and "inured to the work required" of them. A New Orleans resident received a similar assessment from Singapore, which he chose to share with fellow southerners. A sugar planter there, formerly of the West Indies, paid his coolies from China and India wages that made Louisiana's enslaved labor expensive in comparison. Not only was free labor cheaper, as an investment strategy book avowed, coolies themselves also appeared to profit from their new surroundings. T. Robinson Warren, whose vast antebellum travels included Asia and South America, was "very favorably impressed with this new system of labor" in Peru, where the demand for Chinese workers rivaled Cuba's. After eight years of service under conditions "a thousand times superior to the greater part of the laboring portion of the community of England, Ireland, or of France," Warren insisted, the coolie was "free for life." And the widespread "misery and starvation" of his homeland was replaced by a "happy" and "far superior" position in Peru.[15]

These sanguine accounts convinced some antislavery critics to acquire a faith in coolies' potential to serve as a conduit toward abolition, including in the U.S. South—peacefully, gradually, and profitably. In a series of editorials in 1852, the *New York Times* implored U.S. slaveholders to emulate their competitors in the British West Indies, Cuba, and Hawai'i. Addressing Louisiana sugar planters in particular, whose estates accounted for nearly all U.S. sugar production before the Civil War, the newspaper claimed that the Cuban example had verified the profitability of substituting "a more intelligent grade of labor at less expense" for "the reckless, indolent *abandon* and passion for amusement, characteristic of the African" in sugar production. If the Louisiana planter did not heed the lesson, then "how shall he sustain himself, against the shiploads of orientals imported, or about to be, by the enterprising Spaniard?" "Some happy medium must be struck," the *New York Times* charged, "and the only medium between forced and voluntary labor, is that offered by the introduction of Orientals."[16] Neither free nor enslaved labor, coolies signified an ambiguous contradiction that seemed to hold the potential to advance either.

Coolies and Slavery

Humphrey Marshall, the U.S. commissioner to China, likewise felt that coolies would spell the end of American slavery. "Should that power [Britain] seriously undertake to populate her West India possessions and her colonies on the coast of South America with Chinese laborers, who have no idea, however, of the right of popular participation in the direction of government," he informed the secretary of state in 1853, "the effect . . . upon the industrial interests of the planting States of the United States, and upon the institutions of the republics of South America, must necessarily be most disastrous to them." Marshall, a Kentucky planter and a future member of the Confederate military and congress, estimated that each Chinese contract laborer cost eighty dollars per year to employ, "far below the cost of slave labor, independent of the risk which the planter runs in his original investment." The Chinese were "patient of labor, tractable, obedient as a slave, and frugal . . . [and] will compel from the earth the maximum production of which it is capable, and, under whatever circumstances, will create a competition against which it must be difficult to struggle." On behalf of American slaveholders, Marshall hoped the president would establish a policy to prevent American ships from advancing the profits of British interests, against whom the United States was competing in the production of tropical goods and Asian commerce. Coolies, he believed, threatened both American imperial ambitions and American slavery.[17]

Marshall articulated a short-lived ideological convergence between U.S. diplomats and slaveholders that would decisively bind coolies with slavery in

American culture. In the years following his appeal, U.S. officials stationed abroad cast coolie labor not only as cheaper than slavery but as a brutal form of slavery that demanded federal intervention. Proslavery ideologues heartily agreed, even as they bristled at the notion of federal meddling in the domestic institution of slavery. The advent of a new system of slavery after emancipation in the Caribbean, they argued, warranted international scorn and laid bare the duplicity of abolition. American slavery, in their view, deserved protection more than ever. On the eve of the Civil War, New England abolitionists and southern fire-eaters could find common ground in the coolie problem, issuing equally strident condemnations that clarified and blurred the limits of slavery and freedom in the process. American calls for the prohibition of coolie labor abroad, in turn, also justified and fueled U.S. expansionism in Asia and the Caribbean. Joining the international movement to suppress the trafficking of coolies—commonly called the coolie trade—legitimized the U.S. diplomatic mission in China; the abuse of coolies in Cuba seemed to affirm the need for American annexation of the Spanish colony, for many, as a slave state. In and through coolies, American diplomats and slaveholders found ways to promote the U.S. empire as a beacon of freedom and slavery in the age of emancipation.

Marshall's admonition against the coolie trade conveyed the United States' longstanding commercial aspirations in China,[18] an economic motive that was in full display in response to the tragedy aboard the U.S. ship *Robert Bowne*. In 1852, Captain Lesley Bryson transported a cargo of contract laborers to Hawai'i and then returned to Amoy the following month to carry another 410 workers, ostensibly to San Francisco. On the tenth day out at sea, the Chinese passengers rebelled against the officers and crew, killing Bryson and six others and ordering the surviving crew members to guide the ship to Formosa. Instead, the ship ran aground near a small island on the Ryuku archipelago, to which American and British ships were dispatched to round up as many of the "pirates" as possible. Most of the Chinese passengers were never accounted for—only about a hundred were captured—and hundreds probably died from gunshot wounds, suicide, starvation, and disease in addition to the eight who had been killed during the original insurrection. Peter Parker, the chargé d'affaires of the U.S. delegation in China, conceded that Bryson had administered "injudicious treatment of the coolies"—such as his order to cut off their queues—but insisted that recent mutinies by "this class of Chinese" aboard French and English ships indicated that the uprising might have been "premeditated before the vessel left port."[19]

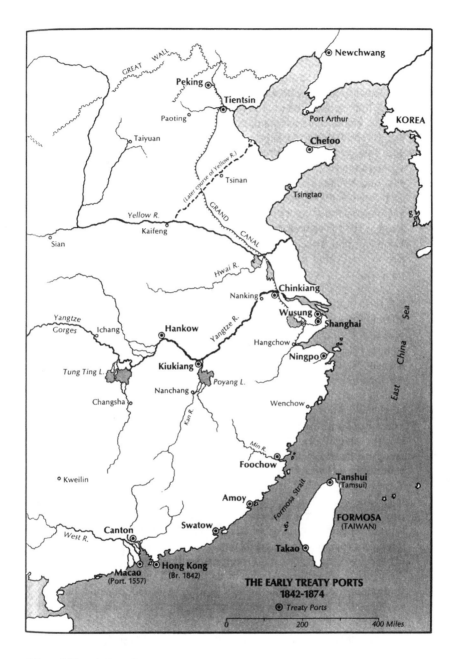

Map of China's Port Cities.

From Immanuel C. Y. Hsü, *The Rise of Modern China*, 5th ed. (New York: Oxford University Press, 1995), 217. Used by permission of Oxford University Press, Inc.

The mounting evidence against the American captain and the coolie trade in general had no effect on Parker's blind defense of his deceased compatriot and U.S. national honor. Bryson's ship was involved in an intensifying trade in Chinese workers around Amoy operated by European and American shippers and their local suppliers, Chinese brokers (or *crimps*). The insatiable global demand for coolies manifested locally in the early 1850s in an upsurge of kidnappings and fraudulent schemes, coercive tactics that drove Chinese residents to equate the trade to "pig-dealing."[20] The growing infamy of the coolie trade in Amoy could not deter Parker's quest for justice on Bryson's behalf. Although he claimed U.S. jurisdiction over the entire affair, Parker agreed to hand over seventeen individuals, those deemed the "principal actors" by a court of inquiry aboard a U.S. frigate, to Chinese authorities for a speedy trial and punishment. A month later, however, Parker regretted the "most flagrant breach of good faith" committed by the Chinese commissioners who, from the testimony of the accused, had censured Bryson for engaging in "the style of thing called *buying pigs*" and treating his passengers in a "tyrannical" manner. Only one man was found guilty. The U.S. official angrily defended Bryson as "a kind and humane man" and dismissed the suggestion that the passengers had been coerced into signing contracts. "Hereafter the United States will execute their own laws in cases of piracy occurring upon the high seas," Parker declared.[21]

Parker's absolution of U.S. coolie traders, however, quickly became untenable, especially as more and more American clippers entered the troubled yet profitable trafficking business in the second half of the 1850s. "There seems to be a rage at this time for speculating in Chinese . . . the trade, which gives enormous profits, is engaging the attention of the first commercial houses and largest capitalists of this city," the U.S. consul in Havana reported in 1855. "Chinese are coming in fast; and . . . these laborers are, on some plantations, treated no better and even worse than negro slaves." The mass influx of Chinese workers, he added, failed to "diminish the trade in African negroes, which are imported in large numbers, brought, many of them, to the environs of the city and sold, in a measure, openly." The brazen nature of these transactions astonished the U.S. official, who wished to dissociate his nation from what he regarded as a nefarious and deadly slave trade. "For my part," he wrote to his superiors in Washington, "I assure you that I regret very much to see vessels under our flag engaged in such a traffic."[22]

U.S. officials in Asia also dispatched frightening accounts of the trade that Americans back home read about, including the infamous case of the Boston-based *Waverly*. In September 1855, the *Waverly* left Amoy with 353 migrants and added 97 others in Swatow before embarking on its chartered voyage to Peru. Within a short span, four passengers had "sprung overboard" and drowned, while a "good many" fell ill, among them the captain, who died soon afterward. Under the circumstances, the first mate, now the acting captain, decided to switch course to the Philippines. Two more Chinese died before the ship reached Manila, where Spanish authorities placed it under quarantine. Difficult to control from the outset, the new captain wrote in his log, "all of the coolies came aft, with the intention to kill" him two days later. The crew killed "about four or five" in the ensuing struggle and "drove them all down below, between decks"; the captain later killed another "very impudent" passenger. When the others attempted to break through the forward hatch, the crew "shoved them down again and shut the hatches on again." Eight hours later, when the captain finally decided to allow the passengers on deck, he discovered a grisly scene below. Only 150 persons remained alive. The captain's account of coolies attacking him and then killing one another, however, could not be corroborated by witnesses, who testified that he had killed and injured the passengers without provocation. The U.S. consul in Manila reported that "the unfortunate beings had perished by suvocation."[23]

Amid such calamities, U.S. officials moved to prevent American citizens from transporting coolies, a trade that appeared to threaten America's commercial access to China and its international standing. Four years after his defense of the *Robert Bowne*, Peter Parker heard about the *Waverly* disaster en route to take up his appointment as the new U.S. commissioner to China. Armed with verbal instructions from the secretary of state to "discountenance" the coolie trade, he wasted no time in issuing a strong "public notification" in January 1856. Parker denounced the trade as "replete with illegalities, immoralities, and revolting and inhuman atrocities, strongly resembling those of the African slave trade in former years, some of them exceeding the horrors of the 'middle passage,' . . . and the foreign name has been rendered odious by this traffic, hundreds and thousands of lives having been inhumanly sacrificed." Parker instructed U.S. citizens "to desist from this irregular and immoral traffic" that imperiled "amicable relations" and "honorable and lawful commerce" between the United States and China, whose government prohibited it. "No felon in a European prison is more securely incarcerated than these Chinese," he later remarked after visiting a coolie barracoon in Macao, "and why? . . . If they are voluntary emigrants, what fear of their deserting?" When a Boston firm involved in the coolie trade suggested its legalization and regulation, Parker resolved more than ever that the "cause of humanity" would be best served instead by "western nations concentrating their influence to discontinue the traffic altogether."[24]

Parker's proclamation generated immediate public outcries back home that further coupled coolies with the banned African slave trade. The abolitionist *Liberator* featured articles on the "new slave trade" and chastised northerners participating in it as "doughfaces." Indeed, the growing ties between the Northeast, a region identified with the antislavery movement, and the coolie trade turned into a source of humiliation and contempt. A Boston merchant visiting Asia chronicled American clippers, many from his hometown, departing daily for Havana and Callao, part of a "most unchristian trade . . . worse than the slave trade" that forcibly placed the Chinese "in the iron bondage of Cuba or South America." Reports like this compelled the *New York Times* to reverse its earlier depiction of coolies as a vehicle to free labor. It now pressed the federal government to sustain Parker's declaration "with corresponding vigor" and suppress "this abominable trade." By April 1856, both chambers of Congress felt enough political pressure to pass resolutions requesting documents from the president on, as the House version put it, U.S. citizens "engaged in the slave trade, or in the transportation in American ships, of coolies from China to Cuba, and other countries, with the intention of placing or continuing them in a state of slavery or servitude, and whether such traffic is not, in his opinion, a violation of the spirit of existing treaties, rendering those engaged in it liable to indictment for piracy."[25]

Back in China, the new U.S. minister to China came to the conclusion that the trafficking of coolies amounted to violations of federal slave trade statutes. Almost immediately after being appointed to the post in 1857, William B. Reed was forced to contend with the trade that had haunted Parker. The issue was "of painful interest and some perplexity," he wrote initially, since "the written law does not seem to be against it, but the spirit of all law which is meant to protect humanity is." Like Parker, Reed found that shippers blatantly disregarded his public intimidations and general allusions to Chinese and U.S. laws and treaty obligations. In January 1858, he decided to fortify his warnings with a federal statute already on the books, an 1818 law that prohibited U.S. citizens and residents from transporting from Africa or anywhere else "any negro, mulatto, or person of colour, not being an inhabitant, nor held to service by the laws of either of the states or territories of the United States, in any ship, vessel, boat, or other water craft, for the purpose of holding, selling, or otherwise disposing of, such person as a slave, or to be held to service or labour, or be aiding or abetting therein." Despite "some uncertainty" of its applicability and its original intent for "a different evil," Reed argued for the law's relevance. A "Chinese cooly," he rationalized, was surely "a man of color, to be disposed of to be held to service in Cuba."[26]

In contrast to Parker, who had distinguished between the illegality of the "coolie trade" and the legality of "voluntary emigration of Chinese adventurers," Reed felt that coolies raised questions far more significant than coercion. It was, to him, a matter of U.S. racial, national, and imperial interests. Beyond "the practical enslavement of a distant and most peculiar race," the prospect of mass migrations of "free" Chinese male laborers also troubled Reed. Such a demographic shift, he believed, would strengthen "the decaying institutions of colonial Spanish America" that ran contrary to U.S. interests. The Chinese would "either amalgamate with the negro race, and thus increase the actual slave population, or maintain a separate existence, their numbers only to be recruited by new arrivals." Reed thought the latter more likely and, alluding to the Chinese in the Philippines and the Dutch Indies, envisaged a "bloody massacre" borne from the oppression of "a vast aggregation of troublesome populace" in a foreign colony. "Viewing it in any light as a matter of humanity and policy," he concluded, "I deem it my duty to condense this traffic, and to beg the early attention of the government to its repression, so far at least as it is conducted in American vessels."[27]

Incensed by the impotence of his legal threats, Reed soon amplified his rhetoric to a level that exacerbated the general confusion. He stressed that "whether the coolies go voluntarily or not to Havana" did not make "the least difference" under the law, if they were transported "under a contract 'to be held to service.'" "I am resolute to do all in my power to put an end to this infamous traffic," Reed exclaimed after a particularly frustrating encounter, "in this instance carried on in defiance of all admonition, by a most discreditable combination between an American master and lawless British shippers." He issued a course of enforcement that U.S. consuls ought to follow, claiming that "the employment of American ships in carrying Chinese coolies to be held to labor is illegal." If warnings by consuls and correspondence with Chinese officials failed, Reed threatened, he had "no other resource than to expose the individual ignominy which a share in such a trade involves, and to bring the guilty parties to punishment."[28] His reasoning had come full circle. In his search for a law to suppress the coercive and corrupt trade in coolies, Reed turned to a slave-trade prohibition that, in turn, defined a coolie. A coolie, in his mind, was "a man of color" shipped to labor abroad, a gendered, racialized, and classed figure whose migration, voluntary or not, signified the bounds of slavery.

Reed left his post in November 1858, months before federal officials in Washington rescinded his application of the 1818 statute to the coolie trade. Secretary of State Lewis Cass, who criticized British and French efforts to obtain coolie and African labor for their colonies, had referred Reed's concerns to Attorney General J. S. Black in April 1858. Black finally ruled almost a year later that he considered the coolie trade outside the purview of slave trade prohibitions and other "existing laws." "The evil is one which Congress alone can remedy," he concluded. Washington's delayed and deflective reply provided little comfort or direction to the U.S. legation in China, which continued to witness the horrors of the trade firsthand. The "cooly trade to the West Indies," Reed had pleaded repeatedly, was "irredeemable slavery under the form of freedom," with results worse than the African slave trade. The "Asiatic" faced a doomed fate in the Caribbean, he prophesied, marked by racial isolation and "a certain and fatal struggle, in which the Asiatic, as the weakest, fails."[29] To U.S. diplomats in China, it was a matter of life and death, a matter of slavery and freedom.

By 1859, the coolie trade from China generated diplomatic crises that both undermined and bolstered Western imperial designs in China. Popular outrage in southern China against kidnapping and deception, sometimes boiling over into mass antiforeigner riots, drove the Chinese imperial court to request assistance from Western diplomats to suppress a trade that flagrantly violated its prohibition against all emigration. The British—motivated by West Indian planters' demand for labor and London's desire to protect its international image—requested a legalized and regulated system of migration instead. The military occupation of Canton (Guangzhou) by British and French troops beginning in 1858 allowed them to exact such a system. Long aware that the imperial decree on emigration carried no weight among Western shippers, Chinese officials in Canton felt empowered and compelled to collaborate with the British to implement a more pragmatic policy. In November 1859, British and local Chinese motives coalesced into a system of voluntary contract migration to the British West Indies from licensed depots in Canton, with regulations intended to avert the violence heretofore employed in the recruitment of coolies. Lao Ch'ung-kuang, the provincial governor general of Guangdong, then called on other foreign consuls to instruct their citizens to conduct all emigration through Canton under the same guidelines. British and French troops subsequently headed north to Peking (Beijing) and pressured the imperial court to recognize the right of Chinese subjects to emigrate to foreign lands in October 1860.[30]

Even as the Canton system appeared to portend a new era of legal regulation and international cooperation, the coolie trade continued to vex U.S. officials in China. To begin with, American and other foreign shippers shifted their operations beyond Canton's city limits, especially to nearby Whampoa, immediately testing the new regulatory regime and exposing the contradictions inherent in Western moralistic claims and imperial ambitions. Fearing that a U.S. ship, the *Messenger*, was about to leave Whampoa for Cuba with a full cargo of coolies in January 1860, Lao asked the U.S. consul in Canton to help his deputies examine the passengers on board. The joint inquisition determined that twenty-eight individuals were on board against their will and, after examining two additional U.S. ships, released fifty into the care of Chinese officers. Not satisfied with these results, Lao refused to grant clearance to the American captain until all 578 aboard the *Messenger* were delivered to Canton for inspection. Everything seemed to work as planned until the agent for the ship's charterer, a British firm in Hong Kong, transferred the recruits to a Macao barracoon. The detention of a now empty American coolie vessel placed the U.S. legation in a quandary, its wish to assist Chinese officials compromised by its mission to protect and advance U.S. commercial interests. John E. Ward, a Georgia Democrat who replaced Reed as the U.S. minister to China, objected to what he deemed an unwarranted detention and wished for a U.S. law to place the entire matter under his power.[31]

The final outcome of the *Messenger* fiasco reaffirmed what American diplomats and many back home had been contending for years: the use of coolies marked a vicious and treacherous form of slavery. After a month of delay and negotiations, Lao and Ward arranged for the examination of 432 passengers by Chinese and U.S. officials in Canton. Their testimony, the secretary of the U.S. legation reported, "exhibited a dismal uniformity of the acts of deception, violence, intimidation, and crafty devices practiced by native crimps, to beguile or force them to go on board boats where they were compelled to assent to the demands of their captors, and go with them on board ship or to the barracoons at Macao." All were released. The liberation of this cargo barely tackled the gross abuses of the trade. Upon receiving its clearance papers at last, the *Messenger* simply proceeded to Macao and then departed with upwards of 400 workers for

Cuba. Ward had no legal authority under Chinese or U.S. law to interfere with American vessels transporting coolies from a Portuguese colony to a Spanish colony. Nor did he consider consular inspection adequate to the daunting task at hand. "When the consul visits the ships to examine into their condition," Ward observed, "they are questioned under the painful recollection of what they had already suffered, and what they must still endure if a ready assent to emigrate is not given."[32] The United States had an obligation to outlaw coolies on American ships, Ward and his predecessors urged, for the sake of free labor and free trade.

Immigration or Importation

Excepting U.S. diplomats in China, no group of Americans studied and criticized the transport of coolies to the Caribbean more assiduously than southern proslavery ideologues. They, however, drew conclusions that had little to do with ending coercive practices in Asia and the Caribbean; rather, their obsession with the Caribbean and coolies developed into a moral rebuttal to abolitionism. The racial and economic failings of emancipation and coolieism, proslavery forces argued, confirmed the natural order of slavery, an order that fanatical abolitionists and politicians had destroyed in the Caribbean. While U.S. officials in China appealed for a federal legislation to suppress the coolie trade, slavery's supporters emphasized the futility of state intervention in matters concerning race and labor. American slavery, they asserted, protected the nation from the utter decay experienced in the Caribbean and thereby justified its renewal through new importations from Africa and its expansion southward to Cuba and beyond. Their arguments led to neither but contributed to the emerging consensus in antebellum America that coolie labor was an evil to be expunged from America's ships and shores.

Not long after the legal end of slavery in the British Empire, American slavery's defenders charged again and again that abolition heralded a new era of duplicity and hypocrisy, characterized by semantic games rather than genuine humanitarianism. British imperial authorities had imposed the slave trade and slavery upon their colonies in North America, the *United States Magazine* claimed, and now ruled over millions of "absolute slaves" in India and elsewhere. Worse yet, they continued deceptively to sell "negroes" into slavery as "immigrants" and inaugurated "the blackest and worst species of slavery" by transporting "Indian Coolies" to the West Indies. "Humane and pious contrivance!" James Henry Hammond accused the British in his widely circulated letters in defense of slavery. "To alleviate the fancied sufferings of the accursed posterity of Ham, you sacrifice, by a cruel death, two-thirds of the children of the blessed Shem, and demand the applause of Christians, the blessing of Heaven!" Under the ruse of "immigration," Hammond added emphatically, "THE AFRI-CAN SLAVE TRADE HAS BEEN ACTUALLY REVIVED UNDER THE AUS-PICES AND PROTECTION OF THE BRITISH GOVERNMENT." West Indian emancipation was a "magnificent farce" that his "humanity" and American slavery's "full and growing vigor" could not allow on U.S. soil. Rev. Josiah Priest likewise castigated the British for "inveigling . . . a yellow, swarthy race" to labor on the other side of the world, a system at odds with "their seemingly noble generosity in manumitting their slaves" but consistent with their recent indenturing of "the negro"—"ignorant" of legal contracts as a "monkey"—in Africa.[33]

New Orleans-based journalist J. D. B. De Bow was perhaps the most influential figure to incorporate British hypocrisy, conspiracy, and degeneracy into the proslavery argument. A study of scientific racism and the British West Indies in the 1840s, he wrote in his regional journal *De Bow's Review*, led him to conclude that *"the negro was created essentially to be a slave, and finds his highest development and destiny in that condition."* Great Britain had been the greatest slave dealer, whose conscience turned to "philanthropy" only out of economic self-interest. De Bow's theory of British conspiracy was straightforward: *"Liberate your West India slaves; force them [other nations], as you can then, to liberate theirs, and you have the monopoly of the world!"* The true lesson of emancipation, in his estimation, was that West Indian planters should have "defied and resisted" the imperial decree, "even unto death." Black "barbarism" without slavery and the failure of other races in tropical agriculture, including coolies, meant that "the doom of the British West Indies is irrevocably sealed." His personal mission was to protect his beloved South from the same fate.[34]

De Bow increasingly concentrated his attacks on coolies in the second half of the 1850s, as the abuses of the China-Cuba trade came to public light and the sectional conflict over slavery intensified. Diatribes against Caribbean coolieisms, in turn, became integral to his defense of American slavery. Following up on the Senate resolution to investigate the coolie trade in 1856, which signaled its "world-wide importance," De Bow published a series of exposés on its "widespread evils." "Neither the oceans of blood which she [England] sheds in Asia, nor the hundreds of thousands of apprentices whom she decoys from Asia and Africa," he declared, "will supply the place of the negro slaves of Jamaica, Barbadoes [*sic*], Guiana, and her other slave colonies." No one could escape the science of race. Emancipation not only reverted former slaves to "a state of Pagan cannibalism" in the colonies but also drove up the prices of tropical products at home, conditions that "made fillibusters [*sic*] and buccaneers of more than half of christendom." British and northern abolitionists, De Bow reported, were now shipping "Coolies and Africans" in a "new system" that was "attended with ten times as much of crime and sacrifice of human life" as the slave trade and slavery. Government and newspaper reports on the *Robert Bowne, Waverly*, and other disasters, which he quoted extensively, illustrated the "enormities" being committed everyday in Asia and the Caribbean.[35]

To De Bow, the Caribbean demonstrated the moral superiority of the South and the dire consequences of interfering in the racial order. The "humane conduct" of American slaveholders, he argued, "preserved" human life—contrary to "every stigma and opprobrious epithet that ingenuity could invent!"—and the four million American slaves deserved to be spared "the risk of being exposed to evils" characteristic of other plantation societies. After surveying the various migrant contract labor systems of British, French, and Spanish tropical colonies, particularly the "truly frightful" mortality rates on ships and plantations, De Bow wondered how they could be accorded "the specious title of *free labor*." "What is the plain English of the whole system?" he asked. "Is it not just this?—that the civilized and powerful races of the earth have discovered that the degraded, barbarous, and weak races, may be induced *voluntarily* to reduce themselves to a slavery more cruel than any that has yet disgraced the earth, and that humanity may compound with its conscience, by pleading that the act is one of *free will*?" Platitudes on "humane principles" and "righteous decrees" might be "all very plausible and very soothing to the conscience" but the truth, he believed, exposed the unconscionable hypocrisy of abolitionists. De Bow demanded that "decisive means" be taken "to arrest this evil in its infancy," lest the entire world be cursed with the "ineradicable evils" of the coolie trade, including the specter of race wars between "half savages and half-civilized idolators" in the tropics. Although slavery protected the South for the moment, he concluded, "a successful insurrection of the negroes" incited by abolitionists would prove "an enormous impulse" toward the introduction of coolies to the United States.[36]

While De Bow and many other writers emphasized the need to protect the United States from Caribbean influences altogether,[37] other proslavery propagandists like Daniel Lee proposed that American slaveholders ought to emulate their southern neighbors' policies on "immigration"—not to abolish slavery, which he likened to industrial education, but to extend it. "Without making the disastrous sacrifice that ruined the planting colonies," Lee wrote, "we may, if it be wise to do so, import Coolies or Africans, under reasonable contracts to serve for a term of years as apprentices, or hirelings, and then be conveyed back to the land of their nativity." The system would not only fill the South's demand for "a muscular force worthy of its destiny," he argued, but also civilize Asia and Africa as these "pupils" returned home, enlightened. Lee's ultimate objective, however, was to reopen the transatlantic slave trade, a movement that witnessed a resurgence in the late 1850s. By 1858, he abandoned the idea of recruiting new races of laborers and advocated the sole importation of "African immigrants" under fourteen-year indentures or longer, as Louisiana legislators were then considering. He claimed that the system, once begun, would convert northerners to the wisdom of southern ways, allowing the extension of "the term of the African apprenticeship from fourteen years to the duration of his natural life." Lee's reasoning was, in effect, the mirror image of William Reed's attempt to apply the slave-trade laws to the coolie trade: since the coolie trade and African "immigration" to the Caribbean were like the banned African slave trade, the slave trade itself ought to be legalized.[38]

Some of Lee's ideological allies saw no need for legal or verbal subterfuge in demanding a resuscitation of the transatlantic slave trade. And the existence of the coolie trade and African "immigration" proved instrumental in demanding more slaves outright. George Fitzhugh, a prominent southern conservative, argued that the slave-trade laws had created systems worse than "the old orthodox Guinea trade" in the form of "Coolie apprentices" from Asia and "negroes" seized from "slave ships" in Africa. Great Britain was "but the eagle, hovering over the coast of Africa, to pounce upon and rob the fish-hawk of its prey." The "new form of slave trade" was worse, he argued, because Asian and African "apprentices" were worked "with careless cruelty" and "to death" by "masters" who saw them as merely temporary workers. "Such a trade would be endless," Fitzhugh concluded, "whilst the African slave trade might die out of itself after the market is supplied." Edward Delony, a Louisiana state senator, claimed that the federal government's prohibition reflected its historical "usurpation" of power, a "false policy" detrimental to southern interests. "Would a Louisiana planter, in going to Havana, and purchasing half a dozen negroes for his plantation, believe that, in so doing, he was any more guilty of an infamous act or a piracy than if he should go to Richmond and do the same thing?" he asked.

Delony called for the legalization of slave importations from abroad and the
territorial extension of American slavery to Cuba and Central America.[39]

The drive to enslave peoples, at the same time, did not stop proslavery forces
from imagining themselves and their nation as liberators—would-be liberators
of coolies across the oceans as much as U.S. diplomats. U.S. expansionism in
the Caribbean, they suggested, would result in the deliverance of slaves and
coolies from backward despots. Rep. Thomas L. Clingman of North Carolina
attempted to shed light on "how this system of transporting and selling into
slavery these Coolies is managed by Great Britain and Spain," to drum up congressional support for a more aggressive policy toward "our American Mediterranean" in peril. The mass importation of Chinese coolies, Mayan Indians, and
Africans intermixing with "the present black and mongrel population," he argued, threatened to make Cuba and other islands "desolate," the permanent
"abode of savages." Instead, some *"Norman* or *South-man* fillibuster [*sic*]" ought
to go down and force "Cuvee" to produce tropical goods, "which Providence
seems to have intended these islands to yield for the benefit of mankind." Senator John Slidell of Louisiana likewise called for the U.S. acquisition of Cuba.
In January 1859, he presented a bill to that effect on behalf of the Committee
on Foreign Relations, whose accompanying report forecast the humanitarian
and financial benefits to come. The United States would put an end to the slave
and coolie trades—the latter of which resulted in mortality rates and suvering
"far worse" than slavery—and thereby improve the value and treatment of
Cuban slaves and allow American slaveholders to dominate the world sugar
market.[40]

The proslavery argument's critique of Caribbean coolieisms, at the least,
frustrated abolitionist attempts to draw sharp contrasts between slavery and
freedom and revealed the complex global ties that slavery and coolieism had
forged. The "savage howlings" against the coolie trade and the antislavery
cause, as an abolitionist newspaper put it, muddled the national debate over
slavery. Developments in Europe, the British West Indies, Cuba, India, China,
and Africa produced new anxieties and hopes that informed and challenged universalizing notions. Were the British West Indies really free after emancipation? Weren't Asian and African immigrations merely legalized slave importations? The transport and employment of coolies in the Caribbean rendered
such questions—whether in diplomatic correspondence from Asia or proslavery pronouncements from the Old South—beyond a black-and-white issue.
Initially cast as the "free" advancement from coerced labor, coolies came to

epitomize slavery in the United States at a time the national crisis over slavery was about to erupt in open warfare. On the eve of the Civil War, the coolie and slave trades had become so intertwined in American culture that an encyclopedic entry for "Slaves and Slave-Trade" devoted a section exclusively to the "Coolie Trade." Coolies, at the same time, continued to traverse geopolitical and ideological boundaries, enabling a broad assembly of antislavery, proslavery, British, northern, and southern writers to call for—on behalf of freedom and slavery—a regulated system of migrant labor from Africa and American imperial expansion southward. Coolies reflected and complicated the shifting and expanding terrain of slavery and freedom in the nineteenth century.[41]

Importation and Immigration

The convergent and contrasting denunciations of coolies by American diplomats and slaveholders generated simultaneous but distinct initiatives to outlaw coolies on U.S. vessels and U.S. soil. Indeed, after years of inaction (other than investigative resolutions), Congress finally began deliberations on a federal law to extricate Americans from the coolie trade. In March 1860, Rep. Thomas D. Eliot, a Republican from Massachusetts, tried to introduce a bill and its accompanying report by the House Committee on Commerce (charged with inquiring into the "expediency" of banning American participation in the coolie trade to the Caribbean). Withstanding a series of procedural objections and a lone substantive protest against "the principle of the bill" by Rep. Henry C. Burnett of Kentucky, Eliot convinced his colleagues to permit him to introduce the bill and to print the report. In return, he agreed to send the bill back to the committee.[42] Despite the tepid reception, the report's publication represented a major breakthrough. For the first time, the U.S. Congress voiced its strong opposition to the coolie trade and, by extension, slavery.

Eliot's report encapsulated the frustrations and aspirations of U.S. diplomats in China far more than those of proslavery critics. Rather than using the coolie trade as a vehicle to disparage the British Empire or to reopen the slave trade, the Committee on Commerce took an unequivocal stand in favor of the British state system and against the slave trade. Eliot and his associates took great pains to distinguish between the status of coolies in the British colonies and in Cuba. The transport and employment of "East Indian coolies" in British Guiana, Trinidad, and Mauritius, the report argued, were characterized by voluntary contracts and government supervision that obviated outside interference. "It has not been the policy of the American government," the committee claimed, "to place obstacles in the way of intelligent and voluntary emigration." Chinese migration to California was also "voluntary and profitable mutually to the contracting parties" and, at any rate, already subject to federal statutes on passenger ships. The "Chinese coolie trade" to Cuba, on the other hand, was categorically unique and warranted immediate congressional action. That particular trade was "unchristian and inhuman, disgraceful to the merchant and the master, oppressive to the ignorant and betrayed laborers, a reproach upon our national honor, and a crime before God as deeply dyed as that piracy which forfeits life when the coasts of Africa supply its victims." Although the report targeted "American shipmasters and northern owners" engaged in a trade "as barbarous as the African slave trade"—not southern slaveholders—its antislavery message was inescapable.[43]

Consistent with a longstanding imperial rebuke of Cuba as morally backward, the report's geopolitical boundaries also reflected the Republican party's growing faith in nation-state authority and enduring hope for a peaceful end to slavery. The British Empire stood for state protection, progress, and freedom; the Spanish Empire exemplified state failure, stagnation, and slavery. Antislavery forces therefore vigorously contrasted what the *New York Times* called the "Chinese Coolie-trade" to Cuba and Peru and the "Hindoo Coolie-trade" to the British West Indies, which was "not the ally, but the enemy of Slavery." The "East-India Coolies, taken to the British Islands," John S. C. Abbott wrote in his antislavery tract, seemed to "have their rights carefully protected by the British government," whereas "in Cuba the Coolie trade is merely a Chinese slave-trade under the most fraudulent and cruel circumstances." Juxtaposing the "human misery" in Cuba against the "joy and gratitude" in postemancipation British West Indies, Abbott prayed that "the execrable institution" of slavery would "speedily go down" in the United States, "but not in a sea of flame and blood."[44] State regulation and supervision, it seemed, would guarantee and, in essence, define freedom for all.

A diplomatic squabble between the United States and Britain, on the other hand, captured the proslavery argument's derision of the British Empire and state intervention. In the summer of 1860, Lord John Russell, the British foreign secretary, put forward the idea of employing Chinese labor to fill the persistent demand for "laborers suited to a hot climate" as part of the international campaign to end the slave trade. "By judiciously promoting the emigration from China, and at the same time vigorously repressing the infamous traffic in African slaves," he wrote, "the Christian governments of Europe and America may confer benefits upon a large portion of the human race, the effects of which it would be difficult to exaggerate." Replying on behalf of President James Buchanan, Acting Secretary of State William H. Trescot, a Democrat from South Carolina, refused to meddle in Cuban and Spanish affairs or to sanction a new trade marked by "fraud and violence" reminiscent of "the middle passage." The importation of "heathen coolies" to the United States, he stated, would cause "a most deleterious influence" upon every region, demoralizing "the peaceful, contented, and orderly slaves" in the South and undermining "our own respectable and industrious laborers" in the North. Russell, obviously irritated, countered that he had never pondered the introduction of coolies to the United States, for he was referring only to Cuba. But Chinese migration to the British West Indies and Mauritius, he added, had not produced "the evils and inconveniences" that Trescot imagined.[45]

Slavery's defenders had no patience for drawing distinctions among Caribbean coolieisms and demanded the exclusion of coolies from America's shores so as to preserve domestic slavery. Between Lincoln's election and inauguration—and during the secession of one state after another—proslavery unionists desperately turned to the Caribbean and coolies to sustain their lost cause, with President Buchanan going so far as to propose the acquisition of Cuba. At a convention called to draft a constitutional amendment to avert a war in February 1861, a delegate from New York recommended the preservation of slavery as a state institution and ridiculed its abolition in England and France. "True, they have abolished slavery by name," he argued, "but they have imported apprentices from Africa, and Coolies from Asia, and have placed them under the worst form of slavery ever known." In considering a provision to prohibit the importation of slaves from abroad, the convention added the phrase "or coolies, or persons held to service or labor" upon the suggestion of a Kentucky delegate, who contended that "the importation of coolies and other persons from China and the East" was "the slave-trade in one of its worst forms."[46]

In a fracturing nation, those who were fighting hardest to uphold slavery attempted to criminalize coolie importations first. In March 1861, congressional leaders of the compromise movement proposed multiple drafts of a constitutional amendment that included the retention of slavery below the 36°30′ parallel line and the prohibition of the "foreign slave trade" involving "the importation of slaves, coolies, or persons held to service or labor, into the United States and the Territories from places beyond the limits thereof." At the exact same moment in Mobile, Alabama, the constitutional convention of the Confederate States of America considered an identical clause against "the importation of slaves, coolies, or persons held to service or labor into the Confederate States and their Territories, from any places beyond the limits thereof." Politicians on different sides of the secession crisis figured that the preemptive exclusion of coolies might shore up slavery in the South.[47]

Antislavery Republicans also moved to put a stop to coolie importations during the first year of the Civil War. After settling for congressional resolutions requesting more documents from Buchanan and then Lincoln, Eliot and his allies renewed their own legislative effort against the coolie trade in the now Republican-dominated Congress. In December 1861, eight months into the Civil War, Eliot attempted to introduce his bill to the full House for a vote, only to have it referred back to the Committee on Commerce again. Lincoln's administration, meanwhile, submitted recent diplomatic correspondence on the "Asiatic coolie trade" to the House, as requested, on December 23, 1861. The documents confirmed Americans' persistent participation in the trade and its attendant violence, despite steps taken toward government inspection.[48] About a month later, Eliot proposed an amended bill (H.R. 109) for the House's consideration and pleaded for its passage. Aside from procedural objections, Eliot argued, he had heard from his colleagues only "a solitary objection" to his earlier bill. "I refer to Mr. Burnett, who is now doing what he can to pull down the Government which he was then under oath to sustain and support," he explained, "and that objection, as I recollect it, was based simply upon the assertion that . . . it might by possibility affect some of his constituents who, as he declared, had some cooly laborers upon their plantations." The House passed the bill.[49]

The Senate then made a significant modification to Eliot's bill. Senator John C. Ten Eyck of New Jersey recommended on behalf of his chamber's Committee on Commerce that the phrase "against their will and without their consent" be stricken from H.R. 109. "The committee are of opinion that the cooly trade should be prohibited altogether," Ten Eyck argued. "They are of opinion that persons of this description should not be transported from their homes and sold, under any circumstances; being, as is well known, an inferior race, the committee are of the opinion that these words will afford very little protection to this unfortunate class of people." His racial and moral argument carried the day. The Senate passed the bill with Ten Eyck's amendment; the House concurred two weeks later. And Lincoln finally signed "An Act to Prohibit the 'Coolie Trade' by American Citizens in American Vessels" on February 19,

1862.[50] Signaling the beginning of the Republican program against slavery, the statute anticipated the party's ambivalent and hesitant role in the abolition project and unwittingly framed the postbellum struggle between federal officials and Louisiana planters over coolie labor.

The final version of Eliot's bill reproduced the racial logic of the age of emancipation, which made the practical enforcement of prohibiting the coolie trade a confusing and impossible endeavor. What exactly constituted a coolie? And could one ever be emancipated from the status of a coolie? The new law answered neither question. Its first section prohibited U.S. citizens and residents from acting as "master, factor, owner, or otherwise, [to] build, equip, load, or otherwise prepare, any ship or vessel . . . for the purpose of procuring from China . . . or from any other port or place the inhabitants or subjects of China, known as 'coolies,' to be transported to any foreign country, port, or place whatever, to be disposed of, or sold, or transferred, for any term of years or for any time whatever, as servants or apprentices, or to be held to service or labor." It was from this section that Ten Eyck removed the words "against their will and without their consent," a clause that might have classified coolies more conclusively. Instead, the legislation simply outlawed any shipment of Chinese subjects "known as 'coolies'" abroad "to be held to service or labor." Virtually all Chinese subjects leaving China were known as coolies. But another section of the law left the door open to Chinese migration, proclaiming that "any free and voluntary emigration of any Chinese subject" should proceed unabated so long as a U.S. consul attested to the voluntary status of the migrant through a written certificate.[51] The two sections presumably went hand in hand. The United States deplored the importation of human beings; it embraced immigration.

Passed in the throes of military and political battles over slavery, the anticoolie-trade law marked a critical turning point in U.S. history. It was, in a sense, the last of America's slave trade laws, unambiguously framed as such by Republican legislators. "Let us here, by legislation, declare it illegal—not a piracy; this bill does not so designate it," Eliot had argued, "and yet no statute pirate who has brought slaves from the coast of Africa more truly, in my judgment, deserves execration than those men who knowingly . . . have engaged in the work of bringing coolies from their native homes to the island of Cuba."[52] The law was, in another sense, the first federal statute to restrict immigration into the United States. Chinese migrants henceforth would have to prove to U.S. consuls that they were "free and voluntary" immigrants—and not coolies, although they could be both under Ten Eyck's calculation—and therefore worthy of legal entry. The 1862 law paved the way for the Page Law that targeted coolies and prostitutes by reinforcing the earlier law's dual framework of illegal importation and consular inspection in 1875.[53] Seven years later, Congress would outlaw the entry of "Chinese laborers." The last slave-trade law, from this angle, was simultaneously the first immigration law. Coolies bridged the legal and cultural gap between the national exclusion of slaves and immigrants, liminal subjects that were neither yet both in the age of emancipation.

CHAPTER TWO

Envisioning Freedoms

William J. Minor, the owner of three large sugar plantations in Louisiana, expressed his vision of freedom to a federal commission immediately after the Civil War. "The only certain remedy that we know of is, to take us back under the Constitution & establish things as they were," he explained in April 1865, "but perhaps under some other name." Asked if he meant the retention of slavery, Minor assented eagerly. "Yes Sir, I think this state & all the states would come back under the Constitution Sir," he replied. "I am the more inclined to think so because I was one of those who were altogether opposed to going out in the beginning." Nearly three years of wage labor under Union military occupation, according to Minor, had proven that sugar production would cease without slavery. Louisiana, he insisted, was too cold for sugarcane cultivation without enslaved labor—winter frosts were a perennial threat to ripened cane stalks after October—and too hot for white labor. He felt that "the white man can not bear the climate or sun & he can get as much as we can afford to give, elsewhere." Increased foreign imports would eventually drive down agricultural prices and wages, making white labor impossible to control "to any extent" or to attract "to live among mosquitos & mud" of southern Louisiana. "When emancipation is perfected," Minor stated resignedly, "we will have to get 'Cooly labour' or some other,—labourers that can stand this Climate."[1] Envisioning freedom, like defending slavery, implicated exploiting coolies.

Forswearing coolie labor in the name of slavery, alongside slavery itself, was a casualty of the Civil War. As in the Caribbean decades earlier, slavery's death generated a planter demand for Asian coolies in the South. This racial logic, however, never materialized uniformly across postemancipation societies. In addition to depictions of Asian labor before the war, local wartime developments, themselves shaping and shaped by events near and far, drove former American ex-slaveholders to seek coolie labor after the war. Louisiana sugar planters, in particular, exhibited a swift and high demand for coolies, although they were by no means the only former slaveholders and proslavery ideologues to look to the Caribbean for historical guidance. Southern Louisiana was not an exception, but its distinctive history of colonial subjugation and sugar production made it as much a part of the Caribbean as the Old South. Political, economic, and social networks that stretched across the Gulf of Mexico in tandem with the revolutionary potential of the Civil War propelled New Orleans and its surrounding sugar-producing parishes to the forefront of postbellum movements for and against coolies. Although Asian workers remained on the margins of antebellum and wartime struggles over sugar production, their arrival in Louisiana so soon after the war was ultimately and intimately tied to the violently competing visions of freedom among planters, workers, and federal officials. Federal policies to sustain and then abolish slavery, driven by the words and actions of planters and workers, ironically would recast coolies as potentially free immigrants in American culture during the Civil War.

The Ties That Bound

Sugar and slavery—the twin forces that enriched western Europe, enslaved western Africa, and colonized the Americas for centuries—emerged and died in Louisiana during revolutionary times. Before the late eighteenth century, French and Spanish attempts to establish a plantation slave regime comparable to Saint Domingue had failed miserably, finding neither a viable staple crop nor a controllable labor force. The encroachment of American Indian lands, the importation and enslavement of Africans, and the production of plantation staples proceeded haphazardly in the lower Mississippi Valley, marred and jarred by African and American Indian insurgencies (real and feared), maroon communities, and competitive and fickle markets. Throughout the eighteenth century, slave importations from Africa and the Caribbean, intensely pursued at times, were forbidden repeatedly to guard against slave uprisings. Aspiring planters often found producing foodstuffs for sale within Louisiana and export to Saint Domingue, Martinique, Mexico, and Cuba more profitable than plantation staples like tobacco or indigo. For about a century after the French began colonizing Louisiana in 1699, mercantilist ties oriented Louisiana to the south, making it a northern colony within what some historians have aptly labeled the "Greater Caribbean." It, however, seemed incapable of producing the kind of wealth generated by Caribbean sugar colonies, even as its military and commercial significance grew over time.[2]

Louisiana, a stop along what Peter Linebaugh and Marcus Rediker call "the planetary currents around the Atlantic," profoundly felt the reverberations of revolutionary currents in the 1770s and beyond. Revolutionary ideas and peoples traveled across the seas, as did violent campaigns to expurgate them. The American Revolution extended into the lower Mississippi Valley, where U.S. and British forces met in battle. Spanish forces soon took over British territories, inciting enslaved peoples to flee to wherever freedom seemed most likely. News of the first modern republic in the Americas was then drowned out by stories of Jacobin uprisings in Paris and Saint Domingue, France's most prized colony, that fundamentally transformed Louisiana's physical and social landscape. The French Revolution, and its radical, Haitian incarnation ignited kindred hopes (and fires) in the streets of New Orleans and among a motley crew of Louisiana's working peoples. As French revolutionaries beheaded King Louis XVI and abolished slavery in all French colonies—an act spurred on by the mass slave revolt that would create Haiti, the second republic in the Americas—Spanish authorities in Louisiana did everything in their power to suppress, deport, and execute revolutionaries. But it proved impossible to contain the ferment encircling and engulfing the Atlantic world in the 1790s. Maritime workers and soldiers delivered the latest news; enslaved peoples and their allies organized and rebelled.[3]

Whispered reports of worldwide struggles for *liberté, egalité, fraternité* convinced many in Louisiana to claim their freedom. "We are free, but the settlers do not want to give us our freedom," a black Louisianian was overheard saying

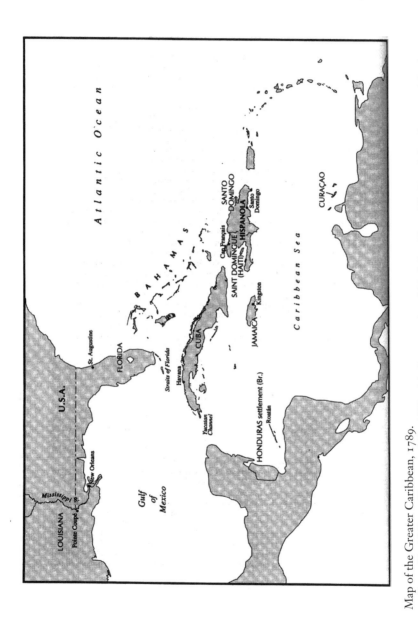

Map of the Greater Caribbean, 1789.

From David Barry Gaspar and David Patrick Geggus, eds., *A Turbulent Time: The French Revolution and the Greater Caribbean* (Bloomington: Indiana University Press, 1997), 76. Used by permission of Indiana University Press.

in 1795. "We must wipe them all out. We have enough axes and sticks to kill them." Centered in Pointe Coupée but extending miles to New Orleans and Opelousas, a plan for a mass uprising involving countless numbers of slaves (African-born and creole), free people of color, and some local whites was revealed in the spring of 1795. The Pointe Coupée conspiracy was not the first or the last to be uncovered, but it was perhaps the greatest. Spanish officials hanged and decapitated twenty-three slaves, nailing their heads on posts up and down the Mississippi River, and sentenced thirty-four others, including three whites, to imprisoned hard labor abroad. The convicts were first taken to New Orleans, a city teeming with supporters and arsonists, before being secretly shipped off to Havana. The alarmed captain general of Cuba received them begrudgingly and begged Louisiana officials to "send such individuals to some foreign country" in the future. The Pointe Coupée convicts, some of whom traced their roots to Saint Domingue, undoubtedly took their insurrectionary notions with them to Cuba.[4] The revolutionary currents of the Greater Caribbean were contagious.

The Haitian Revolution (1791–1804) and corollary conspiracies and rebellions in Louisiana had ramifications far and wide. The Spanish crown, constantly on guard for slave unrest, lost interest in maintaining the unruly colony and agreed to return Louisiana to France in 1800. Napoleon Bonaparte, in the meantime, was busy turning back the revolutionary tide in Europe. Planning to force Saint Domingue into colonial submission, he hoped the revival of its vast plantations would resuscitate the French Empire—Saint Domingue had accounted for 40 percent of prerevolutionary France's external trade—that again included the lower Mississippi Valley. The disastrous results of Napoleon's grand military expedition to the Caribbean killed his western imperial designs, reportedly leading him to exclaim in January 1803: "Damn sugar, damn coffee, damn colonies." The United States would benefit from the triumph of black Jacobins in Haiti later that year when diplomatic negotiations yielded more than 800,000 square miles of land claimed by France. But Americans inherited more than land. Fears of another Haiti or Pointe Coupée led federal legislators and territorial governors to prohibit slave importations, especially from the Caribbean. "I am particularly desirous to exclude those slaves who (from late habits) are accustomed to blood and devastations," the governor explained, "and whose Counsel and communication with our present black population may be pregnant with future mischief." The passage of time could not extinguish the nightmares and hopes that Haiti represented in Louisianians' minds, kept alive most vividly by local conspiracies and outright revolts.[5]

If the Pointe Coupée conspiracy exposed Louisiana's revolutionary potential to turn the colonial world upside down, an experiment downriver by a sugar maker from Saint Domingue spawned an altogether different kind of revolution with no aspirations for liberty or equality. In 1795, after decades of sporadic and disappointing attempts at sugarcane cultivation and granulation, Antoine Morin demonstrated decisively the adaptability of sugar production to Louisiana's alluvial soil. With the capital investment of a frustrated indigo planter and the labor of forty enslaved workers, Morin successfully oversaw the production of twelve thousand dollars worth of sugar. Thus began the sugar revolution in Louisiana at a critical historical juncture within the Greater Caribbean. Sugar and slavery—the generators of wealth in Saint Domingue that the Haitian Revolution dismantled—were regenerated elsewhere, especially in Cuba, Trinidad, the Guianas, and Louisiana in the nineteenth century, often by the experience and capital carried by Saint Domingue refugees and their enslaved laborers. The destruction of Saint Domingue's plantation society stimulated and facilitated the creation of a similar society in Louisiana, but it also created a major obstacle. At a time when would-be sugar planters stridently demanded more and cheaper labor, Spanish and then American authorities continually closed off Louisiana to the slave trade in the name of public safety. Greed ultimately prevailed. Beginning in 1805, U.S. authorities allowed Louisianians to import slaves from any state in the union. And they did.[6]

Sugar and slavery expanded rapidly in southern Louisiana in the first half of the nineteenth century, fueled by dreams of immense wealth and realities of coerced labor—bound, shipped, and sanctioned by the whip, the slave market, and the state. By the time the United States purchased Louisiana in 1803, there were already eighty-one sugar plantations on the richest lands bordering the Mississippi River that consumed enslaved labor far faster than the local market could supply. Inundated with complaints over prohibitions on the slave trade, the territorial governor wrote to President Thomas Jefferson in 1804 that "the most respectable characters, cou[l]d not, *even in my presence*, suppress the Agitation of their Tempers, when a check to that Trade is suggested." Louisiana's prominence in the flourishing domestic slave trade—New Orleans was home to the largest slave market throughout the antebellum period—would ease some of those tempers and enable hundreds of individuals to establish sugar plantations of their own, initially led by French creoles (and some free people of color) and steadily joined and surpassed by Anglo American migrants. By 1853, scarcely a half century after its founding, Louisiana's cane industry was producing nearly a quarter of all exportable sugar in the world.[7] The enormous profits falling into slave traders' and slaveholders' pockets flowed from the backbreaking labor of Louisiana's enslaved women and men, whose numbers increased exponentially in the decades before the Civil War. This was true for the lower South in general, but southern Louisiana stood out.

Sugar marked the difference. Combining field and factory work, modern sugar plantations were, in the words of anthropologist Sidney W. Mintz, an "industrial enterprise," subject to the agricultural rhythms of the cane fields and the industrial discipline of the sugar mill. Planters eager to optimize production levels not only embraced advances in cultivation and manufacture but also demanded particular types of workers—enslaved, young, male. "I will give the highest price for likely young negroes, say from 10–25 years of age," an antebellum advertisement announced. "Fellows will be preferred with proper certificate for the New Orleans market." The rigors of sugar production demanded laborers in their prime; if female, they had to be "stout young women," as a slave trader put it. Around two-thirds of the slaves imported into Louisiana's sugar region were male, in contrast to a more balanced sex ratio in the cotton districts. Reminiscent of and parallel to the disastrous demographic characteristics of the Caribbean, the enslaved peoples on Louisiana's sugar plantations had inordinately low birth and fertility rates, their increase mostly due to large-scale importations.[8] It was a legal, brutal system of migrant labor. About twelve years old when she and her family were sold from South Carolina to St. Bernard Parish, Ceceil George recalled it was like arriving in "a heathern part of de country." "Everybody worked, young and old," she explained. "If you could only carry two or three sugar cane [stalks], you worked . . . And if you say, 'Lawd a-mercy,' de overseer whip you. De old people, dey just set down and cry."[9]

As American slaveholders, Louisiana sugar planters held a common political agenda with cotton planters to the north, especially as the conflict over slavery intensified. At the same time, they shared wishes and struggles with sugar planters in the Caribbean. As late entrants in the sugar rush, by which time empires and nations had begun repudiating the transatlantic slave trade, planters in Trinidad, British Guiana, and Cuba, too, complained bitterly about labor shortages, importing enslaved and indentured laborers from wherever possible, legally and extralegally, and demanding young male workers in particular.[10] Although incomparable to the scale of legalized migrations within the United States, labor migrations sometimes crossed national and imperial boundaries in the Greater Caribbean, the boundaries themselves constantly shifting and being redrawn. British West Indian planters recruited free blacks from the United States between 1839 and 1847; slave smuggling, including shipments from Cuba to Louisiana, lasted into the 1860s in the United States. If not for U.S. annexation, slave vessels docking in antebellum New Orleans with thousands of human beings might have sailed from Africa and Asia, as in Havana, rather than from Richmond. Their domestic origins did not diminish the human suffering and terror.[11]

Ideas, peoples, and capital moved around the Greater Caribbean in myriad ways, across geopolitical boundaries. It is not surprising, then, to discover that coolies—or, at least, ideas about them—made their way to Louisiana by the mid-nineteenth century. As planters and lawmakers pointed to Caribbean importations of African "immigrants" and Asian coolies to drum up support for the reopening of the African slave trade in the late 1850s, other Louisianians simultaneously pursued Chinese workers directly from Cuba. As early as February 1859, several merchants had taken steps toward the transport of coolies from Havana to New Orleans, going so far as to inquire if the local customs collector would consider the project a violation of federal slave-trade laws. Treasury department officials, as confused as other federal agents, declined a definitive answer and instructed the customs collector to use his discretion in dealing with such shipments. "The mere description of persons as Coolies, does not appear to indicate whether they come within the laws prohibiting the Slave trade, or not," wrote Secretary Howell Cobb. "Without any special knowledge of the meaning of this term, it is supposed to refer to *laborers*, in oriental countries, whatever may be their condition." By way of coolie vessels or some other means, there is evidence to suggest that some Chinese entered Louisiana from Cuba before the Civil War.[12]

Geopolitical boundaries, at the same time, mattered a great deal to sugar planters, particularly in light of the industrializing economy, which deeply affected sugar-producing regions of the world. Sugar production and consumption patterns, in many ways, acted as an index of world capitalist development, centered around the north Atlantic. The incorporation of sugar as "a virtual necessity" into the British industrial working-class diet by 1850, for instance, placed a premium on a greater supply of sugar at lower prices. These coterminous developments operated hand in hand, according to Mintz, as "sugar and other drug foods, by provisioning, sating—and, indeed, drugging—farm and factory workers, sharply reduced the overall cost of creating and reproducing the metropolitan proletariat." The institution of "free trade" policies over the rancorous protests of British West Indian planters in the second half of the nineteenth century attested to the political triumph of industrial capitalists within the British imperial economy. To a great degree but later in time, this was a struggle that sugar planters encountered everywhere. In an industry renowned for its high capital requirements—in land, machinery, and labor—as well as high profits during the height of mercantilism, sugar planters' fates depended on industrial markets far away, markets determined previously by tariff protections and more and more by global competition. No matter how wealthy sugar planters became in southern Louisiana—and they were among the wealthiest slaveholders in all of the United States—they were entering a vulnerable industry, susceptible to increasing foreign competition in addition to spring floods, winter freezes, and disgruntled workers.[13]

The Civil War would lay bare these vulnerabilities, but, encouraged by new cane varieties, federal tariffs, and high prices, Louisiana's sugar industry experienced phenomenal growth in the antebellum decades. Louisiana produced about five thousand hogsheads of sugar in 1803 and nearly doubled that figure within seven years. The intensity and scale of sugar production increased sharply in subsequent decades, reaching the antebellum record of 495,156 hogsheads by 1853. Throughout the 1850s, Louisiana averaged more than 300,000 hogsheads per season, which coincided with an explosive jump in U.S. sugar consumption.[14] An expanding market and federal protection not only made sugar planters wealthy men but also attracted wealthy men to become sugar planters. With easier access to manufacturing equipment, improved lands, and enslaved labor, an elite corps of planters came to dominate southern Louisiana by the eve of the Civil War, enlarging and consolidating sugar plantations over time. In 1860, 525 large planters (owners of fifty or more slaves), though only 12.6 percent of the sugar region's slaveholders, owned about two-thirds of all improved lands and enslaved laborers and accounted for more than three-quarters of the state's sugar production. Capital flowed upward in southern Louisiana, the top twelve individual sugar planters alone representing nearly a tenth of the 1859 crop. None of this growth would have been possible without the labor of bound women and men, whose numbers increased from about 10,000 in 1812 to 88,439 in 1860. Outnumbering whites (60,356) by a significant margin, the enslaved population reflected sugar planters' labor preferences, men exceeding women 1.4 to 1.[15] They bore the deep human costs of sugar and slavery.

Saint Domingue Redux

Enslaved laborers of Louisiana made the war between the Union and Confederacy a revolutionary moment, fomenting a crisis that would lead to the abolition of slavery and the near annihilation of sugar production. On the eve of the Civil War, Louisiana's sugar industry was valued at $200 million, more than half of that figure being the value of the enslaved labor force. By the end of the war—after the physical destruction of sugar machinery, depreciation of land prices, and, most of all, emancipation—the industry would lose approximately $193 million of its antebellum assessment.[16] In claiming their freedom and their bodies, slaves effected a radical redistribution of wealth that their forebears had imagined possible for generations. A tradition of slave rebellions, that of running away, stretched back to the earliest days of slavery—sustained through French, Spanish, and American rule—and shone bright as thousands personally bid farewell to slavery before formal abolition. No one recognized this better than their owners. "As far as the memory of man can go," a distressed planter stated in 1862, "there has existed among the negro population a tradition which has caused us many a sleepless night."[17] The Civil War caused planters more sleepless nights than ever before. To slaveholders and slaves alike, the war was nothing short of revolutionary Saint Domingue resurrected on U.S. soil.

Even before Louisiana's native son, Confederate general Pierre G. T. Beauregard, ordered the first shots of the Civil War on April 12, 1861, tension and excitement filled the humid air. Rumors of an impending war and possibly emancipation gripped the countryside, from the plantation mansions to the slave quarters. "Shucks we knew everything de master talked about," recalled Elizabeth Ross Hite, a former slave. "De house girl would tell us and we would pass it around. Dats how we knew dat master was afraid of de Yankees. My mother says dat one day she heard master say dat de Yankees would kill dem and take all de slaves and free dem." Planters and local police juries (governing bodies at the parish level) took precautionary steps whenever they learned that, as a planter put it, "the Negroes have got it into their heads they are going to be free." They raised slave patrols, reinforced the pass system, and banned slaves from possessing a boat or a skiff. Planters' confidence in the slavery regime nonetheless suffered severe blows everyday, with military preparations and maneuvers providing an ominous backdrop. Within days of Beauregard's shots on Fort Sumter, N. P. S. Hamilton, in charge of a sugar plantation in Lafourche Parish, summoned Allen Collins from the slave quarters, to no avail. When Collins

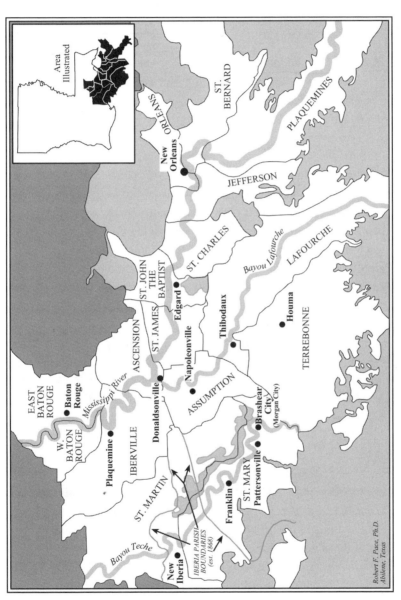

Map of Louisiana's Sugar-Producing Region.
By Robert F. Pace, Ph.D., Abilene, Texas.

finally showed up, Hamilton "slap[p]ed him in the face" to teach him a lesson. Collins promptly ran away.[18] This was but the beginning of a deluge.

As Union forces captured New Orleans in April 1862 and then marched through the heart of the cane region, Louisiana's slaves formed a considerable portion of what W. E. B. Du Bois labeled the "general strike" of half a million African Americans, which determined the fate of the Civil War. They ran to Union lines, to freedom. In 1861, Octave Johnson was sold by his New Orleans owner to a planter in St. James Parish. Working by the task as a cooper, he figured he could get away with not responding to an early morning bell. "For this the overseer was going to have me whipped," Johnson recounted, "and I ran away to the woods, where I remained for a year and a half; I had to steal my food . . . before I left our number had increased to thirty, of whom ten were women; we were four miles in the rear of the plantation house." After narrowly evading the bloodhounds on their trail, Johnson and his cohorts "jumped into" a bayou before finally finding refuge in a Union military camp. When federal forces made their way up the Mississippi River to Baton Rouge in June 1862, a West Baton Rouge planter noted in his diary the names of those slaves who had "Gone to Federals," including "Antony & Achille . . . in Tony's skiff—a most daring achievement."[19] The imperative to run away spread like a wild contagion wherever Union soldiers went.

Desperate to contain and maintain their human property, Louisiana's sugar planters resorted to costly preventive measures. "I tell you, a man that owns ten, twenty, or thirty thousand dollars in *Slaves*," observed a New York soldier, "*will not* give them up without a struggle to maintain their (so-called) rights." Planters who "used to count their money by thousands" displayed a "brutal ferocity" worse than that of "the Savage." In September 1862, the Roman family of St. James Parish sent some of their slaves farther behind Confederate lines, but the new surroundings failed to stem the tide of runaways. "Now, let me tell you that I have no news of your servants . . . I am looking for them and if they are found they will be caged up right fast," wrote Célina Roman to her son. "I have three of them in prison now. This costs $36 a month[;] when we find a way to send them to the country I shall send them back and I beg you to put them to work in the fields and lock them up in the evenings and on Sundays." She slapped Rosalie, a bondwoman who threatened to leave, and thought such actions were necessary to demonstrate her authority. A week later, Roman was begging her son to punish Rosalie harshly, if found, for she had run off with some others. "I do not want any more Negroes around me," Roman exclaimed, "with what pleasure I would sell them all." Instead, she took great pains to keep her "negroes" around.[20]

When Union troops organized an offensive down the Bayou Lafourche in October 1862, John Williams, a sugar planter who would play a leading role in recruiting coolies after the war, knew what would happen next. Just six days into the campaign, a Union general was complaining that he had "already twice as many negroes in and around my camp as . . . soldiers within."[21] Along with many of his neighbors, Williams decided to seek refuge in Texas. He directed his daughter Mary W. Pugh to pack and prepare her husband's slaves for an imminent departure. "I rode up to Dixie, sent for all of the negroes & told them there was a strong probability of the Yankees coming," Pugh reported to her husband Richard, a Confederate soldier, "in which case it was your desire that I should move & take care of them, that you had plenty of money to support them until they could return home (*a big story* isn't it?) & that you would certainly take care of them as long as possible, &c. . . . they have behaved as well as possible since we started notwithstanding they have had every example to do otherwise." The trip had been a disaster. "The morning we started about 29 of Pa's had disappeared, amongst them Jim Bynum (will you ever have faith in one again?) . . . the first night we camped Sylvester left. the [*sic*] next night at Bayou Boeuf about 25 of Pa[']s best hands left & the next day at Berwicks Bay nearly all of the women & children started," she explained, "but this Pa found out in time to catch them all except one man & one woman. altogether [*sic*] he has lost about sixty—many of them his best men—he bears his losses very cheerfully *all things considered* & says he thinks he was fortunate in saving what he has done." A fellow planter decided to turn back after most of his "best hands" deserted him on the road. Pugh was "grateful" and "proud" of her own slaves, but, to protect against future losses, she "brought their winter clothes along in bundles," so " if any of them ran off they should go without any."[22]

The precipitating event varied from plantation to plantation, but the world that slaveholding families had made came crashing down. Like so many Confederate women whose husbands joined the military or escaped westward, Josephine N. Pugh witnessed the revolutionary change among her labor force alone. "They saw their masters leaving their homes . . . their faith could not stand the test, and numbers flocked to the Yankee Standard, forming a motley, grotesque, and increasing multitude," Pugh wrote. She resolved to stand her ground, hoping that "demoralization would be less complete at home." She was wrong. The Union Army entered and left her Lafourche plantation in a single day—albeit with all the plantation livestock and "negro men, they could lay hands on"—but her troubles remained. Early the next day, her "confidential man" in the slave quarters reported that "the servants yet remaining, dissatisfied and sullen, refused to work." Pugh was confident she could mend matters by speaking to them directly. "I was among a strange people, and was unprepared for a change so great," she wrote. "I looked vainly in familiar faces for the old expression." When her "voice faltered" and her eyes filled with tears "unbidden," Pugh saw the "pleasure" and "triumph" in her workers' expressions. She composed herself into "a countenance as hard as their own" and instructed them to work as long as they remained on the plantation, wondering all the while if their "relationship" was "so soon severed" and "an antagonism already arisen" between them. All but "one invalid family" left within twenty-four hours.[23]

The revolution afoot in Louisiana's sugar region was a primary reason behind the postbellum initiative to recruit coolies. Before the war, it would have been nearly inconceivable to imagine scores of Chinese migrant laborers at work on Laurent Millaudon's vast sugar estate, valued at upwards of $1.25 million. But everything changed in the fall of 1862. Relations between overseer William P. D. McKay and the enslaved labor force had grown extremely tense when Millaudon's son paid a visit in October. Henry Clement Millaudon reproached George Windberry, the alleged "ringleader," and threatened to hit him if his "rough manners" did not cease. Windberry refused to back down and, upon being struck with a whip, knocked Millaudon down. The scuffle ended when the planter pulled out his pistol and shot "sideways" at Windberry's retreating figure. Windberry reemerged shortly thereafter and charged at Millaudon with an axe, at which point another bondman intervened. Windberry fled into the cane fields. Millaudon then left the place in McKay's charge, evidently with instructions to shoot in case of further trouble. The overseer did precisely that later the same day, injuring two men and endangering many others, including Freeman Washington, a slave not involved in the earlier altercation. "When McKay shot at me I made up my mind that if he shot again, I would shoot him," Washington testified later. The overseer was shot dead; the remaining 150 or so slaves left the plantation en masse. Within eight years, Boston investors would purchase the estate for merely $175,000 and recruit more than 140 Chinese migrant laborers.[24]

Louisiana planters could not have foreseen all of the changes looming ahead, but they certainly felt the immediate shock of the labor insubordination and military occupation that would overthrow slavery, although Lincoln's Emancipation Proclamation conspicuously exempted southern Louisiana. By the summer of 1863, Union forces had captured almost the entire sugar-producing region, westward to Bayou Teche and northward to Alexandria. The level of disruption and defiance stunned and overwhelmed planters and Union troops alike. "All or nearly all of the plantation hands come within our lines and planters in consequence are unable to use their plantations," reported a Union general looking to "remedy" the situation. Andrew McCollam had no remedies. Most of the planter's slaves had "cleared out" of his Terrebonne Parish plantation by March 1863 so that in 1864 he could only hope to cultivate enough cane to use as seed with his remaining force, some of whom were "not more faithful than" those who had fled. A regiment dispatched to Duncan F. Kenner's estates found willing and able assistants, his daughter noted, "the negroes" disclosing the whereabouts of the hidden wine and silver. The prominent planter narrowly escaped arrest, but everything valuable was found and confiscated.[25]

Despair among planter families manifested in a range of emotive responses. Mary C. Moore, whose husband had relocated to the Confederate interior, fell into a deep depression. "Your letters are written more in a style of business than . . . that of protecter [*sic*] . . . ," she wrote him, "no one can im[a]gine the suffering I have undergone mental and bodily . . . I am this moment the worst off of any woman in the place . . . I am failing so much in flesh that I fear I may never see you again. I feel so desolate and cast down . . . my very heart sickens with despondency, every thing seems so changed, my thoughts are all of gloom." The arrival of Union troops and the likelihood of emancipation at times triggered violent outbursts. Carlyle Stewart's owner was usually "good to us," the former slave recalled, "but when we was freed, one of the bosses kicked my ma in the face." The same turn of events outraged Henrietta Butler's plantation mistress, who was already "mean as hell." "Never will forget how she said," Butler remembered decades later, "'Come here, you little black bitch, you!' and grabbed my finger [and] almost bit it off."[26]

The spirit of Pointe Coupée and Saint Domingue was very much alive in southern Louisiana. From plantation to plantation, parish to parish, slaves waged war against slavery, the Confederate cause. The results were profound, as realized on the sugar plantations of Louisiana's Confederate governor Thomas O. Moore in the spring of 1863. The arrival of Union forces, his neighbor John H. Ransdell reported, drove the slaves "crazy" and "utterly demoralized at once and every thing like Subordination & restraint was at an end." Three bondmen "forcibly put a confederate soldier in the stocks at your place on Saturday night a week ago," Ransdell continued. "They abused him too, very much." The soldier finally managed to escape near dawn the next morning. A high proportion of Moore's labor force left with the Union troops, taking with them plantation stock and supplies. "Demoralization" persisted after the soldiers' departure. One of the overseers was "determined to chastise" a slave named Nathan who had been "acting badly" the following month, but Nathan "showed fight" and vowed he "was ready for him." The overseer subsequently beat him "pretty severely & put him in the stocks." Ransdell nonetheless recognized that the workers' outlook had changed fundamentally, and he pledged a new course in plantation management. "*My feelings*, too, have entirely changed towards the Negro," he informed Moore. "I now care nothing for them save for 'their work.'"[27]

The British West Indies Redux

The kind of labor sugar plantations would employ was the driving concern of not only Louisiana's planters and slaves but also, with the de facto dissolution of slavery, federal officials in charge of the state. Indeed, wartime reconstruction in Louisiana, which was to be the blueprint for postwar national Reconstruction, highlighted the central role the federal government would assume in U.S. society. Louisiana sugar planters had long appreciated the power of the nation-state, with their profits heavily dependent on sugar tariffs. Although as obsessed with the protection of slavery as any group of slaveholders in the Old South, many had resisted secession from the Union until it became a foregone conclusion.[28] Louisiana slaveholders' resistance to federal authority over labor relations would prove much more durable. For most of the war, however, Union military officials attempted foremost to assuage planters' anxieties and to revive their unionist sentiments. Quite apart from the revolution that they, by and large unintentionally, sparked, these northerners were no revolutionaries. Denying, misconstruing, and repressing the cataclysmic changes in their midst, they prolonged the institution of slavery by implementing what was, in effect, an American equivalent to British "apprenticeship," the netherworld between enslavement and emancipation that pleased no one but its creators. Union officials turned repeatedly to the British West Indies rather than Haiti for historical inspiration and justification, reflective of the wide gulf between themselves and the thousands of slaves around them.

Gen. John W. Phelps, an abolitionist from Vermont, articulated early on the vast promises and grave limitations that the Union forces brought with them.

In December 1861, from a Mississippi island before the Union invasion of New Orleans, he proclaimed the North's determination to destroy slavery, long before Lincoln and others were ready to do so. Slavery, Phelps argued, was a "monopoly which excludes free-labor and competition," and which kept slaves in "comparative ease and idleness" in the South and confined "free white laborers" to the North where they were "often distressed by want." He was fighting for free labor, "the granite basis on which free institutions must rest . . . [and] the right of five millions of our fellow countrymen in the Slave States as well as of the four millions of Africans there." He encouraged Louisiana's slaves to flee to Union lines, openly welcoming them to his base near New Orleans beginning in May 1862. Two months later, Phelps decided to organize the escalating number of fugitive slaves into military units, in his mind "the best way" to channel them away from "a general state of anarchy" and toward a Union victory. Ending slavery, however, was only the beginning. Phelps assumed emancipation would necessarily involve "a well regulated system of apprenticeship" to last between five and fifteen years.[29]

Although unmistakably ahead of his peers and superiors in lashing out against slavery, Phelps's beliefs rested fundamentally on the free labor ideology at the core of the Republican party in the 1850s and 1860s. Republicans saw the world in dichotomous, individual terms, insisting on the utter incompatibility of slavery and free labor, and shifting the abolitionist focus on the personal sin of slaveholding to slavery's degradation of free labor. Slavery, Republicans argued, denied individuals the right to realize their full potential, the right to advance from wage labor to self-employment, the ultimate objective of all free laborers. Slavery not only extinguished any hope of free labor—the drive to become an independent producer—in the slave South but threatened the aspirations of northern whites by its expansion to new territories, the underbelly of America's "manifest destiny." Slavery, not capital, was the enemy of free labor. Indeed, capital and labor were deemed partners on an endless path toward general prosperity and individual mobility, purportedly the hallmarks of northern society. The antislavery stress on social values (industry, frugality, enterprise) as the key ingredient to a free society ironically prevented nearly all Union military leaders from envisioning a policy that would enable slaves to become independent producers.[30] A revolution in values was not a revolution in property; it was hardly a revolution. Even to a man like Phelps, ever impatient to wage war against slavery, freedom was a gradual matter, a matter of the mind. It would involve years of adjustment, of inculcation, of "apprenticeship" or the like.

Unlike Phelps, the commanding Union generals of the Gulf Department were all too eager to delay the abolition of slavery. First to take charge, Maj. Gen. Benjamin F. Butler, a Democrat from Massachusetts, initiated a cautious course to appease Louisiana slaveholders. In May 1862, while his subordinate Phelps embraced fugitive slaves, Butler "directed all not employed to be sent out of my lines, leaving them subject to the ordinary laws of the community in that behalf." That is, he threw them back into the hands of slaveholders, whom he generously characterized as "passive rather than active in the rebellion." A policy of virtually confiscating slave property, Butler reasoned, was "manifestly unjust" and equal to "an actual confiscation of all property, both real and personal, of the Planter, if we take away or allow to run away his negroes as his crop is just growing." He objected to the institution of slavery—"a curse to a nation"— but was willing to accept "its present existence" to avert a crisis. "What would be the state of things if I allowed all the slaves from the plantations to quit their employment and come within the lines," he concluded, "is not to be conceived by the imagination." Moreover, he objected to the "employment of negroes in arms" and deemed them unfit for military duty, alleging that the British failure to capture New Orleans half a century earlier was due to their reliance on a black regiment from the West Indies.[31]

Pressed by circumstances beyond his control, Butler slowly came to recognize the centrality of slavery in the war, albeit long after Louisiana's slaves, months after Phelps, and weeks after federal officials in Washington, D.C. In July 1862, Congress authorized the confiscation and emancipation of Confederate-owned slaves as "captives of war" and the employment of African Americans in military labor or service. Around the same time, Lincoln's treasury secretary instructed Butler to demonstrate clearly that he was "no proslavery man." In these changing times, the general could only intimate warnings against an imminent "negro insurrection," another "San Domingo," to defend his hard-line stance. By August, however, he felt enough pressure to reverse his policy on runaways, whose numbers showed no signs of diminishing, and to reconstitute the Native Guards, formerly a Confederate regiment made up of Louisiana's free people of color. Still wary of arming slaves, an issue over which Phelps tendered his resignation, but desperate for troops, Butler formally allowed free blacks to enlist in the revived unit. He proudly pointed out his policy's consistency with Confederate policy. In practice, as Union forces suffered their worst military setbacks, anyone who swore to his "free" status was allowed to enroll.[32]

Months after his Louisiana tour, which ended in December 1862, Butler reflected on his experiences before a federal commission. His testimony—sprinkled with metaphors and allusions to the Caribbean, however misapplied or misinformed—revealed not only a staunch disciple of the free labor ideology but also the severe limitations of that ideology and his policies. A belated convert, Butler became a vocal proponent of black military service. Asked about the likelihood of a slave insurrection, he again invoked Haiti. "Not if you will arm the negroes, and give them officers of their own color," Butler replied. "Do you suppose if the French General at St. Domingo had given Toussaint a captaincy, there would have been any trouble? I have always thought not." His mission had been to thwart, to co-opt a revolution, not to promote it. Butler was against slavery, believing its abolition essential before northern ideas could take root in the South. But emancipation had to be implemented gradually, with "remuneration to the masters" of perhaps one hundred dollars per slave. "I think any change should be gradual," he said. "All natural changes are gradual." He envisioned "a military supervision" of the South "for a series of years" necessary to instill free labor values in blacks and whites.[33] His testimony was an apt reflection and justification of Union military policies on Louisiana plantation labor, during his tenure and afterward. They were a peculiar variation of British apprenticeship, concocted in wartime conditions more analogous to Saint Domingue. And they were bound to fail.

As in the British West Indies—where the first four years of emancipation had compelled the freedpeople to remain with their former owners as "apprentices"[34]—Butler attempted to reconcile the fundamentally irreconcilable contradiction between masters' claims to slave property and slaves' claims to freedom. In an agreement reached with "loyal" planters in St. Bernard and Plaquemines parishes in October 1862, the U.S. government vowed to employ "all the persons heretofore held to labor . . . as they have heretofore been employed and as nearly as may be under the charge of the Loyal Planters and overseers" and to "authorize or provide suitable guards and patrols" to maintain law and order. Planters, for their part, were required to pay ten dollars per month, three dollars deductible for clothing, to "each able-bodied male"—the rate set by Congress for military laborers—and less to women and children, in addition to furnishing food and medicine to all laborers and their dependent relatives. Planters were barred from inflicting "cruel or corporal punishment"; instead, they were to report cases of "insubordination or refusal to perform suitable labor" and other offenses to local provost marshals, who would administer the appropriate punishment, "preferably imprisonment in darkness on bread and water." Slaves belonging to "disloyal" planters (and "loyal" planters refusing to enter the agreement) could "hire themselves" out to "loyal" planters of their choice. Butler subsequently extended the arrangement to the Lafourche district, where "thousands of hogsheads of sugar of the value of at least a Million of Dollars" were at stake. Labor was in high demand for the grinding season, when workers harvested the cane and manufactured it into sugar.[35]

Although Butler excitedly forwarded "the first sugar ever made by *free black labor* in Louisiana" to President Lincoln in November 1862, his policy hardly heralded a new era of free labor and prosperity. Individual slaves' consent to contract, the most basic tenet of nineteenth-century understandings of freedom, was completely absent in his arrangement. It was rather a contract between "loyal" planters and their government, with the laborers' interests presumably represented by the latter. Even on government-operated plantations, those confiscated from "disloyal" planters, laborers were cheated out of what had been promised them. Due to malfeasance, insolvency, or both, many employers, including lessees from the North, did not pay their laborers after the 1862 grinding season, causing another exodus from Louisiana's plantations.[36] The sugar industry was in a dire crisis. Planters, who had been unable to market much of the 1861 bumper crop (459,410 hogsheads), already owed their New Orleans factors about $20 million. The disastrous results of the 1862 season (87,231 hogsheads) brought down the industry at all levels. Only six of the thirteen New Orleans banks in business before the war remained open after February 1863; only a handful of the five hundred antebellum factorage firms, dependent on bank loans, survived beyond 1863.[37] Those at the bottom, the workers, were the first to go unpaid.

Union occupation put southern Louisiana in limbo under a plantation labor system that was both compulsory and compensatory, neither slave nor free. In December 1862, planters and workers, frustrated and infuriated by the first mass experiment in black wage labor, anxiously cast their eyes on Maj. Gen. Nathaniel P. Banks as he took over the Gulf Department. The moderate Massachusetts Republican quickly made it clear that he would stray little from his predecessor's compromising ways. On Christmas Eve, in a tense atmosphere created by slaves' anticipation of emancipation and planters' fears of the same (as well as slave revolts), Banks stressed that Lincoln's Emancipation Proclamation would not apply to southern Louisiana. He advised slaves "to remain upon their plantations until their privileges shall have been definitely established," suspending "unusual public demonstrations" and restricting the Native Guards' role. Banks, like Butler, tried to entice slaveholders to the unionist cause by suggesting that slavery could be preserved if the rebellion ceased and "the former constitutional relations be again established." At the same time, he reiterated the federal statute against military officers' returning fugitive slaves and counseled planters to reserve "an equitable proportion of the proceeds of the crops . . . for the support and compensation of labor."[38] Slavery was not over, but compensatory labor ought to proceed.

Declaring war against "idleness," "vagrancy," and "crime," Banks initiated a new labor program in February 1863 that further confused the boundary between slavery and freedom. Provost marshals would induce "negroes . . . to return to their families and the plantations where they belong" and take their physical presence as "proof of their assent" to contract. They would then make sure laborers worked "diligently and faithfully" with "respectful deportment to their employers, and perfect subordination to their duties" on the plantations to which they were "bound" for the year. Employers, in turn, agreed to provide food, clothing, proper treatment, and due compensation in the form of wages (sharply reduced to between one and three dollars per month) or one-twentieth share of the crop at the end of the year. Louisiana's working peoples, the majority of whom formally remained slaves, were nowhere closer to economic independence under Banks's system. Many refused to be "induced" to return to their old plantations, a group of workers on a plantation near New Orleans collectively vowing they would "rather die" than labor under the new rules. Union officers, moreover, often ended up taking on roles previously held by slave patrols and overseers. Not only did they compel blacks to work on plantations or public works projects, they collaborated closely with planters to discipline workers, at times displaying a viciousness that rivaled the worst of the slavery regime. Planters nonetheless decried the new system as "an actual and immediate emancipation" of Louisiana slaves.[39]

The British West Indies seemed to afford the only argument in favor of Banks's labor regulations, which satisfied neither slaveholders nor slaves. George H. Hepworth, a "warm Abolitionist" chaplain, arrived in Louisiana in January 1863 skeptical of Banks's plan, personally favoring a more radical plan of confiscating and distributing plantation lands to black families. He, however, changed his mind after touring southern Louisiana and later championed Banks's system in northern antislavery circles. It was the "first grand step" toward freedom, he wrote, "very like the apprentice system in the West Indies between

1834 and 1840, except that, in this case, the black man had more privileges." The plan was "satisfactory to the planter and the negro," affording the latter "an experience which will do much to fit him for the freedom which he is destined if the war continues." But African American struggles for freedom would not wait. "The negroes come back on to the plantation," a provost marshal reported, "with altogether different feelings . . . a spirit of independance [*sic*]— a feeling, that they are no longer slaves, but hired laborers; and demand to be treated as such." Confronting workers demanding wages and privileges that Banks denied them, planters grew frightened and frustrated. "The wish of the negro is now the white man's law," William Minor lamented. "A man had as well be in purgatory, as attempt to work a sugar plantation under existing circumstances."[40]

Responding to critics near and far and another dreadful season (76,801 hogsheads), Banks took formal steps to abolish slavery and to introduce free labor ideas and institutions in Louisiana. In January 1864, Banks suspended the slavery provision of Louisiana's state constitution until the adoption and ratification of a new constitution that abolished slavery. Then, in February, he established new labor regulations that finally gave laborers (or "hands")—no longer slaves—the right to choose their employers. In addition to increasing workers' monthly wages and shares of net proceeds, Banks also included provisions on schools for black children and land allotments for laborers' private use. These were significant advances. But teaching the freedpeople "the necessity of toil," despite "the revolution through which we are passing," remained paramount in Banks's agenda. Once laborers chose their employers, they would be "held to their engagement for the year, under the protection of the Government." Instances of malingering, disobedience, indolence, insolence, and crime would be punished by the forfeiture of wages and "labor upon the public works, without pay." To further insure a full year's labor, Banks required that at least half of the monthly wages be retained until the end of the season and advised employers "to discourage monthly payments so far as it can be done without discontent, and to reserve till the full harvest the yearly wages." Banks, at the same time, pledged the crops toward the payment of laborers to assure final compensation.[41]

Although Union officials acknowledged at last what Louisiana's slaves had envisioned all along—that slavery would not survive the war—they continually failed to grasp the limits of their own ideology. What ultimately ended slavery and inaugurated the elusive search for freedom lay within the enslaved peoples themselves, whose visions of freedom extended beyond Union labor regulations. Never losing sight of their own interests, they sought the kind of economic independence that northerners' sermonettes told them they ought to desire. In 1863, a group of "old and crippled" slaves in Terrebonne Parish, for instance, were allowed to work their runaway planter's estate—the planter had taken all of his able-bodied slaves to Texas—without any assistance. "No White men in Louisiana could have done more or better than these Negroes[,]" remarked a federal official, "& they well deserve the reward of their labor (the Crop) and the Encouragement of the Government." But the federal government provided little to no encouragement to such promising efforts.[42] The vast majority of the freedpeople had no choice but to sign labor contracts as directed and compelled by Union officials. Within these confines, however, they struggled to increase their independence, preemptively seizing Saturdays and holidays as their own time and preferring to tend to their garden plots over plantation crops. Women, the majority of the labor force in war-torn Louisiana, often took the lead. "They seem to think they can leave work when they please," a planter complained of his female workers.[43]

Over the course of the war, Union labor policies gradually, though never completely, accommodated laborers' insistent demands and complaints. Maj. Gen. Stephen A. Hurlbut, Banks's replacement, issued new labor guidelines in March 1865 which expanded laborers' rights and wages, including a stronger clause on liens against crops and other property to insure payment. Hurlbut's order, however, retained his predecessors' structure—lengthy labor contracts that combined compensation and compulsion—and reproduced their racial logic. Contract violations, including leaving a plantation without permission, would still result in the forfeiture of all earned wages and "forced labor on public works, without pay." Union officials continued to assume that Louisiana's freedpeople lacked the motivation to work, the individual initiative that defined a free labor society. To underscore this point, Hurlbut imposed a poll tax on "all colored persons" in the Gulf Department "so that the active labor of this race may contribute to the support of their own helpless and disabled."[44] These were the regulations in place as the war drew to a close.

The contentious dynamic forged by laborers, planters, and federal officials during three tumultuous years would outlive the Civil War, with no party able to determine Louisiana's fate alone. The war unleashed the revolutionary consciousness deeply engrained in the minds of Louisiana's enslaved workers, a force that destroyed antebellum social relations, if not to the extent they had hoped for. Planters longed for the old regime. Only "corporal punishment"—rather than "increased pay"—would effect "obedience, honesty and faithful labor," a planter stated, among "a people entirely oblivious of moral obligations resulting from their contract." By the spring of 1865, planters had no choice but to concede acrimonious negotiations over labor contracts as a sad fact of life. After a disappointing season, many of A. Franklin Pugh's laborers either searched for new employers or held out for a contract under Hurlbut's terms, flatly rejecting the offer of a share of the crop. "It was very distasteful to me, but I could do no better," Pugh admitted. "Every body else in the neighborhood has agreed to pay the same and mine would listen to nothing else."[45] Indeed, planters ignored at their own peril federal authority over labor (and, as before, over sugar markets) and laborers' demands. As the work of reconstructing their plantations and the nation-state began, Louisiana planters found themselves envisioning a different kind of freedom, the kind they knew to exist in the West Indies after "apprenticeship."

Eyeing Coolies and Cane

Louisiana sugar planters looked abroad to cope with their postwar predicament because the world they knew and ruled was no more. The state's once thriving sugar industry was on the brink of extinction, with no better prospects on the horizon. The last wartime harvest from the 1864 crop had yielded only 10,387 hogsheads of sugar, not even enough to meet the local market that had to resort to imported Cuban sugar. Less than 200 of the 1,291 antebellum sugar plantations remained in operation by 1865, one after another a casualty of war, debt, and other forces beyond the planters' control.[46] Many planters were pressed to liquidate their estates on terms that an Ascension Parish planter called "a Suicidal Sacrifice of property." Two years after the war, a Freedmen's Bureau agent still noted numerous plantations "not cultivated owing to the insolvency of their owners or proprietors." Above all else, Louisiana planters blamed emancipation for their woes and demanded that the federal government deliver them from the throes of wage labor. "History proves that the labor of free negroes can not be made profitable," a planter argued before a federal commission. "The negro population is so large in comparison with the white, and the territory so great, that I don't see how it is possible that the parties can exist free together." Sugar production, he insisted, could not survive in units smaller than five hundred acres, given the high capital requirements, or "without an absolute certainty" of labor.[47]

Louisiana sugar planters also faced greater competition from abroad, their wartime demise—not unlike Saint Domingue earlier—contributing to major shifts in global sugar production. The Civil War provided a major impetus to sugarcane production in Hawai'i, a kingdom that had fallen increasingly dependent on the U.S. economy throughout the first half of the nineteenth century. By 1850, haoles (white foreigners) had engineered a transformation of the islands into a model of capitalist social relations, transferring most of the land, capital, and government positions into their own hands. The stage was set for a haole oligarchy, whose sights fixated on sugar beginning in the 1860s when Louisiana's secession and destruction opened up the West Coast market.[48] On top of Hawai'i and Europe's budding beet sugar industry, Louisiana planters continued to face their venerable rivals from the Caribbean in a national market that they no longer controlled. A St. Louis merchant had informed his brother, a Louisiana sugar planter, during the war that prices were "altogether governed by values in the New York market," which relied on Puerto Rican and Cuban sugar imports. The future looked bleak. The lack of "sufficient protection from the General Government" and "unfair competition in Cuba," mourned the *New Orleans Times*, would likely worsen as "the people at large are much more interested in obtaining cheap sugar than in fostering the sugar producing interests of Louisiana."[49]

Asian migrant laborers, the so-called coolies, played a pivotal role in the global expansion of sugar production in the second half of the nineteenth century, a development not lost on Louisiana sugar planters. Exporting cheap sugar became synonymous with importing cheap Asian labor, both integral aspects of a worldwide system of capital accumulation. The "pacific domination" of the industrial working class in western Europe and North America through mass sugar consumption, as Sidney Mintz argues, was intricately tied to the brutal domination of enslaved African labor and, increasingly, Asian indentured labor in the Mascarenes, the Caribbean, and the Pacific.[50] Within this context, and as the congressional passage of the anti-coolie-trade law in 1862 indicated, the Civil War by no means halted American renderings of Asian coolies. To the contrary, as Americans (and Confederates) wrestled with conflicting visions of freedom, they were again drawn to coolies, whose wartime representations reproduced their ambiguous and contradictory antebellum status. Asian coolies recurrently and paradoxically embodied the hopes, fears, and anxieties of those struggling to sustain and abolish slavery.

Eager to cultivate a climate favorable to abolition, antislavery writers of the Civil War era studied postemancipation societies in the Caribbean for relevant precedents and lessons. The West Indies held the hidden truths behind the "recuperative power in Free Trade" and "Free Labor," Lydia Maria Child argued in a tract on the economic benefits of abolition. Hers was just one of many antislavery pamphlets produced to refute a popular perception, and a favorite proslavery argument, that emancipation had failed miserably in the Caribbean.[51] The logistics and ramifications of postemancipation Asian migrations formed a topic of considerable import in these historical and travel accounts, such as in William G. Sewell's widely circulated and excerpted testimonial on the British West Indies. Unlike Child, Sewell expressed "no sympathy with the argument of the Abolitionists" and framed emancipation primarily as a "commercial" question. He visited the various British West Indian islands in 1859 and 1860 with no intent to draw "any inference" or "any conclusion" on slavery in the United States. His letters, originally written for the *New York Times*, were collected and revised in a book that went through two editions during the first years of the war. His timing could not have been better. A nation at war over slavery craved news from the Caribbean.[52]

Sewell rekindled the idea that Asian coolies marked an advancement from slavery, a mark of free labor that would bear profits for both capital and labor in the right settings. Trinidad, in his estimation, was a prime example. It was an island with "a curious mixture of races—European, Asiatic, African, and American," with almost a quarter of the entire population "Eastern laborers," mostly "Indian coolies . . . fast giving to the island its only want, a laboring class." The "Creoles of African descent," the majority on the island but a diminishing minority on its plantations, were headed "not downward in the path of idleness and poverty, but upward in the scale of civilization to positions of greater independence." Everyone in Trinidad benefited from the system of migrant labor, entirely directed by "government supervision" that was "perfect and complete, and the consideration paid to the wants and comforts of the immigrant is carried to a point that many consider injurious to the planting interest." The "immigrant laborer" was "removed from the over-populated districts of the East to these sparsely-settled islands of the West," free of charge and for a new life of "social and moral progress" and decent wages. Asian workers thus took the place readily vacated by "West Indian Creoles," whose "increased intelligence" guided them to "a more independent mode of life." Both "Creoles and immigrants" had "in their respective spheres, materially improved, and live together in perfect harmony and contentment." Jamaica, Sewell insisted, likewise required "the contract or permanent labor of coolies" to resurrect its economy.[53]

Sewell's observations of coolie labor in the Caribbean paralleled and bolstered Union rationalizations of wartime labor policies in Louisiana. However much Sewell found the "West India negro . . . doing exactly what a white man would do under the same circumstances," white supremacy pervaded everything he saw and wrote. "Let me not be mistaken," he assured his readers. "I am not setting up the West Indian Creole as an object for hero-worship. I do not place him on an equality with the American or the Englishman." The "untutored negro," after all, was utterly unfit for democracy, the "most easily influenced by a bribe" in the world. Sewell, however, celebrated the emergence of a Creole middle class, a testament to the unyielding power of free labor to overcome racial deficiencies. How, then, was he able to reconcile the universal appeal of free labor and the institution of coolie labor? Like Union officers in Louisiana, Sewell turned to race to justify a government-supervised system of compulsory plantation labor. Coolies, already beneficiaries of socioeconomic mobility through migration, were not equipped for anything else, at least for the moment. They were "industrious and intelligent" but "mild in disposition almost to effeminacy, docile and obedient, contrasting very favorably, in this respect, with the negro, who has more force and character, and the Chinaman, who has more cunning." Their migration was "decreed in the providence of God" to make "these fair and fertile islands" into "an asylum for millions of wanderers from heathenesse" for their own "elevation" and "the restoration to prosperity of a splendid inheritance."[54]

In and through the British West Indies, Sewell, if unwittingly, bore witness to America's own potential, the wisdom of the North's past and the South's future. "Truth, we are told, will prevail," he wrote, "and freedom, we know, is truth." And "immigration" formed a centerpiece to a free society. Sewell warned that it had to be "a free immigration, violating in no points of theory and in no details of practice the grant of liberty conferred by the Act of Emancipation upon these islands and their populations forever." "Immigration" under contract was nothing less than tutelage for "a degraded people," managed by a benevolent and neutral government. Beyond laborers, Sewell beckoned "settlers and farmers from Europe or America, who will stimulate, by the force of example, the sluggish energy of the Creole peasantry . . . who will create an independent public opinion, and who will elevate the middle classes of Jamaica far above the present standard of questionable civilization." A free labor advocate through and through, Sewell envisioned the West Indies on a path toward general prosperity and individual mobility, with "the Anglo-Saxon's rapid and determined strides" leading "negroes and half-castes" and "coolies" to opportunities unavailable under slavery or in Asia.[55]

Racial arguments on behalf of coolies could be directed just as easily against them, romantic racialism and moral uplift giving way to racial dystopia and moral degeneracy. In his prize-winning book on the French West Indies, translated into English in 1863, Augustin Cochin made observations similar to Sewell's on the overall economic success of abolition and the racial traits of Asian workers, but he could not have drawn a more contrasting conclusion on "immigration." The "East Indian" was "sober, more intelligent than the black, but less robust," he wrote, while the Chinese were "generally robust and laborious" and acclimated to sugarcane production. Although he found neither group objectionable on these grounds, he explained that his opposition "rose from the ruling cause in every question of race—the cause on which religion alone can act,—morals." Only "one power alone could conquer" the "immorality of the Chinamen and Indians," but "these are the races of all others most difficult to convert to Christianity." Cochin dreaded their addition. "Baleful to the freedmen, an evil counsellor to the colonists, immigration creates above all a permanent danger to the social and moral state of the colonies," he implored. "On thinking of these nooks of the globe, where crowd and mingle together masses of negroes, Indians, Chinamen, and Malays, with a handful of whites, one shudders for the race, threatened by deplorable mixtures, and for morality and good order, afflicted by this invasion of a heathenism which Christianity has not time to break through." Lest his readers miss his point, he exclaimed: "Fancy a St. Domingo peopled by Coolies!" Cochin advised that energy be directed toward aiding the freedpeople instead.[56]

Comparisons of the racial and economic merits of black and Asian labor generated contradictory conclusions regarding both groups. If the "negro" was "universally preferred" in the West Indies, as Cochin argued to defend emancipation and to condemn coolie labor, other observers exploited the same logic to defend slavery and to condemn coolie labor. Around the time Union troops took over New Orleans, *De Bow's Review* published an article that claimed abolition as a British ploy to monopolize the world market in "tropical agriculture" by eradicating the "slave-labor sugar of Cuba and Louisiana" and resorting to "cooly labor" in its own colonies. "We fight against nature's laws in seeking to impose tropical field labor on the white and olive races, and to release the black race from it," it concluded, "and we, moreover, violate true liberty in so doing." A delegate at Maryland's wartime constitutional convention made a similar argument against abolition, stating that "the English nation . . . the great champions and advocates of freedom for the negro race, have themselves repudiated their own doctrines . . . and under the garb of coolie apprenticeship reintroduced slavery where they had once abolished it, and in a manner and by means much more objectionable than it any where exists in the United States."[57] Coolies in the Caribbean were some of the final straws clutched by proslavery propagandists in their struggle to hold onto their vanishing "peculiar institution."

The Civil War broke the antebellum consensus that the migration and employment of Asian coolies signaled a form of slavery, a consensus that had culminated in the passage of a federal law ostensibly designed to protect these unsuspecting subjects from their cruel captors. The consensus was broken not by proslavery ideologues—who continued to denounce British hypocrisy—but by free labor advocates. In a nation at war, with Union officials besieged by runaway slaves and in search of law and order, the British West Indies represented a beacon of hope. Government-sponsored "apprenticeship" and "immigration" afforded a historical justification for Union wartime policies, appearing as a hopeful harbinger of things to come, namely a peaceful, gradual, and profitable transition to free labor through long-term contract labor. If the British West Indies illustrated the profits of the rule of law, Saint Domingue epitomized the destruction of revolution, a fate to avoid at all costs. The revolutionary potential of the Civil War caused Union officials and antislavery writers, already partial to British imperial decrees, to accept, indeed to champion, state intervention as the most sensible and judicious path to freedom, even as they perpetually compromised their own notions of free labor in the process. The federal prohibition of the coolie trade, Union labor policies in Louisiana, and positive assessments of emancipation in the West Indies—even Sewell's and Cochin's divergent conclusions on coolies—were logical products of the free labor ideology refracted through white supremacy and exigencies of war.

Race had lain at the heart of antislavery and proslavery criticisms of Caribbean coolieisms before the war, but its significance grew as northerners came face to face with the task of applying their free labor principles to a people identified with slavery, free labor's antithesis. During the war, federal officials found it more convenient to rebuke slavery and slaves (and then ex-slaves) than to interrogate the limits of their own ideology and policies. In Louisiana, as elsewhere, they rationalized compulsory practices with assumptions on racial shortcomings. In a pattern that would become more pronounced after the war, as historian Thomas C. Holt argues, emancipators in the British West Indies and the

United States increasingly explained the freedpeople's resistance to their edicts with overtly racist theories, allowing "the reformers to maintain their faith in their liberal democratic ideology which justified the bourgeois world they had created."[58] In the same vein, as northerners looked abroad for historical guidance, they came upon another group of workers seemingly ignorant of what they deemed free labor's inherent and universal virtues, a godsend in Sewell's view and in Cochin's a recipe for nightmare.

The intellectual ethos behind antislavery arguments and the social and political ferment of emancipation, in the end, generated new American perspectives on coolies during the Civil War. First, coolieism was once again hailed as a free alternative to enslaved labor, a civilizing mission that benefited the coolies as much as anyone else. Second, the institution of coolieism was assailed for its inhumane conditions and its inferior human subjects. Neither perspective was unprecedented per se, but the varying ideas embedded therein had melded into new contradictory positions and juxtapositions neither possible nor desirable before the war. No one, for example, had suggested, as Sewell did, that the *success* of free labor among the freedpeople had created a legitimate demand for coolies in the Caribbean. And neither antislavery diplomats in China nor proslavery ideologues in the Old South had concentrated on the inhumanity of coolies in their opposition to coolieism. As long as slavery existed on U.S. soil and its defenders and foes fought over its relative morality and brutality, debates over the nature of the institution (coolieism) had taken precedence over the nature of its victims (coolies). As free labor advocates strove to resolve free labor's universalism with the realities of long-term contract labor in the South, they intensified the racial scrutiny of coolies (and blacks), within and beyond the United States.

Edgar Holden's elaborately illustrated article, "A Chapter on the Coolie Trade," exemplified how anxieties surrounding emancipation affected wartime interpretations of Caribbean coolieisms, including the China-Cuba coolie trade, long the object of American scorn. Published in *Harper's New Monthly Magazine* in 1864, Holden could not have been more unambiguous in his antislavery sympathies. "Gigantic outrages have been enacted," he declared, "but more than this, an old form of slavery has been instituted under a new name, and many a deluded Coolie is to-day under a more hopeless and terrible bondage than the African from the Gaboon." His "very brief account," he hoped, might provide insights on "one of the greatest problems of the age—the finding [of] an efficient substitute for slave labor." From kidnappings and farcical inspection in China to sale and abuse in the Americas, the entire trade smacked of human bondage in the worst form. Up to this point, his account merely reinforced the resounding sentiment against the trade, a sentiment that federal legislators had encoded into law. Holden's portrayal, however, took a curious turn as he shifted from a broad historical overview of the coolie trade to the voyage of the U.S. vessel *Norway*, a ship filled with a cargo of 1,037 coolies, "our crew" numbering sixty, and "several lady passengers and children" on their way back to the United States via Cuba. He foreshadowed the ill-fated voyage by quoting a letter from Havana on the "malicious and vengeful disposition" of the coolies and the likelihood of "a serious outbreak, perhaps revolution" if "the present system of oppression" persisted.[59]

Rather than demonstrating the inhumane aspects of the trade, Holden's words and accompanying pictures dehumanized coolies. Aside from casual asides on

"Preserving the Peace," *Harper's New Monthly Magazine* 29 (June 1864): 5. Edgar Holden's article, "A Chapter on the Coolie Trade," condemned the inhumanity of the coolie trade.
Courtesy of University of Washington Libraries, Special Collections, UW2364oz.

"On the Lower Deck," *Harper's New Monthly Magazine* 29 (June 1864): 10. Holden's article also dehumanized Chinese migrant laborers in the process.
Courtesy of University of Washington Libraries, Special Collections, UW23641z.

the "barbarians" committing suicide or "constantly quarreling," he devoted the bulk of his article to "a plot the most cold-blooded and inhuman," divulged "in the heat of passion and revenge" by a coolie engaged in a "not unusual quarrel" below deck. "The leaders were desperadoes who had voluntarily come to the barracoons," Holden revealed, "having studied the plot for weeks; and ere they had been on board an hour were at work, urging, with every plea of cupidity or revenge, the rising *en masse*, murdering every man who opposed, seizing the ship and cruising as they chose." The rebels planned to set fire to the vessel and, as the crew ran to put out the flames, "to rush up" and "massacre every man as he came in their way, and thus gain possession." Two days later, as foretold, the crew awoke in the middle of the night to flames and "a yell like that of ten thousand demons" and instantly managed to lock the main hatch and arm themselves with every weapon on board. The initial uprising had been contained with minimal injury, only an officer wounded and a coolie shot in the breast.

The crew then threw tarpaulins over the hatches, aimed a "stream of water" below, and "shot down with remorseless vengeance . . . till ere long not one could be seen from any point on deck."[60]

The rest of the narrative, framed as a classic battle between the forces of evil and good, recounted the violent struggle between the "foiled wretches" and the outnumbered but better-armed crew. Amid the "ominous lull" following the original outburst, the crew found cracks through which "the miscreants could be seen gliding hither and thither, their dark forms tinged with a dusky red glare from the smouldering flames, or grouped together in consultation." For two nights, the coolies periodically, "with terrific yells" and "as if animated by one impulse," rushed "from one end of the deck to the other, making one's blood almost curdle at the conviction that they had actually found a way of escape." Four coolies chained above deck tried "to join in the melée," only to be discovered and beaten or shot. Refusing to surrender as ordered, one of the "rioters" "dipped a stylus in the blood upon the decks" and demanded that the ship proceed to Siam, where "a certain number may leave her," before resuming the original course. The ship would burn otherwise. The captain, crew, and ladies "bravely" worked together to suppress "the fury of the mutineers" who ultimately capitulated and "sued for pardon." By the time the ship disembarked in Havana, 130 Chinese had died, 70 from the "mutiny" and the rest mostly from a dysentery epidemic.[61] Holden's story essentially was a tale of Saint Domingue (or any other slave rebellion), except, this time, the white minority won. That the crew and human cargo eventually landed in Cuba, where slavery and coolieism reigned, was a fitting conclusion.

Holden's article conveyed, at best, conflicting messages that emblematized the countervailing judgments on coolie labor swirling across the seas. Coolies were all over the map. They suffered under horrid conditions but rebelled for no reason and therefore deserved violent repression. From Hawai'i came early accounts of the "vicious" and "inefficient" nature of "Chinese coolies" and better hopes for "Hill Coolies of India" or "coolies from Polynesia" during the wartime sugar boom.[62] Other prognostications had coolies bound for cotton production in Algeria and the U.S. South and American "free negroes"—acclaimed as a cheaper and superior labor source than "Coolie Importation"—for sugar production in the British West Indies. The colonization of blacks abroad, a vision of freedom popular among Republicans, deeply troubled *Harper's Weekly*, which warned against a "negro empire . . . rearing its head menacingly somewhere on our Southern border" and the replication of "systems of coolie and negro immigration" in the United States. Republicans in Congress and American missionaries in China, meanwhile, continued to demand the prohibition of the "coolie slave-trade" that ensnared only "reckless and profligate fellows" and "ignorant and unsuspecting villagers."[63] Characterized as slaves and immigrants, rebellious and docile, male and effeminate, and neither black nor white, coolies were thrown back into the netherworld between slavery and freedom during the Civil War. The indeterminacy of their status was an opening that Louisiana planters would exploit in their drive to establish what William Minor hoped would be slavery "under some other name."

CHAPTER THREE

Demanding Coolies

In April 1861, Raphael Semmes arrived in New Orleans to assume the command of CSS *Sumter*, the first naval vessel to fly the flag of the Confederate States of America. After converting to "war purposes" the packet ship, which formerly plied between New Orleans and Havana, Semmes and his crew made their way down the Mississippi River toward the Union blockade in the Gulf of Mexico. In June, they broke away from Union ships on their trail and headed to the Caribbean, where they would spend the rest of the year enforcing their own blockade of sorts. The *Sumter*'s primary mission was to disrupt American trade in the West Indies, arresting, confiscating, and setting ablaze U.S. vessels as Semmes saw fit. "Our first prize made a beautiful bonfire and we did not enjoy the spectacle the less because she was from the black Republican State of Maine," he wrote elatedly in his log. The *Sumter* came upon a wide array of vessels—American, Spanish, Dutch, French, British, Prussian, Danish, and Swedish—engaged in all kinds of trade, including the shipment of sugar and provisions to and from sugar-producing colonies. For six months, the Confederate steamer cruised around the Caribbean, stopping over in Cuba, Curaçao, Venezuela, Trinidad, Cayenne, Surinam, Brazil, and Martinique. In each port, Semmes liked to recount, government officials and local residents often "expressed a warm sympathy in our cause."[1]

There was no question in Semmes's mind that the Confederacy was "fighting the first battle in favor of slavery" against "Yankee and English propagandists." Everything he observed in the Caribbean seemed to confirm his proslavery worldview. The disastrous results of "free niggerdom" in British and French colonies led to their downfall, he believed, the "negro race" proving to be "idle and thriftless" everywhere. In Surinam, where Dutch authorities maintained slavery, Semmes found a landscape reminiscent of the South and "evidence of more prosperity . . . than we had seen either in Trinidad or Cayenne." The Dutch colony's fate was nonetheless doomed, as "the slave tenure" was "very precarious" and racial mixing all too common. "All classes are being mixed here, and all these Guianas, in course of time," he predicted, "will follow the fate of the West Indies and be owned and governed by a mixed race of whites and blacks." The "Yankee consul" there, whose wife was "a dark mulatto" and "the owner of slaves," appeared to herald the downward march, a "worthy representative of Yankeedom and negrophilism." The consul not only offended Semmes's racial sensibilities but also tried to prevent the *Sumter* from receiving coal. The Confederate commander detested the "Connecticut man."[2]

The Caribbean revealed more than a morality tale involving whites, blacks, and mulattoes though. Semmes could not ignore Asians in his midst. On his last day in Surinam, he discovered that two of his stewards had deserted the *Sumter* and instantly concluded that "they were seduced away by the U.S. consul, a man of no character . . . and some Yankee skippers that were in port." He identified one of the deserters as "my body servant and a slave" and the other as "a Malay." Semmes solicited the aid of the colonial governor and police chief and issued a reward for their capture, all in vain. The local police determined that the two runaways had gone to the "bush," beyond reach. Semmes vowed to return or to dispatch another vessel for the fugitives, emphasizing to local officials that the "negro" was "not only bound to service on board this vessel" but "also valuable private property, so recognized by the laws of Holland and of the Confederate States, . . . subject to the reclamation on other grounds than as a deserter." In addition to the wayward Malay, Semmes saw in the West Indies hundreds, if not thousands, of Asian workers to whom he tenuously accorded "white" status.

To underscore the venality and hypocrisy that he claimed to have witnessed in Trinidad, Cayenne, and Martinique, he condemned the myriad coolie ships arriving daily. He had "found the coolie trade in full activity in the English and French colonies," which seemed "intent upon retrieving their error of liberating the black man by enslaving the white man."[3]

In his Civil War memoirs, originally published in 1869, Semmes recalled these events in a slightly different light. A New Orleans friend, he explained, had given him the enslaved steward, Ned, "a good-tempered, docile lad" who had become his "right-hand man." Then, the "Connecticut miscegenist (and slave-holder, at the same time)" lured Ned away and forced him to work on a plantation owned by his "negro wife." "Ned's head was rather too woolly to enable him to understand much about the abstractions of freedom and slavery," he wrote, "but he had sense enough to see, ere long, that he had been beguiled . . . and . . . began, like the prodigal child, to remember the abundance of his master's house, and to long to return to it." Ned, according to Semmes, escaped to England "in quest of the *Sumter*" and subsequently returned to the United States and "died miserably, of cholera, in some of the negro suburbs of Washington City." Semmes erased the Malay runaway altogether in this retelling, although he later mentioned "my faithful steward, John (a Malayan, who had taken the place of Ned)." He also revised his disapproval of coolie labor. The devastating failure of freed black labor, Semmes now believed, compelled West Indian planters to introduce coolies, whose "skilful and industrious cultivation" restored their "lost prosperity." Cast originally as a fellow deserter and an enslaved "white man" in 1861, both the Malay steward and the coolie had become perfect replacements for enslaved black labor by 1869.[4]

Semmes's reactions and recollections represented the deep transformations wrought by the Civil War and the prominent yet marginal—and always contradictory—role of coolies therein. After 1865, those who had been among the most vehement critics of coolieism, slavery's defenders, became its fervent champions, demanding and importing coolies as never imagined before abolition. In the years after the war, Americans witnessed with horror, joy, and confusion the arrival of Asian workers in the United States via New Orleans. Their status in the wake of the Thirteenth Amendment bewildered the reunited nation. Asian migrants had already become a fixture along the West Coast for close to two decades, also suffering under the racial epithet *coolies*, but they had been generally divorced from the debates on coolie shipments to the Caribbean that had led to the federal law against the coolie trade.[5] Asian migrants in postemancipation Louisiana, on the other hand, had closer connections to the Caribbean than to California, at least initially. As the politics of coolieism merged with the politics of Reconstruction in Louisiana and the rest of the South, Asian coolies kindled new dreams, anxieties, and antipathies that defined postbellum America. They remained an enigma, a cultural figure identified with the past (slavery) and increasingly with the future (industrial capitalism and free trade). Were they slaves or immigrants, black or white, an asset or a deficit to America's progress? In an industrializing and expanding nation trying to recover from a devastating war, they were all those things and much more.

From Cuba to Louisiana

The ties between Louisiana and the Caribbean, particularly Cuba, deepened immediately after the Civil War, with many Confederates finding a haven in the Spanish colony. Eliza McHatton-Ripley and her family, for example, had fled their sugar plantation near Baton Rouge in December 1862 and made their way to Havana. Landing in "the loveliest gem of the ocean" just before Lee's surrender, McHatton-Ripley marveled at the "animated and gay" scenery, the sugar boom having made Cubans "fairly drunk with the excess of wealth and abundance." Havana, she noted, was "thronged with Confederates as homeless as ourselves," with their numbers increasing daily. "Scarcely a day passed that news of fresh arrivals did not reach us," she recalled, "and we met many friends on that foreign shore whom we had not seen since the first gun was fired at Sumter." These Confederate exiles, including Louisiana governor Thomas O. Moore, had found refuge in a slave society, as Saint Domingue's planters had in Louisiana decades earlier. They eagerly looked forward to "steamer days," when news and letters arrived from their old homes on the other side of the Gulf of Mexico.[6]

News and peoples traveled in the other direction as well, including those focusing on coolies. With the war's embers still smoldering, southerners with Caribbean connections began fanning the flames for coolie shipments to the postemancipation South. John S. Thrasher, a resident of Cuba and Louisiana and a leading filibuster before the war, argued in the summer of 1865 that the "advantages of Coolie contract labor" had "been abundantly demonstrated in Cuba" and ought to initiate "a combined effort" by "our responsible planters" to invest in a similar project. Cuba's success, he stated, was due to "a full and explicit code of free labor regulations" and their strict enforcement, a precedent that portended the necessity of federal legislation and state recognition of multi-year contracts. No "scheme of legislation," on the other hand, would "make the freed blacks as a mass industrious." Thomas M. Boyle, a former commander of a U.S. vessel engaged in the coolie trade between China and Cuba and a renowned figure in New Orleans and Mobile, proposed to transport coolies to southern ports, first from Cuba and then directly from China, under eight-year contracts. And Charles de Gaalon, a native Louisianian who had been a sugar planter in Guadeloupe, pontificated on the "docile and respectful" outlook of "Hindoo Coolies" over the "vicious, insubordinate" tendencies of the Chinese, whose "tenderer skin" could "not endure the sharp edges of the cane leaves." The prosperity of French colonies after emancipation, he insisted, derived from the mass importation of "Asiatic laborers" coupled with a "rigid police and vagrant system" for former slaves.[7]

Indeed, Louisiana appeared poised to implement de Gaalon's dual prescription of systemic importation and strict enforcement by the end of 1865. In March, Lieutenant Governor J. Madison Wells, a Unionist planter from Rapides Parish, ascended to the governorship and soon aligned himself with ex-Confederates, many of whom he appointed to state and local offices. Complemented by President Andrew Johnson's liberal amnesty proclamation at the national level, Louisiana planters and their supporters regained their old seats of power and began passing local ordinances that virtually reinstituted the antebellum slave codes. And after sweeping the state election of November 1865, Louisiana Democrats passed a series of laws—cumulatively called the Black Codes—that severely undermined the freedpeople's rights as workers. Omitting overt references to race in laws that otherwise targeted African Americans, they compelled agricultural laborers to contract for the year within the first ten days of January and authorized voluntary indentures of up to five years. Failure to contract left them subject to being arrested as vagrants and hired out to private parties or public works for up to one year without compensation. Other prohibitions against enticing or employing laborers already under contract and trespassing on plantation property further empowered the state to restrict ex-slaves to plantation labor.[8]

Louisiana planters and merchants simultaneously set out to import coolies en masse, fully expecting an endorsement of their project from the state legislature. Reports and rumors on coolie labor spread throughout the countryside and converged in New Orleans, the South's leading port city. "The Chinaman is naturally industrious and obedient, as he is, also, intelligent and ingenious,"

a planter rhapsodized in a New Orleans newspaper. "He understands the cultivation of rice, cotton, and sugar in his native country . . . he is also usually honest, inclined to fulfill to the letter his contracts, and is not disposed to shirk or
slight any labor or responsibility." The "working classes" of China were "content to labor all their lives, scarcely thinking of any recompense above a scanty
subsistence" and "never have shown any disposition to meddle in politics." He
urged an association of planters to charter a ship and export goods to China and,
on the return voyage, import laborers under long-term contracts. By November 1865, "large planters" from nearby parishes convened in New Orleans to
test the "public sentiment" on "coolie labor" and to take steps toward forming
a company "for immediate importation" into Louisiana. "To bring coolie labor
in competition with negro labor—to let the negroes see that laborers can be had
without them—is the main feature of the plan," a reporter noted, "and these
planters are sanguine in the belief that after a few cargoes had been brought in,
there would be no want of labor on the cotton or sugar plantations."[9]

Confident of the local demand and state sanction, various merchant houses
took concrete steps to supply and profit from the burgeoning market for
coolies. Samuel Rainey of New Orleans—representing an "enterprising firm"
with "abundant means, foreign connections, and familiar with the whole business, of coolie importation"—inquired in August 1865 if the secretary of state
would permit the importation of "immigrants from China." F. Reimonenq of
Soubry and Company, a French commercial firm that operated five steamships
transporting coolies from India to the French West Indies, likewise opened an
"Immigration Agency" in New Orleans in November 1865. He solicited planters
in Louisiana and neighboring states to sign contracts for migrant laborers from
India or China, hailing the "Orientals" of India as superior plantation laborers
and asserting the legality of their transport to Louisiana. Reimonenq hoped to
sign contracts as soon as "the question of reconstruction" was resolved or earlier if planters were willing to incur the political and financial risk. His company
announced that if agreements were signed over the next two months, it could
import two thousand laborers per month beginning in April 1866. William
Hunter and Company, another New Orleans commission merchant and shipping firm, also wished to enter the business but, like Rainey and Reimonenq, requested the federal government's seal of approval.[10] It would never arrive.

Amid the tensions arising from war and emancipation, the coolie question
emerged as an early cause for federal intervention in the South. The Bureau of
Immigration, an agency the Republican Congress created within the State

Department in 1864, tried to discourage such projects early on by noting its inability "to grant special commissions or to give subsidies for the purpose of securing Immigrant laborers from any country." Besides, Commissioner H. N. Congar warned, the federal statute against the transport of coolies posed specific "obstacles" to such schemes. Congar later revealed to Congress that his bureau had "received numerous letters requesting authority to bring into the south East Indian or coolie laborers." All correspondents, he reported, had been informed that "the introduction of new races bound to service and labor, under contracts similar to those in the West Indies, is contrary to the true interests, as it is to the laws, of the United States."[11] Congar's successor, E. Peshine Smith, a prominent Republican and free labor theorist, reiterated the bureau's policy, declaring that "the introduction of Coolies into the United States is expressly forbidden." "The whole policy of the Government is in accordance with the Spirit of this Law," he stated in reference to the 1862 law, "and this Office does not feel itself authorized to encourage any scheme for the introduction of coolies into this country."[12]

The prospect of coolie importations into the South quickly became embroiled in the broader political struggle over Reconstruction. Although the creators of the anti-coolie-trade law had fixated on the Chinese coolie trade to Cuba and framed it strictly as a foreign issue, the Bureau of Immigration recast it in domestic terms, applying it to a recalcitrant South seemingly intent on resuscitating slavery. The southern press, in response, examined the law closely and pronounced its inapplicability. "There is nothing in this act which would forbid the immigration of this people to this country, and the making of contracts for labor with them, when each laborer yields his full and voluntary assent to such agreement," the *New Orleans Daily Picayune* announced in an editorial that otherwise reserved judgment on the "coolie system." Louisiana planters and mercantile firms also pointed out—correctly—that coolies from India and voluntary migrants from China fell outside the statute. They demanded the right to import coolies. Reports extolling the merits of the coolie system in British Guiana, Trinidad, Mauritius, and elsewhere circulated even more widely in the South, including claims that either Chinese or Indian coolies (or both) possessed peculiar racial traits—such as "cheerful industry" and indifference to politics—ideal for plantation labor. Journalist Whitelaw Reid reported that he had heard "men of all ages and conditions" exclaim across the region: "We can drive the niggers out and import coolies that will work better, at less expense, and relieve us from this cursed nigger impudence."[13]

The era of the Black Codes and President Johnson's Reconstruction, in the meantime, was coming to an inglorious end. By January 1866, Governor Wells had become distressed by the unrestrained course set by Democratic legislators, who behaved as if the Civil War had never taken place. After several vetoes and attempts to stem the tide, he desperately allied himself with his former Unionist colleagues. They decided to reconvene a constitutional convention to enfranchise African Americans and disfranchise former Confederates. This call, along with the sustenance of the Civil Rights Act of 1866 by the local U.S. district court, aroused white New Orleans residents to take to the streets for three hours of mayhem on July 30, 1866. By the time federal troops descended upon the city and declared martial law, around fifty people were dead—"several cartloads of dead negroes," as a New Orleans merchant put it—and well over a hundred wounded, the vast majority of them African Americans. The riot proved a key factor in the unraveling of Presidential Reconstruction, as Congress passed in March 1867, over Johnson's veto, the Reconstruction Act, which divided the former Confederate states into federal military districts and mandated the reorganization of state governments. To gain recognition by Congress, southern states were required to draft and ratify new state constitutions that guaranteed universal male suffrage.[14]

The genesis of Radical Reconstruction intensified the federal government's vigilance against the extension of the coolie trade to the South. In the midst of its showdown with President Johnson, the Republican Congress reiterated its stand against the trade. In January 1867, Rep. Nathaniel P. Banks, the former Union commander in Louisiana, submitted a resolution condemning it as "inhuman and immoral" and "abhorrent to the spirit of modern international law and policy, which have substantially extirpated the African slave trade." Since the United States could not allow "a mode of enslaving men" through "fraud" or "force," all of its government agencies would henceforth work to prevent "the further introduction of coolies into this hemisphere or the adjacent islands." Unanimous resolutions against the coolie trade by the House and Senate, where Republican Charles Sumner of Massachusetts took the lead, prompted Secretary of State William H. Seward to issue a "Circular Relative to the Coolie Trade." Seward instructed U.S. consuls to deploy "all the authority, power, and influence, at your command, towards preventing and discouraging the carrying on of the traffic referred to in any way." The only exception, he added, was voluntary migration, which required consular examination and certification.[15]

Seward soon learned from the U.S. consulate in Havana not only that the coolie trade was alive and well in Cuba but also that it had arrived on American soil. In July 1867, Vice Consul Thomas Savage reported that "certain parties in the State of Louisiana have been for some time past, and are still engaged in the business of importing into that state from this Island Chinese or coolies under contracts to serve on stipulated wages for a specified time." Among them was J. J. Wyckes, a U.S. citizen who had previously worked on a Portuguese coolie ship sailing from China to Cuba and now sought to transport coolies from Cuba to Louisiana. He recently had dispatched twenty-five coolies to New Orleans on the American brig *William Robertson*, Savage noted, reportedly having "purchased" some of them from their "masters" and entered into contracts that established "the relation of slavery or servitude" in violation of U.S. laws. The consul recommended to Seward that the vessel be investigated upon its landing and related that he had heard of another scheme, possibly already under way, to import coolies directly from China to Louisiana and elsewhere in the South.[16] Seward immediately instructed Savage to send all information on the subject of "procuring by purchase or otherwise in Cuba, of Coolies, with the purpose of reducing them to slavery or servitude in the State of Louisiana." He also forwarded copies of the consul's dispatch to the attorney general and the secretaries of war and the treasury.[17]

Republican federal officials armed themselves for another struggle with Louisiana planters and merchants over the bounds of freedom. The attorney general's office ordered Samuel H. Torrey, the U.S. district attorney in New Orleans, to investigate the *William Robertson* and, if justified, "to interpose promptly the authority of the United States." The secretary of the treasury simultaneously instructed William P. Kellogg, the New Orleans collector of customs, to collaborate with Torrey on the case.[18] On a boat quickly provided by the commander of the fifth military district in early August, Torrey and two other federal officers proceeded to the quarantine station below New Orleans, where they discovered on the *William Robertson* twenty-three coolies under the charge of J. J. Wyckes's son Edward. After interviewing him and taking possession of the original labor contracts, Torrey had the ship seized in New Orleans, "for the emigrants were not provided with the certificates of the consul at Havana showing that their emigration was voluntary." Torrey then ordered the U.S. marshal to file a libel against the ship and to arrest the younger Wyckes and the brig's captain. The ship's owners obtained a quick release of the vessel upon a bond of fifteen thousand dollars, with William Creevy, a leading New

Orleans merchant and ship broker, as one of the sureties. Wyckes and the captain were also released on one-thousand-dollar bond each and scheduled to appear before the U.S. circuit court in November.[19]

Federal officials appeared to have a solid case against the shippers, a case to demonstrate their authority to suppress the latest leg of the coolie trade in its infancy, but the prosecution ended before it had barely begun. Although the transport of coolies potentially violated the Thirteenth Amendment and other federal statutes, as noted by the attorney general's office, Torrey's case rested on the anti-coolie-trade law of 1862. And there was no doubt that the arrested parties were guilty of transporting Chinese subjects "known as 'coolies' . . . to be held to service or labor" for eighteen months in violation of the statute.[20] Shortly after his release, however, the captain, whose main interest was in shipping Cuban sugar, returned to Havana and convinced Vice Consul Savage to exonerate him of any wrongdoing. Identifying the Wyckes and their employers as the true culprits, Savage informed Torrey that the captain had "acted in good faith, and under the impression that the chinese [*sic*] were passengers going to New Orleans as free agents." Torrey then decided to drop the charges against the captain and asked the solicitor of the treasury for permission to dismiss the entire case. He was afraid he lacked enough evidence to present to a jury. The request was granted, leading to the discontinuance of *U.S. v. William Robertson* in October 1867.[21]

The legal proceedings should have ended there, but these were no ordinary times. Edward Wyckes soon filed a lawsuit against Torrey and other federal officers for the papers they had confiscated and ten thousand dollars in damages, as the local press and citizenry lent Wyckes their overwhelming support in his battle against the government. It was this "great pressure" from fellow Louisianians, according to a federal court official, that "forced the opinion" on Wyckes to take action against Torrey, a family friend, lest "his standing in society . . . be ruined." Wyckes apparently "commenced shedding tears of repentance" during an unofficial confession and promised not to pursue the suit further. Nearly two months later though, the attorney general's office in Washington received a copy of Wyckes's complaint and demanded Torrey's explanation for *U.S. v. William Robertson*, including why he had "erroneously" corresponded with the solicitor of the treasury to suspend prosecution. Torrey now had to defend himself against his superiors for doing too little against the coolie trade and against Wyckes and his boosters for doing too much.[22] At no time did federal officials

inquire into the welfare of the twenty-three people whose transport had instigated the legal imbroglio.

Not only had federal officials mishandled what turned out to be a test case
for the anti-coolie-trade law but they also had failed to detect a series of shipments from Cuba to Louisiana, long before the *William Robertson*. The first
shipment of coolies to receive public attention arrived in New Orleans months
earlier in January 1867. Jules H. Normand, a Louisiana native who had lived in
Cuba for a number of years, delivered fifteen Chinese workers to a cotton plantation in Natchitoches Parish and announced that he could have contracted
with five to six hundred others desiring to leave Cuba. "They are stout, hardy
looking young men, and will doubtless prove better laborers than the negroes,
under the present system," the conservative *New Orleans Bee* proclaimed. Normand returned to Cuba and introduced another fifty-five Chinese migrants in
March, scarcely meeting the high local demand for coolie labor. Normand reportedly engaged "the services of those only who have performed their eight
years of apprenticeship in Havana, and in the best circumstances." Normand
and his associate then advertised their business of furnishing "Chinese Coolies"
from Cuba and arranged to register Louisiana planters' orders and inquiries
through New Orleans commercial firms. Perhaps because the Chinese "appren-
ticeships" in Cuba had expired, Normand and local newspapers felt no need to
conceal that the enterprise entailed transporting coolies under multiyear contracts. That was precisely their selling point.[23]

Federal officials had no idea that coolie shipments between Havana and New
Orleans had been established before the *William Robertson* investigation. During
his initial confrontation with Edward Wyckes, Torrey learned of Normand's
March shipment as well as twelve workers transported by the Wyckes in May
1867 to a Bayou Lafourche sugar plantation. The New Orleans firm of Lyle and
Wyckes, in which the elder Wyckes was a partner, also reportedly had contracted
with seventy-two other coolies who were apparently en route to Louisiana in
August 1867. Later in the same month, Vice Consul Savage reported to Secretary of State Seward similar information on Normand's and Wyckes' activities,
in addition to two ventures emanating from New Orleans which potentially involved upwards of one thousand Chinese from Cuba.[24] These findings alarmed
leading Republican officials in Washington, including Treasury Secretary
Hugh McCulloch, who issued an order to all U.S. customs collectors to "inquire
vigilantly" into "an alleged trade in Coolies between foreign ports and this

country" and to report all suspicious cases to his office and to proper U.S. attorneys. The federal scrutiny was hardly foolproof. When the New Orleans customs office followed up on McCulloch's order by contacting Torrey for an update, the U.S. attorney replied that the *William Robertson* was the "only infraction of the law regulating the importation of Coolies" he was aware of. Out of malice, convenience, or incompetence, Torrey forgot to mention what Wyckes had told him just three weeks earlier.[25]

It is impossible to determine exactly how many Chinese workers arrived in Louisiana from Cuba, but it is certain that the actual number exceeded that known to federal officials. In a report published in July 1867, the Havana correspondent to the *New York Times* recounted the makeshift origins of the Cuba-Louisiana migration in 1866 and its enormous growth by the following year. "The importation of coolies, who have completed their time in Cuba, has been carried on extensively for over a year, about 2,000 having left for New-Orleans within that period," the report stated. Over the previous winter, numerous "Southern planters visited Cuba . . . for the express purpose of contracting for coolies, and nearly all took from ten to forty away with them." These small-scale recruitment trips rapidly evolved into a lucrative business below the Republican regulatory radar. Around the time of the *William Robertson* shipment, the Havana correspondent had observed a French steamer shipping a cargo of more than eighty coolies to New Orleans without federal interference. The *New York Times* predicted great change ahead, as the "trade is assuming such proportions" that "Louisiana merchants and planters" advocated "the establishment of a line of steamers between New-Orleans and Matanzas," a city in Cuba's leading sugar-producing province. Spanish officials in Cuba, on the other hand, would likely "prohibit the emigration of Chinese, or, at least, be careful that all those leaving have completed the term of their contract, as cases are known where they have escaped in this manner by mingling with those who were contracted."[26]

The landing of Chinese workers in postemancipation Louisiana by way of Cuba magnified the ambiguities surrounding coolies in American culture. In April 1867, only a month after the passage of the Reconstruction Act, the *New York Times* applauded Louisiana's "gentlemen of means and enterprise" for their propitious introduction of Chinese coolies from Cuba. They were an ideal migrant labor force, much superior to Louisiana's freedpeople, as they were "generally young or middle-aged, strong, athletic, free from bad habits, quiet, frugal, industrious and, above all, willing." And they were "not citizens," unhampered

by politics, wives, or children. But when Louisiana planters and merchants zeal-
ously pursued coolies in the summer of 1867, northern newspapers raised new
alarms that resonated with antebellum images and fears. The *New York Times*
now demanded the enforcement of federal laws to prevent Chinese coolies from
bringing their "annoyance and mischief" into the South and corrupting the
freedpeople. Coolies, it seemed, imperiled emancipation. "These people are the
lowest and in every way the least desirable portion of nations the most alien to
us and our civilization," *Harper's Weekly* editorialized. "They are not needed as
laborers; and their introduction into a section of the country in which the traditions and habits of slavery are still fresh could result only in establishing a new
form of slavery, and infinitely perplexing and delaying the natural and desirable
consequences of emancipation." To "tolerate the cooly importation" would be
as "an incalculable blunder" as countenancing "the African slave-trade."[27]

While these protestations anticipated the rhetoric of Chinese exclusion, those
with heavy investments in transporting and employing coolies promoted an argument at the other extreme. In August 1867, Bradish Johnson, who owned a
sugar plantation in St. John the Baptist Parish, wrote a widely publicized letter to
Treasury Secretary McCulloch on the legality of the Cuba-Louisiana shipments.
"The coolies who came to Cuba eight years ago have served out their time, and
are now well skilled in the cultivation of the sugar cane," Johnson argued, "and
learning that the cultivators in Louisiana are willing to pay fifteen dollars per
month and board, they are desirous of coming to our country, and why should
we forbid them?" Johnson admitted to having ordered and employed such laborers on his plantation, a voluntary migration unrelated to "the infamous coolie
trade, as carried on by Spain." "They are frugal and very domestic in their habits,"
he wrote of his Chinese workers, "and those who have married, have married
white women, and their domestic life seems eminently happy. The children are
healthy and vigorous, and promise to add to the effective labor of the country."
All parties, including the nation as a whole, would profit from the infusion of
"industry and frugality against idleness and dissipation." Johnson contended that
Chinese labor would not interfere with "the colored labor of the South," as there
was plenty of work for all, and that the federal government ought to treat Chinese migrations to the South and California equally.[28]

The image of slavelike coolies replacing and undermining black labor, however, carried too much cultural weight and political appeal to be displaced by a
roseate portrait of Chinese men marrying white women and creating biracial
progeny. Both the proslavery argument condemning Caribbean coolieisms as

worse than American slavery and newfound aspirations to reproduce Caribbean precedents on American soil haunted and attracted would-be traders and employers. They demanded the importation of coolies, not the immigration of social equals, a sentiment individual coolie traders actively cultivated in postemancipation Louisiana. "A young man called in who is engaged in bringing Coolies from Cuba," a New Orleans merchant informed sugar planter Edward J. Gay in September 1867. The man offered to deliver fifty coolies under three-year contracts for two thousand dollars (or one hundred for $3,500), the laborers to receive ten dollars per month in wages as well as rations and "comfortable quarters &c." "He says he is not prohibited from bringing them in on foreign vessels," the merchant added. "The prohibition by Act of Congress is only against American ships engaging in Coolie business." John Burnside, the largest slaveholder and richest planter in antebellum Louisiana, urged Gay to consider the plan, arguing that "the Coolie competition will bring the niggers to their senses."[29]

Although Gay did not take up this particular offer, other Louisiana merchants and planters continued to receive Chinese migrants in the last three months of 1867. In November, the *New Orleans Daily Picayune* announced that a "dozen fullblooded Coolies," whose indentures had expired in Cuba, arrived in the city on the steamship *Star of the Union*. Accompanying them was none other than J. J. Wyckes, who had signed them to one-year contracts that Vice Consul Savage endorsed this time. The vessel was chartered by William Creevy's shipping firm, another party involved in the *William Robertson* affair. On board the *Star of the Union* was a Chinese passenger, whom the *New Orleans Bee* assumed was another coolie. He was Tye Kim Orr, the disgraced missionary from Singapore and British Guiana who would soon become the most renowned "Chinaman" in the South.[30] Orr's unfettered arrival with a dozen Chinese contract laborers signaled the federal government's admission of the 1862 law's confused and confusing provisions. In a year marked by the prohibition of the Black Codes and the imposition of universal male suffrage, the prospect of regular and unregulated shipments of coolies from Cuba afforded Louisiana merchants and planters a glimmer of hope.

Escaping Cuba, Freeing Cuba

To planters like Dr. E. E. Kittredge, the availability of coolie labor from Cuba in the spring of 1867 could not have appeared at a better moment. Planters in Assumption Parish had been desperate for additional laborers to begin the new season, the local Freedmen's Bureau agent reporting "no Idle Freedmen in this Parish." Kittredge, in particular, suffered from the labor shortfall, as the entire workforce on his Elm Hall plantation, the largest in the parish, "quit work" in late January. While his neighbors went "north for hands," Kittredge began looking southward. He received twelve Chinese workers from Cuba through the Wyckes in May 1867 and reportedly contracted for the delivery of another thirty-eight soon thereafter.[31] Describing Kittredge's recruits as "always quiet, and work[ing] steadily all day long, but not rapidly" and "less stoical, and much more passionless than either whites or blacks," a local newspaper editor acclaimed the Chinese as "the laborers for Louisiana." Supervised by a local creole speaking Spanish, he reported, they appeared "peaceable and satisfied, do anything they are required to do without a murmur, and as freely work in a ditch knee deep in mud as in the field." Cotton planters in Natchitoches Parish likewise praised the "deportment" and "assiduity" of their new workers from Cuba.[32]

These happy days would not last. Natchitoches planters recanted their initial appraisal by the fall of 1867, leading the local newspaper to conclude that the "Chinese Coolies" were "a sorry substitute for our former negro slaves." Their "inefficiency" could no longer be attributed to "a change of climate" or unfamiliarity with local tools and cultivation techniques, as first thought. "The fact has become final and undeniable that they are incapable of cultivating the soil profitably and are not to be relied on in making a crop," the *Semi-Weekly Natchitoches Times* remarked. "They are lazy, mutinous, obstinate and thievish." The plantation manager at Elm Hall later drew the same conclusion, denouncing the Chinese laborers as "stubborn, treacherous, and lazy" and stating his preference for "one negro on the place than five Chinese." The Elm Hall experiment ended in 1869 with the violent expulsion of the laborers after they continually refused to work in the field.[33] The patent discrepancy between the racial traits ascribed to coolies and Chinese workers' actual behavior in Louisiana was one of many factors that brought the Cuba-Louisiana shipments to an abrupt end.

Although there was a strong demand for coolies in Louisiana in the early postbellum years, it was a very limited market catering to the sensibilities of elite planters like Kittredge, Johnson, and Burnside. No one else could afford to recruit coolies during the great depression engulfing Louisiana's sugar industry. With so little cane surviving the war, even its most fervent boosters had to concede that sugar production could not resume at a significant level before 1869. After yielding only 15,500 hogsheads of sugar in 1865, Louisiana produced

41,000 in 1866 and 37,647 in 1867, each less than 10 percent of the record 1861 crop. The deep plunge in domestic sugar production, however, had little impact on domestic consumption habits, as sugar shipments from Cuba, Hawai'i, and elsewhere more than made up the difference. Cuba's sharp rise, in particular, coincided with Louisiana's precipitous fall in the U.S. market. Trailing only the British, Americans consumed 467,268 tons of sugar in 1867 and 543,033 tons the following year, the greatest share originating from Cuba. New York alone imported 206,952 tons (260,707 hogsheads) of Cuban sugar in 1868. The scenario clearly frustrated Louisiana's sugar interests. "Do the Republicans wish to encourage slave labor in other countries after taking so much pains to overthrow it in this[?]" the *Planters' Banner* asked at the end of 1867.[34]

Many Louisiana planters came to obsess over Cuba's seemingly endless advantages in sugar production. "As to the future of La & the South generally I can not pretend to judge but if matter[s] become much worse," wrote Andrew McCollam while visiting the Spanish colony in March 1867, "I will come to this garden of the world, if for nothing but to be under a mor[e] free and enlightened rule." P. O. Daigre, a former Louisiana plantation manager who hoped to make a fortune in Cuba as a sugar maker, was most impressed with the island's potential. "I believe if I had one of these places with 200 hands I could make enough money in two years for . . . my life time, particularly with the advantages that I see," he informed Edward Gay, his former employer. Lacking only "industrious & enterprising men," Cuba had everything that Louisiana lacked—a climate suitable for "continual vegetation" without fears of floods or freezes. It also had enslaved and coolie labor, undoubtedly a critical aspect of the "enlightened rule" that McCollam revered. Daigre promised to write again on the "crop, sugar market and the Coolies" of Cuba, three topics that apparently captured Gay's attention.[35]

Importing coolies, imprisoning labor, and exporting sugar lay at the heart of the Cuban economy and society in the 1860s, but all came under mounting attack from within and without as the decade wore on. The coolie trade from China had grown into a mass-scale enterprise by the second half of the 1850s, with nearly 30,000 laborers conveyed to Havana between 1857 and 1859 alone, mostly on U.S. vessels. When Louisiana planters and merchants descended southward to recruit coolies in 1866 and 1867, not only were 30,000 eight-year contracts expiring but an additional 26,654 laborers arrived on the island directly from China. The Louisianians' timing, in this respect, was perfect. Offering wages significantly higher than four pesos a month, the rate for the initial eight-year contracts in Cuba, made Louisiana plantations an attractive alternative to life in Cuba. The Wyckes, for example, agreed to pay the twenty-three migrants on the *William Robertson* fourteen dollars per month, plus food and housing, for eighteen months, while retaining the customary powers of the Cuban coolie system, such as the unilateral right to transfer contracts to other parties. Louisiana recruiters, in effect, threatened the livelihood of Cuban planters, particularly since the illicit importation of enslaved Africans came to a permanent halt after 1866, owing, in part, to Union vigilance against American slave ships during the Civil War. When Eliza McHatton-Ripley's husband, a Louisiana expatriate, desired additional laborers for the family's new sugar plantation in Matanzas, he visited Havana "to secure the only kind available—Chinese coolies."[36]

As in Louisiana, Cuban planters recognized quickly that procuring Chinese coolies marked only the beginning of their elusive search for an ideal labor force. "Beardless, and with long pig-tails, loose blouses, and baggy breeches, they looked like women," McHatton-Ripley wrote of her first impression of the thirty-five new recruits. Her family "watched with ever-increasing anxiety" as their "stolid, quiet, and undemonstrative" demeanor—accompanied by their "voracious" appetite as a result of their "long privation" aboard "a coolie-ship"— evolved into "refractory discontent" and "angry insubordination" that exploded "in an unguarded moment." "The Chinese were in full rebellion: stripped to the middle, their swarthy bodies glistening in the hot sun," she stated, "they rushed with savage impetuosity up the road, leaped the low stone fence that surrounded the cluster of plantation-buildings . . . brandishing their hoes in a most threatening manner, and yelling like demons, as with hastily grasped rocks from the fences they pelted the retreating overseer." The onset of gunfire and the district captain and his army finally quelled the "insurgent rebels."[37] Chinese migrant laborers also proved to be adept negotiators, with some individuals able to secure wages up to twenty-five dollars monthly from planters fearful of losing their experienced labor to American recruiters like the Wyckes. As early as 1870, Chinese residents no longer under contract (*chinos libres*) began organizing themselves into *cuadrillas* (independent labor gangs) and hiring themselves out to plantations under the direction of a Chinese *enganchador* (labor contractor). Chinese workers, it turned out, fiercely rejected the confines of bound labor.[38]

Beyond leaving with American recruiters or negotiating with Cuban planters, the outbreak of an anticolonial insurgency in eastern Cuba opened another means of escape. Armed with Enlightenment notions of liberty and promises of emancipation, Cuban rebels—a multiracial force encompassing slaveholders, slaves, and smallholders—began waging war against Spanish rule in October 1868, transforming the abolition of slavery from a distant concept to a tangible prospect. Although the prolonged anticolonial insurrection scarcely liberated the vast majority of slaves from lifetime bondage or Chinese coolies from indenture—most resided in the western half of the island, where large sugar estates and Spanish forces continued to reign—its impact on Cuban social relations was widespread and profound. The insurgency's antislavery rhetoric and policies appealed to a broad cross-section of Cuban society, especially among the island's enslaved and indentured workers. The recruitment and participation of enslaved peoples in the liberation army, in turn, speedily (yet haltingly) radicalized the rebel leadership on matters concerning slavery, from hesitant calls for gradual and limited emancipation to a general declaration of abolition. As in Louisiana six years earlier, the promise of freedom, however compromised in principle and practice by insurgent leaders, incited thousands of bound plantation laborers to take flight and, even in areas untouched directly by the insurrectionists, to wage claims against planter authority.[39]

If the Ten Years' War opened new avenues of subaltern mobility, it also drove Spanish authorities and their constituent slaveholders to fortify the institutions of slavery and coolieism, the linchpins to the plantation economy. The insurgency led Spain to adopt a formal plan of gradual abolition in 1870, but Cuban sugar planters, particularly in the western provinces, displayed little inclination to accept a world without enslaved or coolie labor. Although the overall number of slaves declined significantly in the 1870s, the concentration of slaves simultaneously increased in the major sugar-producing provinces. The status of Chinese workers also preoccupied government officials and sugar planters. In July 1870, the Cuban captain general complained to Madrid that Chinese migrants were enlisting in the anticolonial rebellion for their freedom, to the detriment of the colony's economic interests and his campaign to subdue the insurgency. In April 1871, Spanish officials, in response, ordered the suspension of Chinese migration and authorized the captain general to deport any Chinese person not under contract. Planters, exhorting the need for more labor, lobbied successfully to rescind the suspension. The colonial government's authority to banish Chinese residents who refused to recontract, on the other hand, remained on the books. The end results were the continued importation of Chinese workers until 1874 and, under the pretext of potential deportation, the close surveillance of all Chinese migrants in Cuba.[40]

The regulations that Cuban colonial authorities created to check Chinese mobility would have made southern architects of the Black Codes envious. In September 1871, the U.S. vice consul in Havana reported that city authorities had arrested every Chinese resident not under contract "that could be found in the streets, their dwellings or shops." Within two days, as many as two thousand of these "unfortunate beings" had been imprisoned in depots. The local governor notified employers to inspect and reclaim those who had run away before the expiration of their contracts, with the rest to be detained until their purported deportation. "I apprehend that this part of the program will not be carried out to any extent, their labor is needed here and especially on Sugar estates," the U.S. official surmised. As he predicted, the captain general soon mandated that all Chinese residents remain with their particular employers— under contract or temporary "guardianship"—or be incarcerated in depots, as the government undertook a thorough census. Fugitive laborers would be returned to their rightful *patronos* (contracted employers), and others would be obliged to sign another contract or leave the island. Chinese *cuadrillas*, whose members did not directly and individually contract with *patronos*, were expressly forbidden, a ban that would not be lifted until the end of the Ten Years' War.[41]

More than any other factor, the ever-tightening hold on Chinese workers' mobility, a reaction to their struggles against indentureship and Spanish colonialism, put a stop to Louisianians' recruiting forays in Cuba. As the insurgency wore on, additional regulations restricted Chinese migrants not under contract to municipal depots until they consented to new contracts. Despite lip service to Chinese migrants' rights, the only option open to them were bound plantation labor or confinement in depots (which required unpaid work for private parties or public works).[42] The beginnings of a revolutionary war in Cuba ignited and then extinguished the hopes of Chinese laborers, as their previously legal and extralegal paths to liberation—independent negotiations with employers, some of them from the U.S., and participation in the insurrection—were cordoned off. McHatton-Ripley recalled that there used to be "no restraint placed upon the movements" of contract-expired Chinese residents, whose "very valuable" experience had "readily commanded higher wages, though few chose planting as an occupation." The insurgency and counterinsurgency changed everything. "The dépôt was formerly a house of detention for deserters, but at present many of our countrymen who never ran away and who regularly completed their time of service are forced to enter it . . . working in chains, some wearing even two or three, under overseers who with whip and knives drive them to labour," a group of Chinese laborers complained. "The sole object of these cruelties is to oblige them to enter into new contracts with the wealthy proprietors . . . and when the new engagement is over, they are sent back to the dépôt and successively dealt with in the same manner. Is it not real slavery for life to which Spaniards condemn us?"[43] With Chinese workers in Cuba cut off from further recruitment, those Louisiana planters and merchants who could contemplate importing coolies were forced to pursue them elsewhere.

Revival in the Age of Capital

By the summer of 1869, China and California surpassed Cuba as potential sources of coolie labor for the South. In addition to Spanish laws, the Cuban connection inexorably triggered the suspicions of Republican federal officials, who recurrently received and rejected proposals to transport coolies from the Spanish colony to the United States. "Enquiry has frequently been made at this office," reported the U.S. consul in Havana in May 1870, "as to whether the laws or policy of the United States would be contravened by the emigration to our country from this island of Chinese subjects who had arrived in Cuba under the Coolie system." He personally did not think so as long as the arrangement violated no Spanish law and the Chinese left of their own accord. The State Department's headquarters went further and instructed the consul to inform inquirers that contracts with such laborers would be difficult to enforce in U.S. courts and that the anti-coolie-trade law probably "embrace[d] not only the case of coolies transported directly to the United States, and in vessels of the United States, but also those who having been originally carried to Cuba in violation of the policy of that law, may afterwards be shipped to the United States from Cuba in either American or foreign vessels."[44] The effective suppression of Cuba-Louisiana shipments, however, failed to curb the surging demand for coolies across the South.

A tangled web of regional, national, and global factors rejuvenated American planters' demand for coolies in 1869. In southern Louisiana, the news of rebellion and turmoil in Cuba enhanced the optimism already springing from the 1868 sugar crop (84,256 hogsheads), which outproduced the two previous seasons combined. "Revolutions seldom go backward, and the trouble in Cuba I think has only begun," a New Orleans merchant predicted in February 1869. If the rebellion succeeded, as he speculated, "a general disturbance of the labor system must ensue, and a great deal of money may be made in sugar." Other

New Orleans observers heartily shared what they had heard from Cuban refugees "arriving by every steamer," that there was "no progress made in putting down the insurrection" and that "the insurgents have no idea of giving up." They eagerly projected that the insurgency would lead to the inevitable overthrow of slavery and "its effects shown upon our market next year as well as this." For the first time since the Civil War, Louisiana sugar appeared once again as a sound investment. After failed postwar attempts at cotton cultivation, a Freedmen's Bureau agent reported in December 1868, "very fine machinery has been put on many of the plantations, much improvement has been made to the buildings, which evidently shows an intention to cultivate the cane only."[45]

Domestic political developments, too, lifted Louisiana planters' spirits on the eve of 1869. The U.S. Congress legislated the Bureau of Refugees, Freedmen, and Abandoned Lands (the Freedmen's Bureau) out of existence in July 1868, ordering all its activities outside of education and veteran bounty payments to cease by the end of the year. Always conceived as a temporary agency, the bureau, to most Republicans, became an anachronism once the freedmen received the right to protect their interests through the ballot box. Hampered from the outset by inadequate resources and President Johnson's generous restoration of property rights to ex-Confederates, the bureau had proved incapable of assisting the freedpeople to become independent landowners, which had been one of its original mandates. The bureau nonetheless had become a vital institution through which the freedpeople pursued their interests against their employers, albeit within an annual contract labor system that, as in Union wartime policies, emphasized the inculcation of free labor values to southern employers and laborers.[46] The closure of what was essentially the proselytizing instrument of the free labor ideology and its bastardized southern creation, the contract labor system, pleased employers far more than laborers. On December 31, 1868, an agent in Louisiana reported that laborers had been "swindled right and left in their final settlements" and exhibited "great anxiety" as the bureau prepared to close its field offices forever. Several employers, he added, "have deferred paying off their hands until the first of January with a view (as they say) of getting the Bureau out of the way."[47]

Less than two years after the inauguration of Radical Reconstruction, moreover, the presidential election of 1868 foretold the fragility of multiracial democracy and the power of white supremacist organizing in Louisiana politics. Black Louisianians wielded their newly won voting rights in stunning fashion, with thousands of men defiantly marching down to register to vote and men and women actively participating in political rallies and clubs. In a series of elections in 1867 and 1868, black male voters enabled the drafting and ratification of a new state constitution and swept Republicans into state and local offices. The plantocracy's reign was unequivocally over, or so it seemed. There was an "ill[-]feeling" in the heart of Louisiana's sugar-producing region, a Freedmen's Bureau agent reported, as the presidential election drew near. "The freedmen have the stamina to maintain their views politically, and defend the principles they advocate," he explained, "which as a matter of course the planter contends against, and tries to win them to the belief of his creed." Unable to influence the black vote peacefully, planters and their allies unleashed a campaign of terror that yielded an overwhelming majority for the Democratic presidential candidate. Paul L. DeClouet, a sugar planter and a member of the Knights of the White Camellia, was ecstatic. "Not one of the negroes left here to go & vote today," he wrote in his diary. "This has been a glorious day. All White!!!"[48]

Louisiana planters' political euphoria did not last long. Along with heavy winter rains that dampened their prospects for the new season, they encountered a labor force as stubborn as it had been before the bureau's withdrawal. "They demand higher wages than our sugar planters feel warranted in giving," declaimed the *West Baton Rouge Sugar Planter* in January 1869. The "caprices and whims of the freedmen" and their demands for excessive wages, the editorial continued, threatened to drive planters away from sugar production or Louisiana altogether. Just when the stars seemed to line up in the planters' favor, the freedpeople threw everything back into flux. To set them aright, Louis Bouchereau, the sugar industry's postwar statistician, proposed that "some concerted effort should be made to invite capital into the State, and to introduce a new class of field laborers, if we hope to continue the cultivation of sugar on a large scale or to reclaim the many fine plantations now lying waste and idle for the want of labor to work them." "Coercive measures being, as things now stand, out of the question," he conceded, "a more efficient system of compelling laborers to comply faithfully with contracts can only be hoped for by increasing the number in the State and thus creating competition and a spirit of emulation among the negroes."[49] As planters turned to solve their vexing labor problem once and for all, questions on the composition and location of their future solution remained wide open.

The steam engine's extension across the oceans and continents, in no small measure a result of Republican policies, greatly widened Louisiana planters' range of possible solutions. The 1860s was a decade full of advances in transportation and communication throughout the world, from the opening of the Suez Canal to ever-expanding networks of steamship lines, railways, and telegraph cables. It was the age of capital, in the words of historian Eric Hobsbawm, when a progressive, materialist spirit fueled and justified industrial capitalism's march to all corners of the world, vastly increasing global exchanges of products and peoples. With the aid of congressional subsidies, the Pacific Mail Steamship Company launched its transpacific service between Hong Kong and San Francisco in 1867. Reflective of the Republican belief in government-funded transportation projects as a cornerstone of economic development, the federal government likewise laid the groundwork for the construction of the first transcontinental railroad during the Civil War. Capital's expansion produced a bigger yet smaller world. From the home of the reunited nation's capitalist market in 1868, *Harper's Weekly* anointed the United States "the great highway between Western Europe and Eastern Asia" and New York "the centre of the commercial world." The completion of the transcontinental railroad in May 1869 only intensified the journal's unrestrained jubilation. Featuring a picture of "a medley of Irishmen and Chinamen" at work, *Harper's Weekly* concluded that "the very laborers upon the road typify its significant result, bringing Europe and Asia face to face, grasping hands across the American Continent."[50]

Though alienated from the national epicenters of capitalist development, southerners were by no means impervious to the pervading ideology of material and moral progress through trade and enlightenment, an ideology that, especially within the U.S. context, focused heavily on Chinese trade and labor. The editors of *De Bow's Review* suggested in 1868 that a steamship line be established between China and the isthmus of Central America (Panama), whereby New Orleans would become the major U.S. port of entry for the transpacific trade. Newfound dreams of the China trade also revived dreams of coolie labor—directly from China rather than by way of Cuba. "Those pent-up millions of Asia want room, want food, want the opportunity to work; we, in the Valley of the Mississippi, want labor; we must have it; we have farms for millions, work for tens of millions," an advocate claimed in 1868. "Here is the demand; there the supply. Those plodding, rice-eating, polygamic, idol-worship[p]ing Orientals, live on the other side of the world; but steam will soon bring us together." Celebrating the first direct shipment of Chinese products to the Crescent City in 1870, the *New Orleans Daily Picayune* observed that China had "more labor and more of the products of labor than her toilsome hordes can use" and now sought "a natural exchange" of goods and labor "in accordance with the great law of

"Work on the Last Mile of the Pacific Railroad—Mingling of European with Asiatic Laborers," *Harper's Weekly*, May 29, 1869. The completion of the transcontinental railroad renewed the imperial imaginations of Americans across the nation and their demands for coolies.

Courtesy of University of Oregon Libraries, Special Collections.

supply and demand." New Orleans and the South stood to profit immensely from the "equalization and exchange" between the two great empires.[51]

If the early postwar recruitment of coolies from Cuba, like the Black Codes, signified a rejection of emancipation, the post-1868 demand for Chinese labor bore the imprint of the New South creed. Beginning in 1869, a growing body of southern promoters attempted to distance themselves from the rhetoric of the past in calling for political and economic reforms, even as they strove, first and foremost, to revert (or "redeem") the region back to the old racial order and labor control. The search for Chinese labor, thus, reemerged as a regional imperial project, an indication of southern Democratic leaders' readiness to enter the age of capital, with their old tools of white supremacy and enslavement recast in terms that northern industrialists might appreciate. Their mission, too,

was about conquest and progress. "Now, if the opportunity were offered to
the people of the South to go to China and control her commerce, superintend
the construction, equipment and operation of the thousands of miles of railways . . . to build navies of steamships and navigate them—in other words, to
rule, govern, control, and be profited by the wealth and labor of that people,"
a newspaper leading the campaign for Chinese labor argued, "there is not a
question but that we would go and take possession." That was "not possible,"
the editorial concluded, but "we may move as much of the Chinese population
here as we wish; we may make this great country of ours what she ought and will
be—the seat of Empire on this continent."[52]

New modes of transoceanic and transcontinental transportation made such
imperial visions possible, as did the celebrated accounts of Chinese railroad
workers in the American West. From 1865 to 1869, the Central Pacific Railroad
Company, in charge of building the original transcontinental route eastward
from Sacramento, recruited and employed thousands of Chinese laborers, dra-
matically increasing the number of Chinese migrants entering the United States
and transforming the lives of Chinese residents already in California. Railroad
work drove independent Chinese miners to wage labor and Chinese merchants,
who had catered principally to the miners, to labor contracting. Similar to the
cuadrilla system in Cuba, Chinese merchants organized their compatriots into
labor gangs, from whom they exacted fees for finding work and supplying provisions.[53] As early as 1866, ambitious merchants from San Francisco explored
the idea of supplying Chinese labor gangs to the South, in part through publicized
interviews with Governor Wells and other Louisiana officials in New Orleans.
Their visit in September 1866, in turn, invigorated the local demand for coolies,
who were a particularly inviting prospect since, as a New Orleans newspaper put
it, "to political theories they carry the oriental philosophy of indifferentism to
the extreme." Although scattered reports suggested that "a goodly number" of
"Coolie labor" arrived in the South as a direct result, any Chinese laborers in the
Mississippi River Valley before 1869 almost certainly came from Cuba rather
than California.[54] Recruiting in Cuba was cheaper and easier.

Within a span of several years, however, California and China became more
accessible—materially and psychologically—to Louisianians and other southerners as the national economy and consciousness absorbed the American West
(which, in many ways, extended to the Pacific and Asia) and its laboring peoples.
"With the Pacific Rail Road you are brought quite near to our common country, only six days and some hours, for instance from this city," a New Orleans

resident wrote to his niece in California. "And on our Christmas dinner table we had fine luscious pears from California that were without even a bruise." Alongside fresh fruit, reports on Chinese labor's unmatched traits and feats flowed from California and accelerated the southern demand for coolies. A California correspondent to the *New Orleans Daily Picayune* portrayed the Chinese as "good general servants, and possessing the very desirable qualification of doing as they are bid." These "half cared for hardworking respectful people," he argued, contrasted sharply with the "sleek, fat, well fed and well clad lazy insolent niggers" common "in palmy days of prosperity" in the South. His editors in New Orleans, in turn, praised the "patient, quiet and persevering" Chinese character that obviated "any fear of the Chinaman becoming a citizen and voting." So indifferent was the "Chinaman" to his new surroundings that he would not bother "to exercise this privilege, so-called, as to take the trouble to be naturalized." His track record as the "better railroad building laborer than any other" demanded his introduction to the cane, rice, and cotton fields of the South.⁵⁵

Concrete plans to recruit Chinese laborers from California came from all parts of the South in the summer of 1869. Parties in St. Louis organized a company to transport Chinese laborers from California by railroad and then to distribute them under contract to southern planters. The "solution" to the South's "labor question," the company's agent argued in a circular letter, was "most readily and most successfully found in the vast and overflowing population of China, the cheapness of Coolie labor, the peculiar adaptedness of that race to the climate of the South and to the production of Southern staples, and in the cheap and convenient transportation afforded by the Pacific Railroad." Not to be outdone, Louisiana sugar planters revamped their determination "to embark their capital in a systematic plan" to introduce Chinese labor. Led by "our largest planters" and "large capitalists," the *New Orleans Times* reported, the new movement was different from earlier postwar efforts that had languished under the debate over a federal law and a delusive faith in former slaves. The "two dissuasives" existed no more. "We must be limited to the negro, made lazy, insubordinate and unreliable, from a too sudden introduction to political rights and equality with the white race," the newspaper stated, "or we must bring to bear upon him the counteracting influence of the rivalry of another class of equally capable and far more docile and manageable race." St. Mary Parish's "larger planters" were also "secretly negotiating" for "coolie labor" around the same time.⁵⁶

Grand Coolie Dreams

The overlapping yet distinct movements for an economic New South and Chinese labor diverged and then converged in New Orleans and Memphis, the leading commercial cities in the Mississippi River Valley. In May 1869, each city hosted a regional commercial convention to consider and advance economic development in the South, appealing for, among other things, increased transportation and trade links with the West and federal aid to Mississippi River levees. Heralded as harbingers of a new era of regional prosperity, these commercial conventions indicated the South's willingness to remake itself through investment and reform. The idea of recruiting Chinese labor, however, received a lukewarm hearing at best, confined to a motion to employ former Central Pacific laborers on southern railroads. Otherwise, there was only opposition. Aspiring to develop the South largely in the mold of the North, most of the conventioneers supported immigration from Europe and rejected coolies from China. In the meantime, planters near Memphis, like their counterparts around New Orleans, organized their own meetings, which advocated Chinese labor exclusively. In June 1869, they incorporated the Arkansas River Valley Immigration Company with the aim of transporting two thousand laborers directly from China to New Orleans. The *Memphis Daily Appeal*, insisting that the labor question outweighed all issues addressed by the recent commercial convention, wholeheartedly endorsed the company and urged "our merchants, property holders and capitalists to step forward and take the initiative in working up this great matter." Memphis civic boosters responded right away.[57]

Located in a border state, which had given birth to the Ku Klux Klan and its brand of paramilitary violence and which more recently was spearheading the march to respectable "redemption," Memphis was a fitting site for the South's elite to discuss the fate of race and plantation labor. On the heels of a commercial convention designed to attract capital, could the New South ideology conceal its Old South roots in matters regarding race and labor? The revitalized quest for Asian labor put this question to its early and trying test. In a meeting at the Memphis Chamber of Commerce on June 30, 1869, the city's "prominent and influential citizens" resolved to organize and host a Chinese labor convention in two weeks' time, inviting delegates from every city and county in the South. The short notice conveyed the meeting's urgency; it was an emergency gathering to tackle what was presented as the preeminent crisis in the postbellum South. For more than a week, Memphis leaders had been urged and hounded by a barrage of editorials and reports in the *Memphis Daily Appeal*. "Already *the negroes are forming combinations to make their own terms with their employers next season,*" the newspaper warned. The "quiet, orderly, good-tempered, docile, cheerful, willing workers" from China, "easily controlled, and so intelligent," were the people "to take the place of the labor made so unreliable by Radical interference and manipulation." "Organize and go to work," implored another editorial, "and do not let this fair land degenerate into a second Jamaica."[58]

J. W. Clapp set the tone for the new campaign at the Chamber of Commerce gathering which echoed earlier pronouncements by coolie traders from Cuba. Like delegates at the commercial conventions, Clapp endorsed European immigration to develop small farms upland and manufacturing in the South. But "in the alluvial lands—the swamps . . . we need dark-skinned laborers, Mongols or Africans, who luxuriate where the white man would perish," he argued. "This shows the wisdom of God who has thus ordained that the human race is to go forward and develop the whole earth to its nethermost parts." While other speakers related the terms under which the Chinese worked in California, Clapp emphatically turned everyone's attention southward to what he considered the true historical guide:

> From Madagascar to Canada that country does not exist where the negroes engage in voluntary labor. They had him in the West Indies, and he converted them into a garden, but when the negroes ceased to be guided by the whites the Islands became a wilderness, and the inhabitants became savages again . . . As to the mixture of races—have we not a mixture among us now that cannot be worse? Have not the most stolid and ignorant race been made the governing power? . . . [The Chinese] don't come among us to mingle in politics; they do not seek to be naturalized even. They come here from their teeming hives, and expect to go back, carrying with them the scanty pittance that they have earned. . . . As to the internecine struggle between the Chinese and negro that we hear about, we don't know that that is any affair of ours. I have a kindly regard for the negro, but I don't want him to be hung as a millstone around our necks. Extermination is his doom. The supremacy of the white race must be vindicated under all circumstances . . . There will be no amalgamation. The superior race will not come down to the inferior.

The audience reportedly listened to Clapp with rapt attention and applause.[59]

On July 13, 1869, around five hundred delegates from Alabama, Arkansas, California, Georgia, Kentucky, Louisiana, Mississippi, Missouri, South Carolina, and Tennessee—an assembly reputedly "of the most solid and businesslike" ever seen in Memphis—convened at the Greenlaw Opera House "to devise ways and means to inaugurate the importation of Chinese or Asiatic labor" to the South. Perhaps fired up by his earlier performance and reception, Clapp again stood up to define the convention's mission, which, in his mind, was the South's mission. Fixated on the Caribbean, he discarded the New South camouflage altogether. In the South and the Caribbean, he argued, "experience taught that the great staples could not be produced by voluntary labor, but under coerced labor systematized and overlooked by intelligence . . . labor that the owner of the soil can control." Clapp unabashedly expressed his overriding wish—labor "you can control and manage to some extent as of old." "These same islands now employ a coerced labor, and again blossom like the rose; again they are an earthly paradise," he continued. "Whose labor is it that has done this? India and China answers. Asiatic labor supplies the place of that stricken down by emancipation, and the country again commence[s] to be what it once was. Shall we not profit by its example?" Although Clapp, like the other delegates, repeatedly stated his "most kindly feeling toward the African race," he had no qualms about verbalizing his impassioned longing for a new system of "coerced" labor.[60]

Throughout the three-day convention, speaker after speaker drew references to Cuba, Hawai'i, and other plantation societies, a predictable but surprising development given the very recent completion of the transcontinental railroad to California. Tye Kim Orr, the disgraced evangelist of British Guiana and Freedmen's Bureau schoolteacher of Louisiana, was one of these speakers. Invited to the convention by the Louisiana delegation, whose members figured prominently in the proceedings, Orr delivered a "semi-colloquial" address on the second day that made him an instant sensation. "His enunciation is very clear and good, resembling very much that of an educated Spaniard," observed the *Memphis Daily Appeal*, "differing in that respect very widely, however, from the Lascars and Manillamen usually found on the coast." Orr, an indefatigable opportunist, exploited his sojourn in the Caribbean to advance his newfound ambition in the field of labor contracting:

You want to know about the Chinaman labor. I will tell you my candid opinion; but I left home six years ago—in 1863, and since then I have traveled a great deal in West Indies and South America . . . Now we have heard of the emancipation and land going to waste, unless we get labor. In the West Indies I studied the character of the people. You know they had emancipation—that was in 1830 something. The negroes, after emancipation, degenerated and would not work. To remedy that they imported Chinese. I can't say how many. In British Guiana there are 12,000. In Surrinan [*sic*], Martineque [*sic*], Gaudalupe [*sic*], there are also some. I don't know the statistics; but they all are getting along well.

Orr was ready for his main argument and punch line. "I know the Chinese are heathens," he said, "but you want cotton and cane—and if he makes them you will not object very much to him."[61]

After the applause and laughter died down, Orr impressed upon his would-be patrons that they were embarking on a civilizing mission that would not only generate handsome profits into their pockets but also enlighten the dark masses of the world. The Chinese, he said, would arrive in the South "benighted as they are, and lie at your door, and say, 'do, massa, teach us!' " Adeptly updating the message he had presented before London missionaries five years earlier, he called attention to the industrial age's promise. "What are the railroads for? What are the telegraphs for? What is this the 19th century, for, if not to bring 'The Word' to the people who have it not? . . . You may be the means for evangelizing them," he argued. "The Chinese are a docile, patient, susceptible people, and will follow and love those wh[o] try to teach and benefit them. Love begets love." Orr was by no means proposing an era of amalgamation and equality. "Your land is your own," he assured his audience. "They are physically strong, but they have good intention. They can't do so much as white man, but do different kind of work. If you have a grand house you want a cook. If you have a big table you want a footstool." Performing for an impetuous and credulous audience, Orr, who likely knew nothing about labor recruitment in China, stepped into the role of a resident expert without missing a beat. "I went to the West Indies, there I found nothing but misery," he warned. "You must not take the wharf-rats; you must get them from the rural districts of China . . . where the people are agriculturist, what good could a barber do in the field?"[62]

Warmly received as he was, Orr was not the main attraction. As he fielded questions from the audience, Cornelius Koopmanschap arrived at the opera house and immediately took the spotlight. Advertised as the featured speaker, Koopmanschap was a source of intrigue and mystery. Rumored to be Chinese, Russian, or German, the only certainty seemed to be that he was a famous "importer of Chinese goods, wares and men." Born in Holland in 1828, Koopmanschap moved to California during the gold rush in 1851, apparently by way of the Dutch East Indies, China, and New York City. With his connections in

Hong Kong, he subsequently established a flourishing business as a commission merchant and labor contractor in San Francisco, specializing in the recruitment and distribution of Chinese labor.[63] Koopmanschap, "astonished" at the size of the convention, spoke briefly on the varying wages Chinese laborers received, from eight dollars per month in Cuba and Peru to thirty-five dollars per month in California. He believed that the South could procure them at twelve dollars per month, provided planters did not try to outbid one another. The Chinese, he warned, could not be "relied upon to carry out contracts" if offered higher wages elsewhere. After Koopmanschap's remarks, the convention's chairman Isham G. Harris, the ex-governor of Tennessee and former Confederate exile in Mexico, appointed a committee to confer with Orr and Koopmanschap.[64]

Already inclined to trust everything the two speakers uttered, the committee fully endorsed the project of recruiting contract laborers from China. Koopmanschap indeed offered an impressive résumé, with letters of reference from the governor of California and the president of the Central Pacific Railroad Company. He claimed that his firm, Koopmanschap and Company, had already imported and delivered thirty thousand Chinese laborers to California. The transpacific voyage to San Francisco, he estimated, would cost about thirty to forty dollars per laborer and the transcontinental railroad trip to Memphis another sixty, a voyage that would have been unfathomable just a few years earlier. For his part, he promised to travel to China in early September and to transmit specific details upon his return in November. This was precisely what the committee and the convention had hoped to hear. "There is no doubt but a supply of Chinese laborers can be had to meet all the demands of the South," the committee reported the following morning, the last day of the convention. "It will be a question of time." The key was to make contracts in China, where "sometimes good guarantees can be had from the Mandarins or Governors of districts, for a faithful performance of the laborers['] contract." The length of contracts could last from two to five years, and possibly up to eight years, at wage rates from eight to twelve dollars per month. Reaffirming Orr's caveat, the committee emphasized that "if you want farm laborers you must go to the rural districts."[65]

The committee's report seemed to reflect the meeting's purpose. It recommended that Orr and "some well known, competent, reliable business man" familiar with southern planters' needs be dispatched immediately to China to secure one thousand laborers as an initial experiment. If proven successful in a year, the project could be extended "until the South is fully supplied." "I see no future for the South except by them," explained the committee's acting chairman. "Like other speakers here, I am not for pouring forth tirades against the negro . . . We understood him as a slave, and we know him as a freedman. In his present condition he can never be useful to us." The transcontinental railroad, he argued, "puts us in direct communication with San Francisco," which was "in direct communication with China," all part of a providential design to allow the South to tap "a country teeming with the best labor in the world" and to "Christianize them." Refraining from heated racist tirades and rejoicing in material and moral progress through global exchanges, the committee appeared to capture the aims and means of the new movement for Chinese labor and later put forward a resolution to raise eight hundred to one thousand dollars to send an agent and an assistant to China for five hundred to one thousand laborers.[66]

The committee's cautious resolution, however, conflicted sharply with the ambitious and acquisitive atmosphere permeating the convention and the nation. It was time for mass mobilization and investment, not tentative trials. Gideon J. Pillow of Tennessee, chairman of the finance committee, suggested an alternative plan, which, he insisted, "had been matured after consultation with merchants and capitalists, many of whom would embark their money in it." He proposed the immediate formation of a joint stock company, the Mississippi Valley Immigration Labor Company, with a capital base of $1 million (and possibly up to $2 million) at a rate of one hundred dollars per share. Once organized, the company would "take the most active measures for carrying into effect the objects of this organization, by bringing into the country the largest number of Chinese agricultural laborers in the shortest possible time" in accordance with all federal and state laws. It would be based in Memphis, where Chinese migrants would be afforded "proper accommodations" until "engaged in fair contracts with employers" all across the South, with stockholders' orders given top priority. Pillow's proposal also called for the company's legal incorporation and its protection of laborers' rights in all contracts, provisions that conferred an additional measure of legitimacy in the nation and the world. All "capitalists and planters" were invited to subscribe to the company, whose founding investors, if they raised at least $100,000, would hold an organizing meeting in a month.[67] This was a proposal seemingly more attuned to the South's deep crisis and determined resolve.

In introducing his proposal, Pillow preemptively enjoined the New Orleans delegation not to turn "the cold shoulder to us," an insinuation that sparked a bitter quarrel in the generally unified proceedings. He anticipated objections to the company's location in Memphis, which, he pleaded, was "only a faubourg of New Orleans" and would fulfill its "humble capacity" as "the agent that collects and distributes the labor throughout the country." Should New Orleans balk, Pillow threatened, he would raise the necessary capital in New York. "New Orleans ought not to do this, for she has to look to the Mississippi Valley for her wealth," he argued. "She cannot look southward. The Gulf of Mexico cannot furnish her with it." Louisiana's delegates took umbrage at Pillow's "mild reprimand" and swiftly rose to their state's defense. Moses Greenwood pointed out that Louisiana had "brought the only genuine Chinaman"—Tye Kim Orr—to the convention. A fellow Louisianian explained that the New Orleans Chamber of Commerce, which alone appointed twenty representatives to Memphis, had not authorized them to endorse any specific measure. The entire delegation, however, stood ready to extend "their moral and intellectual aid." Pillow replied that he was "pained and chagrined at the failure of the Louisiana delegation to give the movement that moral aid and support that he thought he had a right to expect." The entire convention grew uneasy as the "controversy" dragged on and the hour of adjournment neared.[68]

After dismissing a motion to remove "Chinese" from Pillow's proposal in favor of "laborers" and "immigrants" in general, the convention proceeded to vote on the two resolutions before it. Pillow's plan to organize the Mississippi River Immigration Labor Company passed easily "with but one dissenting voice." The other modest resolution to recruit fewer than one thousand laborers, "vigorously opposed" by Clapp and others, initiated a lengthy debate before being "finally voted down almost unanimously." Despite some internal bickering, the convention's final resolution and vote projected a united and confident South. Summing up the three-day gathering, the Committee on Chinese Immigration, headed by Clapp, concluded that "China, especially, is capable of supplying us with a class of laborers peculiarly adapted to our circumstances and the necessities of our situation." The South afforded "ample room and superior inducements . . . to European immigration" but had no choice but to pursue "the teeming population of Asia" for agricultural recovery and industrial development. The convention then ended as it had begun, on a high note, concluding with rounds of applause and tributes resembling a religious revival meeting or a political convention.[69] Many southerners had acquired a faith in Chinese labor. More than ever, they believed.

The Memphis meeting, in the end, embodied and encompassed the contradictions of a region and nation in transition, its origins and deliberations shaped by romantic visions of plantation slavery and old ties to the Caribbean as much as grandiose dreams of industrial development and new ties to California and China. Struggling to cope with emancipation, Radical Reconstruction, and global competition, delegates heard and endorsed Clapp's brazen calls for "coerced" labor as warmly as Pillow's entreaties to capitalists everywhere. In lobbying for his proposal, Pillow announced that Nathan Bedford Forrest, a delegate who left the convention early, had pledged five thousand dollars toward the new company on behalf of the Selma, Marion, and Memphis Railroad and vowed to employ one thousand Chinese laborers. Here was a man committed to rebuilding the South anew. But Forrest represented much more. Formerly a prominent slave trader, planter, and Confederate commander, he was also the founding Grand Wizard of the Ku Klux Klan. That the Memphis convention brought him side to side (and eye to eye) with Koopmanschap, who likewise pledged five thousand dollars, and Tye Kim Orr attested to the complex links that slavery, coolieism, and capitalism had forged.[70] In the summer of 1869, these men from the Old South, imperial Europe, and colonized Asia shared a hope of making money by cultivating and catering to the postemancipation demand for coolies. This growing demand revealed and resolved southern planters' multiple desires, serving at once as a testament to slavery's resiliency and an instrument to welcome the age of capital.

CHAPTER FOUR

Domesticating Labor

Southern planters' swaggering pronouncements on race and labor captured the nation's attention in the summer of 1869, a moment when the nation itself was being redefined. In a speech delivered in Boston, Frederick Douglass, the former slave and eminent abolitionist, disparaged the "Southern gentlemen who led in the late rebellion" for "they believed in slavery and they believe in it still . . . They would rather have laborers who will work for nothing; but as they cannot get the negroes on these terms, they want Chinamen who, they hope, will work for next to nothing." In the end, he warned, they would regret their foolish notions. "But alas, for all the selfish inventions and dreams of men!" Douglass exclaimed. "The Chinaman will not long be willing to wear the cast off shoes of the negro, and if he refuses, there will be trouble again." He challenged his compatriots to reconstruct the United States truly as a "composite nation" with "human rights" for all. "I want a home here not only for the negro, the mulatto and the Latin races; but I want the Asiatic to find a home here in the United States, and feel at home here, both for his sake and for ours," he concluded. "Right wrongs no man. If respect is had to majorities, the fact that only one fifth of the population of the globe is white, the other four fifths are colored, ought to have some weight and influence in disposing of this and similar questions."[1] Douglass's eloquence stood out, but his views did not stand alone.

Indeed, the surging demand for coolies confronted a widening movement for multiracial democracy and class struggle. Within days of the Memphis gathering of southern employers, the State Labor Convention of the Colored Men of Maryland resolved to organize a national conference, in part to consider the "Contract Coolie Labor" question. Black workers and leaders across the nation responded enthusiastically to the call, selecting and sending 214 delegates to Washington, D.C., for the Colored National Labor Union's founding convention in December 1869. The meeting denounced the classification and exclusion of laborers based on "a geographical division of the globe in which they or their forefathers were born, or on account of statutes [*sic*] or color," as "a disgrace to humanity." "While we extend a free and welcome hand to the free immigration of labor of all nationalities," a resolution read, "we emphatically deem imported contract Coolie labor to be a positive injury to the working people of the United States . . . the system of slavery in a new form, and we appeal to the Congress . . . to rigidly enforce the act of 1862, prohibiting Coolie importation, and to enact such other laws as will best protect, and free, American labor against this or any similar form of slavery." In rejecting slavery and racism of any kind, the delegates hoped to build a labor movement without regard to "nationality, sex, or color," "a superstructure" to unite workers of all backgrounds—Irish, German, "poor white" southerners, northern whites, blacks, and Chinese.[2]

The nation was at a crossroads in 1869. African Americans and Radical Republicans forged ahead to recast the United States into a multiracial democracy, making the first significant strides toward disaggregating race and American citizenship. Southern planters, on the other hand, plunged into the global competition for plantation labor, fueled by revamped dreams of white supremacy and enslaved labor. Asian coolies figured prominently yet tenuously within and between these competing visions, as impassioned reactions to the Memphis convention would reveal. After a two-year hiatus, political battles between federal officials and Louisiana planters and merchants over the status of coolies erupted again. Champions of coolie labor, moreover, encountered an obstacle far greater than Republican politicians. In contrast to their imperial ambitions, they turned out to be decidedly minor players on the world stage and, after a series of frustrating attempts abroad, would concentrate increasingly on domestic sources of migrant labor, eastward and westward, to check the effects of black enfranchisement and labor struggles. The contradictions of emancipation and imperialism thus generated new opportunities and migrations that brought Asian and black bodies next to one another, first in Louisiana planters' minds and then on their plantations. The contested status of coolies, at the same time, proved critical in the regeneration and reracialization of American nationalism in an era marked by overtures to nonracial citizenship. Through the recruitment and exclusion of coolies, the United States would be reconstructed as a white nation of immigrants, a pale reflection of the radical "composite nation" that Douglass imagined possible in 1869.

Importation to Immigration

As the five hundred or so delegates left Memphis and headed home in July 1869, they found their meeting the object of widespread acclaim in the South. The arrival of "the Chinaman," the *New Orleans Daily Picayune* rejoiced, would teach the freedpeople "the hard lesson, as yet unthought of by them, of the struggle of poor men with each other in the competition for employment, and . . . through trials, and failures, and long sufferings, the virtues of steadiness, patience and frugality, as indispensable to maintain and elevate themselves." The *New Orleans Times* presented the Chinese as the vehicle to kill the Fifteenth Amendment, which was to extend the ballot beyond "the intelligent white or Caucasian race," many of whose members, let alone blacks and Asians, lacked the "capacity" to vote. "Admit our principle," an editorial challenged Republicans, "and you will exclude the African and the Asiatic; deny it in regard to the African and adhere to it as to the Asiatic, and you proclaim yourselves arrant knaves and hypocrites." The newspaper was convinced that the Chinese would side with "the conservative white vote of the South" or, more likely, "prefer their own institutions, refuse to have anything to do with our politics, or take the least interest in them." In column after column, conservative voices heralded the Memphis meeting as the harbinger of southern prosperity and political salvation.[3]

The northern press likewise paid close attention to the Memphis proceedings, but concluded that nothing could be worse for the South and the nation.

"A Coolie is a Chinese slave, bound for a longer or shorter time," *Harper's Weekly* charged, "and in February, 1862, Congress very properly forbade the importation of coolies from China." Sentiments expressed by J. W. Clapp and Cornelius Koopmanschap, the journal reported, indicated the South's demand for "an ignorant, brutish, servile population of laborers, instead of intelligent, industrious, self-respecting workmen." The United States—extending "an endless welcome for the industrious laborer who comes hither to secure larger opportunities for himself and his children"—faced enough "difficulties" from "honest emigration" and therefore had a foremost "imperative" to prevent "this illicit emigration." In a similar tone, the *New York Evening Post* rued the "pitiful" southerners "still drivelling about 'new ways to develop' their states, and catching eagerly at every means of reviving that system of slave labor which has been the curse of the southern states." Unlike the "cheap" and "certain" nature of free labor, "'coolie' slaves" would "bring only more barbarism, more violence, more disorganization, vice and lawlessness, and will drive off, as surely as the old slave labor did, the free laborers, the enterprising, active, intelligent, industrious population, on which every state must depend for its glory and true prosperity." Labor projects like those proposed by Koopmanschap and Orr, the *Post* added, would violate the federal statute against the coolie trade.[4]

Federal officials, however, remained perplexed over the 1862 law's provisions and applications. At root, they asked, who exactly was a coolie? This question surfaced anew in May 1868, months after the *William Robertson* debacle, when an American businessman acting as the Hawaiian consul general in Japan dispatched 149 migrants to Hawaii's plantations under three-year labor contracts. Japanese officials, who never authorized the shipment, filed a complaint with the U.S. minister to Japan. Surmising the migrants to be coolies, the U.S. official immediately decreed the "act of Congress to prohibit the coolie trade, &c., approved February 19, 1862 . . . framed with regard to China," henceforth "applicable to Japan." His ruling was consistent with the popular usage of the term *coolie* in the 1860s, when Webster's American dictionary defined it as "a laborer transported from India, China, &c., for service in some other country" and a magazine portrait of Japan featured a "coolie, in full dress." Secretary of State William H. Seward disagreed though. He commended the "spirit" of the minister's actions but ultimately found them "without sufficient foundation in law, and . . . therefore, invalid and ineffectual." He nonetheless promised to recommend that Congress amend the law "to provide a remedy against the newly discovered evil" in Japan.[5]

About a year later, William Creevy, the New Orleans shipping merchant who had been involved in earlier coolie shipments from Cuba, hoped to settle the matter for good, seeing a potentially lucrative market for coolies in the South. The recently signed Burlingame Treaty with China, Creevy wrote to the Treasury Department in 1869, seemed to abrogate the anti-coolie-trade law altogether, as it granted Chinese subjects the right to migrate freely to the United States. "On the Pacific slope of the United States I believe I am accurate in saying coolies from China are constantly arriving in American ships, and in unlimited numbers," Creevy argued. "Can it be, therefore, that such immigration is permissible and lawful in California, and not permissible and lawful on the American territory of the United States on the Gulf of Mexico?" Secretary of the Treasury George S. Boutwell, a Radical Republican, directed Creevy's query to James F. Casey, the New Orleans collector of customs, with comments on the department's resolute stance against the coolie trade two years earlier. Casey conferred with Creevy, who left the meeting unsatisfied and formally resubmitted a request for further explanation. The customs collector, characterizing Creevy as one of "our most reliable businessmen," forwarded it again to his superior in Washington.[6]

Boutwell minced no words in his subsequent instructions. Perhaps irritated by Creevy's insistence or driven to action by what he read in the newspapers, he waited nearly a month to pen his reply, a week after the Memphis convention. In a widely published and publicized letter, Boutwell wrote that Creevy was "in error" in assuming the revocation of the ban on transporting coolies. The Burlingame Treaty, he countered, reinforced the 1862 law by making "it a penal offence to take Chinese subjects from China without their free and voluntary consent." "Such being the facts in the case you are hereby authorized and directed to use all vigilance in the suppression of this new modification of the Slave trade," he instructed Casey. Boutwell's letter instantly checked the momentum generated in Memphis. William R. Miles had attended the convention and then proceeded to San Francisco to procure Chinese labor on behalf of the Vicksburg (Mississippi) Chamber of Commerce. He marveled at what he heard and saw, proclaiming that "for the present at least, and possibly for all time" the Chinese were "not only the best and cheapest, but perhaps the only labor that we can get to fill up and cultivate our waste and unoccupied land." Miles arranged for the transport of upwards of ten thousand laborers from China, only to find Boutwell's letter all over the newspapers. Calculating "the risk of the great outlay" and "probable" federal intervention too great, the party he had been negotiating with backed out of the deal. Miles returned to Vicksburg empty-handed.[7]

The Memphis convention and Boutwell's letter received nationwide attention because the prospect of coolies in the postemancipation South resonated with the most pressing political and social issues of the day. Over the previous four years, the nation had abolished slavery and begun establishing the principle of racial equality in its Constitution and laws. In February 1869, Congress had approved the Fifteenth Amendment, introduced in the House by Boutwell, prohibiting the denial of U.S. citizens' access to the ballot on racial grounds. Although the final wording gravely disappointed those lobbying for universal suffrage, feminists in particular, the amendment's impending ratification again raised fundamental questions about federal authority, racial equality, and national identity, questions that pertained not only to blacks in the South but also increasingly to the Chinese out West. By 1869, Chinese migration and employ-

"The New Comet—A Phenomenon Now Visible in All Parts of the United States," *Harper's Weekly*, August 6, 1870. The South's demand for coolies reverberated across a nation struggling with emancipation and industrialization.
Courtesy of University of Oregon Libraries, Special Collections.

ment in California and vehement opposition thereto—led by the state's trade unions, anticoolie clubs, and Democratic party—had become a staple news item across the United States. With the completion of the transcontinental railroad in May 1869, moreover, industrial employers' vocal demands for Chinese labor, including as strikebreakers, could be heard frequently in the Northeast and Midwest, threatening to export the Chinese "problem" and white labor's mobilization against it eastward.[8] Like no other single issue, the specter of former slaveholders' importing coolies to restitute slavery and the federal government's determined opposition touched on the panoply of recent and imminent changes the nation faced, coast to coast.

The South's demand for coolies, situated geographically and ideologically somewhere between the Caribbean and California, threatened to unify the nation's heretofore seemingly distinct racial and regional problems. "A new problem of race presents itself to the people of this country," the *National Anti-Slavery Standard* argued in the summer of 1869. The longtime antislavery organ delineated two distinct aspects of the "Chinese question." California's "workingmen's movement" and "Sham-Democracy"—"the implacable enemies of the negro" who opposed the Fifteenth Amendment—subjected the Chinese to "invidious taxation" and "unbridled brutality and ruffianism." They demanded an end to Chinese migration. At "cross-purposes" with such sentiments were "the former slave-owners of the South," who, "born of their spite against the negro as a freeman," favored Chinese migration "as a means of reestablishing something as near like slavery as possible . . . They wax eloquent in anticipation of the importation of another 'inferior' class of men, who cannot be elected to their Legislatures, or sent to Congress, at least till they have been here long enough to be naturalized." The *Standard* ultimately reproached both regions for violating U.S. traditions and laws and appealed for immigration with naturalization and equal rights wherever the Chinese went, North or South. But great differences lingered. California violated "civil rights"; the South sought to restore "chattelism."[9] Between the two remained the legal and cultural gulf dividing "immigration" and "importation."

Koopmanschap's publicity drive only sustained the view that a new system of slavery was about to take root in the South. He left Memphis for New York City, where his newfound fame awaited. In interviews with reporters, Koopmanschap announced his intention to bring 100,000 coolies—all men who would then "import" women "for themselves"—into the United States within a year and unabashedly positioned the South next to Cuba, Peru, and the West

Indies. "Nothing but coerced labor will bring about prosperity," he stated matter-of-factly. "The products of tropical climates or semi-tropical, are brought forward by great attention and care." The Chinese were the "peculiar race" perfectly suited for postemancipation plantation labor. "European laborers are not going into the swamp . . . which is most fertile and prolific, and it is no inhumanity to put the Chinaman there," he noted. "It does not hurt him." Nor would "the introduction of these yellow men" hurt blacks. "Well, we cannot let our interests perish for the negro," he said. "We cannot commit suicide for him. Thistles and thorns will grow up in our idle fields if we rely on the help of negroes. But, then, there is plenty of work for him if he will do it." He dismissed fears of "a deluge of idolatry" and "amalgamation," since "there is no danger of our people taking a fancy to them." "Ours is a superior race," he assured his audience, "our God is the true God."[10]

While Koopmanschap headed back to San Francisco by train in July 1869, southern champions of coolie labor had to deal with the crisis engendered by Boutwell's letter and exacerbated by Koopmanschap's statements. Their first task was to dissociate their project from importation, coolies, and the Caribbean. The *Memphis Daily Appeal* rose in defense of J. W. Clapp, whose oration frequently bore the brunt of northern rebukes. Clapp, the newspaper claimed, had expressed "only the Southern animus of extreme liberality towards all immigrants and warmly declare[d] the unanimous Southern interest and intent to 'make them political and social equals' with ourselves." Biased excerpts and "disgraceful" misrepresentations by the Republican press, the *Appeal* insisted, were "disingenuous if not malignant" efforts to undermine "truth" and "peace" in the reunifying of the nation. Clapp, in reality, had emphasized differences between European and Chinese migrants, the former to become "our political and social equals" and the latter to work "our vast extent of alluvial soil" under planters' supervision. In the wake of potential federal intervention, the Memphis newspaper collapsed Clapp's racial divisions and remade coolies into "immigrants." A series of editorials claimed that the South had no interest in coolies, just the "voluntary immigration of willing workers" from China who deserved to be treated like all other immigrants. Anything less would be an "un-American impolicy."[11]

Envisioned and advertised as a weapon against free labor, Chinese migrant labor ironically had to be advanced as a paragon of free labor, beyond the reach of federal law. Conservative New Orleans newspapers, for their part, fully endorsed Creevy's project and framed the political controversy as the latest manifestation of Reconstruction's injustice. Creevy, the *New Orleans Daily Picayune* editorialized, faced no legal obstacle "in bringing Chinese immigrants here, provided they come by their own choice, and not as bondmen." The newspaper rejected the notion that the New Orleans merchant planned to import "unwilling" laborers to the United States, where persons could not be imprisoned for debts or contract violations, and added that no provision of the federal statute applied to the landing of Chinese in U.S. ports anyway. The *New Orleans Times* concurred, declaring defiantly that "the preparations to secure a large influx of Chinese labor to the South are going on, and will go on, just as though he [Boutwell] had never written." "The Coolie trade, as proposed here, and as sanctioned in California," the *Times* maintained, "is very different from the Coolie trade as conducted in the West Indies in 1862 . . . when a rabid state of feeling was at its height against slavery, and everything savoring of the slave trade." Boutwell and his ilk objected to the movement solely because they saw "in the immigration of the Mongol the overthrow of their negro empire." The "coolie," in fact, would be afforded "the same protection and redress under the law as the negro enjoys today."[12]

The affirmation of Chinese "immigration" celebrated it as the latest chapter in the quintessential American experience of upward mobility, with the Chinese not too distant from whites in the racial hierarchy. If the "semi-barbarian" people "just released from the thralldom of slavery" insisted "insolently" on "equality and fraternity" with "the white man, with his centuries of civilization," an editorial on the "labor problem" reasoned, "how much better fitted . . . is the patient and industrious representative of a civilization which dates back far beyond the Christian era!" "They are superior to the negro or the Indian," remarked the *Jeffersonian*. "Much as they have been opposed in California, they have always been preferred before the African or the savage." The agricultural and "superior mechanical capacity" of the Chinese, the *Picayune* chimed in, meant they "will be our drudge but for a little while." Like whites, they would "soon be the independent producer of wealth" and "a leader in improvements of all kinds." "The Chinaman, it must be understood, is a thoroughly intelligent human being, who is not able to get along at first among [u]s, because he is a stranger," another editorial added. "As soon as he becomes familiar with our language, laws and course of business, which he may do as readily as a German, if not an Irishman, he will ask equal privileges and get them." Any talk of "importing" bound Chinese laborers, as voiced by speakers at the Memphis convention, was mere "folly" that only provoked Republican hostility.[13]

To be almost white (and not black), however, was not the same as to be white. Advocates of Chinese labor never imagined the kind of racial inclusion and equality suggested by Frederick Douglass and others in 1869. The Chinese, the *Memphis Daily Appeal* proposed, would provide "still another infusion of character and here the four races of mankind, Caucasian, Indian, African, and Mongolian, will fight the last battle for supremacy and existence." But the battle's outcome was never in question. "As the Chinaman is superior to the negro, who has clothed and enriched and civilized the white race," an editorial claimed, "so the millions of China will take up the task where the African abandons it and perfect the providential scheme which the negro inaugurated." This newspaper, purportedly welcoming Chinese "immigrants" as equals, also gleefully pointed out that the Chinese could not become U.S. citizens or voters, since they were not "free white persons"—as required by the Naturalization Law of 1790. A writer in *De Bow's Review* likewise emphasized that the Chinese would remain aliens, workers. They "will perform with equal contentment gang labor on large plantations and labor in detail upon smaller farms," he declared, "placing it in the power of every land owner to become a planter." Not likely to "covet ownership of the soil" or to "become a politician" because of their ingrained attachment to their homeland, he informed white southerners, "there will be no trouble about Chinese equality [a]nd brotherhood."[14]

Paying homage to America's inclusive reputation (immigration) and exclusive tradition (naturalization) yielded political dividends in 1869, at once granting Chinese "immigrants" the liberal subjectivity that the federal government demanded and reaffirming the white exclusivity that the Fifteenth Amendment threatened. It enabled former proslavery southerners to shake off their antebellum past and the Reconstruction present, to exorcise the old ghosts of slavery and coolieism. Promoting Chinese immigration, they asserted, fell outside the scope of coolie trade prohibitions and universal male suffrage, as encoded by federal and state governments. The 1868 state constitution of Texas, for instance, forever barred "importations of persons under the name of 'coolies,' or any other name or designation . . . whereby the helpless and unfortunate may be reduced to practical bondage." The intense public scrutiny of coolie schemes in the postemancipation South would persist as long as Reconstruction persevered, but the immediate uproar over Memphis faded as the months passed. Koopmanschap returned to the East Coast in September 1869, freshly versed in the finer politics of Reconstruction. He publicly disavowed any connection with the coolie trade, arguing that coolies received only four dollars per month whereas the "Chinamen" brought to the South would earn ten to fifteen dollars per month plus rations. The latter would be voluntary immigrants in search of better wages, Koopmanschap told Boutwell in a personal interview, with full knowledge of their contract terms before departure. The treasury secretary promised not to interfere as long as the labor agent violated no law. Koopman-schap had already secured orders for more than five thousand Chinese laborers in Texas.[15]

The effervescent excitement over the Mississippi Valley Immigration Labor Company, in the meantime, flattened and then dissolved. In August 1869, after weeks of "indifferent" response, Gideon J. Pillow and other backers of the company organized a local meeting to stimulate investment and to deflect federal intimidation. Pillow remonstrated before "a goodly number of respectable citizens" that President Ulysses S. Grant would more than likely support the project if "properly informed" and that he had received favorable responses from New England cotton manufacturers. Unanimous resolutions were adopted to correct the "erroneous opinions" that resulted "in opposition to the movement by many honest, well-meaning persons." It was "not the desire or intention of the people of this section of the country in inaugurating this movement to violate or evade any of the existing laws or regulations of the United States governing immigration," they stated. "But that we only desire to procure voluntary immigration and labor suitable for our lands and climate." After securing $100,000 in stock subscriptions and electing officers, the company foundered. In November 1869, the Tennessee state legislature, in considering a bill to incorporate the company, voted for an amendment to prohibit the "importation" of Chinese into the state.[16] The company soon vanished from public light, a victim of grandiose dreams crashing into the realities of capital scarcity, political and otherwise. The prospect of Chinese "immigration," on the other hand, remained politically viable.

Grand Bankrupt Schemes

After his interview with Boutwell, Koopmanschap arrived in New Orleans in October 1869 to appoint a local agent and to extol the virtues of Chinese labor. He impressed the local audience. "It does not need any information to tell that he is a Hollander—his face, temperament, or what we call 'style,' bespeaks it," gushed the *New Orleans Times*, "and the same personal characteristics show he is a man of surprising energy, one who would not fail to round off and complete any undertaking which he would take up." Koopmanschap emphasized that the Chinese were "patient and willing" workers who would abide faithfully by their contracts, normally for five years at eight to ten dollars per month. Their single-minded goal, he related, was "to secure five hundred dollars in five years and go back . . . home." Koopmanschap selected the commercial firm of John Williams and Sons to receive planters' orders for Chinese labor in New Orleans. In mid-October, the firm announced its intention "to be the means of aiding the Planter in securing good and reliable labor from the rural districts of China, (which, we are informed, is of the best character and far superior to that in and about the cities,) and on such terms as will be acceptable." The laborers would arrive under five-year contracts, every single one of them coming "voluntarily and cheerfully."[17]

Williams, perhaps the leading expert and advocate of Chinese labor in the South, was a logical choice. Having abandoned his Bayou Lafourche sugar plantation in 1862 and gone to Texas with his enslaved laborers, many of whom ran away en route, he returned to Louisiana after the war. His New Orleans firm was likely among the first to transport coolies from Cuba to Louisiana, reportedly arranging for the delivery of two thousand Chinese laborers in the summer of 1867. Two years later, Williams served as a prominent delegate at the Memphis convention, where he formed critical business contacts and apparently made up his mind to recruit laborers directly from China. Probably stunned by Boutwell's letter, he immediately asked his lawyers to clarify the legal state of affairs in the summer of 1869. They replied that Louisiana laws allowed adults, regardless of their present domiciles, to contract up to five years of service in the state and empowered the state courts to enforce such contracts. The federal statute of 1862, they added, was "not designed to interfere in the carrying of passengers from Oriental countries to the United States." The law only forbade U.S. vessels from carrying "the involuntary" between "Oriental nations and foreign countries," while "authorizing the conveyance of the voluntary" with proper government certification. To avoid difficulties, his lawyers recommended that Williams secure consular certificates attesting to the "perfectly free and voluntary" nature of the labor contracts.[18]

Williams liked what he heard, particularly since he had already begun arranging for the recruitment of contract laborers from China to Louisiana on his own, even before his appointment as Koopmanschap's New Orleans agent. He most likely agreed to advance funds to an aspiring recruiter, George W. Gift, at the Memphis convention, a personal investment that had probably driven him to write his lawyers in the first place. Reassured, Williams decided to invest further in Chinese labor in August 1869, almost certainly spurred to action by his neighbor along the Bayou Lafourche, Tye Kim Orr. Orr, too, had returned to Louisiana after his arousing performance in Memphis and continued to trumpet Chinese contract labor, announcing to local newspapers that he would operate a sugar plantation near Donaldsonville with Chinese workers in 1870. Williams soon entrusted his son Frank and Orr to procure laborers directly from China to work on Lafourche Parish sugar plantations, including his own. Orr and Frank Williams left for China the last week of August 1869.[19] Despite all the attention paid to Koopmanschap, Williams's personal arrangements with Gift and Orr would turn out to be the earliest ventures to realize the grand southern dream of competing in the burgeoning Asian market for plantation labor.

Gift had been a proponent of Chinese labor long before the Memphis convention. He had become familiar with Chinese laborers in California, where he had lived for years before the Civil War, and championed their introduction to his native South after his service in the Confederate Navy. As early as September 1866, he had written articles in favor of Chinese migrant labor which grew increasingly passionate with the onset of Radical Reconstruction. "The negro possesses a sort of monopoly, not only of political rights, but of labor," he had proclaimed. "The only remedy I know against monopolies, is COMPETITION! and competition we must have against the negro monopoly." Noting the incompatibility of European immigrants and the "miasmatic climate" of the South, he selected the Chinese—accustomed to such a climate and to sugar and rice cultivation from birth—as the appropriate alternative. "Like a hive of bees they are always busy," he wrote of the Chinese in California. It was California's history he wished to imitate, Gift emphasized, not Cuba's. The importation of "Coolies or persons who are *forcibly compelled to leave their homes*" violated U.S. laws and, in the long run, the laws of economy. "Let no more INDIA RICE be sold in your marts, but let the INDIA LABORER make it better on your own broad fields," he implored Georgia's planters in particular. "Don't stand idle, whilst California is importing Chinese labor by ship loads, and wait for the negro to 'come to his senses.'"[20]

Mimicking and competing with California, however, proved far tougher than Gift ever imagined. Appointed the recruiting agent for an Arkansas-based immigration company and backed by Williams's investment, Gift left Memphis a week after the Chinese labor convention. He first went to California to recruit several hundred Chinese laborers, but found the prevailing wage rates—up to thirty dollars in gold per month—too high for his purposes and means. With great expectations for the second leg of his trip, he departed San Francisco for Hong Kong in September 1869 to secure one thousand laborers for the Arkansas River Valley. "Nothing can equal the misery and destitution here," Gift beamed upon his arrival in the British colony, "or the desire of the inhabitants to come to America." But the local Chinese, he soon learned, had no desire to go to the South, a destination they dreaded even worse than Cuba or Peru. "It seemed impossible that we, who had owned slaves, would be more reasonable or humane, than the Spaniard or Peruvian," Gift reported. "They had proven themselves infamous, and we only lacked opportunity to do likewise. In fact, our record, according to popular romances was already quite abominable. So under these difficulties I began my work in Hong-Kong."[21] As in U.S. government reports, Chinese popular lore placed the South more in the Caribbean than in "America."

Gift encountered a series of other unforeseen delays and difficulties. It took him two months simply to familiarize himself with the intricacies of life in Hong Kong. "*I am the Chinese Immigration* and must go wherever there is most to be done *and made*," he wrote to his wife in December 1869, "and concerning the latter I am beginning to see my way pretty clearly." He hoped his ships would soon "spread their broad wings and speed away around the Cape of Good Hope with the China boys who are to help our poor country, I sincerely trust, out of her difficulties." His optimism turned to weary frustration as another month passed and political bureaucrats stood in his way. Gift derided British "red tape" and "*mock* philanthropy" in Hong Kong, remarking bitterly that the "bloody Englishers are greatly averse to some things, African slavery for instance, but they poke opium on to the Chinese whether or no."[22] He had to contend not only with British efforts to regulate Chinese emigration from Hong Kong but also with U.S. officials baffled by his undertaking. Would the federal government derail his mission on the other side of the world?

Gift's request for consular certification, the first by a southerner to ship Chinese laborers to the South, drove the local U.S. consul to pore over the anti-coolie-trade legislation and to write to his superiors in Washington for further instruction in November 1869. Seven years after the law's passage, consul C. N. Goulding became the first U.S. official to identify explicitly its contradictory and ambiguous provisions. "*What constitutes a free and voluntary emigrant?*" he asked the secretary of state. The law prohibited U.S. vessels from transporting "the inhabitants or subjects of China known as 'Coolies'" abroad, he explained, but another section endorsed the "free or voluntary emigration" of Chinese subjects. "Does any conflict exist in this law? What is a 'Coolie' as here defined, and what is a free emigrant?" Goulding demanded to know. With Gift's request sitting on his desk, he summed up his quandary in more direct terms. "Can an individual or Company come here and engage Chinese to be employed for a term of days, months or years in the United States," he asked, "and legally demand of the Consul the certificate contemplated in the 4th section of the act aforesaid[?]"[23]

The 1862 law still flummoxed federal officials. In his reply two months later, Assistant Secretary of State J. C. B. Davis conceded that there was no clear legal definition of a *coolie*. He, however, stressed that federal policy had been guided by "the subjects of the commerce known as the Coolie Trade," which differed from the slave trade "in little else than the substitution of fraud for force in obtaining its victims." "The fact that an emigrant embarks under a contract by which he is to reimburse the expenses of his transportation by personal services for a period agreed upon," he stated, "does not deprive him of the character of a free and voluntary emigrant, if the contract is not vitiated by force or fraud." Davis concluded that specific instructions would be unnecessary, as each consul ought to rely on "local knowledge and experience" to suppress the "Coolie Trade without impeding immigration really free and voluntary" in scope. The extirpation of all migration by fraud and force, Davis added, would require more than formal questioning of emigrants aboard ships. He offered no other resources or procedural suggestions, leaving the matter up to individual consuls. Even as State Department officials refused to outlaw Chinese contract labor migration in this instance, five months later they treated more stringently a similar inquiry from Cuba. The migration of Chinese subjects from Cuba to the United States, even if voluntary, they ruled, would violate federal law.[24]

Gift, in the meantime, finally fulfilled his mission in February 1870 after four months of setbacks. Goulding subjected every migrant aboard the French bark *Ville de St. Lo* to "a very severe and rigid examination as to thier [*sic*] knowledge of the country they were going to, the wages &c they were to recieve [*sic*] and length of time they Expected to remain." Hong Kong authorities, the consul reported, also attested to the migrants' health and the ship's capacity, which left little doubt of their status as "free and voluntary emigrants" under the law. He also reassured his superiors that he had not allowed Gift to make contracts before embarkation and was "satisfied that no attempt was made in that direction."

Goulding figured this was "probably the first emigrant ship which has sailed from China to the East Coast of the United States." Gift, whose own report indicated engaging workers to three-year contracts, was relieved. "I have done here what I was told could *not* be done, & I feel correspondingly proud of my achievement," he wrote. "I *shall send the first ship to the South!*" He would have preferred consigning the *Ville de St. Lo* to Savannah, but, since John Williams and Sons had "advanced us the requisite funds," he was "compelled to send the ship" to New Orleans. "Well the agony is over," Gift sighed, "the first ship . . . has sailed, and my weary heart is at rest."[25]

New Orleans residents were bubbling with anticipation when the *Ville de St. Lo* docked in their city on June 2, 1870, after a 107-day voyage across the Indian and Atlantic Oceans and around the Cape of Good Hope. The long trip had taken its toll, 20 of the original 189 passengers having died at sea near the West Indies. The mortality rate failed to dampen the festive welcome. "Physically they are fine specimens, bright and intelligent," announced the *New Orleans Times*, "and coming, as they do, from the low districts of China, within the tropics, there is nothing to be apprehended on the score of climate." The newspaper could not help but project the region's fate onto this inaugural shipment. "The Chinese are industrious, mild and easily governed . . . With two hundred Mexican dollars they can return to their native districts, buy a wife and settle down in easy circumstances for the remainder of their days. This is their ambition, and this is why they are here." They, however, seldom settled back in China. "A taste of the West has unsettled him for a life in China; hence it is that he remains a few months, enjoys his ease and honeymoon," the *Times* continued, "and then, accompanied by several of his relations, makes another trial." This system of migrant labor, already established in California, promised to "destroy a labor monopoly" and revitalize New Orleans and the entire region to antebellum glory.[26]

Racial images of coolies endured no matter how the Chinese migrants acted or called themselves. After an arduous journey across the oceans, Gift's recruits were exhausted and in no mood to be categorized as coolies. They "indignantly repelled" such rumors and proclaimed themselves "free and voluntary emigrants, and not forced or kidnapped men." This news story, which pleased the anti-Republican *New Orleans Times*, ironically ran alongside a column announcing the arrival of "coolies." Meanwhile, Gift joined his recruits in New Orleans—having traveled separately by steamship across the Pacific, a much shorter voyage—for the last leg of the trip up the Mississippi River to Arkansas.

He found many of the men "quite ill" and recorded another death en route. What happened next surprised Gift. The comprador, who had recruited the men in Hong Kong and now acted as their supervisor and interpreter, ordered a couple of men to bury their compatriot. "One flatly refused whereupon a row ensued and the disobedient fellow got several cuffs & hard ones too," Gift noted, "which persuaded him to do his duty." Attributing the altercation to the Chinese being "singular and very unfeeling sort of wretches," Gift envisioned no further trouble ahead. "I have *every confidence* in the *entire* reliability of the people," he wrote. "They are so very tractable & obedient, and I trust that this is but the beginning of a great enterprise." Their "disobedient" behavior, in Gift's mind, could never change their "tractable & obedient" character.[27]

Back in Hong Kong, Frank Williams and Tye Kim Orr confronted their own problems and delays. Williams's woes, according to Gift, originated "from placing too much confidence in the Chinaman he brought with him and attempting to get to[o] hard a contract." Orr's rhetoric in the United States far outpaced his performance in China. Gift felt compelled to stay in Hong Kong later than he had desired because Williams, "in distress," begged him "hard to remain and get his ships away." Despite Gift's aid, Williams and Orr were not able to dispatch their chartered vessel, *Charles Auguste*, until April 1870, more than seven months into their ill-fated trip. Consul Goulding cleared "the second ship loaded with coolies for the Atlantic coast" by certifying the 213 "Chinese passengers, all free and voluntary emigrants within the meaning of the law." The *Charles Auguste* took twice as long as the *Ville de St. Lo* to reach New Orleans, making an extra stopover in the French colony of Martinique to pick up additional Chinese laborers. The vessel finally arrived in New Orleans on October 7, 1870, with about 220 Chinese workers, six months after receiving Goulding's clearance in Hong Kong.[28] What nearly everyone had predicted as the dawning of a new migration stream in the summer of 1869 turned out to be a trickle defined by, above all else, inexperience and ineptitude. It had taken Williams and Orr more than a year to recruit a single shipload of workers.

The racial fantasies spawned by coolies, however, were too precious to surrender. After what was at best a moderately productive trip, Gift boasted that no one, including publicity-driven Koopmanschap, knew as much about China as he did. His own "energy, untiring and devoted," had beaten everyone in the field, and he anticipated returning to China to expand his new enterprise. Before boarding the steamer for Arkansas in New Orleans, he met with John Williams, who was "very anxious to work the matter up into a large company" with him and interested banks. Whether alone or in partnership with Williams, Gift confided to his wife, "I am pretty safe to do a good business myself." Neither Williams nor Gift would realize their extravagant dreams. The first two shipments of laborers from China to New Orleans would end up being the last; Williams's attempt to contract with a ship captain to transport coolies from Martinique to Louisiana would also flounder. All of this would become evident eventually, but, for the moment, the elation over the two shipments generated more rosy prognostications and speculative schemes. In the popular imagination, the Chinese remained ideal migrant laborers, young men whose labor was always available without the added social, political, and economic costs of settled families. They were, as the *New Orleans Times* put it, constitutionally "mild and easily governed"—feminized men, unlike white and black men (after emancipation)—which resulted in a peculiar admixture of passivity and industry perfect for plantation labor after slavery.[29]

George E. Payne of Louisiana caught the coolie fever soon after the *Charles Auguste* disembarked in New Orleans. His life, like Gift's, had been fundamentally altered by the Civil War. He had abandoned his sugar plantation in St. Charles Parish when Union troops arrived, helpless against the U.S. government's confiscation of his property. Payne, along with the vast majority of absconding planters, succeeded in recovering his estate after the war, but he lacked the means to carry on its operation. In early 1866, he placed his "very desirable" plantation for sale and joined a growing list of former sugar plantation owners during the early postwar years.[30] Payne's close association with leading merchants and planters, especially Leverich and Company of New York and New Orleans, opened doors to other opportunities. In 1870, he became the plantation manager for Mary Porter, an indebted client of Leverich and Company, and received a handsome salary of three hundred dollars per month. The arrangement was otherwise a disaster. Payne continually complained of the "negroes" throughout the season, such as their "keeping high holiday" on July 4 and the "day hands (all wenches)" striking for higher wages on the eve of the grinding season. He later described the entire ordeal as "the most unpleasant twelve months of my whole life." The Porter family, feeling as if he had been "thrust upon them," held him accountable for the meager sugar crop. Payne, in turn, went to New Orleans to launch his "China enterprise."[31]

In January 1871, Payne announced in local newspapers that he intended to travel to China "for the purpose of procuring a large emigration of those people to our Southern States." Having lived in California for six years and visited

Canton, Macao, and Hong Kong, he had come to recognize "the great intelligence, patient industry, sobriety and superior good conduct of the Chinese, as compared with the people of other nations." Ever since emancipation had become "a fixed fact," Payne explained, he had advocated Chinese labor for the South to avoid "the disastrous result" of slavery's end in the British West Indies. The "almost unlimited supply" of Chinese labor—"far more desirable to the country than the African ever had been"—would lead to "a return of prosperity to these States," he claimed. "Chinamen are not uncivilized, uneducated, ignorant savages," he added. "And although it is true that their civilization differs from ours, it is also true that it is much older, and who should say that ours is the best[?]" The Leverich family lent their support, having contemplated the idea of recruiting Chinese laborers on their own as early as February 1869 after "a general stampede among the negroes." "The negroes require competition . . . to work at reasonable wages—they are asking $20 pr. mo. house & provisions," Henry S. Leverich had written then, "which is higher than white labor at the North, & they feel at liberty to quit at the busiest season." They ordered one hundred Chinese laborers for the Porter estate.[32]

Louisiana's elite sugar planters, a select group with the capital to invest in such an undertaking, provided the credit Payne needed to embark on his trip to China. In early February 1871, John Burnside, the state's largest sugar planter, who had expressed interest in Chinese labor for years, answered Payne's solicitation for funds. Burnside agreed to advance Payne more than four hundred pounds to recruit laborers in China on his behalf, the advance to cover "the incidental expenses in China, of collecting together and placing said emigrants on board of Ship, making small advances, printing and brokerage." The planter, at the same time, demanded a guarantee on his investment, requiring Payne to repay the advance in full if he could not "procure said emigrants on the terms authorized" in China. Payne evidently promised to procure Chinese laborers bound to five-year contracts, through January 1, 1877, an offer hard to resist among planters in search of a stable labor force and wage rate. Encouraged by arrangements with Burnside, Duncan F. Kenner, who was authorized to receive additional orders, and other planters, Payne made plans to leave for China in February 1871. Within three months, he reportedly contracted with one thousand laborers in Hong Kong "for a term of years, at $8 per month, in gold." Bradish Johnson, a sugar planter who already employed Chinese labor from Cuba, hurriedly submitted an order for fifty laborers before it was too late.[33]

Payne's auspicious beginnings ended in dismal failure. His sporadic correspondence conveyed little good news over the summer months. He still "had
done nothing" by mid-June; his prospects dimmed to "not very good" by early
August. A month later, Payne sent word that he might be able to dispatch his
recruits by steamship to San Francisco and thence to Louisiana by railroad.
Leverich and Company, excited by the news, began looking for rice suppliers
in preparation for the laborers' arrival. Their hearts sank in early October when
Burnside informed them that Payne was having trouble recruiting agricultural
laborers. Finally, in November 1871, Payne telegraphed Leverich and Company that the "British authorities prevented consummation of my business." He
returned to the United States with nothing but curios "made by the very best
workmen in China" and ten boxes of tea.[34] Payne's project failed largely because of the intensifying global censure of the coolie trade, particularly in China
and Britain. Due to mounting public pressure, the governor of Hong Kong was
instructed to prohibit the emigration of contract laborers to destinations outside the British Empire on May 30, 1870, less than two months after Orr and
Williams received their clearance. British authorities refused to allow Payne to
charter a ship for his large contingent of recruits. By January 1872, a year after
his China odyssey began, Payne was in Washington, D.C., to pursue his claims
against the U.S. government for damages sustained during the Civil War. Re-
alizing the sore limits of his imperial reach, he struck out against antislavery enemies closer to home.[35]

During Payne's misadventure abroad, Louisiana sugar planters entertained
other ambitious projects to transport laborers from China to Louisiana. In March
1871, an agent of the London-based Oriental Steamship Company offered to
contract with local planters for the delivery of Chinese laborers to New Orleans,
"the contracting party paying $150 passage for each man and $8 gold per month
with 5 years contract." The company reportedly owned "the finest vess[e]ls ever
built" and, by using the Suez Canal, "could deliver the chinamen in a comparatively short time." The agent had already secured contracts for five hundred
laborers and waited only to fill a minimum balance of one thousand laborers to
commence his operation. Planters themselves organized the Louisiana Immigration Company, involving "some of the most honored and substantial men of
New Orleans," to introduce Chinese labor "in sufficient number to render
every planter independent." In June 1871, they began "securing the co-opera-
tion of planters throughout the whole State" and raising $250,000 in stocks.
The company's founders and subscribers represented the sugar planter elite,

many of whom had pending orders with Payne. The company, in the end, failed to attract enough subscribers or to collect payments from subscribers, most likely the same fate suffered by the Oriental Steamship Company.[36]

The misfortunes of these grand schemes, from the Mississippi Valley Immigration Labor Company to the Louisiana Immigration Company, had been shaped by forces greater than Hong Kong's governor or Treasury Secretary Boutwell. First, those laborers portrayed as docile coolies rose up defiantly against their captors and employers—in India and China, aboard ships, on sugar plantations across the Caribbean, in the Cuban independence movement, and before various inquiry commissions—bearing witness to coolieism's origins in slavery and their own humanity. Without their relentless struggles against the contradictions of emancipation and imperialism, no liberal humanitarian group or government official would have ever taken notice of their plight.[37] Second, would-be coolie traders, or promoters of Chinese "immigration," in the postbellum South also fell victim to the proslavery ideology, whose vitriolic spokesmen had berated Britain, Cuba, and Caribbean coolieisms. Their belated defense of immigration could never eclipse the broader association of coolies with slavery in American culture. Third, projects to import thousands of workers from China conveyed goals and sentiments beyond the reach of a region marred by political and economic crises, particularly without the support of governing authorities in Washington, London, and China. The coolie fever might have died in Louisiana at this point, but it did not. The daily struggles between planters and black laborers kept it alive, in the process reshaping the search for Chinese migrant labor.

Black Migrant Labor

Payne's mission to China produced a host of hopes and anxieties back in Louisiana. After futile attempts to sell the debt-ridden Porter estate, Leverich and Company took over plantation management in March 1871. Although the Leveriches had earlier advertised the adjoining Oaklawn and Dogberry plantations as possessing a "large force of reliable laborers," the future shipment of one hundred Chinese laborers was integral to their plans. They demanded that the Porters bear the recruiting costs, estimated at ten thousand dollars, and that the entire managing arrangement be annulled if Payne's venture failed. "If it should happen that the Chinese are not procured," Henry Leverich advised his family firm, "you c[an] not agree to go on with negro labor . . . in that case you could only agree to do the best in y[ou]r power." Thomas J. Foster, the newly appointed plantation manager, grew extremely uneasy as the 1871 season progressed, repeatedly demanding updates on Payne's work in China. When he received favorable reports in September, he immediately began "making Bunks, cleaning & fitting up quarters" for the Chinese laborers. He had high expectations of their role in taking off the cane crop and asked Leverich and Company to purchase additional mules to accommodate their arrival.[38]

As much as Foster and his employers laid their hopes in Chinese labor, they readily explored other labor options. Decrying the shortage of "first class labor" in May 1871, Foster suggested that laborers be recruited from Virginia and the Carolinas. He later changed his mind. "About getting them from other states and giving them less," he wrote, "I don[']t think will do for they will not remain with us after we have incurred the expense of transportation &c unless we give them the same they can get at other places." As the grinding season loomed, the competition for labor stiffened in Louisiana, the reason behind Foster's elated anticipation of Payne's Chinese recruits. Disappointed by their delay, he procured additional "negro labour" for the grinding season. Foster's labor troubles, however, worsened. In the height of the busiest season of the year, laborers on Oaklawn and Dogberry caused "a great deal of anxiety" by striking for higher wages. Foster refused to give in and hired workers nearby and "from up above" to break the strike. "They are the hardest set to manage that I ever had anything to do with—have no doubt that they can be brought under a good di[s]cipline," he remarked of the entire labor force, "and have accomplished a good deal this year in that way, but there is a good deal yet to do." Foster planned to hire forty "negroes" from "the poor hills of the cotton country" in Alabama through a labor agent and to "make a good many" of his old laborers "emigrate."[39]

The emotional vicissitudes and hiring patterns on Oaklawn and Dogberry reflected southern planters' postemancipation transformation from, in the words of economic historian Gavin Wright, "laborlords" invested in high slave prices into "landlords" in search of cheaper labor. Payne's failure to tap into the transpacific labor market hardly extinguished Foster's interest in Chinese labor. Evidently abandoning his Alabama plan, he hired local laborers "on the same basis as last year" in January 1872, commencing the new season with "as many hands" but "under better control than the beginning of last year." An excited Foster reported the following month that he had contracted with twenty-four Chinese laborers, who "have been working in the count[r]y some two years[,] must be acclimated, and have some skill as laborers."[40] Over the span of a calendar year, Foster and his employer Leverich and Company contemplated or hired a wide assortment of migrant laborers—Chinese laborers already in the United States and from China, as well as black laborers from nearby plantations and parishes, Alabama, Virginia, and the Carolinas. As grand schemes abroad turned into implausible dreams, Louisiana planters resorted to established and emerging interstate networks to discipline and supplement local supplies of labor. Louisiana planters' vast experience in recruiting and employing African American migrant contract laborers, in turn, would guide the interstate migrations of Chinese laborers in the early 1870s.

Intraregional migrant labor had been vital to the South's plantation economy for decades. The domestic slave trade had flourished before the Civil War, especially after the national prohibition of the transatlantic trade in 1808, and encompassed approximately 200,000 enslaved peoples per decade between 1820 and 1860. The Gulf states, particularly Louisiana's sugar-producing region, became leading importers of slaves from the Upper South, a system of coerced migrant labor that increased Louisiana's slave population from 109,588 in 1830 to 244,809 by 1850. The New Orleans market, which supplied the surrounding sugar and cotton plantations, attracted speculators from across the South and formed the receiving end of perhaps the most prominent link in the slave trading network, the Richmond–New Orleans trade. After the war, the Freedmen's Bureau actively encouraged the relocation of freedpeople, as Commissioner O. O. Howard's office put it, "with the design of bringing labor and capital together." "Should there be an excess of labor in one quarter of the state and a demand for it in another," the commissioner told the head of Virginia's office in February 1866, "the surplus negroes from the overstocked districts should be removed to where they can find employment; those only, going, who can be induced voluntarily to do so." Offering free transportation to freedpeople on government support—or likely to be so in the future—who contracted with employers elsewhere for "comfortable homes and reasonable wages," the Freedmen's Bureau assisted in the migration of at least 29,402 freedpeople in the postwar years.[41]

Like his colleagues in the State and Treasury Departments, however, Howard looked askance at migration proposals that prompted associations with the slave and coolie trades. Unlike his adjutant general, who eagerly entertained and promoted requests for African American laborers from Peru and Hawai'i, Howard remained skeptical of plans that hearkened back to antebellum colonization schemes. Howard's misgivings about resettling freedpeople abroad intensified in the fall of 1866, when the U.S. consul in Peru reported that a Lima resident had recently left the city to recruit two thousand African American families. "This speculation is under the color of free colonization," it was reported, "but in fact the negroes are to be sold in the same manner as the Chinese coolies for the term of eight years." Amid the rising local interest in coolies from Cuba, the *New Orleans Daily Picayune* immediately spoke out against meddlesome federal officials in Washington. A lengthy editorial on the viability of coolie experiments in Louisiana emphasized that the Peruvian government had recently instituted reforms "in the work of suppressing the fraudulent, violent, and inhuman features of the cooly trade." Neither the export of former American slaves to Peru nor the import of coolies into Louisiana, the newspaper suggested, warranted federal intervention.[42] Howard disagreed.

Any migration scheme associated with coolies inexorably stirred up great alarm among federal officials. Upon receiving the consular report, Secretary of State William H. Seward wrote to Commissioner Howard that "plans are on foot to lead freedmen to move abroad and in particular to Peru, upon a promise of higher wages than they receive at home, and probably by other inducements." Seward recommended that Howard instruct all bureau agents "to advise the Freedmen to be cautious how they conclude bargains to go to foreign countries." "As there is reason to believe that these promises will not be fulfilled," he explained, "it is deemed to be the moral duty of the Government to prevent the Freedmen from being imposed upon by them." Howard circulated Seward's letter to all field agents, with an additional warning that contracts requiring migration "beyond the limits of the United States" fell outside the bureau's purview. Such contracts remanded the attention of proper authorities in Washington.[43] Once again, the possible extension of the coolie trade to the United States—involving the freedpeople, in this case—exacted a swift response by Republican federal officials, underscoring the fluidity of transregional notions of race and labor within the Americas in the age of emancipation.

If the Lima labor recruiter ever reached the U.S. South, he entered a competitive and flourishing field of business. Like the promoters of coolie labor, many in New Orleans commercial circles saw an opportunity for a quick profit and organized agencies "to procure HANDS to Planters and EMPLOYMENT to Laborers" in exchange for commission fees. The emergence of private labor agencies, and planters' growing dependence on them, produced distress as much as relief in Louisiana. "The old swindling game has been revived in New Orleans, and it deserves the attention of the city authorities, or at least the Freedmen's Bureau," the *West Baton Rouge Sugar Planter* editorialized in 1867. "Hands are hired from agents—part of the pay is advanced by the planter—the freedmen go on board the steamer, and at the first place she lands, they go ashore . . . These agents should be held strictly accountable for such behavior; and perhaps a little time spent in the Penitentiary, with their associates, the freedmen, might open their eyes to the absurdity of such financial operations." But planters felt they had no choice. "There are people from all parts of the South who are looking for hands . . . and runners want big pay to look for Negros," a Louisiana planter reported from North Carolina. "There is no use in trying to get hands without the assistance of these men."[44]

The reliance on "runners" and laborers from afar, as distasteful and costly as it was to planters, seemed to be the only way to combat the constant barrage of work stoppages and negotiations that defined the social relations of sugar production. Upon hearing rumors of an impending strike "for big wages" in December 1867, Roman Daigre of Iberville Parish vowed "to make a clean sweep of all, and get in an other sett [*sic*]." He managed to avoid a strike on his plantation but then faced the onerous task of contracting for the new season. When the laborers made "no definite answer" to his offer in January, Daigre told them they had a day to accept or vacate the premises. They apparently agreed to stay for the year. Within a month though, the planter was complaining of his laborers' being "tampered considerably" by Bayou Teche planters and becoming "very much dissatisfied and trying to force me to raise my wages." "I hope they will not bring it to a focus before the end of the month, in the meantime please find out if hands can be had at Vicksburg or Natchez, because it is such a bad pri[n]ciple to yield to them," he informed his business partner. "I would rather turn them all off, and get others even if I must pay higher wages. I will not yield if I can pos[s]ibly help it."[45]

As with Chinese laborers, planters' faith in black migrant laborers' docility proved unfounded, with unforeseen consequences. In the midst of his showdown with his labor force, Daigre was relieved to learn that his neighbor Thomas S. Garrett, whom Daigre had recently berated for driving up local wages, successfully procured laborers from Mississippi. Combined with his own decision to discharge some of his workers, Daigre reported, "the negroes are very uneasy and now know that we are independent of them." Garrett was also satisfied with the effect that his Mississippi recruits—"very obedient to my orders"—had on his "old hands," who reportedly became an "*anxious sort*" after his gambit. They nonetheless continued to resist contracting with him again, a holdout that made Garrett very anxious. Though "content and satisfied," the Mississippi recruits knew nothing about sugar production. "I will have to be patient, and wait untill I can learn them," Garrett resolved. "I hope soon to be able to get some hands of experience to assist in teaching them." Already deep into the planting season, he impatiently received eight of his former laborers and contemplated discharging several of the "trifling" recruits who had "worked enough to pay all advances" paid. Garrett, in the end, was the one who had learned a hard lesson. He was determined henceforth to pay his laborers promptly. "The only *recommendation* I have with the *freedmen*, is punctuality—and the only way I can *secure* labor or *retain* it is by being *punctual*," he concluded.[46]

Planters' fierce competition for labor, especially during grinding and planting seasons, drove up wage rates throughout Louisiana and the South, a product of wider transformations in the social terrain. J. T. Rogers, hired by Edward J. Gay to recruit laborers downriver in 1867, dreaded the difficulties of his new enterprise. "This is a horrible business I certain[ly] have never done anything more humiliating than mixing with those miserable drunken wre[t]ches and talking on terms of familiararity [*sic*] in order to obtain their services," he complained. "They feel themselves better than a white man when they have a few dollars in their pockets[;] we have from five to eight different parties here all the time wanting hands all equally anxious to procure labour." Rogers only contributed to the frenzy, eagerly advertising Gay's "most liberal" wages to entice laborers upriver. Induced in part by the Freedmen's Bureau's offer of free transportation, Gay also hired N. G. Pierson to recruit laborers from the Carolinas, with no better results. "I have Made But Little progres in getting Freeadmen it is a verrey uncertin Buisaness after thay sine a contract it is verrey uncertin if thay ar got tow place of Destination," Pierson reported. "The hole countrey is Fluded With Men From all parts of the South Hunting Freeadmen and offering Fabules prises to get them, and Rezorting tow Evrey Manner of Means to get them." He ultimately returned to New Orleans with twenty-seven laborers, having expended $1,111 during his seven-week sojourn.[47]

Appeals for solidarity echoed in vain as planters engaged in local and distant bidding wars for labor. "Don't go out to look up hands, by any means," pleaded a Georgian, who felt that "*planters* from out west" had driven wage rates beyond his reach. A Virginia planter lamented that the "'almighty negro' has literally taken his flight from this parts [*sic*] of the county—and what few are left are worthless as laborers." Many Virginians spread false rumors to stem the exodus, including tales of recruiters' enslaving and selling freedpeople to Cuba. Any semblance of planter unity or decorum flew by the wayside in Louisiana, as sugar planters set their sights on a big sugar crop in 1869. "I found here *your* cousin James trying to hire the hands that I have already cont[r]acted with," a plantation manager exclaimed to his wife. Local newspapers assailed sugar planters' "suicidal policy" that would prove "disastrous" in the long run, advising them to consider "fresh hands . . . from more distant sections of the South" rather than an "impolitic competition between the agents, planters and farmers . . . for the limited supply of good field hands" already in Louisiana.[48]

It was within this local context that ideas on how best to resolve the chronic labor problem percolated and circulated. Planters in St. Mary Parish, who boasted the highest wages in the state and perhaps in the South in 1869, acknowledged the need to band together to secure a long-term solution. They decided to organize the Labor Association to solicit migrants to the Attakapas region. "Let us do this," urged the association's vice president, "and abandon the error some planters have adopted of believing that the increase of wages will proportionately increase the supply, as absurd as expecting 1 × 1 to give 2 as its product." But planter unity, even within a single parish, did not last. Months after the organization's founding, members apparently could not agree on "what class and race of people" to recruit, leading the local newspaper to pronounce it "an utter failure." In the summer of 1869, when the cry for coolies reached a feverish pitch in Memphis, St. Mary's planters abandoned their nascent organization and scattered across the nation in search of migrant labor, including some "quietly feeling for Chinese labor."[49]

Dreams of transporting black and Asian workers to the Louisiana countryside materialized side by side and more often than not elicited stark racial comparisons. As the Memphis labor convention made clear, Chinese labor had its share of fervent boosters. The idea of importing an unfamiliar people also drew many detractors, who presented black migrant labor as racially preferable. "The natural tendency of the race is southward," argued the *New Orleans Commercial Bulletin*. "They drifted that way before emancipation, because they were at once healthier and more profitable in low latitudes." The *West Baton Rouge Sugar Planter* hoped that labor supplies "in the late northern slave States . . . be exhausted before attempting to import labor from abroad." Not only were laborers there "more reasonable in their demands than those we have at home," it stated, the vast majority of planters preferred "the negro" to "the much talked of Chinese." The Upper South, another newspaper urged, afforded "a much more reliable, and cheaper mode of obtaining hands than to send to the other side of the world for them, and get men who know nothing about our mode of cultivation and who would prove a curse to the rising generation." A "very intelligent Radical" correspondent alternatively recommended "Cuban negroes" over "freshly imported Chinese" or "newly imported Africans." They knew "a good deal about work" and could communicate with "our plantation negroes," he wrote in the *Planters' Banner*, even though many were "little better than savages."[50]

As disappointment over the 1869 crop turned into optimism for the new season, black and Chinese migrant labor competed for public attention in Louisiana. Although unfavorable weather had largely accounted for the low yield, only about three thousand hogsheads above the previous season, planters and their allies directed their anger at the local labor force. Labor relations, Louis Bouchereau observed, had created "a tendency to place the planter, under the entire control of the laborer, [and] to create hostility among the planters" rather than the other way around. Louisiana required an influx of additional laborers, he concluded, none "more suitable" than the Chinese.[51] George Gift, Frank Williams, and Tye Kim Orr were then in Hong Kong but moved too slowly to meet Louisiana planters' urgent needs. The DeClouet family, for example, began the new season with their old laborers "in an uproar" and "not yet decided to go or stay." All but nine deserted the estate when confronted with an ultimatum, leaving the DeClouets with no desirable recourse but to hire laborers from Virginia through a professional agent. Other planters followed the same path. A report from Richmond in late 1869 related that "the trains going South" had been "crowded with colored people," who were "daily leaving the State, under contracts, in parties varying from twenty-five to one hundred." The mass migration drove a former proponent to regret that Bayou Teche would be "Africanized again." By February 1870, Virginia labor agents put forward proposals to convey up to twenty thousand "able-bodied negroes" southward, schemes that rivaled the grandest of Koopmanschap's and Gift's Chinese proposals.[52]

If Louisiana planters assumed that African American laborers from Virginia would settle their labor woes, they were sadly mistaken. Edward J. Gay and Company, a New Orleans mercantile firm, and its associates discovered this the hard way. With local laborers reluctant to contract for the 1870 season, the firm decided to invest heavily in recruiting laborers from Virginia. William T. Gay, Edward's brother and fellow sugar planter, first dispatched his overseer Joe

Munn "to try Lynchburg & Richmond or thereabouts until he could pick up 25 to 30 good hands with their famili[e]s." With family ties in Virginia, Munn quickly secured agreements with the desired number of laborers, only to lose many of them when Gay and Company balked at his request for $1,200 to seal the deal. Each laborer required ten dollars in advance, four to five dollars worth of food, and two cents per mile for transportation. When the contractual struggle with local laborers showed no sign of improving in Louisiana, the firm not only sent Munn the requested funds but advanced $3,450 to three planters—Roman Daigre, Thomas Garrett, and Charles H. Dickinson—to recruit additional laborers in Virginia. By the end of January 1870, though, the competition had grown so intense that Munn gave up on the idea of enlisting more laborers and departed for Louisiana with his remaining recruits. After drawing another $2,000 to attract workers, his fellow Louisianians did the same, just in time, it seemed, to rescue the planting season.[53]

The long journey from Virginia to Louisiana presented dangers of its own, as employers along the route held no qualms about enticing migrants with better offers. Many migrants, in turn, felt no obligation to remain with their original recruiters. Munn lost thirteen recruits and returned to William Gay's plantation in February with only "16 men & 7 women & some boys & little children" at a total cost of $1,800. By the time Dickinson—who had left with "50 effective hands" and thirty-five others, most likely family members—reached Mobile, Alabama, around fifteen recruits had deserted him. Twenty others ran away during a stopover in that city. Garrett and Daigre fared no better, losing twenty-two of their recruits in Mobile and arriving back home with twenty laborers. The three planters expended about $6,000 to hire seventy migrant laborers from Virginia, a turn of events that Gay and Company deemed "almost a complete failure attended with great expense and loss." Daigre explained that they "could not help it" and were lucky to have retained the number they had, noting that "for a while we thought we would have to come back without labor." Garrett likewise defended their meager results and deemed the remaining recruits "satisfied" and "obedient to all orders" on the plantation. He complained that "if the *mean* white men will let them alone," he would "have no trouble with them" whatsoever.[54]

Blaming "mean white men" and casting Virginia laborers as "obedient" were nothing more than pathetic attempts to justify their costly endeavors, which became more expensive over time. Garrett's recruits apparently worked satisfactorily after their arrival in February 1870, although many fell ill in March.

Picturing them as a lasting source of labor, the planter adamantly implored his factor for prompt payments to convince them of his trustworthiness. In May, he pleaded for "a good article" of clothing for the laborers because he was "anxious to give satisfaction." "Some of my new Laborers are giving me some trouble," he explained, "but I think I will git [sic] things strai[gh]tened after a while." Within days, however, one of them ran away. "I made ev[er]y effort to have him arrested," he reported, "but have not succeeded." His Virginia recruits turned out to be as troublesome as local laborers. The DeClouet family experienced worse setbacks. Their migrant laborers, hired through a labor agent, began fleeing within a week of debarkation. By June 1870, four months later, more than half of their work force from Virginia had left the plantation. Other Louisiana planters encountered similar problems. William Gay, like many others, had grown so frustrated by the enterprise that he was ready to get rid of his "biggest lot of fools." "I think I am thro[ugh] with importing such live stock," he declared.[55]

By the summer of 1870, when Gift's shipment of Chinese laborers docked in New Orleans, an increasing number of Louisiana planters grew disposed to invest in another "race" of migrant laborers. "The whole system of importing our labor from Virginia has proved an expensive failure and will be abandoned by anybody who ever tried it," the *New Orleans Times* editorialized. Proving to be "utterly unfit" for sugar production, it argued, "the negro" felt "no such gratitude for the assistance rendered to him, and when he arrives here looks around and makes the best bargain he can." The *Times* denounced the fees exacted by Virginia "brokers and agents" in particular and suggested that planters direct their attention to agents soliciting Chinese labor from California instead. Indeed, Louisiana planters had already begun making the transition westward, a transition grounded in their dealings with labor agents and interstate migrant labor from the Upper South. When a Louisiana planter arrived in Virginia in August 1870 to recruit laborers, he noticed the contrast between the ubiquity of labor agents and the slackened demand. A fellow Louisianian there had declined "to take Negroes as he prefers China men & will engage to get 100 from Calafornia [sic]."[56] Many others made the same decision.

Aliens and Citizens Naturalized

Nearby, in the nation's capital, the U.S. Congress also weighed in on the racial characteristics of Asians and blacks; its proceedings would continue to make Chinese labor an attractive alternative to black labor. It was a discussion no one could have foreseen when the House of Representatives resolved to pass a law modifying the nation's naturalization laws to check "fraudulent practices" and "illegal voting" in the wake of the 1868 elections. As the House's Judiciary Committee introduced a bill in June 1870 to criminalize the use of false testimony, impersonation, or documentation in obtaining naturalized citizenship or voting rights, everyone recognized that its purpose was to eradicate the corrupt schemes ascribed to New York City's Democrats and their foreign-born Irish constituents. Surprisingly, Republican legislators from the Pacific Coast registered the loudest objections. Thomas Fitch of Nevada and Aaron A. Sargent of California protested vehemently against the implied inclusion of Asians in the nonspecific rubric "aliens," casting them as "races of tyrants and slaves," "idol worshipers," "imperialists," "polygamists," altogether "a race without love of liberty." Fitch moved immediately to add the phrase "except natives of China or Japan" after "aliens" in the bill to foreclose the possibility of their naturalization. Excluding the Chinese from naturalization, Sargent insisted, was "in strict harmony not only with the letter but the intention of the fifteenth amendment." Congress had not banned "nativity" in voting restrictions, he argued, in deference to the "Chinese question" out west.[57]

The western duo's uncontested diatribes reinforced other objections to the bill which also dwelled on the politics of race and Reconstruction. A Wisconsin Democrat lambasted the bill as "a party measure . . . invented by selfish, reckless, and unprincipled partisans for the preservation and perpetuation of party power." "It is not, perhaps, as desperately cruel and barbarously wicked as the disfranchisement of the cultivated and refined men of our own race and the subjugation of their women and children, at the point of the bayonet, to the rule and government of the ignorant and brutal negro," he said, "but the spirit and purpose is the same." It was an anti-Democratic, anti-Catholic, anti-immigrant measure, he charged, that would extend "the same invitation of citizenship to all India, Japan, China, and Africa" as to "the intelligent Christian of our own race and blood!" In less impassioned speeches, a handful of representatives of both parties defended the immigration and naturalization of Europeans as the bedrock of American civilization, a blueprint the bill jeopardized by placing undue burdens on European immigrants' claims to American citizenship. All of the nation's achievements, a New York Democrat declared, "belong to our progenitors, the white people who earlier or later came from Europe." Over the simultaneous racial pronouncements *against* Asians and blacks and *for* European immigrants, the House easily passed the bill. Fitch and Sargent ultimately voted for the measure, perhaps satisfied that the 1790 Naturalization Law would continue to prohibit Asian migrants from obtaining U.S. citizenship.[58]

The relatively brief deliberations in the House foreshadowed the Senate's strident debates on the nation's racial past and future. Rather than forward the House bill intact, the Senate's Judiciary Committee proposed a detailed substitute to standardize naturalization proceedings within the federal bureaucracy and to empower the federal courts and marshals to supervise elections, all with the same goal of cleaning up New York City's Tammany Hall. The substitute bill garnered little support. With sanctimonious verbiage, senators of both parties stepped up to object to what they deemed unfair, indeed un-American, hindrances to immigration and naturalization. An Indiana senator was "unwilling to adopt any provision of law which shall create an obstacle to naturalization," particularly since "the intelligence of this goes to Europe, and has the effect to check immigration to our shores." Race and Reconstruction, the preeminent political issue of the day, initially entered the debate only to highlight the injustice contemplated against white immigrants, those crossing the Atlantic in search of "the asylum of the oppressed." Backers of the measure were "benighted," a Delaware senator charged, "because they love darkness rather than light, by incorporating such a large negro population into the element of voters and by wanting to exclude light voters." The Senate overwhelmingly rejected the bill.[59]

Such was the unlikely and unpropitious scenario in which Congress would pass the most progressive revision of naturalization rights in U.S. history until the twentieth century. Amid the self-congratulatory speeches on the nation's inclusive character, the old Radical Republican from Massachusetts, Charles Sumner, proposed an amendment to remove the word *white* from the 1790 Naturalization Law "so that in naturalization there shall be no distinction of race or color." His proposal instantly altered the tenor of the debate. The Senate's consideration of the original House bill receded, as did all the rhetoric of extending equality and justice to immigrants. Some senators, most conspicuously the other Massachusetts senator, Henry Wilson, objected on procedural grounds. He hoped to rectify "the loose, corrupt, and corrupting administration of the naturalization laws" and to protect "the purity of the ballot-box" through the law, which was "endangered" by what he saw as an unrelated amendment, however justified in its own merits. Wilson vowed to vote against the amendment in this context, a promise he carried out to the very end. Numerous pleas to withdraw his amendment for the sake of the legislation merely drove Sumner to dig his heels in further. He had tried repeatedly for three years to introduce a separate bill on the matter, he explained, only to see his efforts languish in committees. He was not about to let this "golden opportunity" slip away. "Senators will vote as they please; I will vote for it," he replied.[60]

If Wilson was unprepared and unwilling to discuss Sumner's amendment, anti-Chinese legislators from the West Coast were more than prepared and eager to deploy their political weaponry to kill it. Armed with a counter-amendment just for this occasion, Republican George H. Williams of Oregon moved immediately that "this act shall not be construed to authorize the naturalization of persons born in the Chinese empire." The debate on naturalization, originating from the perceived perils of the Irish in New York, hereafter shifted to considering the racial fitness of the Chinese for U.S. citizenship. Republican William M. Stewart of Nevada launched the case against the Chinese, branding Sumner's measure "a proposition to extend naturalization, not to those who desire to become citizens, but to those who are being imported as slaves." Before Stewart or anyone else could elaborate, the Senate proceeded to vote on Sumner's amendment. Losing by a single vote in the first round, it passed the second time by five votes on July 2 and became part of a bill likely to pass both houses. The United States stood on the verge of permitting anyone to become a naturalized citizen without regard to race, perhaps the closest the nation would be to such inclusiveness until the World War II era. Stewart was dumbfounded. He unleashed a tirade against the Chinese, setting the tone for the rancorous debates that would resume on July 4, the date Sumner and his allies proclaimed as the most fitting for passing his amendment.[61]

Although often couched in nonbiological terms, arguments against the Chinese harped on their racial incapacity for republican citizenship. Ever mindful of his own party's stand for racial equality, Stewart continually pointed to his own Republican credentials—his state was the first to ratify the Fifteenth Amendment, he was a longtime "best friend" of the Chinese, a champion of their "civil rights"—and tried his best to sanitize his racist invective. The Chinese were "pagan imperialists," whose allegiance to their homeland knew no bounds and whose oath to the United States would be as worthless as that taken by "the wild beasts of the forest." They were "hostile to free institutions" and, unlike blacks, would remain so. "Because we did an act of justice, because we enfranchised the colored man, must we therefore necessarily abandon our institutions to the Chinese, or to the people of any other country hostile to those institutions?" Stewart asked. "The negro was among us. This was his native land . . . He was an American and a Christian, as much so as any of the rest of the people of the country. He loved the American flag. Although he was ignorant, although he had been a slave, it became important that he should be enfranchised, so that he might protect himself . . . in a free government, where every man must take care of himself."[62]

The "pagan" charge could be discounted easily enough—for instance, by pointing to the sanctity of the separation of church and state—but a cultural figure almost impossible to dispel proved to be the coup de grace of the anti-Chinese faction: coolies. "These people are brought here under these infamous coolie contracts," Stewart exclaimed, "the same contracts that have disgraced humanity in the taking of these poor people to the West India islands and various portions of South America as slaves." He was "anxious that they shall be liberated," but "do you want to extend naturalization to men who are liable to be dictated to by their masters who brought them here as to how they shall vote?" Congress needed to break up "coolie contracts" first or risk rendering "American citizenship a farce." He presented himself as a neo-abolitionist, a defender of civil rights and American freedom. Stewart expressly had no problems with European immigrants, who were "of our own race" and "assimilate rapidly, and aid in the development and progress of our country." "Asiatics," on the other hand, had "another civilization at war with ours," which imperiled the social order. "They work in your mines and on your railroads; but they have not their families with them . . . this is only their temporary residence." When pressed by Sumner and others, Stewart admitted that U.S.-born Chinese would deserve equal citizenship rights but quipped, "Did anybody ever hear of a Chinaman being born in this country?"[63]

In speaking to the racial, gender, sexual, and class anxieties that defined a nation experimenting with multiracial democracy and experiencing rapid industrialization, condemnations of coolies won nearly universal support and in the process normalized the heterosexual, patriarchal Victorian family ideal and the European immigrant, even the suspect Irish. Henry W. Corbett of Oregon argued that boatloads of Chinese laborers and "women of the most deplorable condition and the most lewd class [were] . . . not only interfering with the family relations, but in every conceivable way . . . introducing the most corrupt practices into our community, which has heretofore been moral, religious, and not surpassed by any of the New England States." Male coolies and female prostitutes, he predicted, would engulf the nation, taking over "the labor of Americans and Europeans" and their moral standards. The Chinese "question," his fellow Oregonian insisted, would dwarf the "civil questions" rising out of slavery, a point he and his associates underscored with frequent allusions to the Caribbean and the South. "Let it be understood that the pro-slavery, negro-hating part of this country are in this programme for supplying the cotton, rice, and sugar fields of the South with coolie labor," Williams appealed to Republicans, "and for the displacement of the black man by such labor . . . a part of the same programme that these coolies shall be scattered from one end to the other of this nation for the purpose of reducing the price of wages and increasing the profits of capital."[64]

Sumner's defense of his amendment hardly made a compelling case for Chinese inclusion, focusing instead on the plight of black aliens and the principle of racial equality. "I have here on my table at this moment letters from different States . . . all showing a considerable number of colored persons—shall I say of African blood?—aliens under our laws," he argued, "who cannot be naturalized on account of that word 'white.'" The clause was "disgraceful to this country and to this age," incompatible with the Declaration of Independence and the Constitution. "The word 'white' cannot be found in either of these two great title-deeds of this Republic," he said. "How can you place it in your statutes?" Sumner, for good measure, stated that he was striving "to imitate the fathers" and "complete our great work of reconstruction." If the "peaceful and industrious" Chinese come to the United States for citizenship, rather than merely for labor, "how can their citizenship be the occasion for solicitude?" When asked if "a Chinaman" possessed "a natural and moral right" to American citizenship as much as "a colored man," Sumner replied that he did not think so. "I do not say that we are bound to admit everybody to our naturalization," he added, "but I do say . . . that if we undertake to legislate on the subject, we can make no distinction of race or color."[65]

Given the debate's origins in regulating the naturalization of Irish immigrants, it was striking that senators' racial comparisons, whether they were for or against Sumner's amendment, centered almost exclusively on blacks and Chinese. A Wisconsin Republican, who openly supported "suffrage without distinction of sex, color, or birthplace," wondered why those in his party would "exclude Chinamen from the benefits . . . extended to the freedman." The ultimate effect of the anti-Chinese provision would be to allow Democrats to revive "their objections to the enfranchisement of the African." Lyman Trumbull of Illinois stood firmly behind Sumner's efforts, noting that the Reconstruction amendments had done away with racial distinctions. "This whole opposition to the naturalization of the Chinese grows out of their race and color. They are Asiatics, and the color of their skin is yellow. It is not long since the color of the skin being black deprived an individual of all his rights." If those from Africa were eligible to naturalization, he asked, why not "the patient, the laborious, the industrious, the skillful, the intelligent Chinaman"? Predicting the growing enormity of the "Chinese question" even in comparison to the "negro question," a Kansas Republican pleaded for Sumner's amendment to ward off a potential "backward" step in "a revolution of this kind." "I cannot understand 'the races' of men, but only the human race," he said. "I do not know of any 'races' of men, but only that one race."[66]

Senators on the other side of the debate not only reified and reinforced racial hierarchies but also exploited the proceedings to reproach the enfranchisement of blacks. A Democratic senator, espousing "consistency" as a "jewel," moved to exclude "persons of the negro race of foreign birth" on top of those born in the Chinese empire. Senator Williams, the Republican from Oregon who introduced the counter-amendment, never tried to conceal his disdain for the principle of racial equality. "Does the Declaration of Independence mean that Chinese coolies, that the Bushmen of south Africa, that the Hottentots, the Digger Indians, heathen, pagan, and cannibal, shall have equal political rights under this Government with citizens of the United States?" he asked. That was Sumner's "absurd and foolish interpretation," which was at odds with America's history. Like "Indians" and "persons of African descent in this country," "Mongolians" were "a peculiar and separate people" who would never "amalgamate with persons of European descent." Unlike the "fading" "red man" or the "enslaved" and "Americanized" blacks, however, the Chinese presented a "practical difficulty" in that "when you open the door to one you open the door to four hundred millions, who are now looking with longing eyes to the shores of this beautiful, attractive country . . . Allow persons born in Africa, or upon the islands of the sea, to become naturalized if you please; but the practical question before us now is to deal with this mighty tide of ignorance and pollution that Asia is pouring with accumulating force and volume into the bosom of our country."[67]

July 4, 1870, a day Sumner had hoped would preserve and broaden multiracial democracy in the United States, was anything but a day of national inclusion for Chinese and African Americans. With renowned Republicans joining the chorus against "the importation of coolies" and proclaiming their unfitness for American citizenship—even as many proceeded to affirm the fitness of voluntary Chinese immigrants—the Senate voted to reconsider Sumner's amendment. In the third vote on his measure in as many days, Sumner suffered an overwhelming defeat. Republican Willard Warner of Alabama then moved to extend naturalization rights "to aliens of African nativity and to persons of African descent," a provision the Senate adopted by a single vote. After voting in favor of the inclusion of blacks, Sumner and Trumbull pressed again to excise the word *white*. It would not be Trumbull's finest hour. The adopted amendment "opens the whole continent of Africa, where are to be found the most degraded examples of man that exist on the face of the earth, pagans, cannibals, men who worship beasts, who do not compare in intelligence at all with the Chinese," he argued. "Are we now going to place ourselves in the condition of authorizing these Africans to be naturalized . . . and deny that right to Chinamen?" His foes had a simple answer. Only "a few" persons of African descent might come from "the West India islands," they countered, but none from Africa, as "there is no opportunity for them to come." The Senate resoundingly defeated Sumner's amendment for the last time, along with Trumbull's last-ditch effort to add the Chinese to Warner's provision.[68]

These were the extraordinary proceedings that concretized America's self-image as the "nation of immigrants" and consolidated the "immigrant" as European *and* white, processes that rested fundamentally against representations of Asians (who would arrive in "hordes" as "coolies") and, to a lesser degree, Africans (who could never come). The denial of naturalization rights to the Chinese was framed as a pro-immigrant measure that would save whites, blacks, and the reconstructing nation. The racial divide facing the nation, as Representative Fitch had put it, was "between the Asiatic and the European." And Europeans—"from the Alps to the Adriatic, from the Rhine to the Northern sea, on the islands of the ocean, by the shores of the Mediterranean"—were presumed to be white, their desire for republican citizenship attesting to their whiteness. "In every European country on the face of the earth, in every kingdom and empire and principality in Europe," he said, "there are people who will make good American citizens, because they are attached to republican institutions, and who have aspirations for republican freedom." Coolies, in stirring up fears of chattel slavery and "wage slavery," came to epitomize the enemy of emancipation, freedpeople, free laborers, and, indeed, "immigrants." The Chinese would "drive out the negro laborers" from the South and "weed out the white laborers" in the North, to the benefit of "slave lords" and manufacturers, and to the detriment of "American citizens" and "white families."[69]

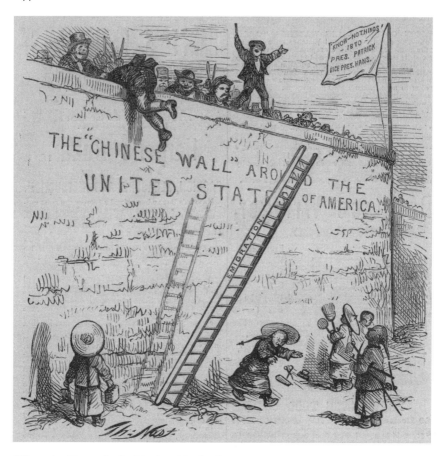

"Throwing Down the Ladder by Which They Rose," *Harper's Weekly*, July 23, 1870. The movement against the Chinese seemed to threaten America's self-image as the "nation of immigrants," but attacks against coolies actually preserved it by racializing immigrants as white and European.
    Courtesy of University of Washington Libraries, Special Collections, UW23643z.

At a moment that had the potential to dislodge national myths and to fracture the white racial category—or, more radically, to rid the nation of racial binaries and hierarchies altogether—Congress turned to coolies to reproduce whiteness. The racial logic of emancipation not only pitted Asians against blacks but also defined the "immigrant" against Asians, making all Europeans appear "white." Asian exclusion sublated the tenuous status of European immigrants and allowed for the begrudging acceptance of blacks. Over the span of a few days in 1870, and for decades to follow, those immigrants accused of corrupting the workings of the American republic—the Irish, for example—simultaneously came to serve as the exemplars of the nation, a white nation of immigrants. In contrast, efforts to recast coolies as "immigrants"—a publicity campaign driven by would-be coolie traders and, from another vantage point, liberal reformers—made little headway against dominant racial formations. The insistence that the word *coolie* was "wholly inappropriate to the Chinese immigrating to this country," as a Presbyterian missionary proclaimed, fell largely on deaf ears in Congress and across the United States.[70] The exclusion of Asians from naturalization and their cultural location opposite immigrants, however, did not yet prohibit their migrations. And the demand for coolies would continue to flourish in light of black political and labor struggles. The allure and rejection of coolies rechristened the United States as the "nation of immigrants" after emancipation, helping to sustain both the legal mirage of racial equality and the harsh reality of white supremacy in American culture.

CHAPTER FIVE

Redeeming White Supremacy

Long before Congress voted to prevent Asians from acquiring U.S. citizenship, Hinton Rowan Helper issued similar admonitions on the ruinous effects of slavery and Chinese migration. In his infamous antislavery treatise *The Impending Crisis of the South* (1857), this son of a North Carolina yeoman farmer bewailed the plight of the South's silent majority—nonslaveholding whites. Slavery and its keepers, Helper argued, extinguished their dreams of economic independence, dreams that, if nourished, would generate true regional prosperity and progress. The South, he proposed, required racial homogeneity and economic diversification to create a society free of self-engrossed planters and enslaved blacks. Like many antislavery Americans, he advocated the colonization of African Americans abroad, claiming that the South was "too cold for negroes," who ought to be "entirely receded from their uncongenial homes in America" to open up a "full and undivided place" for whites. Helper's egalitarian and exclusive impulses were influenced, significantly, not only by his experiences in the Old South but also by his failed sojourn in gold rush California. "Certain it is, that the greater the diversity of colors and qualities of men, the greater will be the strife and conflict of feeling," he had written in 1855. "Our population was already too heterogeneous before the Chinese came . . . and I should not wonder at all, if the copper of the Pacific yet becomes as great a subject of discord and dissension as the ebony of the Atlantic."[1]

Helper's eclectic brand of white supremacy, endorsed by Republican party leaders and berated by slavery's defenders, pointed to a contradiction in U.S. racial ideology which would not disappear with the end of slavery. His pariah status in the South, indeed, betrayed an antislavery, racist ethos that would prove fundamental in the reconstruction of white supremacy in the age of emancipation and industrial capitalism. Helper's ideas, even if not attributed to him personally, circulated widely in war-torn Louisiana and resonated with Union military officials and white unionist Louisianians. Dispossessed whites, many suggested, held the key to Louisiana's salvation. The land monopoly by the "master class," a member of the American Freedmen's Inquiry Commission stated, was wholly incompatible with "the existence of a free, independent, democratic yeomanry, or with the development of free democratic institutions." The "mastership" therefore had to be "overthrown," if not for "the emancipated colored people" then for "these poor whites, these most pitiable men of our own race." Nonslaveholding whites also took up their own cause, most notably at the 1864 constitutional convention. They adopted, in the words of historian Roger W. Shugg, "an extraordinary document" that "remedied the chief grievances of which farmers and laborers complained before secession." The enfranchisement of African Americans was conspicuously absent among provisions on the abolition of slavery, universal public education, and progressive taxation and representation. "The emancipation of the African," a delegate exclaimed, "will prove to be . . . the true liberation and emancipation of the poor white laboring classes of the South."[2]

The "white" race, of course, was a historical fiction in Louisiana as much as anywhere else, but its postwar regeneration rested fundamentally on its antebellum roots and local crises. The reconstruction of whiteness in Louisiana, at the same time, revealed the transregional links forged by capitalism, which melded what Helper had called "the copper of the Pacific" and "the ebony of the Atlantic." As in the halls of Congress, the "white" identity derived its meanings from "negroes," "coolies," and "immigrants," but these racial formations took shape somewhat differently in the Louisiana countryside. In a curious twist of

Reconstruction politics, a contingent of local, die-hard anti-Republicans—Helper's intellectual descendants—came to oppose coolie labor as much as Republican federal officials did. Joining and replacing blacks in the antislavery, racist thought, coolies formed an enemy around which whites rallied together. The movement against coolies in Louisiana, in this respect, mirrored and merged with the nationwide anti-Chinese movement. It also spawned a movement to attract "immigrants," would-be "settlers" and landowners, and opened up an avenue to critique the plantocracy at a political moment marked by rampant appeals for white unity against blacks and Republicans. By directing their ire downward against Asian coolies more than upward against rapacious planters, however, the simultaneous movement *against* coolies and *for* immigrants ultimately justified the consolidation of capital in sugar production and prolonged the phantasmal life of the Jeffersonian agrarian ideal. The inheritors of Helper's ideology enabled not the revolution of emancipation and multiracial democracy but the counterrevolution of "redemption" and postbellum white nationalism.

Great Depressions

In the decade following the Civil War, Louisiana's once thriving sugar industry endured a long-term crisis that, in many ways, prefigured the worldwide depression of the 1870s. To planters and merchants, the liberation of black workers meant far more than the loss of labor. Emancipation demolished the entire pyramid of borrowed capital that rested on the market value of black bodies, planters' most prized possessions. With "the interest on a heavy mortgage staring them in the face," a Union officer observed in 1863, planters begged to "get their niggers back." At the close of the war, Louisiana merchants and planters frantically pursued one another to collect old debts so as to avoid foreclosures. "I am exceedingly sorry things have come to this pass," petitioned an indebted planter's son, ". . . but it is so almost universally in L[ouisian]a—every man, woman & child had run into debt as deep as possible; the consequence is that nearly the entire state is or will be for sale." It would be a buyer's market. Two years after the war, *De Bow's Review* reported that plantation sales fetching a quarter of their antebellum assessment were comparatively "good."[3]

Always a capital-intensive crop in a region full of intrinsic hazards to cane cultivation—especially in the form of spring overflows and winter freezes—sugar production recovered slowly and unevenly in Louisiana, leaving individual planters and merchants in a perpetual state of dread. For more than two decades, the sugar crop never came close to the record 1861 season, the benchmark against which postwar recovery was measured, and inconsistent production spelled disaster for an industry in dire need of capital. In the spring of 1868, a disillusioned New Orleans resident, pronouncing the city's commercial life "dead," decided to try his luck out west. Regardless, every winter and sometimes well into the spring, financially strapped yet "proverbially hopeful" planters, as W. W. Pugh described them, descended on New Orleans in search of credit for another season. Debt and desperation mounted. "Money tighter than a brick every-where!" a merchant exclaimed in 1872. "Planters cry next year! next year! next year!" For many, there would be no next year. A short crop combined with "ruinously low prices" left Andrew McCollam's plantation in the red like many of his neighbors in 1872. "Business is positively stagnant in New Orleans," his daughter wrote despondently. "All the merchants complain of the hard times such times as the City has never known before. The 1st of January will probably see many houses fail . . . Every New Years brings more sorrow and trouble to us."[4]

Even as family after family fell from the ranks of the planter class, a testament to the old regime's demise, huge sugar plantations continued to dominate southern Louisiana's physical and social landscape. Of the 154 planter families owning at least fifty slaves and five hundred acres in four parishes (Ascension, Assumption, Iberville, and Lafourche) in 1860, 71 managed to hold onto their large estates (at least 500 acres) until 1873 and, among them, only 49 until 1880. Neighboring parishes exhibited similar patterns. Despite high turnovers in ownership, the number of large plantations actually increased after the war and the long-held tradition of large planters' owning the most and best land showed no sign of reversal in Louisiana.[5] The dramatic and often traumatic reconfiguration of plantation ownership, in turn, produced a climate inconducive to class solidarity among planters, at least in the short run. In February 1870, a handful attempted to bring together "sugar planters and other persons interested directly or indirectly in the culture, manufacture and disposal of sugar grown in this State" under the Louisiana Sugar Planters' Association (LSPA), seven years before its more lasting namesake would be organized. The original LSPA's history ended after only two meetings, far short of its grand plan of three statewide meetings a year. Most Louisiana planters had more pressing concerns, namely, to stay afloat in a sea of roving sharks. The idea of paying twenty dollars to sit next to their predators three times a year failed to catch on.[6]

The formation of the postbellum planter class was a messy affair that bred intense enmity and strange partnerships among merchants, planters, and laborers; this complex dynamic defined Alexis Ferry's strained relations with Edward J. Gay and Company. Having married a daughter of Valcour Aime, one of Louisiana's richest planters, Ferry's financial prospects before the Civil War could not have been brighter. In 1853 alone, Aime's estate in St. James Parish had generated an income of more than $78,000. The war changed everything. After his father-in-law's death on the fourth anniversary of Lincoln's Emancipation Proclamation, Ferry and other family members struggled to pick up the pieces of his decaying empire. Ferry must have been relieved to contract with the New Orleans mercantile firm bearing the name of a prominent sugar planter, Edward J. Gay, for the 1870 season. Securing a New Orleans factor, or commission merchant, was an essential first step to large-scale sugar production. Factors provided to planters advances for the entire season which made possible the hiring and payment of workers and the purchase of supplies and rations. For their services, which culminated in the sale of the resulting crop, factors levied interest and commission fees on every transaction. Planters thus strove to make their sugar sales exceed their growing debits on their factors' account books, almost a sure outcome in the boom days of old but a tenuous uncertainty in the postbellum years. For many planters, sugar turned into a big gamble that landed them in an unyielding cycle of debt.[7]

Edward Gay profited handsomely from those debts, accruing financial claims over a multitude of relatives, friends, neighbors, and associates. In 1867, the Erwins, a planter family related to Gay's wife, gratefully signed a mortgage with his firm to retain their estate. But Isaac Erwin soon recognized his family's hopeless predicament, jotting in his diary that he had "no doubt but Mr[.] E. J. Gay who furnishes the Negroes & Mules will eventually own this Shady Grove Plantation in the End." Whenever expedient, Gay pressed his clients to settle their debts through a cheap sale or else took them to court for a sheriff's auction, from which he, like so many creditors, consistently emerged as the new owner. "It will be an object to buy the property at as low a rate as the appraisement will permit," he instructed his son-in-law before a sheriff's sale, "and the purchase in my name's necessary." His unrelenting pursuit of defaulters, however close in relation, in fact, had given birth to the firm Gay and Company in 1868 following the collapse of his previous mercantile enterprise, William Edwards and Company. Edwards, in "truly disastrous" debt to his longtime partner, had hoped to exit New Orleans gracefully and return to his old grocery trade in St. Louis, Missouri. Gay humiliated his old friend instead. "Because I did not give him up every thing I had in the World," Edwards protested, "he brought suit by attachment yesterday and . . . we have a notice from EJG. this morning in the paper announcing dissolution of partnership &c."[8]

As high hopes for the Valcour Aime estate turned sour, differences between Ferry and Gay became starkly evident. Samuel Cranwill, the managing partner of Gay and Company, in 1871 criticized Ferry's "very poor green gray sugar," an inferior grade in "almost no demand—except at extremely low prices." In contrast, Gay's own plantation, with its new vacuum pans and centrifugals, produced "a beautiful yellow clarified" sugar that "attracted much attention." Ferry congratulated Gay on his success, adding bitterly that that was "*the Only true Way* of *making Sugar*." He, too, would have installed the latest machinery, but asked, in reply to another round of rebukes from his factor, "what do you Want a poor man to do?" Unlike Gay and his deceased father-in-law, Ferry simply could not afford new technology. Never confident of his standing with Gay and Company, he had enough trouble obtaining advances. After another disappointing season in January 1873, Gay angrily walked out of a meeting with Ferry, uttering not "a Single Kind Word" to his "unfortunate and unprotected friend." Ferry recounted, "I Went home to Kiss my Children . . . and . . . to tell the daughter of Valcour Aime, that, we had four dollars left, and that Mr[.] Gay had not Said a Word in the Shape of an answer to my request."[9]

If not for his laborers, who were neither paid nor fed during this particularly acrimonious standoff, Gay and Cranwill would have happily dropped Ferry as a client and filed claims against his insolvent estate. Although unmoved by his pathetic pleas, they simply could not dismiss a lawsuit initiated by his laborers against the planter for owed wages, an action that Ferry himself sanctioned. The lawsuit jeopardized Gay and Company's legal claims over Ferry's crop and property, some of which were seized immediately on behalf of the workers. In January 1873 and again a year later, Ferry connived to play the role of an accommodative middleman, stuck between a party that had extended credit to him in the form of labor and another that had loaned him capital. Prompt advances to settle with his laborers for the old season and to contract for the new, he proffered, would serve everyone's interests. Cranwill ruefully acknowledged the workers' legal standing above the firm's, a state of affairs that infuriated him. He detested planters like Ferry. "Finding the cane yielding poorly, and worse than poorly in many instances," he complained, "they lay by a large planting for the coming year—then refuse to ship their present crops till the laborers are paid." Pitting one creditor against another, to Cranwill's chagrin, was an effective weapon that "needy and delinquent" planters like Ferry still had.[10]

Ferry's political analysis and outlook, however, ultimately contravened his periodical alliances with workers and his growing resentment of planters and merchants like Gay. He despised the former; he aspired to become the latter. Amid his deteriorating relations with Gay, Ferry felt that "planters of Some reputation before the war" had failed "to Obtain from the black man, the quantity and quality of work for the amount of money paid him." From that failure originated the insurmountable odds they now faced. Ferry became inured to his troubles over time. "Sometime[s] I feel lively, but . . . to day, without any particular causes, I feel despondent," he wrote after another miserable season. "I am an Old man of Sixty, who has always been [p]laced in easy Circumstances, and now, when I look a head, I behold a complete ruin." He could no longer identify with the likes of Gay, who still found sugar a "sensible business," but retained enough racial arrogance to identify with the anti-Republican crusade. Almost a decade after the war, it was clear in Ferry's mind that he had been "ruined by his northern brothers the puritans." Everyone recognized that he and Gay no longer stood on the same ground though. As Ferry's brother-in-law put it in reference to Republican property tax assessments, "were I Edward J. Gay, or John Burnside, or Bradish Johnson, I would not only counsel, but practice, resistance." He could not advise the same to Ferry, who could only beg Gay and Company to pay his taxes before he incurred fines.[11]

What increasingly set Gay and the emergent planter class apart from the rest was their unbroken access to capital in a tightening market that enabled and encouraged their simultaneous experiments with new machinery and migrant labor. Nearly everyone associated with the management of sugar plantations sought to produce high-grade sugar and to undercut local laborers' struggles, all to increase their profit margins, but only a small minority could act on those desires. Unlike Gay, Ferry could scarcely fantasize about hiring migrant laborers from nearby parishes. With his requests for additional workers routinely rejected by Gay and Company, one year he went ahead and unilaterally hired six laborers from northern Louisiana for fifty dollars in recruiting fees. "I hesitated a long time about furnishing the $50—but his letter being so pressing and importuning and picturing his *necessity* in having the laborers," Cranwill sighed, "I concluded it might be best to let him have the $50—so as to allow no excuses hereafter,—in regard to saving the crop."[12] For destitute planters like Ferry, the thought of expending thousands of dollars to recruit laborers from Asia, California, or the Carolinas was as unimaginable as overhauling his sugar mill. As elite planters such as Gay, Burnside, and Johnson pursued their dreams of an ideal migrant labor force, fellow white Louisianians took note. What was a poor man to do? If the movement against blacks and Republicans unified whites and relieved class tensions, the movement for coolies had the opposite effect.

California Dreaming

On October 26, 1870, dozens of Chinese and European workers arrived on Edward Gay's St. Louis plantation in Iberville Parish. After hearing stories of coolies for years, the Gay family took special pleasure in finally seeing Chinese workers from San Francisco in their midst. Gay's son Andrew, a planter himself, found the Chinese "the queerest looking creatures he ever saw," while his daughter "laughed till she cried when they came stalking off the boat." Gay's wife tried to categorize them within the local racial landscape, believing them to look from a distance like "a mixture of mulatoe [*sic*] & Indian." After receiving regular plantation work clothes, they were ordered to the fields right away; they wore their "Chinese dress" only on Sundays and wrapped their queues "around their head[s]" to fit under "the usual hat[s]." The European immigrants recruited from Chicago also commenced work immediately, joining a multitude of black and Chinese laborers in the cane fields of postemancipation Louisiana.[13] East and West, North and South converged and commingled on St. Louis in the fall of 1870. The paths that brought Chinese workers eastward and European workers southward, however, revealed anything but identical forces at work. Neither group was black, but the Chinese emphatically were not white in Gay's and the nation's racial calculus.

Gay's decision to recruit from San Francisco reflected a general shift away from seeking Chinese labor in Cuba and China in the 1870s. Finding workers in California, for one thing, entailed fewer political roadblocks. Famed Dutch labor agent Cornelius Koopmanschap attempted to implement what he had broadcast at the Memphis labor convention in July 1869. Within six months, he reportedly had contracted to send five shiploads of workers to the South and had gone to Europe to secure steamers to ply between China and Louisiana. Although neither venture panned out, he initially refused to give up his transoceanic ambitions. He was "disgusted" with Chinese laborers in California, whom he considered too settled and expensive in comparison to fresh recruits from China's rural districts. But schemes like this still provoked unwanted attention from Washington, D.C.

Days after amending the nation's naturalization law in 1870, the U.S. Senate passed a unanimous resolution instructing President Ulysses S. Grant to report "if Chinese coolies are being imported into the United States in violation of the act of February 19, 1862." His secretary of state reported none, regarding the recent "voluntary emigrants" from Hong Kong to New Orleans legal, but vowed to devote "serious attention" to the matter. Koopmanschap ultimately maintained his operations in San Francisco—beyond the reach of British mandates and American consuls—and dispatched nearly one thousand Chinese laborers to Alabama in the summer of 1870 alone.[14]

John G. Walker followed Koopmanschap's path. Long familiar with "the industrial and economical value of the Mongolian race" on the West Coast, he contracted with 250 Chinese laborers in San Francisco on behalf of the Houston and Texas Central Railway Company. In January 1870, he accompanied them to Texas, traveling through America's new heartland and inaugurating what *Harper's Weekly* called the "Mongolian invasion" of a "peaceful army" eastward. Walker then proceeded to New Orleans to found an agency devoted to Chinese migrant labor. Characterizing both "negro laborers" infatuated with politics and "Caucassians" as unfit for the South, he invited orders for "any required number of able-bodied, docile and experienced agricultural laborers, to be drawn from the interior Chinese provinces, whose climate most nearly resembles that o[f] the cotton and sugar regions of the South." A transpacific migrant labor system, with shipments directly from Asia, however, simply proved politically and financially prohibitive in postemancipation Louisiana. Even if individual merchants and planters were able to overcome political resistance in Hong Kong and Washington, D.C., as John Williams did, most lacked the enormous capital necessary to recruit and transport cheap labor across the seas. His one shipload of laborers from Hong Kong and Martinique in 1870 reportedly cost Williams $30,000, an outlay he had trouble recuperating from. Walker and his partners abandoned their global aims within three months and instead advertised the availability of Chinese laborers from California.[15]

Turning to labor agencies from California, indeed, yielded valuable political dividends, shielding planters from the watchful eyes of federal officials, who perpetually threatened to intervene in supranational schemes involving the South. Louisiana planters and their supporters continually claimed not to contemplate anything beyond northern employers' designs. Pointing to the uproar following a shoe manufacturer's resort to hiring Chinese laborers from San Francisco to break a strike in North Adams, Massachusetts, in June 1870, the

"Chinese Coolies Crossing the Missouri River," *Harper's Weekly*, January 22, 1870. Louisiana planters and merchants increasingly turned their sights from Cuba and China to California in their recruitment of Chinese workers.
Courtesy of University of Washington Libraries, Special Collections, UW23642z.

New Orleans Times presented a sharp contrast between the North and the South. "Whilst our bretheren [*sic*] of New England . . . are . . . passing most sanguinary and menacing resolutions against the inoffensive, industrious and highly productive Chinamen, we, in this far off benighted region of the Union, give them a cordial welcome and offer hospitable homes and the kindest treatment to the enterprising Orientals, who have wandered so far from home, in order to exercise that great natural right, more valuable than any conferred by the Fourteenth or any other amendment of the Constitution, of subsisting by their own labor, and, in Yankee phrase, of bettering their condition." Unlike black workers, moreover, the Chinese would remain aliens in the reconstructing nation and laborers, as a planter put it, whose expenses were fixed, with claims to "no women, no children, no hogs, no ponies, no 'forecastle lawyers,' and no howling preachers."[16]

California also afforded convenience by 1870, as a parade of established and aspiring labor agents, Chinese and white, joined Koopmanschap and Walker to promote and supply a growing demand for coolies in the South. A San Francisco resident originally from Alabama announced his willingness to negotiate with Chinese merchants for "coolie labor" that, he claimed, would "work faithfully, and not bother themselves about suffrage." J. M. Hixson, a veteran California labor agent, likewise exalted Chinese laborers as "naturally sober, industrious and tractable," undoubtedly "the best 'help' the South ever had; far preferable, as a rule, to the negro." Several Chinese mercantile firms based in Hong Kong and San Francisco opened New Orleans branches in the early 1870s to penetrate a potentially lucrative market. The Chinese Emigration Company, which had tried to establish itself in Louisiana years earlier, offered "good and reliable Chinese L A B O R E R S" for "Sugar, Cotton and Rice Plantations" and "Domestic purposes." "We guarantee all Chinese Labor furnished by us to give satisfaction," the company promised, "or no pay." Fou Loy and Company, meanwhile, first specialized in selling groceries, teas, "curiosities," and laundry services to the general public and supplying daily provisions, including Louisiana rice, to Chinese laborers on nearby plantations. By October 1871, they decided to expand their business to labor recruitment, announcing their intention to convey 1,500 Chinese laborers to work on sugar plantations. Other Chinese merchants advertised similar services in goods and laborers.[17]

These proposals circulated at a propitious moment when optimism pervaded Louisiana's sugar industry. Despite delays in the 1870 planting season due to labor disagreements, the summer months proved extremely favorable to cane cultivation, which boosted planters' expectations to an unprecedented level in postwar Louisiana. Political developments abroad also delighted local sugar interests. Samuel Cranwill of Gay and Company was very pleased by the ongoing uprising in Cuba and its likelihood of abolishing slavery, "which would immediately destroy the sugar Planting interest of the Island." The outbreak of the Franco-Prussian War, though tightening the global monetary supply, lifted his spirits as well. The failed sugar-beet crops in France and Germany, Cranwill believed, would increase the demand for cane sugar all over the world. "At all events a home market will certainly be found for all the sugar Louisiana will have to furnish from the coming crop and I think at very fair prices," he surmised. Neither the Cuban insurrection nor European hostilities would derail the long-term transition to imported sugar in the U.S. market and beet sugar in world production, but Louisiana planters and merchants could hope otherwise for the time being. Several years later, Gay's son-in-law, Lawrence L. Butler, wished the United States would intervene in Cuba, noting that since "we all suffered by the civil war I hope one with Cuba may take place in order to give value to Plantations & add to the value of crops now being made."[18]

Motivated by brightening prospects and expedient proposals in the summer of 1870, Louisiana's elite planters decided one after another to invest thousands of dollars on Chinese migrant laborers and, in the process, raised their collective profile in debt-ridden Louisiana. For more than a decade, John Burnside had been at the top of Louisiana's planter circles. He had purchased his first planta-tion and 550 enslaved workers in 1858 for $1 million and became Louisiana's largest slaveholder and sugar producer within two years. The emancipation of his labor force, then numbering nearly one thousand and valued at about $500,000, set him back financially, but it did not liquidate him. Burnside re-sumed his buying spree after the war, reportedly doubling his holdings by 1875 and reviving "plantations which had been nearly abandoned, and left in waste and decay." In August 1870, Burnside concluded that Chinese labor would be in-tegral to his future prosperity and signed a contract with J. M. Hixson and Com-pany for 130 "first class Chinese Laborers" from California. In doing so, he com-mitted himself to an initial outlay of $6,500 in transportation fees, an enormous sum from which he expected high returns over the next three and a half years, the duration of the contract. Burnside secured a fixed wage rate ($14 per month), with a portion ($4) deferred until the contract's expiration, and a delayed monthly payment schedule for Hixson's commission fees, "due at any time after the month's labor has been performed."[19]

Amos B. Merrill, a retired Boston lawyer, and Oakes Ames, a Massachusetts Republican congressman and notorious railroad promoter, represented an-other constituency within the postbellum planter elite, the so-called carpet-baggers who arrived in Louisiana with capital in hand. In 1868, they and their associates purchased the grand Millaudon plantation, once valued at $1.25 mil-lion, for $175,000. At such bargain prices, Merrill quickly enlarged his hold-ings, reportedly owning five additional plantations by 1871. In the summer of 1870, these New England investors engaged the services of A. Kissam and F. W. Gardner to procure more than 140 Chinese laborers from California, at a cost of $64 per laborer or about $10,000 total. It was no trifling investment. Arriving in Louisiana on July 4, 1870, these laborers were under contract for three years at a fixed rate of fourteen dollars per month plus housing and rations, an arrangement that figured to "add greatly" to Ames's "already enormous fortune." The *New Orleans Times* exuberantly embraced this partic-ular Republican's experiment, albeit in anti-Republican terms. His Chinese recruits, an editorial proclaimed, were "young, athletic, intelligent, sober and cleanly," with " little of the appearance of slaves as any laborers we have ever seen." They were so superior to "the vast majority of our African population, to whom the political power of the State has been confided" that any compar-ison "would be the saddest manifest[at]ion of prejudice, bigotry, hypocrisy and downright falsehood and dishonesty that can be found, even in New England history!"[20]

Gay and Cranwill remained circumspect but soon resolved to join their peers in the mad rush for Chinese workers. Recalling the disappointing results of earlier trials with Chinese labor in Louisiana immediately after the Civil War, they initially considered another recruiting trip to Virginia a safer option. But testimonials by fellow planters and labor agents infected the Gay clan with a fever for coolies in the summer of 1870. Gay's son related that Burnside and other leading planters had recently placed orders for hundreds of Chinese laborers and suggested that his father do the same. "I think that is cheaper [*sic*] than sendind [*sic*] to Va for negros as they are so uncertain after you get them and it costs just as much," he explained. His son-in-law, L. L. Butler, agreed that Chinese workers on multiple-year contracts seemed "better than green negroes at a $100 a piece with a twelve months contract." Corresponding with Kissam and investigating his recruits on Millaudon sold Cranwill on the idea of Chinese workers. He learned that they "worked well for green hands," were "rather slow, but systematic" in disposition, "improve[d] rapidly," and would "soon be superior to negroes, and they are more reliable." Able to withstand "hot weather and field work equally as well as the negro," he informed Gay, they were "very quiet and industrious,—and will have nothing to do with the negroes."[21]

Gay's exasperation with black migrant labor proved to be the final straw that convinced him to recruit Chinese workers in California. In the drive to make the most of the "luxuriant" cane crop, Louisiana planters competed fiercely for additional laborers in preparation for the grinding season. In July and August 1870, Butler, in charge of his father-in-law's home plantation, grew alarmed by his inability to hire laborers to cut wood for the sugar mill. In response, Cranwill negotiated with a New Orleans "colored Broker" for several shipments of laborers, most of whom "marched off" the plantation almost immediately. Butler found satisfactory only three of the twenty-seven recruits—"Kentucky negroes" who were "green but not such rascals as the City trash." Probably "deceived" by "his own darkies," he complained, the labor agent was "as great a humbug as that class of people usually are." Cranwill concurred, deeming it "disgusting to have any business with negroes." The impending grinding season nonetheless compelled planters and merchants to scour the city and the countryside for local and interstate labor recruiters and laborers, driving up wage rates in excess of fifty dollars per month by late summer. The growing dependence on black migrant workers, Cranwill concluded, demanded a drastic racial solution. "The negroes are becoming so saucy and unreliable, they are intolerable," he stated. "Then they must have their *horse*, their *cow*, their *pig*, and *such extras* . . . 'Tis well some resort is left to show them the planter is not wholly dependent on their caprice, and obliged to suffer their impertinences."[22]

With confidence borne from his vast capital reserve, extensive experience with labor agents and interstate migrant labor, and growing faith in coolies, Gay dispatched his brother William to San Francisco to procure Chinese laborers for their plantations in September 1870. William Gay realized only a few days after his arrival that California differed little from Louisiana and Virginia insofar as labor agents were concerned. They, too, were "a set of irresponsible men who are trying to make their commission" and nothing else. A couple agents who had received orders for one thousand laborers in Louisiana at fourteen to fifteen dollars per month, he informed his brother, were "unable really to get a man." He discovered that laborers had no incentive to abandon California's employers, who offered them wages as high as two to three dollars per day in the mines. Discouraged but not devastated by what he saw, William Gay vowed to locate "the right Kind of parties, here, who can fill my order with expedition," claiming that "the right Kind of men . . . properly managed by a proper headman, would be fully as good for our purposes as negro labor & more reliable."[23]

William Gay's frustration mounted in California. His short-lived excitement over an agreement with a "first rate Chinese House" for one hundred "agricultural laborers" dissipated when the laborers failed to materialize. The South's distance and reputation, he reported, did not help matters. The recent receipt of "several hundred letters" from "friends in different parts of the south" which expressed "dissatisfaction in a great many instances" compounded the "exceedingly suspicious" nature of the Chinese and made "those willing to go even more timid." "Nearly any of the agents will profess ability to get the hands, "he grumbled, "but no one has them or has any control over them & in many instances after they have been persuaded to come together for shipment, some outside agency will get an unfavorable report of their employers or prospective treatment & they will scatter at once." Gay had never dealt in "a business so unsatisfactory," run by "trifling worthless agents of no responsibility" and "people, who have no confidence in the word or agreement of a white man & who cannot understand the language." When another agreement fell through, he condemned "Chinese headmen" as "the sharpest of the sharps" and accused white labor agents of engaging "coolies from cities in China" who were unfit for field work. Gay did not want to end up like an Arkansas planter who had advanced twenty-six dollars cash to each of the one hundred men he contracted with. Forty abandoned him before the train left San Francisco; others ran away in Sacramento.[24]

With the diminishing prospect of securing laborers in time for the grinding season, William Gay contacted Koopmanschap, whom he considered his last and best option. Things looked so bleak in California that he actively encouraged his brother to follow up on the news that Chinese laborers already in Texas might be available. Back in New Orleans, Cranwill concluded that Kissam, the labor agent who had proposed the Texas scheme, could not be trusted and lobbied for another investment in Virginia laborers. Amid the scramble for grinding laborers, Gay finally saw a ray of hope in California. Having collected nearly seventy of the one hundred laborers that Gay had requested, Koopmanschap advised shipping them out right away, before any of them changed their minds. Gay agreed to pay a flat fee of sixty-five dollars for each laborer delivered to Louisiana—in lieu of commission and travel costs—and arranged to have Koopmanschap fill the balance of the order at the same rate. On October 8, 1870, he shipped fifty-two Chinese laborers to Louisiana, half for his Oaks Plantation in West Baton Rouge Parish and the other half for his brother's in Iberville. At last, Gay could leave California. It had been a most unpleasant trip.[25]

The news from San Francisco provided an emotional boost to those in charge of the Gay plantations, where conflicts with local workers intensified. With the grinding season fast approaching, laborers were all too aware of the increased value of their labor and let planters know it. "The difficulty now is that the women have all stopped work on the back place for the present," Butler reported from Edward Gay's estate. There was a more widespread disturbance at the Oaks. J. T. Nolan, the manager, had been troubled by his boss's delay in contracting with Chinese laborers, noting that the early "competition & contention for hands for the grinding" had raised daily wage rates up to two dollars per day. William Gay's belated success must have relieved Nolan greatly, as he promised to be "prepared for the 'Celestials.'" While the Chinese were en route, however, he faced a mass uprising that threatened to hold up the grinding season. The Oaks laborers demanded a raise and, upon Nolan's refusal, organized a strike just days before the sugar mill was scheduled to start up. Perhaps heartened by the imminent arrival of the Chinese, for whom he was then "putting up Bunks," Nolan chose to retaliate against his workforce. "Some of the strikers (about half the force) went to work yesterday," he reported. "I discharged the ring-leader & think all will go to work today."[26]

The contracting of dozens of Chinese laborers in California failed to allay Edward Gay's fears of a short-term labor shortage, a scenario that revived his interest in European migrant workers. More than a year earlier, he had responded to a solicitation by the Danish Emigrant Agency of Chicago for "a good class of reliable help and Emigrant settlers" from northern Europe. Gay ordered and received laborers in the spring of 1869 and then again during the height of the grinding season. In November, twenty-three men and two women arrived on Gay's plantation, "a fine hardy looking set fresh from the old country, very few speaking english [*sic*]." "We fixed them up very comfortably at the hospital," Gay's wife remarked. "The women cook for them, and they look very comfortable and I hope will do good work." Gay was upset from the beginning though. Five of the men shipped down never arrived, and the rest refused to comply with the labor arrangement. All of the Scandinavians then deserted the plantation within a month, except for "one or two in the garden," who eventually left in May 1870 fearing Louisiana's hot summer. In the months following this experience, Gay evidently turned down a series of proposals to send European workers, including "very stout" and "sober proper looking" Germans.[27]

Edward Gay's ability to entertain and pursue a variety of migrant workers—from California, Virginia, and Illinois—reaffirmed his elite status in Louisiana's planter circles. During his brother's struggles in San Francisco, he changed his mind about European immigrants and dispatched his son-in-law immediately to Chicago. After some difficulty tracking down a labor agency, Butler contracted for thirty-five Scandinavian and German laborers at the rate of "$20 per month for picked men & board, with transportation to the Plantation provided they work faithfully for *four months*." On top of advances for transportation, estimated at twelve to thirteen dollars per person, Butler promised to pay a nine-dollar commission fee to the Chicago labor agency for every laborer delivered to the plantation. The laborers agreed "to do all farm work & to work full ten hours per day, also to work half the night when called upon for fifty cents per 1/2 night." Altogether, Butler left Chicago with forty-four men and two women, "*real wives* of two of the men," who he hoped would prove "useful to the men when they arrive, in cooking &c." On their way down the Mississippi River, Butler and his recruits nearly crossed paths with the fifty-two laborers making their way from California. Traveling by railroad to St. Louis, Missouri and then by steamer to Louisiana, the Chinese concluded their long journey on October 26, 1870, the same day as the Chicago contingent.[28]

Beyond their coincident arrival lay a world of difference defined by race. In the contract signed in California, the Chinese agreed to "labor faithfully & satisfactorily" for either of the Gays "or their assigns" for three years at a rate of sixteen dollars per month. The Gays agreed to pay for the passage to Louisiana and back to San Francisco at the expiration of the contract and to advance each laborer sixteen dollars in gold, to be deducted later from their "first wages or earnings." The Chinese would also receive "sufficient provision, consisting of rice, pork, fish or beef, vegetables and tea, water, fuel, good quarters and weatherproof sleeping places, free of charge." The Gays had so much faith in Chinese labor as a long-term investment—cheap and dependable laborers for others to emulate—that they paid Koopmanschap and Company $4,812.04 for the recruitment of fifty-two laborers.[29] Forty European laborers from Chicago—four apparently abandoned Butler en route—cost Gay merely $1,149.07, most of the sum going toward advances to be repaid by the laborers for food and, if they stayed for less than four months, transportation. The Europeans were promised wages roughly equal to what African American men contracted for the year were then receiving ($19.50 per month) but far below the prevailing rate for extra laborers during the grinding season, and they had no obligation to remain on the plantation, other than a relatively meager financial incentive (passage fare).[30] In Gay's mind, they were only a stopgap measure to save the 1870 crop.

The exorbitant expenses of procuring coolies ultimately meant that only the wealthiest planters and merchants could afford "cheap" Chinese labor. Even with all of their resources, Gay and his colleagues must have been taken aback by how much Koopmanschap and others charged for their services. Instead of accepting various labor agents' proposals, including another by Kissam, Gay attempted to organize a select group of planters in November 1870 behind a local venture with T. B. Stevens, a former resident of China and the Philippines, but received an apprehensive hearing, at best. Within a short span, the "Chinese coolie business" had gone from "such a favourable aspect" to "a standstill" among leading planters, Stevens reported. Gay's brother William withdrew his support, and John Burnside and Duncan Kenner took a "doubtful" view of the project. Bradish Johnson, one of the earliest planters to experiment with Chinese labor in Louisiana, "refuses, is going to get white labour and does not believe in Chinese." But all of these planters would soon renew their demand for Chinese labor. In June 1871, Kenner and Johnson joined a band of influential planters to invest in a company planning to transport Chinese migrants en masse.[31] Although such projects often failed to generate tangible results, much like the original founding of the LSPA, they conspicuously marked these planters apart from bankrupt counterparts like Alexis Ferry. And through heated objections to coolies and planters who could afford them, dispossessed white Louisianians acquired a distinctive political voice.

Rejecting Coolies, Inviting Immigrants

If planters expected to treat European immigrants like Asian coolies, they had to overcome historical, transregional racial formations that linked coolies with slavery and immigrants with freedom. In Louisiana, as in the halls of Congress, coolies solidified "immigrants" as European and white in the age of emancipation, the latter's arrival acclaimed as the key to the redemption of the region and nation. Reminiscent of Hinton Helper's antebellum worldview, white supremacy's exhorters appealed for the replenishment of the white race and the banishment of all others. The last thing the postemancipation South needed was the "importation" of "a new class of servile workers with yellow instead of black skins," the *New Orleans Times* argued in advocating the "immigration" of "white labor."[32] Although contrasting visions of coolies—ideal plantation laborers or slavish barbarians—exposed an ideological schism between the planter class and other whites, they further fortified the idea of a common white identity. In either instance, coolies represented what whites were not, and any attempt to employ whites as perpetual wage laborers faced overwhelming political and cultural obstacles. Permanent plantation labor was the province of coolies and blacks, not immigrants. The racial underpinnings of immigration during Reconstruction not only reified antebellum notions of whiteness but also would have a lasting influence on defining social relations of sugar production in the age of capital.

J. D. B. De Bow established the racial logic of the immigration movement in the first postbellum issue of his popular regional journal *De Bow's Review*. The South's backwardness, he claimed, was due to a labor shortage that had driven "many among us" before the war "to theorize upon the reöpening of communications with the coast of Africa, and with Asia, for the purpose of securing laborers, either as coolies, apprentices, or under some other name." No one had contemplated "free white immigrants," whom he was anxious to court now that emancipation had been "forced" upon his region. *"The South,"* he emphasized, *"must throw her immense uncultivated domain into the market at a low price; reduce the quantity of land held by individual proprietors, and resort to intelligent and vigorous measures, at the earliest moment, to induce an inflow of population and capital from*

abroad." Only through the encouragement of white immigration and the adoption of northern institutions would the South ever catch up economically and
politically. De Bow's own postwar views on coolies were unclear—limiting his
coverage to periodical reports on the "most lively interest" among some circles—but his ringing endorsement of white immigration held at least an implicit rejection of coercive labor systems envisioned by coolie promoters.[33]
Africa and Asia certainly could not supply the immigrants he pined for.

De Bow also published the Old South's leading intellectuals, who likewise
came to shun coolies and to embrace immigrants. Dr. Josiah C. Nott, a prominent scientific race theorist, claimed after emancipation that the "white race
enjoys a higher degree of *pliability* of constitution than the black" and was therefore fit to labor in most locales. Wherever "the white man can live and prosper,"
he continued, "he drives all others before him." Since additional "inferior" races
would only encumber this preordained process, Nott opposed the "slave trade"
and the "Coolie system" and demanded a "nation of white men, whatever may
be the difficulties on the question of labor." Unlike Nott, George Fitzhugh at
first could imagine nothing worse than the extermination of the "negro" race.
Both "native whites" and white immigrants, in his mind, were worthless as
"hired field hands" in the South, where "one negro laborer, be he free or not, is
worth three white laborers." The dawning of black suffrage convinced Fitzhugh
otherwise. Fearing a mass exodus of whites northward and an influx of blacks
southward, he pictured a "wholly and thoroughly Africanized" South, far worse
than the "St. Domingo tragedy." The South, then, would turn to "cheating and
enslaving the yellow races of Asia, and to murdering the Indians of America,
under the lead of the fashionable caprice of modern philanthropy." The federal
government, he argued, ought to compel blacks to work, under slavery if necessary, and encourage immigration to give "a decided preponderance to the
white element in society."[34]

Soon after De Bow's death in 1867, his successors explicitly reached the conclusion that he had been moving toward, taking a decisive stand against "many
Southern planters, and men of influence" pressing for the introduction of
coolies. Beginning in 1868 and especially during the summer of 1869, when the
Memphis labor convention made the nation's headlines, *De Bow's Review* pum-
meled its readers with editorials excoriating "the importation of Asiatic labor"
and offering "some substitute for it." The thorough adoption of fertilizer and
labor-saving machinery, which the editors had been promoting for years, would
allow planters to "escape the necessity of importing Chinamen and Coolies to

infest our country, already embarrassed by the African social and suffrage questions." Integral to "progressive" agriculture, they insisted, was an infusion and profusion of "European whites," as in the North and West. Their admiration for northern economic development notwithstanding, editor-in-chief William M. Burwell and his colleagues despised northerners for Reconstruction and for what they branded as its progenitors: the slave trade and slavery. Slavery was "a God given institution" that the magazine had fully endorsed, but it was fundamentally "a foreign substance in a body otherwise healthy." The coolie system would again infect the South's "rapidly strengthening" body. "Shall the world dump out its negroes and mulattoes to reduce the cost of its shirts and chemises? . . . Shall the world arm the negroes and Chinamen with the ballot to make us support its reconstruction?" they asked. "We demand what the South fought for: 'a white man's government.' "[35]

Regretting that some planters would go ahead and import coolies no matter what they editorialized, Burwell and his associates openly questioned their racial and regional allegiances. Recalling those who "fought very valiantly" and "suffered infinitely for the common cause" but who could not "produce cotton or sugar" or "own coolies," they defended the interests of planters' erstwhile comrades. "We will never forget the men who fought and the women who suffered for the doctrine of State rights," they wrote, "and will always deem it a sacred duty to aid in their restoration." Immigration figured centrally in their vision of small farms and full employment for whites. "The descendants of white immigrants will be just like ourselves," they insisted. "They will be the brothers, the husbands, the comrades of our descendants and theirs. They will amalgamate with us in sentiment, in interest, in destiny." The presence of "pagans and prostitutes of China and Hindostan" would not only repel prospective immigrants from the South, as Africans had under slavery, but would usher in another round of "outside influence" and "eternal degradation." Asians, in the magazine's estimation, ranked below Africans. Not only "far less docile and respectable" than blacks, they were also inaccessible because "like mules, they must be perpetually renewed." Never surrendering their "unqualified" advocacy of "white immigration, and of white immigration alone," the editors nonetheless favored the organization of "colored immigrants" from the Upper South, as carried on by "nigger traders" before the war, over the pursuit of coolies.[36]

The views expressed in *De Bow's Review* captured and reinforced an anti-coolie ambivalence and antagonism permeating the South and the nation. At a commercial convention in Louisville in October 1869, just three months after the Chinese labor convention in Memphis, delegates from all regions of the United States could not muster the votes to build a consensus on Chinese labor. In a meeting guided by a "happy, significant and all-pervading spirit of nationality," the two hundred or so delegates devoted their attention to developing the South by demanding federal aid in levee repair, railroad construction, and steamship lines as well as relief from federal taxation. Everyone also agreed that the South, like the North, ought to "participate in the advantages of immigration." Asian labor, on the other hand, was a separate issue altogether that elicited a fiery debate. The influx of "cheap labor," a contingent led by the Republican governor of Alabama argued, would injure cotton producers by enlarging production and lowering prices. They also objected to Asian "paganism," contending that the importation of coolies would revive the evils associated with slavery. Unable to bridge the great divide on the "the importation of Chinamen and other Asiatic labor," the convention finally resolved to leave the matter up to individual states and organizations. Koopmanschap, who had been invited to Louisville, must have been disappointed, but he had already sensed that there would be resistance to his designs. Across the South, he said, the "poorer and more uneducated classes thought I was initiating a movement hostile to their interests."[37]

Indeed, if the demand for coolies reflected southern employers' desires to revive the glory days of slavery and to enter the age of capital, the prospect of mass coolie importations conversely generated anxieties that cut across regions and political parties. In the South, still smarting from military defeat and political reconstruction, the idea of a new system of slavery combined with universal male suffrage raised deep-seated fears of the end of white supremacy. Various writers objected to "the importation and admixture of the inferior breeds of men" and demanded "men of the Caucasian race, and, no others, as a reinforcement of our population" or the employment of freedpeople to the best advantage "but in no position that can be better filled by a white man." The coolie plan posed a "serious political obstacle" from the outset, the *New Orleans Daily Picayune* claimed, because it involved a people "difficult to adapt . . . in the course of generations, to our laws[,] our social system, and the duties of citizenship." And the latest news from the U.S. West seemed to portend disaster. California, a newspaper predicted, inevitably would be overrun by Chinese voters once the state was "obliged to conform like the rest of us." Many Louisianians who had moved to California, another published report stated, returned home because "they could not compete with the Chinese who had arrived and who were con-

stantly arriving, and were willing to live wretche[d]ly and work for a mere trif-
fle per day."[38]

The constant flurry of letters, articles, and editorials on the merits and de-
merits of *coolies* and *immigrants* led the editors of the *Southern Cultivator* to plead
in 1869 for "a *calm* and *temperate* discussion." Toward that end, they hoped to
clarify what they saw as a jumbled debate. "Immigration" did not include "obtaining *laborers*, to fill the place hitherto occupied by the negroes." That was an
entirely different issue concerning the Chinese, since they were "the only
laborers from abroad that are *practically* available to us." Since white men "worth
anything as a laborer" would quickly become landowners, the "question of
immigration, therefore, turns in fact upon extending the area of land cultivated,
by increasing the number of *land-owners*—(chiefly small landed proprietors,)
and becomes finally a question of increasing the population, (and by so much as
the immigrant brings money) the capital of the country." Immigration was a
racial issue, a white issue. "Whether an increase of *population* (not laborers
working for wages,) would benefit our planting friends," the editors concluded,
"is now the question." In other words, as a New Orleans newspaper argued,
supporters of "immigrants" confuted those "who yet cling to the idea of wield-
ing the products of large bodies of lands, desire only laborers, and if not able to
get white men, are willing to take Chinese, Hindoos or any other sort of people,
out of whom labor can be bought or coaxed."[39]

Resentment against such "planting friends" formed a foundational aspect of
the immigration movement in rural Louisiana, where a couple of newspaper
editors led a spirited attack on their nominal audience, the sugar planters. In
resuming the publication of the *West Baton Rouge Sugar Planter* after the Civil
War in 1866, Henry J. Hyams assailed the hypocrisy of former slaveholders and
Confederate fire-eaters, many of whom "thought the best way to save the country was to save their niggers first, and then come back in the spring and take care
of the country." Although he advocated a general amnesty for former Confederates, he grew wary of the further consolidation of property and growing class
divisions in postbellum Louisiana. "Small farms," he counseled, "will equalize
the difference between labor and capital, and the quicker understood the better." Daniel Dennett of the *Planters' Banner* likewise railed against the social ills
of land monopoly. The upsurge of northern and western men purchasing vast
tracts of land in the South and West, he warned, "benefits a few" but "injures
the many." A large plantation was but "a little kingdom within itself" that dis-
allowed the "most prosperous, the most independent, the most public spirited,

sociable and happy communities" of "small farmers." He hoped that "no more small places will be absorbed by large ones." "Let a dozen capitalists swallow up St. Mary [Parish], and even the owners of these huge plantations would not live here," he charged. "We would rather live in the pin[e]y woods than in an Africanized parish."[40]

Having little confidence in "the naturally indolent negro" after emancipation, as Hyams put it, neither he nor Dennett voiced opposition to coolie labor in the immediate postwar years. After publicizing the "assiduity" of Chinese recruits from Cuba, Hyams concluded that the greatest "stumbling block" to the recovery of Louisiana sugar production was "the question of secured labor . . . [and] if coolies can be introduced and their labor proves satisfactory, or even reliable white laber [*sic*] be secured, we would have no fears for the result." Dennett was more smitten with coolies. He proclaimed that "African instincts and radical teaching" were "fast leading" local freedpeople "to ruin and extermination." Dennett saw two distinct—but not yet mutually exclusive—paths to Louisiana's economic salvation. "Small farms and white labor or large farms and coolie labor may save the land," he believed. Although Dennett never failed to distinguish the two modes of labor, he strongly endorsed efforts to bring greater numbers of whites and coolies to Louisiana. As late as the summer of 1867, he cast coolies as part of the state's solution, going so far as to proclaim them "the laborers for Louisiana."[41] Within two years though, he would demonize coolies as Louisiana's worst problem, a change of heart that coincided with Dennett's intensifying rage against Radical Reconstruction.

Dennett was a staunch Democrat who used his columns to intimidate "carpetbaggers," "scalawags," and "negroes" before elections. In 1868, he called on "every white man who has a gun, a pistol, or a six shooter, to put it in order, keep ammunition always ready to be used at a moment's warning." He cautioned against "rashness," but, alas, he could "not ask them to stand more than human nature could be expected to bear." His inflammatory writings contributed directly to the reign of terror surrounding the 1868 presidential elections— Dennett himself was an active member of the Knights of the White Camellia— and, as a result, landed him before a congressional committee in New Orleans the following summer. The surging demand for coolies that he witnessed during his visit in June 1869 led him to pen the first of a long series of editorials against Asian labor on behalf of the common white man. "I predict that Radical capital, ships, laws, railroads, preachers, politicians and newspapers will yet favor the flooding of this country with the yellow race of Asia," he declared. "It is a bigger thing than slavery ever could have been in this country, and I believe it will be an everlasting curse to the nation." His editorial was accompanied by a lengthy report on how coolie labor would "make the rich richer and the poor po[o]rer" and "crush our working classes into the dust" across the nation, as in California.[42]

With the consolidation of property killing old agrarian dreams in Louisiana, Dennett and his allies launched an ideological offensive against planters who would import coolies, resuscitate slavery, and thereby exacerbate class divisions among whites. The arrival of coolies, they imputed, would steer their beloved region back to antebellum relations (slavery) *and* forward to industrial capitalist relations (class conflict), a singularly pernicious combination that would eviscerate their newfound struggle for racial solidarity to overthrow multiracial democracy. Beyond his objection to "a still greater commingling of the blood," Hyams elaborated on the dystopia to come:

> We will have again a fat and pampered aristocracy, worse than it ever was, and far more haughty and overbearing. It will then be "how many Coolies does he work?" instead of "how many negroes does he own?" so commonly used *ante bellum*. With Coolies . . . a planter can make more than he did when owning negroes, with less risk and perhaps more satisfaction. To replenish our plantations with such labor will undoubtedly restore them to former prosperity, even if not excelling it; but it will be at the sacrifice of the poorer or middle classes, with their bone, muscle and intellect. No man with scanty means can cope with the wealth of the large property owner.

A small farmer who was a regular contributor to Dennett's newspaper similarly inveighed against the "landed aristocracy" that had stirred up the Civil War but refused to "fight the battles" and now were "determined to come as near slavery as possible again by the introduction of thousands of pumpkin colored helots, returning like the dog to his vomit, and the sow to her wallowing in the mire." The advent of "Coolie labor," he prophesied, would reduce whites to a small minority and lead "all the small farms" to be "gobbled up by the larger landed proprietors in less than a generation."[43]

Less restrained in tone and more brash in imprecating "capital," Dennett emerged as Louisiana's most vigorous opponent of coolies. Racially predisposed to the South's warmer climate, he argued, the Chinese would be welcomed by "men of wealth at the North, the manufacturers, the landholders and capitalists" to "cheapen labor everywhere" across the United States. "Who will be benefitted by plantations each worked by one or two hundred yellow heathen[s] from China?" he asked. "And if capital absorbs the small places, and works large plantations with these yellow Celestials, what will be the condition of society here thirty years hence?" All whites in the South, he believed, had an interest in thwarting this northern conspiracy, which would only enrich a "few absentees" and impoverish the region. Dennett also lashed out against antebellum planters who had "Africanized" St. Mary Parish, "absorbed the small farms," and "almost annihilated white society in neighborhoods eight or ten miles in extent." Such would be Louisiana's fate once again, if sugar planters employed coolies. "We want laborers in Louisiana, but we want no more African slaves, nor coolies, nor peons, nor serfs in any shape." Although his racial and economic arguments unmistakably reverberated with Helper's antebellum views, Dennett refused any association with the Old South's infamous traitor. "Give us a population that will give rise to no more 'Uncle Tom's Cabins,' and 'Helper's books,'" he demanded, "and no more civil wars, and on whose prejudices and ignorance the tricky politician and infamous carpet-bagger cannot play."[44]

Having rejected coolies, self-appointed defenders of white workers hailed immigrants from Europe or the North and West as the only viable option. Rather than depending on "hordes" of "barbarians" catering to planters' "consumptive idleness," according to Hyams, Louisiana would be able to construct a prosperous community of small independent producers. "As to our section of country we hope to see Germans and other European laborers come here and settle," Dennett agreed, "and make it a country that we can hand down to posterity with pleasure and pride." His obsession with white immigration evolved into a personal crusade for what he felt was the panacea to all of Louisiana's woes. There was no doubt in his mind that "white laborers" would "root out and crush out all of the colored races, negroes, Chinese, and Indians." Astute businessmen, too, would see that "if small farmers are encouraged, and prosper, our white voting population will be rapidly increased, the State will be saved from political pirates, our cities and villages will thrive, money will be more plentiful, and our schools and churches will prosper." General Robert E. Lee echoed these sentiments, believing that the South required not only "reliable laborers, but good citizens, whose interests and feelings would be in unison with our own." To him, that meant "the introduction of a respectable class of laborers from Europe" in "entire families" settled on "neighboring farms," not the "importation of the Chinese and Japanese" who might provide "temporary benefit" but an "eventual injury to the country and her institutions."[45]

Advocates of white immigration warned again and again that coolies would disrupt and undermine gender and sexual norms. Hyams pondered the fate of white manhood in a society reliant on the labor of another race. The "honest, manly labor" in farming would produce a "hardy class of yeomen" and cultivate "intelligence and usefulness" in the South, he claimed, instead of the "namby-pamby puling carricatures [*sic*] upon humanity, whose only claim to such would lie in their hounds and gun, their horses and dissipations, and 'my father's coolies!'" Dennett turned to local Caribbean sources to conjure up masculinized perils of another sort. An Iberia Parish "gentleman," a former resident of British Guiana, told him that "the coolies were the greatest thieves, cut[t]hroats and rascals . . . that nothing but brute force could control them, that no planter's wife or daughters were safe when beyond the protection of white men; and that they would kill a white man for pay, or kill each other with no more horror than they would feel in cutting off a chicken's head." A Cuban planter, Dennett reported later, confirmed that coolies were "timid and servile" when "overpowered," as in Cuba, but "brutal and defiant when they have the power in their own hands." A correspondent from Nevada, meanwhile, testified that the Chinese were "not so tractable as is desirable" but were, at the same time, physically wanting, their diet unfit for "a strong masculine laborer" desired by southern planters. The Chinese were "a weak effeminate race," he charged.[46]

As Louisiana planters ignored these admonitions and pursued Chinese labor anyway, Dennett in particular grew alarmed and impatient. He continued to publish reports on Chinese labor's detrimental effects in California, the high costs of transport to and employment in the South, the growing anti-coolie movement among white workers across the United States, and the dismal results of early experiments in Louisiana. When some planters asked him to desist, Dennett fulminated against those he now dubbed "Chinese labor planters." "If he has money to pay, $120. or more, for each Chinaman he needs, and is willing to risk the money, who interposes between him and pigtail labor?" he asked. Professing that most sugar planters actually opposed Chinese labor—along with "nine out of ten of the white people" and "all of the negroes"—Dennett challenged "some of this minority" who wished "to silence every editor in the State" on the topic to cancel their subscriptions instead. In contrast to his earlier editorials in favor of coolies and black migrant labor, he saw no room for compromise or coexistence between white families on small farms and Chinese or black wage laborers on large plantations. "So soon as the Chinese labor theory explodes—and that will not be long—the small farm system will come into use and the whole South receive the benefits therefrom," Dennett predicted. "None but a few antiquated specimens of the old time will cling to large plantations and their fortunes will vanish with their stupidity and pride."[47]

Such rancorous outbursts notwithstanding, there was a general consensus among white Louisianians that permanent plantation labor violated the very essence of whiteness. The *New Orleans Times*, whose views on race and labor evolved opposite Dennett's, gave up on white immigrants by 1869, categorizing them, unlike the Chinese, as unfit for "the drudgery and constant, but not severe, toil of the plantations." The emerging dualism between white immigrants and Asian coolies, however, did not necessarily mean forsaking one over the other. From the earliest promoters of coolie labor, many pointed to their perfect compatibility since, as J. W. Clapp had put it, the "swamps" required "dark-skinned laborers, Mongols or Africans, who luxuriate where the white man would perish." Welcoming "white families," "negroes from Virginia," and "Chinese heathens" at once, the *Louisiana Sugar-Bowl* addressed the underlying coherence of these seemingly contradictory migration campaigns. While preferring settlers of "our own race and blood" from Europe and the North, this newspaper denied "any antagonism" between "the large land-owners and small planters": "We hope that the former may be supplied with thousands of Chinamen and other good laborers . . . to cultivate and manufacture sugar on a large scale, as they have their fields, machinery and quarters arranged for that purpose, but we also hope that all large planters will . . . locate white tenants on the rear of their plantations, who will manage their own crops, raise stock and increase our population."[48]

Reconstructing a White Nation

The immigration movement should have united Republicans and Democrats of the old Jacksonian persuasion far more than large planters and small farmers in the age of emancipation. The Republican party shed its Whig roots and embraced mass immigration and homesteads during the Civil War, co-opting two issues previously identified with the Democratic party. Following the passage of the Homestead Act (1862), federal officials dispatched a special agent to Europe in the summer of 1863 to inform potential immigrants of opportunities west of the Mississippi River. Northern newspapers, among them former nativists, lent support to the cause, in part by reassuring readers that "yellow and brown races" like the "Chinese, Hindoos or Turks" would not come. Two years after prohibiting American participation in the coolie trade, moreover, the Republican-dominated Congress passed a logical extension, the Act to Encourage Immigration, which President Lincoln signed into law on July 4, 1864. It created the Bureau of Immigration in the State Department and the U.S. Immigrant Office in New York City to disseminate information in Europe and to disburse immigrants upon arrival in the United States. Although never funded sufficiently before the law's appeal only four years later, Republican conversion to promoting immigration nevertheless heralded its apotheosis in American culture.[49]

In the wake of the Civil War, state officials and private entrepreneurs in Louisiana, and the South in general, eagerly enlisted in the national project of European immigration. The Bureau of Immigration received favorable reports and inquiries from virtually every former Confederate state, including from Governor J. Madison Wells of Louisiana and J. D. B. De Bow. By the spring of 1866, various southern states had begun creating their own versions of the federal bureau to attract immigrants southward.[50] Democratic lawmakers in Louisiana conferred on the new state agency not only the same name but also an identical mission—to encourage "immigration to the State of Louisiana, by diffusing information abroad, and protecting and assisting such immigrants as may settle therein." Years before Dennett came to champion white immigration, federal and state officials, working in tandem, were on track to realize his future dream of white egalitarianism, a neo-Jacksonian dream shared by Andrew Johnson in the White House. The South, it appeared, would receive its share of European immigrants. "It has been the special aim of the Bureau of Immigration, of late, to lend its aid to all measures tending to the encouragement of immigration to the South; and it has never failed to recognize the importance of such measures," the federal agency affirmed. The bygone sectional conflict, it promised, would "have no effect on the unwavering solicitude of the Bureau for the welfare of the South as a part of this Union."[51]

Regional and partisan apprehensions and divisions, however, quickly drove apart these potential allies. Commissioner H. N. Congar, head of the federal Bureau of Immigration, expressed grave skepticism of southerners' designs. Besides various illegal schemes to import "East Indian or coolie laborers," he reported to Congress, "the agents employed to secure the labor of immigrants for the southern States grossly misrepresent the nature of the contracts to be entered into" and commit "great injustice" toward "the ignorant immigrant" whom his office tried to protect from "their grasp." Newspapers like the *New York Times* also withdrew their support of labor recruiters from the South, who, like the architects of the Black Codes, seemed oblivious to the realities of free labor. The experiences of German immigrants in Louisiana and elsewhere, it was reported in 1867, revealed that planters failed "to recognize how the war has changed the relations of employers and employed" or to "forget the old rule and its methods." German immigrants were forced to live in "abandoned negro quarters, wretchedly fed, and, though frequently dying of fever and other diseases . . . left unprovided with medical attendance." Meanwhile, the state project of immigration was a casualty of deteriorating relations between Governor Wells and Democratic legislators in Louisiana. Wells's appointee to the state's Bureau of Immigration resigned in the spring of 1867 after the legislature refused to fund his salary.[52] Political squabbles would grow worse with the advent of Radical Reconstruction.

The election and appointment of Republican officials isolated Louisiana's bureau from its surrounding immigration movement. James O. Noyes, who took over the agency in 1868, had an ambitious plan to fulfill its original mandate. In February 1869, he recommended that the state legislature reorganize the bureau into the Commission of Immigration and open a labor exchange modeled after the Castle Garden Commission and Labor Exchange in New York. The commission, composed of "citizens of the highest character and responsibility," would supervise the entire operation, its principal objects being "simply to bring the employer and the laborer" and "the seller and buyer" of lands together. Governor Henry C. Warmoth and fellow Republicans followed his advice and created the six-member Commission of Emigration, with Noyes serving as its president and general agent. Overlooking the Democratic origins of Noyes's agency and Louisiana's debt, conservative opponents dismissed state-sponsored immigration as another example of Republican patronage and lavish spending. The commission was nothing but a ruse by "our Legislature Solons" to provide "a stall for some hungry hack at the State crib," a columnist in Dennett's newspaper declared. The *New Orleans Daily Picayune* likewise suggested leaving immigration matters up to "planters and others" rather than to the commission. It was "unwise" to retain "the expensive paraphernalia and costly mechanism here," its "grammatical blunder" and all. Calls for its dissolution hounded the agency, which was renamed the Bureau of Immigration and divested of public funding in 1873.[53]

Although no one in Louisiana worshipped the gospel of white immigration and small farms more than Noyes, his differences with other local boosters of immigration were, on one level, considerable. Free labor, to him, was a universal right, not a monopoly of the white race. All Louisianians, he argued, would profit from the infusion of industry, labor, and capital generated by white immigrants, including "our colored people," the "involuntary immigrants" of yesteryear. Landownership, he insisted, bore "a mysterious something" that "raises the owners to intelligence, power, dignity, manhood" regardless of race. And he unabashedly hoped that "multitudes of those patient, industrious, rice-eating Orientals would flock to the delta of the Mississippi." Racial homogeneity was not Noyes's object, but he was no racial egalitarian. He believed that the "aggressive Anglo-Saxon population" always dominated wherever they settled. Noyes thus welcomed immigrants from southern Europe only if they discarded their cultural heritage to "become Americans." "We wish to become a homogeneous people, speaking the English language, which is fast becoming the language of the civilized world," he stated, "and adopting those free and liberal institutions which are the strength and pride and glory of the nation." In May 1869, Noyes expressed his preference for European immigration but willingness to try the Chinese before a regional commercial convention, a position that put him at odds with local immigration promoters. For his liberal views on coolies, *De Bow's Review* branded him a "stranger" to the South, "alone" in his views on race and labor.[54]

For all his celebration of multicultural Louisiana, Noyes, in concert with his critics, helped to preserve the small-producer ethic as an inherent white right in an era defined by mass industrialization, including in the sugar region. Southern Louisiana never witnessed the proliferation of independent producers during Reconstruction; rather, it experienced a complex proletarianization that tied nearly everyone to the fluctuations of global capitalism. But what historian W. E. B. Du Bois called the "American Assumption"—"that wealth is mainly the result of its owner's effort and that any average worker can by thrift become a capitalist"—survived and legitimized the emerging industrial order. The immigration movement in Louisiana, whether trumpeted by Republicans or Democrats, sustained the American Assumption by conveying its dual message of egalitarianism and white supremacy in ways that ultimately positioned capitalists as allies, models of aspiration, rather than as adversaries. However much they despised Republicans and "Chinese labor planters," Dennett and his fellow immigration boosters never relinquished their belief in the indissoluble partnership between capital and labor, a racial pact enshrined in the altar of white supremacy. The immigration movement became an instrument through which that mirage, paradoxically the defining feature of Republican ideology, persevered in the age of capital.[55]

Far from alienating elite planters, Louisiana's Bureau of Immigration eagerly courted their participation in the campaign for immigrants. Noyes's predecessor J. C. Kathman challenged planters to look after "not only your own interests, but those of the State at large, its development and riches" and, like landowners in other regions, to extend "liberal inducements and facilities towards incoming settlers." Since "large bodies of idle lands" meant only high taxation and impoverishment after emancipation, he informed potential immigrants, they were all "in the market, in lots and prices to suit purchasers." But an aspiring immigrant would have been hard pressed to find land in the sugar-producing region. Of the twenty-four proposals listed in Kathman's pamphlet for immigrants, none involved a planter wishing to divide up his sugar estate, even though plantation foreclosure and bankruptcy sales notices filled local newspapers. Characterized by expensive machinery, expansive cane fields, and, in many cases, debts to a wide web of creditors, sugar plantations were not amenable to easy subdivision. The failure to attract planters' attention did not deter Noyes from adopting the same strategy. Welcoming "all honest new comers with either labor or capital," especially those "able to buy land and willing to work it," he, too, implored planters to share "their wants in the way of labor" and to "communicate, for publication, any facts relative to the climate, health, resources and advantages of Louisiana that may aid in attracting capital and labor."[56]

Contrary to their obituaries for the plantation system and tirades against carpetbagger rule, Dennett and his associates were just as eager to eulogize elite planters, old and new. "The whole South invites capital and welcomes the immigrant," *De Bow's Review* announced in 1867, "but in perhaps no other section can he who has capital invest it more to his satisfaction than in our Louisiana sugar lands." With an infusion of capital, Louis Bouchereau noted in his annual volume on Louisiana sugar production, "we would rapidly recuperate, and progress with the giant strides peculiar to all American enterprise."[57] When prominent northerners purchased plantations in his neighborhood, the rich sugar lands of Bayou Teche, Dennett greeted these "Union men" with open arms. Like Kathman and Noyes, Dennett also concentrated on producing and circulating promotional literature to potential immigrants, first in his newspaper and then in his magnum opus, *Louisiana as It Is* (1876). Ostensibly designed to attract small farmers from Europe and the North, Dennett's publication, at times, seemed to be little more than an advertisement to the richest capitalists of the world. Sugar plantations that had once been worth upwards of $2.5 million, he noted, could be purchased for less than a tenth of their antebellum value, such as the Valcour Aime estate. Acquiring a sugar estate, potentially worth $200,000, for $10,000 might have enticed some northerners, but certainly not the yeoman farmers that Dennett exalted endlessly.[58]

As their dreams of small farms and white families competed unsuccessfully with planters' enthusiasm for recruits from China, California, and Virginia, immigration advocates lobbied for a white alternative. To dampen the rising fever for coolies, *De Bow's Review* suggested "another practical resource" far closer to home than Hong Kong. In cities with established transportation routes to New Orleans—Chicago, St. Louis, Cincinnati, and Louisville—were "thousands of laborers who are thrown out of outdoor employment in the winter." "Why not, then, appeal to this labor? Why not organize its transportation for the cotton and sugar harvests, from the first of September to the first of February?" the editors asked. Aside from meeting immediate labor needs, many might grow to like the South and "become small farmers and settle among us." Dennett, Bouchereau, and others chimed in with ringing endorsements of the idea, proclaiming that it would become "a regular business" within a few years, and many of "the multitudes of Western harvesters" would "eventually locate, purchase farms, and hel[p] improve the country to an extent beyond present comprehension." Northern labor agents marketing white laborers for monthly wages likewise tended to highlight their "settler" qualities, racial traits that cast them apart from coolies and blacks, even as they came to work on the very same plantations.[59] Unlike coolies, hailed and reviled as permanent plantation laborers who would remain aliens in race and culture, immigrants, if afforded kind treatment as temporary plantation laborers, represented the region's permanent population, the future of the white race.

Especially between 1869 and the Panic of 1873, a coterie of planters, including venture capitalists from the North, employed white immigrants through agents to supplement their grinding labor force. T. J. Bronson, who had made a fortune in the grain trade in Chicago, and his partner Charles H. Walker hired 125 white men during the 1869 grinding season and recruited another group of sixty-five German laborers from Chicago the following year. Contracting them for three months at thirty dollars per month plus board and transportation in November 1870, Bronson claimed that Chicago was teeming with immigrants "anxious" for similar offers. When George E. Payne, working as a manager on a nearby plantation before his recruiting trip to China, encountered a strike by female workers, he "im[m]ediately got Walker & Bronson to telegraph to Chicago for 30 Swedes." A steady flow of solicitations by northern and New Orleans labor agencies piqued and complemented planters' interest in recent European immigrants.[60] Edward Gay received numerous offers for white laborers and actively recruited them for the grinding season from Chicago, St. Paul, and St. Louis throughout the early 1870s. John Williams and other merchants, in the meantime, focused on establishing labor migrations directly from Europe to Louisiana. That these planters expressed simultaneous interest in recruiting Chinese and black migrant laborers, albeit usually on different terms, was no accident.[61] They had the luxury to experiment with various labor arrangements at a time when most of their neighbors struggled merely to stay in operation.

As much as Dennett welcomed any and all white immigrants to Louisiana, he constantly reminded planters to treat them as equals, as neighbors. "The true policy of large landholders is to divide and sell to small farmers," he maintained. In 1870, his enthusiasm for a plan to recruit Canadians from Quebec shifted to uneasiness once he learned they would be employed as wage laborers. "We hope they may succeed," he stated, "but we would have more confidence in their success, were they in families and working on the share system." Even those wishing laborers of all colors—"white, yellow, tan or black," as one writer listed them—emphasized that whites would arrive "with the *animo remanendi*" to reclaim Louisiana sooner or later as "a white man's country as well as a white man's government." To expedite the inevitable ending, Dennett became an early champion of central factories so as to decouple cane cultivation and sugar manufacture. "Small farms for those who can purchase them, and leasing plantations on shares to white families, the planter to be the manufacturer," he argued as early as 1870, "seems to be the most feasable [*sic*] mode of cultivation of the rich sugar, cotton and rice lands of this State." Neither Chinese nor black labor figured in the "revolution in the old system of sugar culture." "It costs less to bring white families to this State than the yellow race," he counseled. "The white man must rule this State, and cultivate these lands."[62]

The conversion to central sugar factories gradually came to form an ideological cornerstone of Louisiana's "redemption." After a brief infatuation with cheap, portable sugar mills in the early 1870s, sugar pundits advised planters to construct bigger mills to accommodate the evolving market for higher-grade sugar. "Let Sugar Factories be established in different neighborhoods, and let the producers of the cane *sell* it to the Factory," an expert recommended in Bouchereau's report. Sugar production seemed to be headed in that direction worldwide and, lest Louisiana follow suit, its sugar industry "will become one of the things that were!" Central factories surrounded by small farms, exhorted J. Y. Gilmore of the *Louisiana Sugar-Bowl*, was the ideal mode of production. He publicized the system's success in French colonies, inviting capitalists to construct similar factories in Louisiana, and applauded large landowners willing to rent their "idle lands" to white families. To Gilmore, elite planters like Kenner and Bronson—who adopted "the French system" and spent upwards of $100,000 in a new mill—anticipated a new golden era for Louisiana sugar. That those individuals purchasing the latest machinery were the very planters recruiting Chinese laborers failed to besmirch old agrarian dreams of whiteness. Rental arrangements worked most efficiently with whites, immigration advocates reiterated over and over, since only they possessed the "great energy" required. In such ways, the immigration movement not only made peace with the march of capital but also touted it as a means to facilitate immigration and to exorcise the "political incubus" haunting Louisiana.[63]

Dennett himself embodied the contradictions of the immigration movement, imagining himself a representative of the planter class as much as its archenemy. Despite his harangues against large plantations and their owners, he repeatedly sought their patronage. With William Burwell of *De Bow's Review* and prominent planters, he established the Louisiana Immigration and Homestead Company in February 1873. The corporation strove to introduce "a good class of immigrants" by purchasing and subdividing lands for sale and lease, particularly to "persons of limited means" under lenient terms for permanent settlement. It was the "DUTY of every citizen of Louisiana" to buy shares in the company, a cooperative venture "toward retrieving the State from her fallen condition of poverty, suffering and degradation." The encouragement of this "class," the founders claimed, would pave the way for the "sacred struggle for the redemption and disenthral[l]ment of a common heritage." Dennett, who was appointed the state agent, canvassed the countryside to attract sponsors, especially among landholders. "It looks to me that we *must* succeed, or Louisiana must sink," he pleaded. "Immigration may raise us above Illinois; a want of it put us on a level with Jamaica." Like so many other grand schemes in postwar Louisiana, success eluded the company. Scheduled to commence operations once $100,000 was raised, the Louisiana Immigration and Homestead Company could not have picked a worse time. A financial panic swept the nation in the fall of 1873.[64]

Immigration nevertheless remained atop Dennett's agenda. By December 1873, he had become engrossed in the movement to organize a statewide

Grange. "The money crisis, short crops, low prices, and an unusually bad season, have for a short period checked the interests of immigration," he admitted, ". . . but immigration is not dead." The Grange, he proposed, might serve as a vehicle for its revival. "With such a force we can make a strong and successful effort to redeem the State," he argued. "We can say to our brother patrons of the West and North, come down into the sunny climes and settle among us . . . let us henceforth live together as brothers, and we will do you good." Dennett found support in the cotton parishes but sugar planters, particularly the large landholders, spurned Dennett's invitations to join the Grange. His subsequent project, the Southern Land Company, likewise never coalesced into a widespread movement for radical land redistribution. Whatever his failings, Dennett's indefatigable work on behalf of "redemption" earned him a seat on the ignominious pantheon headed by Andrew Johnson and Hinton Helper. "It was the drear destiny of the Poor White South that, deserting its economic class and itself," W. E. B. Du Bois observed long ago, "it became the instrument by which democracy in the nation was done to death, race provincialism deified, and the world delivered to plutocracy."[65] Dennett and the campaign for immigration fulfilled that destiny perfectly.

CHAPTER SIX

Resisting Coolies

By 1874, bitter struggles over wage rates had become commonplace on Louisiana's plantations, but the devastated money and sugar markets invigorated planters and merchants to reduce production costs as never before. On December 23, 1873, St. Mary Parish planters resolved to contract no laborer for more than fifteen dollars per month in the upcoming season, setting a limit that neighbors in other parishes quickly matched or cut further. In a region where wage rates had climbed to upwards of twenty-five dollars per month for adult male laborers, this was shocking news. As planters complied with their new pacts in unprecedented fashion, partly at the insistence of jittery New Orleans factors, everyone anticipated trouble ahead. Pierre Landry, an African American Republican state legislator, tried to defuse the tense atmosphere at an emancipation celebration on January 1, 1874. He told his constituents that they alone had the right to accept or reject contract offers but advised them to take the planters' financial circumstances into account. "Make the best contracts you can," he said, "go cheerfully and earnestly to work, live frugally, educate your children, be honest and upright in all things, and you will soon see better times." The audience applauded his words, which, upon some reflection, must have rung hollow to many.[1] They were not about to surrender what they had fought for all those years.

Terrebonne Parish would be the site of the most intense struggle. In response to planters' collusion to restrict wages to thirteen dollars per month, two hundred plantation laborers convened at the Zion Church near the town of Houma on January 5, 1874, to organize an association of their own. Given the desperate financial climate, they proposed to form "sub-associations" to rent and work lands independently, pledging to waive their privileged claims over the resulting crop to those who would lease lands and furnish supplies. Amid mass bankruptcies and wage reductions, they figured that rental agreements on crop shares promised greater security. In addition, those contracting for wages vowed to accept no offer below twenty dollars per month, to be paid fully in cash every month. After another meeting three days later to ratify the resolutions, according to the *New Orleans Daily Picayune*, a "mob" fired up by "incendiary speeches . . . paraded through Houma, threatening the citizens, but doing no harm." Over the next several days, it was reported, groups of armed men on horseback "roamed over the parish and forced hands who had begun work on several plantations to quit the fields, th[r]eatening all who showed a disposition to resist with condign and summary punishment." On January 12, Terrebonne's prominent sugar planters—including Henry C. Minor, William A. and William J. Shaffer, and Nolan S. Williams—urged Governor William P. Kellogg, a Republican, to deploy troops immediately, to quell the "terror and alarm" overwhelming the parish.[2]

Kellogg decided to dispatch two officers from the Republican-controlled New Orleans Metropolitan Police to investigate matters instead, a measure that won him no friends on either side of the impasse. The conservative *New Orleans Daily Picayune* accused Kellogg of engaging in partisan politics when "the negro strikers . . . had broken out into open riot and were murdering white people, burning houses, plantation mills and committing the wildest outrages." Striking workers had not committed any of these acts, but their standoff with obstinate planters was heading toward a violent climax on January 14. For two days in a row, Henry C. Minor—reinforced by the local "colored" sheriff, his "posse of white and colored men," and Kellogg's officers—confronted an armed group trying to compel his laborers to join the strike. When ordered to disperse, a

Houma correspondent related, the "negroes insulted the officers, and told them to bring on their troops, for they were armed and were ready to fight them." The strikers reportedly then shot and injured a black worker and a passenger aboard a passing train. "Matters have not been in the least exaggerated," Kellogg's officers telegraphed. "Moral suasion no avail. Send about twenty cavalry to report at Houma." Kellogg sent the troops. After the arrests of the "ringleaders" and speeches by Minor and local black politicians at a mass meeting, laborers finally conceded to the wage reduction. With the Republican leader of Louisiana siding with men of property, the "war" in Terrebonne was over.[3]

The triumph in Terrebonne could not alleviate Donelson Caffery's anxieties. "After seeing the destruction I witness on every hand, and the general poverty and despair of the country," the St. Mary Parish lawyer and sugar planter wrote in June 1874, "I am more bent than ever, on going to Texas." Caffery, as depressed as he was, stayed in Louisiana and soon placed all his hopes in the White League, a new organization that spread like wildfire to all parts of Louisiana in 1874. This type of "political agitation" was necessary "as long as the white people in this State are governed by negroes, & scallawags," he believed, but the White League bore more than a "political character." It originated from a higher objective—"simply for the protection of the white race"— and toward this "redemption," Caffery and throngs of white Louisianians joined together behind the ballot, rifle, and any other "political" weapon they could lay their hands on. The road to "redemption" took an especially bloody turn in 1874, with the White League declaring a political war "not between Republicans and Democrats or Liberals, but between the whites and blacks." The end of Republican rule in April 1877, however, failed to settle Louisiana's troubles in Caffery's mind. "It is not a desirable country to live in, so far as population is concerned," he still complained. "The *very* rich planters are too selfish; the well to do planters are generally too close & ignorant to make a pleasant community."[4]

As spectacular battles over Reconstruction captured the headlines, coolies seemingly disappeared from the social landscape altogether. But Chinese laborers remained in Louisiana, affected as much as fellow plantation workers by planters' unilateral wage cuts of 1874. They engaged in a strike of their own, with their feet. "The pig-tail Celestials are again flocking to town and their old haunts on Lafourche street," the *Donaldsonville Chief* reported during the Terrebonne crisis, "which have for many months been deserted, are filled with the busy hum of Chinese life." Rather than submit to the new order, they retreated to Donaldsonville for a couple months before returning to nearby sugar plantations. These movements, so at odds with the long-term contracts that had brought them to Louisiana, became commonplace. "The pig-tail celestials seem to be of a wandering disposition and unable to stay for any length of time in the same place," the *Chief* surmised.[5] While their itinerant ways rendered Chinese laborers increasingly invisible, particularly in relation to the media frenzy of just a few years earlier, they reflected and shaped the social relations of sugar production after emancipation. Their relative invisibility was a testament to the social integration of these so-called coolies into Louisiana's multilayered, multifaceted class struggles. Their unrelenting struggles, however, did little to erase the broader racial formation of Asian workers as coolies in American culture, an image that fueled their exclusion and, in the process, reconstructed the United States along the color line.

The General Strike

Although the 1870 federal census enumerated only seventy-one Chinese in Louisiana, other contemporary estimates ranged up to two thousand or more.[6] They were becoming familiar sights on sugar plantations up and down the Mississippi River and its bayous. In a tour through Plaquemines Parish in 1869, Daniel Dennett came across not only white men working for wages but also Chinese laborers producing "good satisfaction." "The laborers of this parish, like the mass of the population," he observed, "represent a great variety of races." The reality of Louisiana's diversity, against which Dennett would soon wage war, simply could not be overlooked. Over the course of a single week in 1870, Rev. Edward Fontaine, a missionary traveling through southern Louisiana, presided over a congregation of whites and "quadroon creoles" (seated in the rear) and another of "a half dozen nationalities," including Swedish, Dalmatian, French creole, Danish creole, Irish, and "creoles of various castes." On a previous Sunday, he had preached at Dr. Joseph B. Wilkinson's sugar plantation, holding a morning service for the planter's family, "his white employees, & many of the colored people and Chinese working on his place" and an afternoon service exclusively for "the colored people and Chinese." "The Doctor hired the past year twenty[-]five of these Mongols, and they so far have worked well with more than a hundred negroes," Fontaine noted, "having had no difficulty with them or any one else; and they have not required any punishment, or reproof, in the performance of their tasks." He saw "many more of them" on nearby plantations and hoped "to be the instrument in the Redeemer's hands of bringing some of those pagans to the knowledge of his Truth."[7]

As with the earlier wave from Cuba, Chinese laborers landing in Louisiana after 1869 gained an instant reputation as industrious and faithful workers. A month after his son and Tye Kim Orr returned with 220 recruits from Hong Kong and Martinique in 1870, John Williams expressed his "entire satisfaction" with their performance. "As to the Chinamen, they work slow but sure and nice," his manager concurred. "They are very apt to learn anything. They have planted 300 arpents of cane for me as well as I ever had it planted with slaves . . . The yellow boys do it first-rate so far, so I think that I shall be able to make a crop with them." Thomas J. Shaffer, who employed twenty-five of Williams's recruits, likewise extolled their aptitude for plantation work. During the grinding season, they cut cane "better than any negro" and loaded it onto carts efficiently "from the fact that Chinese are peculiarly strong in the arms and shoulders." When all but three of his black workers deserted him at the end of the season, he relied almost solely on his "Chinamen" to plant the cane. Unlike black migrant workers, whom he hired later in the spring, the Chinese gave him "comparatively no trouble" and were "quiet and perfectly satisfied, and always in a good humor." Several "good negro men" were "quite friendly with them," Shaffer added, "and often say they would prefer to live and work with Chinese than with the common negroes generally found on plantations."[8]

The honeymoon between Chinese recruits and their employers did not last long on most plantations. It was especially short-lived between Amos B. Merrill and 140 laborers from California in July 1870. The Chinese were shrewd and disciplined, a reporter visiting Merrill's Millaudon plantation claimed, listening to every order given by "their head man." "This chief . . . appears to be a man of superior cast[e] or rank," he believed, "and as such commands the respect of his more plebian followers." The reporter was half right: the laborers were shrewd. They had signed three-year contracts that would pay them fourteen dollars in gold per month (defined as twenty-six days worked) plus daily rations of fresh meat, rice, and tea. Not long after their arrival, they noticed that their "colored" counterparts quit work at noon on Saturdays, while they toiled all day. They demanded the same. Merrill refused to credit them more days than they actually worked, agreeing only to record six days every other week if they chose to work five and a half days every week. The Chinese laborers then requested that the planter pay for vegetables that their foreman had purchased on their behalf. Merrill paid the bill but reminded them to expect no more than what they had contracted for. Unfazed, his new employees subsequently asked for ten acres of plantation land to grow and sell their own vegetables. These were signs of things to come.[9]

The laborers, in fact, showed no hint of deference to their primary "head man," Cum Wing, the San Francisco contractor who had arranged their delivery to Louisiana. When Cum Wing visited Millaudon on a Sunday evening to have dinner with Merrill, he was approached by several workers who insisted on a meeting right away. He declined. The laborers reportedly then made "a sudden rush, seized Cum Wing, threw him first on his back, and then in among a crowd of their comrades." Accusing the merchant of fraud, they forcibly carried him to their quarters and demanded a better arrangement. The "crowd of infuriated Chinese laborers" harbored no ill will against the "white folks" or "colored persons" whatsoever, according to newspaper accounts, but Merrill

"'Cheap Labor' in Louisiana—Chinamen at Work on the Mill[a]udon Sugar Plantation," *Every Saturday*, July 29, 1871. Though contracted in the summer of 1870 to work for three years, 115 of the 140 Chinese recruits deserted Millaudon plantation within fourteen months.

Courtesy of the Historic New Orleans Collection, accession no. 1953.73.

found the disturbance grave enough to summon the police. Twenty-five members of the Metropolitan Police rescued Cum Wing and arrested at least fourteen "ringleaders" who "had been most prominent in ferocious gesticulating and posturing" during the abduction. The police locked them up in the old servant's house, from which their "comrades" attempted to liberate them in the middle of the night. The "scuffle" with the police resulted in "no blood shed." Promising no further trouble, the prisoners won release the following morning. Merrill offered to draft a new contract, but all of the laborers decided to return to work under the original agreement, purportedly expressing the "greatest contrition."[10]

Just as one crisis ended on Millaudon, another arose. During the 1870 grinding season, Merrill later recalled, the "irascible old" overseer became embroiled in a "dispute with the Mongolians, which they attempted to decide by belaboring him with sugar-cane." The enraged overseer fired his pistol "indiscriminately" and shot a Chinese laborer in the arm. The "whole heathen gang" then rushed after him "in such a way that he had to seek safety in flight." Law enforcement officers arrived on the scene again to end the skirmish, but the overseer never returned to his post on Millaudon. In Dennett's imagination, this incident took on magnified significance and became a scene right out of revolutionary Saint Domingue. "With heads shaved, queues three or four feet in length, hanging down their backs, their dark yellow countenances distorted, their black eyes flashing fire and fury, brandishing their cane knives and other weapons, an angry jowering running through all their ranks," he wrote, "one would suppose that hell had been attacked with black vomit, and had used the Millaudon plantation for a slop tub." To save the life of the overseer, appropriately named Mr. White, Merrill and the white minority on the plantation pretended to investigate the matter, thereby slowing down the "yellow fiends" and allowing him to escape. The "infuriated celestials" calmed down only when the planter falsely informed them of the overseer's arrest.[11]

As Merrill's reliance on the Metropolitan Police implied, Republican officials' reactions to Chinese labor prefigured Kellogg's stance in the Terrebonne crisis of 1874 and corresponded closely to their contradictory views of black labor. Kellogg, as the New Orleans collector of customs in 1867, had played an active role in the federal campaign against the extension of the coolie trade from Cuba to Louisiana. Republicans meant to prove the sanctity and universality of free labor, which the *New Orleans Republican* saw as the true lesson of the rebellion against Cum Wing. Contrary to the "docile" image of "coolie labor," which had posited the foremost Chinese "passion" as "hard work (the harder the better) and the lowest of wages," the official state newspaper editorialized, "Cum-Wing's fellows show[ed] all the usual characteristics of human beings, even to the extent of assailing their oppressors and fighting for their rights, or for those things they want, which amounts to about the same thing." Yet, from the days of Union officers and Freedmen's Bureau agents, most Republicans were loathe to countenance labor strikes of any sort. When a gang of Chinese workers fled a St. Bernard Parish plantation in April 1871 to file a complaint with Gen. A. S. Badger, head of the Metropolitan Police, they were greeted with nothing but scorn. Badger dismissed their charge against their employer of contract violations and reportedly told them that "this was no place for vagrants, and that unless they went to work somewhere they would be arrested."[12]

Such threats failed to bring collective resistance to a halt in Louisiana. Not long after Badger issued his warning, a fatal confrontation erupted in Terrebonne Parish, where so many fierce battles between planters and laborers took place. By the summer of 1871, William L. Shaffer, brother of Thomas and son of prominent sugar planter William A. Shaffer, employed twenty-three Chinese and seven black workers on his Cedar Grove plantation. After witnessing Shaffer whip a neighbor's "Chinese servant boy" in early September, all of his Chinese laborers protested by refusing to work. Fearing that their compatriot had been killed, they demanded to see him in person. The Chinese were "arming" themselves, the earliest newspaper report stated, and ignoring entreaties by Shaffer and "about a dozen of his friends" to return to work. Lavager Babin, the overseer's brother, "kindly took one of them by the arm, and was trying to persuade him to go to work, when he turned and struck the young gentleman." Babin struck back, at which point "a number of Chinamen jumped at and struck him with sticks, and one fired a pistol." Shaffer's posse was then "forced" to retaliate with gunfire, killing one "Chinaman" and wounding two others. The official inquest by the coroner's jury then concluded instantly, and farcically, that "the deceased Chinaman died from a gunshot or pistol, shot by some one unknown, and that said unknown was acting in self-defence [*sic*]."[13]

That might have been the final word on the death, but the Chinese were determined to have their say. Tsang Afat, the thirty-seven-year old interpreter and foreman on John Williams's plantation in adjoining Lafourche Parish, insisted that the local newspaper also print their side of the story. Tsang had accompanied an American merchant and his family to the United States as a servant in the 1850s, when he learned English and converted to Christianity. He returned to China, married, and then moved back to the United States aboard the ship chartered by Frank Williams and Tye Kim Orr in 1870. Because of his fluency in English, he in effect became the spokesperson for all of Williams's recruits, some of whom ended up on Cedar Grove. The "whites" were responsible for the entire mess, Tsang explained. Babin had actually begun "dragging the Chinaman out of his cabin, who, being bareheaded, wished his hat, but as he was unable to speak English, had his hand raised, to show what he wanted." Babin mistook the innocent gesture as a physical threat and "struck the Chinaman, which so angered him that he returned the blow with a stick he picked up near by." The other Chinese "rushed in to prevent further difficulty," but "the whites, mistaking their motive, opened fire upon them, wounding three, one of whom afterwards died." The Chinese, all unarmed, admitted to being "much excited" and beating Babin with sticks but emphatically denied ever owning or firing a pistol.[14]

In legal proceedings that would have been unimaginable before Radical Reconstruction, Cedar Grove's Chinese workers were able to testify against white men before Terrebonne Parish judge Paul Guidry.[15] Despite rebuttals by "respectable white men" and "reliable colored men," Guidry ruled that Shaffer, Babin, and a third defendant would have to stand trial at the next session of the district court and that they would be detained at a New Orleans prison until then. Just as the defendants were about to be removed, another judge more sympathetic to their interests had them released under a writ of habeas corpus and bail. But Shaffer could not escape his labor difficulties. All of his Chinese workers, bound to three-year contracts, deserted his plantation, representing an immediate loss of $6,000 in recruitment costs on top of impending losses from the imperiled crop. "They have put themselves under the protection of Judge Guidry," it was reported, "and bid defiance to the men that paid their money to bring them to Louisiana." William A. Shaffer, who had recently invested $4,000 to ship sixty other Chinese laborers to Louisiana, complained that if his son's laborers "could not be compelled to return to Cedar Grove and work out their time," then "he never would bring one of them on his place, as it would be money thrown away." A local correspondent felt that "there was never a greater outrage perpetrated on the rights of citizens by local authorities than this same affair."[16]

No one should have been surprised by the resolve displayed by Shaffer's workers, since John Williams's recruits had already established a pattern of quitting work whenever they felt their rights violated. A couple months earlier on Ardoyne plantation in Terrebonne Parish, owned by Williams's brother Nolan, an overseer had tried to assign specific daily tasks to the forty-six Chinese laborers under his charge. They "demurred, and finally quit work altogether" and "remained idle for two or three days," a local newspaper reported. Nolan Williams, who had been away during the dispute, took forceful action upon his return. He rounded up "a party of friends" and "went out among them, prepared for any emergency, and compelled all the grumblers, over forty in number to go to work again—fortunately without violence—and ever since they have worked better than before, performing their tasks regularly." A similar conflict had been brewing on Cedar Grove around the same time but was somehow "easily arranged." Individual Chinese laborers, however, began running away, the first trickles of the deluge to come. At least two laborers from Ardoyne, one from Cedar Grove, and six from John Williams's plantation had run away during the summer of 1871, all unsuccessfully pursued by their employers. The "old and experienced overseer" on Ardoyne, who also supervised twenty-five black workers, retained his hope in the Chinese but learned that they had "to be watched, like all other laborers."[17]

Indeed, the recruitment of Chinese workers only produced new sets of struggles that resolved none of the old, as Edward J. Gay's experiences illustrated. By October 1870, Gay had assembled a broad assortment of workers on his residence plantation, St. Louis, including 101 African Americans, 26 Chinese men from San Francisco, and 40 European immigrants from Chicago. He not only employed diverse peoples but also entered into multiple labor arrangements that reflected his wishes as much as his laborers'. The white recruits had agreed to work for twenty dollars per month and, if they stayed for four months, their transportation costs. Gay hired them primarily as temporary laborers to get through the grinding and planting seasons, the same role that freedwomen, in general, had come to occupy on Louisiana's plantations. Critically weighing the socioeconomic rewards of productive and reproductive labor, women increasingly refused to sign yearlong contracts and engaged in plantation work selectively during times of peak demand. As of October 1870, only five women and girls worked on annual contracts on St. Louis, earning monthly wages of eight dollars (equivalent to 31 cents per day for a 26-day month) or less. All of the other fifteen women, in contrast, worked on short-term bases, at much higher rates ranging from sixty to ninety cents per day. Last but not least, black men contracted for the year at $19.50 per month and Chinese men recruited for three years at sixteen dollars per month represented the most constant, permanent corps on Gay's large payroll.[18]

The arrival of white and Chinese workers seemed to afford Gay greater flexibility and stability to meet his immediate and long-term needs and to reduce his dependence on local workers. He would be terribly disappointed. Although he had imagined the Chicago contingent as transient plantation workers from the outset, Gay soon discovered how ephemeral they would be. Most left his plantation within two weeks. Only twelve worked enough to warrant any monthly payment, and one of them stayed for only a single month before abandoning St. Louis. Gay's daughter probably welcomed their departure, having grown tired of "how busy these old scandinavian [*sic*] and Swedes keep us all." Only eleven of the European recruits, in the end, worked four months through February 1871.[19] Particularly in light of mass white flight, Gay held higher hopes for Chinese laborers, whose recruiting fees alone had cost him thousands of dollars. But their early performance failed to live up to their reputation as models of unparalleled industry. Only one of the twenty-six workers, Yook Chow, worked close to the twenty-six days expected every month, registering twenty-five days and four night watches in November and twenty-six days and four and a half watches in December. All others worked—or were recorded as having worked—far less, a "sickly delivered" among them evidently too sick to work at all for months.[20] This was not the kind of production Gay had envisioned.

If Gay had a right to be upset, his Chinese employees had many reasons to feel betrayed, even irate. When they had signed up to work in Louisiana, they expected to make sixteen dollars in gold every month, perhaps with the exception of the first month. Gay had advanced them between sixteen and twenty-four dollars in San Francisco, to be deducted from their first months' wages. Probably to their dismay, Gay would pay none of them again until January 8, 1871, more than two months after their long journey southward. As they waited in line for their wages, finally, each worker must have walked away shocked. Credited with working fewer than twenty-six days per month and accumulating additional debts for clothing, blankets, shoes, whiskey, and other goods, the vast majority received less than eight dollars. Only three workers earned more than ten dollars, with Chow collecting the greatest amount ($20.77). Even Yu Kid, the foreman who had been advanced fifty dollars in California and earned fifty dollars per month, had a positive balance of only $31.80. Four individuals received nothing, learning rather that they owed their employer money.[21] All of them undoubtedly had become aware of how much more their fellow workers were earning on St. Louis, making their wages appear all the more paltry. This was not the life they had envisioned.

To Gay, the Chinese were failing on multiple levels. They were unproductive and their presence had no disciplinary effect on local workers. The conclusion of the old season and the dawning of another in January 1871 felt no different from past years' struggles. Gay administered the final settlement of wages with black workers immediately after the grinding season to avert trouble, knowing that, as his wife put it, "we cannot tell what changes there will be among them but of course there will be some, and planters all dread the worry & trouble of beginning a New Year." A number of black men began leaving St. Louis plantation within days of final settlement, determined to find a better situation elsewhere. Once L. L. Butler, Gay's son-in-law, heard that several others were thinking of joining them, he felt compelled to extend a raise to twenty dollars per month for "first class" men. Chinese workers provided no relief during the crisis, working only a bit more than they had over the previous two months. Between January 9 and February 1, 1871, when they received their second payment, only Yook Chow logged more than twenty days. Although all but two workers worked their way out of debt, only five received wages more than ten dollars, Chow topping the list with sixteen dollars. Regardless, the Gay family felt fortunate, since "most of the negroes" decided to remain "at home" and, along with Chinese and Dutch workers, made a decent start on the new season.[22]

Probably rankled by their concession to black workers' demands, yet again, Gay and Butler decided to keep closer tabs on the Chinese. Beginning in February 1871, Butler paid them not monthly, as stipulated in the contract, but every twenty-six days worked. Yook Chow finished his twenty-six days on February 28, at least a week ahead of anyone else, and then received an individual raise to seventeen dollars. Conversely, four of his co-workers, censured as "Feeble & Lazy" and "Lazy, with bad influence," saw their wages cut unilaterally to ten dollars per month. Gay and Butler clearly meant to punish Chee Sun, Chan Sing, Lai Gun, and He Choi, since they had been working relatively fast, completing their twenty-six-day cycles by mid-March. Gai Yuk ("crazy, works well") and Gou Ching ("Lazy & worthless"), for instance, finished their "month" a month later, but retained the original wage rate. Nearly everyone, at the same time, was fined for "lost time," again a policy not enumerated in the contract. Workers were to forego wages for days lost to sickness or injury, according to the contract, but there was no provision on fines. Nineteen of twenty-five workers sustained fines before their third payment, generally at a rate of fifty cents per day. These fines, from the workers' standpoint, were not only illegal but capricious and malicious. Some workers endured worse penalties, as high as $1.25

for half a day, while others encountered fines for working at the same pace as fellow workers without deductions.[23]

Just as these workers mulled over the consequences of Gay's flagrant contract violations, he added insult to injury. He hired a gang of seven other Chinese laborers at a higher rate of eighteen dollars per month in early March 1871. Excepting Yook Chow, who received another raise to twenty dollars per month, the rate granted black men, the original California recruits must have felt humiliated and incensed. They started to run away from St. Louis and Iberville Parish. In mid-March, William T. Gay in neighboring West Baton Rouge Parish instructed his brother to "Come up & strai[gh]ten out these Celestials." Fearing that the St. Louis fugitives might hire themselves out to another employer, he promised not to "permit your Chinamen to stop here, but will try & induce them to return." In his judgment, it would have been "a good idea to have the whole lot arrested & put in prison awhile on the ground of obtaining money under false pretences [*sic*]." William conferred with the runaways, who ostensibly agreed to head back. He, however, saw three of his brother's "Chinamen" still "loafing about" near the ferry landing the next day. He vowed to "try & get even with them somehow" but advised "not to reduce their wages as they all seem so bitterly opposed to a change of contract price." William hoped "these scoundrels will get satisfied & quit fooling about & go to work in earnest."[24]

The Gay brothers drew the same wrong lesson from these early instances of unrest, concluding that the Chinese would respond to additional discipline and punishment. With an equal number of Chinese at work on his own plantation, William planned "not to pay again until each man works 26 days & pays in addition for his board. If they stop work in a body pay no more & remove all eatables." Edward Gay, for his part, got even with Gai Yuk and Gou Ching, the slowest of the Chinese laborers, when they finally completed their first twenty-six-day cycle in mid-April. He withheld nine dollars for board, driving their incomes for nearly three months of work down to seven dollars each. The original contract had stated explicitly that the Gays would provide "sufficient provision, consisting of rice, pork, fish or beef, vegetables and tea, water, fuel, good quarters and weather-proof sleeping places, free of charge." Neither laborer appeared on the plantation payroll again. William's confidence in his Chinese labor force, in the meantime, declined precipitously. When his plantation manager experienced trouble with them during William's absence, he resolved to unload them to "some party willing to pay something for them," including his brother at a discounted rate. Within a couple weeks, William expressed his desire to sell his plantation altogether, a decision surely accelerated by his dying faith in coolies.[25]

Taking on more Chinese labor, even at bargain prices, was not a priority on Edward Gay's agenda. He had enough trouble with those he already employed. Rather than tolerating his whims, they soon left him en masse, sixteen of them together with Yu Kid, the foreman. On April 26, 1871, Gay filed civil suits against the foreman and nine individual laborers for transportation and recruitment fees ($65 each), provisions ($60 each), and varying amounts in damages and wages. He claimed to have "fully and liberally carried out" all of his contractual obligations, whereas the workers constantly broke theirs "without any just cause of complaint" against him. Yu Kid bore the brunt of Gay's wrath, having been paid fifty dollars per month but "proved himself utterly inefficient and incompetent as a foreman and when required to work and fulfil[l] his contract . . . refused so to do or to work, and . . . used his influence on other parties of his own race, and prevented the working and complying with said contract." The foreman, Gay argued, owed him $489.20, including $200 in punitive damages. Among the absconding workers, Gay demanded the most from Yook Chow ($257.35), the recipient of two recent raises, ironically seeking revenge for his relative productivity and higher wage payments. All in all, Gay claimed at least $200 from each party, unless they returned to work within three days of court notification.[26]

Gay's legal action accomplished nothing. Only six of the original twenty-six laborers remained on the St. Louis payroll after April, all of whom had some of their wages deducted for "lost time." Among the gang of seven laborers hired in March, meanwhile, only four worked a second "month" (twenty-six workdays), three of whom stayed on the plantation until June. Gay and Butler, in response, continued to intimidate the Chinese through competition and punishment. Sometime in late May or early June, they hired another group of Chinese laborers, three of them at a higher monthly rate of eighteen dollars. Still dissatisfied with the level of production, the planters exacted infractions for "lost time" against all but a lone individual worker in May and June. Meting out fines, in turn, seemed only to hasten the workers' fleeing ways. Gay and Butler finally gave up. On June 21, 1871, Butler settled with the six Chinese workers left on St. Louis, none of them the original recruits from California, and later remarked unceremoniously that "the Chinese all left this morning early." William Gay suffered the same fate. He was still away from his plantation in May when he learned through newspaper reports that all of his Chinese laborers had "gone to New Orleans."[27] Only eight months after their much anticipated arrival, the

Chinese vanished from the Gay brothers' plantations. The entire affair had been an expensive failure.

Amos Merrill could empathize with the Gays. Reflecting on his experiences a year after Chinese laborers had begun work on his plantation, he stated that "they were elegant for every work except ploughing." "They are too light for that," he said. "But I soon found that while I had a set of men who would do first-rate if they would stay, I was losing them one by one." Not only was New Orleans "full of Chinese sharpers," but his laborers were "sharp" as well, "quick at figures" and disposed to cheat whenever possible. "I believe they are entirely destitute of moral principle," he charged. "They are all heathens, and won't become Christians." Regardless, Merrill liked them as workers. He and other grand planters who had spent thousands of dollars to recruit them, however, could not reap the profits of their investment. He explained:

> You see it costs considerable to get them here, and when they run away it's an expensive thing. If you can engage Chinamen without their costing you anything except their wages, then Chinese labor with good management is as good as any man need hope for in the way of labor. But I live too near the city. The sharpers come over and take them away, promising to pay them a sum of money for going to another plantation. They go, the sharper makes something, and I lose the Chinaman's passage money to my plantation. Those fellows make a business of doing that. Every planter wants them. One of the Chinese contractors will go to a planter and engage to furnish a specified number. Then he will entice them from somewhere else.

Like the Gays, Merrill gradually became resigned to his runaway problem. He preemptively arranged for the departure of seventy-seven Chinese laborers, more than half of his recruits, to work for other employers, most likely in exchange for cash payments. With forty others running off on their own, Merrill was able to hold on to the services of only twenty-five Chinese workers by September 1871, merely fourteen months into their three-year contracts.[28]

By the early 1870s, there was no question that Chinese workers had failed miserably as long-term contract laborers, but, as Merrill noted, there was still a strong demand for their labor. The Chinese have "been tried and . . . effectually found—at least, *questionable* as an article of utility," a columnist remarked in the *Louisiana Sugar-Bowl*. For Dennett, that the Chinese turned out no more docile than other laborers, as he and others imputed, only proved his larger point: their entry would resurrect slavery. With a single exception, he wrote, they were "fond of changing about, run away worse than negroes, and . . . leave as soon as anybody offers them higher wages." The exception was due to "a stout resolute overseer," who "whipped" and scared away the Chinese foreman and then "kicked and cuffed" the gang of workers "as though they were dogs," which, he claimed, was the only proven way to manage the Chinese. However much Dennett proselytized against coolies, planters continued to prize them. Merrill himself did not lose faith in "Chinese cheap labor," even as he lost all of his Chinese laborers, and hoped for the mass recruitment of true "agriculturists" from China's interior. So widespread was this sentiment that Boston-based reporters surveying southern Louisiana believed that "the prospect of John's crowding Sambo from the soil may be much nearer than we imagine . . . [as] in the Southern colonies of the Dutch, French, and Spanish."[29]

In the wake of costly shipments from China and California as well as political opposition in Washington, D.C., and Hong Kong, where would "John" come from? Partly from Alabama, of all places. A couple of months before supplying workers for the Gays, Cornelius Koopmanschap had dispatched 960 Chinese laborers from California to work on the Alabama and Chattanooga Railroad in the summer of 1870, the largest single shipment of Chinese migrants to land in the South. He had negotiated with John C. and Daniel N. Stanton of Boston, the company's organizers, who had been awarded $2 million in bonds by the Alabama state legislature. Although the Stantons themselves had little hard cash, generous state subsidies enabled their agreement with Koopmanschap, who charged them sixty dollars for every Chinese laborer delivered. As on Gay's plantation, the Chinese recruits reportedly did "not give satisfaction" early on. Their original superintendent grew so tired of them that he transferred them all to the opposite end of the railroad line. By January 1871, however, a British journalist heard that "their hands were hardening, and they were now on the whole giving satisfaction." The Chinese nonetheless continued to deviate from the racial images preceding them. Contrary to "the alleged saving and economical habits of the Chinese," they freely spent all their wages on "whisky, chickens, and whatever they could buy in the stores" and gambled away every Sunday with fellow black workers.[30]

By the summer of 1871, when the Gays, Merrill, and other Louisiana planters witnessed a mass exodus of their Chinese recruits, most of Alabama's Chinese railroad workers would find their way down to Louisiana. The first signs of trouble surfaced in the spring, when John Stanton took an "adventurer from Louisiana" to court for trying to "entice" away his laborers. Despite his lawsuit, the Chinese began running away in March. A railroad official remarked afterward that "until Chinamen become less clannish, less stubborn, *less Chinese* (until the leopard change[s] his spots) it is labor by no means desired." Approximately five hundred Chinese laborers abandoned the Alabama and Chattanooga Railroad at once, making their way to Mobile and thence to various locales in Louisiana. The Stantons then confronted a worse calamity as their speculative railroad scheme became mired in bankruptcy suits, seizures, and sales. Their multiracial labor force, reportedly unpaid for six months, watched the collapse in horror, many of them storming the railway to prevent its operation. The situation grew so urgent that Koopmanschap, who was unable to liquidate $160,000 in railroad bonds, paid a visit to the 330 Chinese encamped outside Tuscaloosa in July. He provided no relief. Surviving on blackberries, lizards, and crawfish, they did whatever they could to survive. Some found jobs as domestic servants in Tuscaloosa; others went to Mississippi as cigar peddlers. Greater numbers did what their compatriots had done in March and accompanied labor agents to Louisiana.[31] New Orleans and its surrounding sugar parishes were quickly becoming a hub for Chinese migrant laborers.

Sugar and Struggle

For years, New Orleans, Donaldsonville, Franklin, and other towns in Louisiana had attracted plantation workers seeking a better life. In 1867, a distressed Freedmen's Bureau agent had observed that Donaldsonville seemed to be "the centreing [*sic*] point of great numbers of Freedmen, coming from the Western and North-Western portions of the State, occupying every available cabin within reach and with nothing to do and nothing to eat." By the end of 1871, the congregation of Chinese migrants in New Orleans elicited comparable commentary. "A year ago we had no Chinese among us," noted the *New Orleans Bee*, "we now see them everywhere in the streets . . . and they have opened two large stores for the sale of Chinese articles." The influx did not disturb the *New Orleans Times*, which hoped it would de-urbanize the black population. "Many of these Chinamen have come from the plantations, preferring, as they do, the small trades and industries of the city to the dull, plodding work of the plantations," the newspaper stated. "This tendency will prevent the accumulation of large forces on the plantations for some time to come." But the exodus of "a great many Chinamen" from the plantations would "displace the immense surplus of lazy, loafing negroes, who have straggled from the country, where they could be usefully and profitably employed."[32]

With inducements, those in search of the urban life were ready to leave it behind to work elsewhere, even if not permanently. The urban migration of freedpeople had made New Orleans and outlying towns key centers of plantation labor recruitment and professional labor agencies in the postwar years, centers that planters tapped on a regular, ongoing basis.[33] Though on a smaller scale, the same pattern emerged among Chinese workers, a diverse group hailing from Cuba, China, Martinique, California, and many other places. Like the Alabama railroad workers, the 250 Chinese employed by the Houston and Texas Central Railroad in 1870 staged a protest against the company, filed suit for back wages, and then, under the charge of their interpreter, made their services available to "the community at large" in New Orleans. The lives of Chinese workers, however, were oriented more toward sugar plantations than the Crescent City throughout the 1870s. In 1875, Louisiana officials counted 619 residents born in China, only 53 of whom lived in New Orleans. Although these records surely undercounted a highly mobile segment of the population, they clearly reflected the rural bases of Chinese life in Louisiana. There were, according to the census, 178 Chinese in Ascension Parish, followed by 79 in Carroll, 76 in St. James, 62 in Jefferson, and 55 in St. John the Baptist. Except for Carroll, a leading cotton-producing parish, all others were in the heart of Louisiana's sugar bowl.[34]

The simultaneous movements of Chinese workers toward *and* away from Louisiana's sugar plantations pointed to a dramatic transformation in their status in the sugar belt. So many Chinese were entering southern Louisiana in 1871 that a local newspaper predicted that "the influx of Chinamen will naturally continue, without effort on the part of our planters." More than ever, labor agents or contractors approached planters first, some of them still asking for high commission fees for cheap, long-term labor. A. Kissam, the veteran labor agent who had earlier supplied laborers from California to Merrill's plantation, shifted his field of operation to Alabama in 1871 and transported former railroad workers to employers in Louisiana. For thirty dollars per man in commission fees, he promised to deliver Chinese workers contracted up to three years at sixteen dollars per month, an offer that planters like Edward Gay and John H. Randolph continued to entertain and embrace. As late as July 1871, according to William L. Shaffer, a "gentleman" in New Orleans was prepared "to furnish any required number of Chinamen at $8 per month, under an eight years' contract, from among those who have already served eight years on Cuban plantations, and are anxious to come to this country." But such hyperbolic statements, reminiscent of Koopmanschap's and Tye Kim Orr's oratories in Memphis just a couple years earlier, no longer held sway. Orr, for his part, retired from his days as a labor agent to resume his teaching career at a public school in Ascension Parish.[35]

In short order, larger gangs of low-wage workers dispersed into smaller gangs of high-wage workers across Louisiana, a phenomenon that led Merrill to admit that it was "better to work them in small gangs." S. L. James, who leased and ran the state penitentiary in Baton Rouge, was among the first employers to resort to financial inducements, luring Chinese laborers from Alabama and nearby sugar plantations, including Merrill's, at twenty-two dollars per month in March 1871. Anxious to maximize production, James soon employed more than 150 Chinese workers to operate the penitentiary's cotton mills at night to supplement the day shift supply of convict labor. High wages alone, however, proved inadequate to contain and retain them. In June 1871, the Chinese organized an uprising that had to be suppressed by the police. After trying them for a few more months, James reportedly discharged them all "in disgust." Legions of sugar planters welcomed these and other Chinese workers with open arms and pocketbooks. A lessee of an Assumption Parish plantation hired around fifteen Chinese laborers who approached him as a group in the summer of 1871, paying, a local newspaper reproved, "rather high for their services—$20 per month and rations." John S. Wallis of St. James Parish likewise hired forty Chinese workers at twenty-two dollars per month, not including rations, while paying his "colored men" eighteen dollars per month plus rations.[36] Cheap coolies these workers were no more.

John Burnside's series of contracts with Chinese workers revealed how much had changed over the course of a few critical months. His previous arrangements with San Francisco's J. M. Hixson and Company in August 1870 and with George E. Payne in February 1871 had involved mass shipments of workers on multiyear contracts, with wages fixed at fourteen and eight dollars per month, respectively. Given Payne's misadventure in Hong Kong, Burnside decided to pursue Chinese laborers far closer to home, initially at costs rivaling those recruited directly from California. For fifty-five dollars in commission fees per laborer, he reached a deal with Merrill and Kissam for the delivery of fifty-seven Chinese, under contract for three years at fifteen dollars per month. The signed accord, probably involving disgruntled workers on Millaudon, fell through at the last minute, when Burnside took offense at Merrill's insistence on an immediate cash payment. Accusing Merrill of doubting his word, he nixed the deal.[37] Burnside may have had other motivations. By the fall of 1871, there were hundreds, if not thousands, of Chinese workers available for hire, free of exorbitant commission fees, including those running away from Merrill. Most likely having heard of the great difficulties that fellow planters encountered in enforcing long-term contracts, Burnside adopted a different strategy. He quickly signed the first of many contracts with smaller groups of Chinese workers, paying almost nothing for their recruitment.

Burnside agreed to pay in other ways. In October 1871, twenty-nine Chinese laborers contracted to work on his Armant plantation for one year, renewable for two additional years at the planter's discretion, at twenty-two dollars per month, paid in full monthly. Burnside's willingness to assume wages that seemed at odds with old notions of coolie labor—eight dollars more per month than what Merrill was paying his contingent from California—stemmed from a variety of factors. He not only avoided nonrefundable commission fees but entered into a relatively long-term arrangement at a crucial stage in sugar production. As in previous years, workers in the sugar region were all too aware of the increased value of their labor on the eve of the grinding season. There was "a great number of extra Hands on the B[a]you," Thomas Garrett, another planter, complained, "but they will not contract to work, Holding off for higher prices." His subsequent recruiting trip to Mississippi yielded only ten workers, most other potential recruits refusing to leave with him before an upcoming November election. Seven of his new laborers ran away within a week of arrival. Burnside must have been grateful for his gang of Chinese workers, whose hiring freed him from engaging local black workers at $1.25 per day during the grinding season, as Garrett and many other planters were forced to do.[38]

Perhaps more significantly, Burnside sought accountability in a labor market overflowing with labor recruiters and contractors from New Orleans, Mississippi, California, and elsewhere. In January 1872, he advanced D. W. McDonald $1,400 to recruit black workers from Mississippi for the new season. Distressed by dismal results, McDonald gave back $800, with a pledge to pay off the balance as soon as possible. He was no "rascal or swindler," McDonald pleaded, but simply a man who "had too great confidence . . . to procure negroes." Not in a forgiving mood, Burnside threatened to take up the matter in public unless repaid immediately. With the collapse of the Mississippi venture, Burnside hired his second gang of Chinese laborers in February 1872, signing a one-year contract with A. Yune, an agent for twenty-six "Chinamen" in New Orleans. The new contract was nearly identical to the first, with explicit provisions on wage reductions for "any time lost," a garden to grow produce for the workers' "own consumption only," three days off for the Chinese New Year, and workers' restriction from leaving plantation grounds without permission from Burnside or his agents. There were significant differences though. Burnside agreed to pay the new gang twenty-six dollars per month, four dollars more than the first gang, and no longer held a right to renew the contract at his option. He, in turn, exacted concessions from A. Yune, the agent and foreman, who bore the cost of replacing fugitive laborers with "first class chinamen" and transporting all twenty-six workers to Burnside's plantation.[39]

Louisiana planters' increasing resort to small-time labor brokers like A. Yune—"sharpers," as Merrill had called them—signaled more than their labor needs and desires. Chinese workers, too, demanded accountability from their representatives, whom they themselves selected, rather than being appointed by commercial houses like Koopmanschap and Company. Both foremen with whom Burnside negotiated agreed to work for thirty-five dollars per month, certainly more than what the laborers made but far less than what their counterpart had earned on Gay's plantation ($50 per month). The divide between foremen and workers narrowed considerably; foremen, however, continued to occupy a position analogous to assistant overseers, who received comparable salaries. They recognized that workers under their charge, if maltreated, would leave them as fast as they had deserted planters. There was plenty of tension between local Chinese merchants and workers in Louisiana. Fou Loy and Company of New Orleans, a firm supplying rations to laborers and laborers to planters, sued two compatriots for larceny, while Ah Sin of Donaldsonville turned to the local constable in his struggle with workers. He prevented several indebted individuals from escaping aboard a Mississippi River steamer, letting the workers go only when a mutual friend intervened.[40] The persistence of worker turnovers thus made substitution clauses standard in Burnside's negotiations. When he contracted for another gang of twenty-five Chinese workers in New Orleans in the summer of 1872, the foreman guaranteed the replacement of not only absconding workers but his own position as well.[41]

The rapid rise in Chinese wages, at the same time, was symptomatic of deep rifts among Louisiana planters which made unified action on labor impossible. Ever since the Civil War, plantation workers left their employers before and after the expiration of their contracts in search of better opportunities. "The reason why many have left is that the rolling season is about to commence," a Freedmen's Bureau agent had complained in 1868, "and as they can get higher wages for the next 3 months, they have not hesitated to break their contracts." Few planters had qualms about hiring such workers. "There is no system or concert of action with the planters here," protested a Terrebonne planter. "Every one works to his own immediate interest, without regard to his neighbor's, or to the future welfare of the planting interest of the parish." The solution, he proposed, was hiring laborers strictly on an annual basis, lest "hundreds of negro families" continue to reject work "unless it is by the job, and that at prices greatly exceeding any paid before." Countless planter pacts on hiring practices, from understandings between neighbors to parishwide resolutions, rarely survived the demands of sugar production. When planters in Ascension Parish tried to impose a five-dollar pay cut after the 1871 season, workers hit the road at once in search of new homes, threatening to delay the planting of the new crop. Their employers, beginning with the "leading planters," gave in almost immediately.[42]

While planters were willing to suspend disbelief on a regular basis to endorse new collusive pacts, workers and their agents never forgot the tenuousness of planter solidarity. In 1869, Edward Gay and his neighbor A. Thompson agreed not to tamper with each other's workers. But Thompson decided to take on Hacket Doax in late spring, causing, according to Gay's overseer, "quite a stir among the ballance [as] a good many would go from here if he was to agree to take them." Doax, it turned out, had instigated everything. "Hacket went to town and hired a cart and moved from here in the night and stayed on the road till next morning near Thompson[']s house," the overseer explained, "then told Thompson that you had drove him off the place so Thompson says he thought there was nothing [w]rong to hire him as he was moveing [sic]." If a thinly veiled ruse could dissolve neighborly alliances and absolve planters' conscience, smooth-talking Chinese labor agents elicited excitement rather than guilt among planters. John Wallis was ecstatic with his gang of workers, especially his foreman, Yo Tin. They were, he claimed, "just as organized, systematic and intelligent as white men," always "energetic, never lazy, and . . . very careful workers." He felt that everything hinged on Yo Tin, who acted not only as an indispensable interpreter but a strict disciplinarian, docking pay from "lazy" workers and maintaining "a perfect system of accounts" over his gang.[43]

Beyond convenience, Louisiana planters' enduring infatuation with Chinese labor emanated from an unyielding fascination with race, in particular their assumption of an impending racial competition between blacks and Asians.

Coolie promoters, planters, and newspapers took great pleasure in seeing, as George Gift put it, "darkies" "quite crassfallen [*sic*]" and "monstrously exercised" over the entry of Chinese recruits. In July 1869, when the Chinese labor convention took place in Memphis, a local newspaper reported that the "negro population" was "very much exercised at the prospect of Chinese labor," some very "loud-mouthed in their threats of what they intend to do when the Chinese come to town." "For a year or so Sambo regarded himself as master of the Southern situation," the *New Orleans Times* noted gleefully. Their "dream" was rudely "interrupted," as the "coming man from Asia meets him face to face." The "impotent endeavors of Sambo and his Radical allies," the newspaper claimed, could never impede the march of history and Chinese migration. The *Baton Rouge Advocate* believed that "the appearance of so many celestial laborers" was "regarded with jealousy by the colored laborers as the 'coming man.'" Another newspaper's editor verified these reports with a personal survey of planters and overseers. The majority favored "the Chinamen to the negroes," he concluded, because they were "more easily managed, and do better work, although much slower." He had "no doubt that the introduction of a hundred thousand Chinamen into Louisiana would make the negro a much more reliable laborer."[44]

Scattered reports of anxious freedpeople sustained a popular belief in a new kind of interracial rivalry. J. A. Craig, a freedman and a Radical Republican, voiced his opposition to coolies at a New Orleans political meeting in 1867, pronouncing them "ignorant," especially "regards our peculiar civilization" and likely to come "in direct conflict with the natural toilers of the soil." The influx of coolies, he argued, would infringe upon "the natural rights of the American laborer, both white and black." "I have no objections to an immigration which will till our soil and assist in redeeming our waste lands," Craig said, "but an immigration which will fill our jails, our lunatic asylums and our State prisons, I abhor." C. C. Gould, a veteran sugar planter working as a plantation manager, claimed to have met aboard a local train "an old servant of his" who now worked on a plantation employing mostly Chinese laborers. Gould "accosted" him to tell the truth about their performance. "The man, in the presence of a car load of other negroes, described them in glowing terms as being better workers than any crew of negroes he ever saw, caring nothing at all for the heat of the sun, and a more orderly and peaceable set of people he never saw," it was reported. "Mr. Gould says the negro's fellow passengers all looked as if they did not in the least relish the story of their comrade."[45]

Relations between black and Chinese workers, however, turned out to be a splendid failure of Reconstruction. In the summer of 1870, the *New Orleans Republican* interviewed several "colored" laborers on Millaudon plantation to gauge their reactions to their "new competition, and how far they are likely to harmonize together." Although one man believed "the plentifulness of Chinese labor would have the effect of stirring up some of the lazy folks," the newspaper reported, there was generally "no feeling of jealousy among the colored folks in the neighborhood of the Chinese." Another "colored" laborer said that the Chinese should not evoke any sense of competition, "cause you see, boss, dat any man's got a head on his shoulders, an's willin' to use ee arms an' leg, kin allus git wuck in dis country, caze dare allus plenty to do." An "old auntie" characterized her new neighbors as "very good people" who "don't do nuffin to nobody; mind der own bisness." Dennett, a staunch anti-Republican, also confirmed that "Chinamen" and "negroes" were "very friendly" with one another, experiencing "no trouble" whatsoever. "There is a good feeling between them," another journalist concluded, "and they work together first rate." Chinese migrants, excluded from naturalization and voting rights, moreover, held neither the power nor the inclination to undermine black political gains. A Republican rally on the eve of the 1872 elections, a newspaper related, attracted five hundred people, including "White and Colored Men, Chinese, Women and Children" in Donaldsonville.[46]

Isolated conflicts between individual workers proved to be the rare exception rather than the general rule in Louisiana. On an Assumption Parish plantation during the 1871 grinding season, a "muss occurred among the colored and Chinese hands" involving gunfire that resulted in a serious injury to a Chinese worker. Despite numerous arrests, a newspaper expected "considerable difficulty in fixing the responsibility of the affair." Several years later, "a festive youth of the Celestial tribe" was arrested for attempting to shoot a "colored woman" on the streets of Donaldsonville. And in the summer of 1875, two "Chinamen" reportedly shot a "colored" worker, who defended himself with an ax, "whacking one of his assailants on the head, causing a severe but not necessarily dangerous wound." Both of the Chinese, failing to secure assault charges against their foe, instead faced arrests for assault with a dangerous weapon. The columns of the *Donaldsonville Chief,* indeed, indicated that local Chinese residents had regular encounters with the criminal justice system but only sporadically in cases involving disputes with the freedpeople. They were far more likely to come to blows with one another in violent rows that sometimes captivated the town's entire "Chinese quarter" or to become embroiled in legal proceedings with their contractors or employers.[47] The bitter interracial rivalry imagined by coolie promoters never took root in Louisiana.

Away from the cane fields and sugar mills, Chinese and black workers were, in general, kept apart physically. Chinese workers on Thomas Shaffer's plantation in the summer of 1871 lived in two houses on the other side of the bayou from the "negroes." "Instead of having to give each man a separate house, I gave the 26 men two houses, 20 by 40 feet, and they have ample room, and are contented," Shaffer explained. "I have another house 16 by 18, in which all their cooking and eating is done. One regular cook does all the cooking and policing of quarters, and prepares both cold and warm baths, which every man uses twice a day." Shaffer deeply appreciated the efficiency of employing Chinese migrant laborers, whose social costs, in his mind, were fixed and limited. They were all young men, who, if married, had migrated alone to the United States, some by way of the Caribbean; this rendered their familial attachments and obligations nonexistent to planters. A similar arrangement prevailed on the Millaudon estate, where the Chinese lived apart from the approximately three hundred "negroes." "The Chinamen keep generally to themselves," a journalist recounted. "They have a large house where they spend most of their leisure gambling. One of their number takes care of the house and does their cooking, while the rest are in the field."[48] The Chinese ostensibly ate, slept, and essentially lived by themselves, alone and isolated.

Planters' racial notions and segregated housing, however, did not tell the whole story. To rely solely on planter propaganda, as historian Walter Rodney argued in his study of British Guiana, would be to miss a hidden history of shared responses to common circumstances, regardless of race. Much like British Guiana's multiracial labor force, Louisiana's working peoples engaged in what Rodney called "semiautonomous sets of working class struggles against the domination of capital" in disparate yet interrelated ways. In a pattern familiar to so many plantation workers across the Caribbean, Chinese laborers in Louisiana remade themselves from long-term contract laborers to independent, itinerant labor gangs that engaged with employers for brief periods or finite tasks. In doing so, they joined the circuits of migrant labor that young, unmarried black men had established and followed the routines of sugar production that black women had negotiated in postemancipation Louisiana. Transient wage laborers, however much denounced by sugar pundits and planters, became integral to sugarcane production. Higher monthly wage rates failed to increase the num-

ber of regular laborers, the *Louisiana Sugar-Bowl* noted, and "the negroes everywhere seem to avoid the field as much as possible, and find lucrative employment as wood choppers, ditchers and general jobbers, holding themselves in
readiness for the sugar-making season, with the extra high wages to be obtained
in that period."[49] The Chinese, it turned out, behaved no differently.

Life on the road was not easy, but it afforded an escape from year-round reg-
imented toil on plantations and a critical source of leverage against employers.
Entering the vicissitudes of migrant wage labor, economic historian Gavin
Wright reminds us, conferred little socioeconomic mobility or security in the
postbellum South. It appealed mostly to single, young men in a world of very
limited options. Frank Moss, who spent his youthful days in the 1870s and
1880s moving from one job to the next, explained:

> Somehow or other—I can't remember, but I think it was on account of one of the
> boys of our gang—we generally went around together from place to place and from
> town to town. Well, this feller says there's good money in the sugar cane belt, so
> we went out there. For those three, four months we cut cane. After grinding was
> over, we'd high-tail it back to Texas, or we'd high-tail it here to New Orleans to
> knock 'em up and out and [to] have a good time . . . It's a funny thing—and I just
> thought about it—I've worked all through the coast of Alabama, Mississippi,
> Louisiana, and Texas; and did you know I never did work in New Orleans. Not
> once! . . . Sometimes we didn't hit a lick of work in three or four weeks—sometimes
> longer—all depending on how much money we had and how fast we spent it.

Louisiana sugar planters came to count on labor gangs like Moss's, particularly
to weather the exigencies of the grinding season. Armies of workers descended
on Louisiana's sugarcane fields between October and January and, as *Harper's
Weekly* described the scene, "with great dexterity they cut, trim, and lop off the
heads of the plants with the formidable cane knife." Without the added and experienced labor of women and gangs of young men, who together sometimes
outnumbered "regular" workers, planters faced cane rotting in their fields.[50]

Mobilizing Labor

Chinese workers in Louisiana, like gangs of migrant laborers in general, left
behind few written records, all too often making their work anonymous, if not
invisible, in contemporary and historical accounts. What follows is an attempt
to map the movements of these workers, to get a sense of their frustrations and

"Cutting Sugar Cane for the Mill." Sugar planters depended on gangs of young, mobile men during the grinding season.
Courtesy of the Louisiana State Museum.

aspirations, through one planter family's payrolls. Throughout the 1870s, to operate their Houmas and Brûlé plantations in Ascension Parish, Benjamin Tureaud and his son Benjamin Jr. turned repeatedly to gangs of Chinese laborers whose comings and goings they recorded meticulously in wage lists and time books. These largely impersonal snapshots, taken together, reveal a composite portrait of workers' individual and collective struggles within and beyond the strictures of sugar production, as well as planters' evolving and enduring fixation on coolies.[51] The mobilization and mobility of Chinese workers came to define a world shaped by elusive dreams of coolies and cane.

Unlike Merrill, Gay, and others, the Tureauds began their experiments with Chinese workers gradually in 1871. They first employed a gang of fifteen laborers for less than two weeks in July and, after their departure, hired a handful of others in preparation for the grinding season, perhaps to chop wood for the mill. Either satisfied with their performance or irritated by their evanescence—

or both—the Tureauds then turned to Ah Lee, a Chinese labor contractor based in the nearest big town, Donaldsonville. Ah Lee was most likely making the upward transition from a contract laborer to a labor contractor in 1871, having worked on Edward Gay's plantation earlier in the spring. His new enterprise apparently flourished. By June 1872, he would contact Gay again through an assistant, offering his former employer "a choice gang" for five dollars in commission fees per laborer. The Tureauds paid Ah Lee in October 1871 an equivalent rate for twenty-five Chinese laborers, delivered just in time for the busiest months of the year. Although four left before the end of the grinding season, five others joined Ah Lee's gang, so at least twenty-four Chinese laborers worked for the Tureauds in November and December. In contrast to the infrequent payments encountered on Gay's plantation, these workers received their wages weekly, an increasingly common practice in Louisiana during the grinding season to keep the entire labor force satisfied and settled.[52]

Hundreds of Chinese workers would follow the same path through Houmas and Brulé over the next five years.[53] As the 1871 season wound down, the Tureauds evinced a strong interest in contracting Chinese laborers for the next year. In January 1872, they turned again to Ah Lee, who delivered twenty-one laborers to Houmas, only two of whom had worked for the Tureauds the previous season.[54] Thirteen other Chinese workers likewise commenced the new season on Brulé. Of these thirty-four, surviving wage lists indicate that twenty-two, including the foremen, stayed for an extended stretch, at least through October, receiving wage payments regularly once every month. The Tureauds, at the same time, continued to rely on new gangs of Chinese workers for shorter stints, recruiting, for example, seven laborers each on Houmas and Brulé in April, most likely from Donaldsonville.[55] All told, they employed at least sixty-two Chinese laborers throughout the 1872 season but never more than forty-two in any given month, attesting to both the permanence and transience of Chinese workers in Louisiana.

The dual pattern of stability and mobility continued in 1873, a pattern exhibited by sugar workers in general. The Tureauds' consistent payment schedule might have earned them a reputation as reliable employers by January 1873. When Johnny, the foreman on Brulé the previous season, was entrusted with the task of recruiting fellow Chinese workers, he had no trouble assembling seventeen from nearby neighborhoods.[56] On Houmas, foreman Ah Hong and a dozen laborers evidently agreed in January to work the entire year. Seven of them followed through by working at least forty-three weeks through the

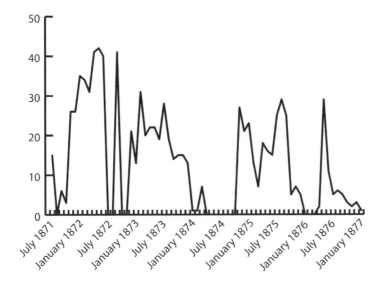

Minimum Number of Chinese Laborers on Houmas and Brulé Plantations.

grinding season. The 1873 season marked the high point of Chinese labor stability on Houmas, where sixty workers averaged almost fourteen weeks of residence. More than half (32) were veteran employees, having worked for the Tureauds in 1871, 1872, or both. The vast majority of Chinese workers, however, belonged to itinerant gangs that appeared and disappeared periodically throughout the year. During the first week of February, for instance, a gang of sixteen Chinese laborers arrived for the planting season and then left together on March 1 after receiving their wages, excepting an individual who had worked only two weeks. The Tureauds, in the end, employed at least nine Chinese workers every week of the year but never more than thirty-one at a time.

Chinese plantation laborers, like fellow working peoples in Louisiana, could never fully control their own destinies, bound as they were to planters' whims and global capitalism's entangled webs of social relations. In February 1872, Thomas J. Foster, who managed Mary Porter's plantations in St. Mary Parish, eagerly welcomed an experienced gang of twenty-four Chinese workers. "Labour is scarce throughout the Parish," he noted, "and planters to get enough are offering high prices." Foster was so pleased with them that he proposed six months later to increase the number of Chinese workers in 1873. He ended up engaging thirty in the new season, a quarter of the entire "regular" force, and

Year	Total Number of Laborers Hired	Total Number of Weeks Worked	Average per Laborer
1873	60	826	13.77
1874	28	235	8.39
1875	65	406	6.25
1876	32	194	6.06

Weeks Worked by Chinese Laborers on Houmas.

inquired into the feasibility of obtaining others from San Francisco. In addition to the 120 monthly workers, he also frequently called upon women on the estate as "day hands." Suddenly in August 1873, on the eve of what would turn out to be a worldwide depression, Foster summarily dismissed all of the Chinese to cut production costs. "Moreover a good many worthless one's [*sic*] had got among them and it was difficult to weed them out without giving great dissatisfaction," he explained. "I thought best to break up the camp by paying them up and discharging all and taking my chances to make a more advantageous contract, with the best of them or others when I will require them which will be about putting up seed cane in October."[57]

The ripple effects of the wider financial crisis touched everyone in Louisiana, none more than its working peoples, including the Chinese. "Property is *Dead*, the Planters are ruined," a New Orleans merchant exclaimed in December 1873, "& many of the merchts. in the same Boat." As planters across the state implemented drastic wage cuts that would culminate in the deployment of state troops in Terrebonne Parish, workers on the Tureaud estates had hard decisions to make. The Tureauds offered "regular" workers only thirteen dollars per month, with five dollars reserved in back wages until the end of the year.[58] The thirteen Chinese laborers on the Houmas payroll at the end of 1873 chose not to return in the new year, more than likely electing to go to Donaldsonville's Chinese quarters to contemplate their options. They were not alone. Among the multitude returning to town may have been a hundred Chinese workers who had left Donaldsonville back in the summer of 1872 to work at a cutlery factory in Beaver Falls, Pennsylvania. A year later, they all returned to Louisiana together after a violent confrontation with a Chinese foreman.[59] Black men on Houmas, meanwhile, also refused to accept the Tureauds' proposal. Although seventy-nine of them eventually agreed to work in January and February 1874, only a quarter of them commenced from the beginning. The vast majority refused to work for weeks, about half holding out until February, and demanded weekly payments, indicative of their strong aversion to the Tureauds' long-term offer.

The Tureauds encountered a highly volatile labor market, especially after the 1873 season that generated ever-shifting hiring practices and patterns. Many Chinese workers rode out the wage reductions in Donaldsonville for as long as possible, until March 1874 when they set off for surrounding plantations. By May, all but a single individual had vanished from the river town. That "crazy chinaman," the *Donaldsonville Chief* reported, was "ostracized by his brother celestials, and now wanders through the streets . . . without shelter, without food, and almost without clothing, presenting a most loathsome and disgusting spectacle." The *Chief* beseeched the mayor "to rid us of this obscene object," surely a casualty of the financial panic as much as local antipathies.[60] Six Chinese workers, in the meantime, went to work on Houmas in early March, joining a lone compatriot already there since late January. All seven received their wages every week, suggesting a temporary arrangement, and then left before the end of the month. Chinese workers then stayed away from Houmas until the grinding season, when high wages probably lured them back. In comparison to the previous season, the Tureauds hired many more black men to operate Houmas in 1874, a reflection more of their inability to hang on to laborers than their success in attracting laborers. Amid high turnovers, they must have been eager to engage a gang of twenty-one experienced Chinese workers, among them a skilled sugar "clarifier," for the last two months of a most unpredictable year.[61]

Chinese workers continually agreed to work for the Tureauds, in part because they could count on consistent payments. Regardless of their length of engagement—from half a day to forty-nine weeks in 1873, for example—all of the Chinese received payments on a uniform schedule, about once a month. This unique schedule applied only to long-term Chinese workers on Houmas, as all other monthly laborers, male and female, collected their wages only once they completed twenty-six days of work, which, in most instances, required longer than a month. All temporary workers, on the other hand, were paid on a regular schedule like the Chinese.[62] In January 1875, the Tureauds attempted to implement a new regimen, apparently convincing Wan Sing, who had worked twenty-five weeks on Houmas in 1873, to accept a monthly rate of $17.50, paid every twenty-six days worked. Six months later, he had worked only three "months" and,

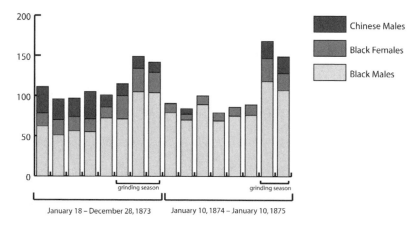

Houmas Labor Force, 1873–74.

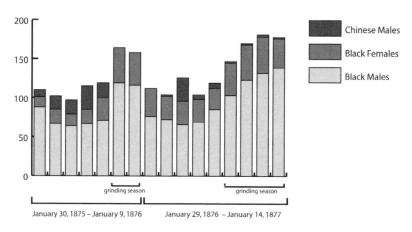

Houmas Labor Force, 1875–76.

subtracting for debts to the plantation store, earned only $34.85 in wages.[63] Five other Chinese workers hired on similar terms in the spring, meanwhile, worked at most two "months" before deserting Houmas. Discouraged by the infrequency and inadequacy of his earnings yet encouraged by the arrival of short-term Chinese workers, Sing evidently persuaded the Tureauds to pay him like the others in early July. He received two payments before leaving "of his own accord" at the end of the month. Another experiment to make the Chinese conform to the twenty-six-day pay schedule likewise failed in 1876.

Perpetually embittered and embattled with the state of labor, the Tureauds tapped multiple sources of migrant labor, not only Chinese workers, particularly to meet seasonal demands. In January 1875, they recruited at least sixty-two men from Pointe Coupée Parish for the planting season, some of them through Alfred Lindsy, a professional labor agent. Months later, on the eve of what promised to be a lucrative grinding season, the Tureauds became desperate for workers. "Get all the hands you can for the coming month," the senior Tureaud instructed his son, "and push everything through as fast as you can." Duncan Kenner, Tureaud's brother-in-law, advised the younger Tureaud to explore the "upper parishes" for extra laborers and, if not possible, to "try & get them in the vicinity, by paying *cash* every Saturday or some other inducement, but as much as possible at plantation rates." The Tureauds turned to Lindsy again. But, by September, planters in Pointe Coupée Parish offered high cotton-picking wages that halted workers' movement southward. The Tureauds, in turn, relied heavily on Chinese and black female workers for the pre-grinding rush (see figures). Perhaps enticed by better offers, none of the Chinese remained for the grinding season, compelling the Tureauds more than ever to recruit additional laborers from Baton Rouge, Plaquemine, Donaldsonville, and Pointe Coupée. On top of professional agents, the Tureauds paid individual laborers upriver to Pointe Coupée or downriver to New Orleans to "return with family & plunder" and other recruits back to Houmas and Brulé.[64]

The recurrent arrivals and departures of workers on the Tureaud estates emblematized the everyday struggles that lay at the heart of social relations of sugar production in Louisiana. Migrant laborers of all backgrounds and Louisiana's working peoples in general proved impossible to control. After surviving the grinding season's demands with boatloads of migrant workers, Tureaud could find no solace in the new season. Unable to secure more than a handful of workers to commence planting, he "fear[ed] we will have trouble starting work." He had plenty of company. "For two weeks past, the roads have been lined with negro carts, laden with the plunder of laborers moving from one plantation to another," the *Louisiana Sugar-Bowl* observed in January 1876. "They seldom better their condition; but then, to change habitations is one of the prerogatives of freemen, and a majority of the blacks are not satisfied unless they indulge in that luxury." Recruited to Louisiana as plantation workers bound to long-term contracts, the Chinese turned out to be equally determined to practice the same prerogative, the same luxury. They, too, were mobilizing for freedom, which Louisiana's working peoples recognized as a moving target rather than a fixed state of being. Small gangs of Chinese workers, "all laden like pack mules" and on the march toward New Orleans, Thibodaux, Donaldsonville, Baton Rouge, and other towns came to be familiar sights in Louisiana.[65] They blended in all too well.

The migratory habits of Louisiana's working peoples tore apart whatever solidarity planters could muster in these uncertain times. "I am of the opinion that some of our neighbors are giving more—others giving land & other inducements which will—I fear—consume the labor of the neighborhood," a planter complained during an unparalleled display of planter unity in January 1874. Roman Daigre was among those who began to buckle under the pressure. Most of his "single men" had "gone away," and some of his "old hands" had begun seeking their own lands rather than submit to the reduced wages. To compete with planters offering shares to his "best hands," Daigre felt he had no choice but to offer twenty rather than thirteen dollars monthly to "each *first class* hand." Three years later, following a profitable crop in 1876, John Burnside decided unilaterally to raise the monthly rate by two dollars, in effect establishing the local wage rate, and, along with a host of other planters, hired Chinese workers in place of black workers. A local newspaper tried to remind planters of the "utter worthlessness" of Chinese laborers, but old racial dreams died slowly. Neither higher wages nor Chinese workers settled their labor "problems" though. By fall, Burnside encountered a strike by "colored" workers, whom his manager discharged immediately. Another planter who, like Burnside, placed his faith in Chinese workers by hiring thirty of them for the entire year found no better results. He fired them all by September.[66] In the endless search for an ideal plantation labor force, race meant everything and, in the end, nothing.

Segregation and Exclusion

The White League gained political momentum across Louisiana amid these struggles on sugar plantations in the 1870s. Following the panic of 1873 and the ruinous spring floods of 1874, the White League proffered an easy solution, a racial panacea. The entire crisis, Alexandre DeClouet exclaimed at a rally, was engendered by "a black league" whose "object" was "the overthrow of the last breastworks of our dearest prerogatives—even to the invasion of the sanctuary of our homes and firesides!" "Are we prepared to surrender our manhood," he asked, "to give the lie to the superiority of our race, to our past history and to bequeath to our children and to future generations the burning shame and opprobrium of an Africanised and disgraced country?" White Republicans, a St. Mary Parish newspaper suggested, ought to be "*reckoned negroes*" and branded "Pariahs, forever cast out from all association with the Caucasian race." From all corners of the state came cries for racial unity and charity. Another newspaper urged that white men's "*patriotism*" obliged them to join the White League, a movement that "aroused planters and land holders generally to a sense of duty toward poor white men" of Louisiana. The Grange appealed to their members' sense of racial responsibility, announcing the availability for hire in New Orleans of "white mechanics and farm hands" thrown out of work by the financial crisis.[67]

The racial politics of the White League meshed closely with the immigration movement in Louisiana, making their messages and constituencies largely interchangeable and indistinguishable. Immigration, many suggested, was essential to "redemption." J. Y. Gilmore, editor of the *Louisiana Sugar-Bowl*, prefigured the fusion of the two reactionary movements in 1873. When some white businessmen and black leaders in New Orleans proposed an interracial alliance to support racial equality under the law in return for political and economic stability, he emphasized the need for white unity and immigration. "In plainer terms, Louisiana wants a sufficient number of white votes to thoroughly neutralize the vote of the black element, now so powerful at the polls and so weak at the plow," Gilmore lashed out. "She wants white votes enough to enable her to place the source of governmental power where it rightfully belongs— among the intelligent masses—and white hands enough to re-establish her upon her past agricultural footing." He would throw his full editorial weight behind the White League the following year. DeClouet, a White League organizer, had similarly helped found one of Dennett's projects in 1873, the Louisiana Immigration and Homestead Company.[68] Immigration and white supremacy were inextricable.

Integral to this vision of a white nation was the reservation for whites of not only political rights but all opportunities for economic independence, especially share arrangements. Even in the sugar region, where wage labor dominated postemancipation production, shared divisions of the final crop between planters and workers were not uncommon. Cash-strapped planters in post-bellum Louisiana had no choice, "a straw grasped by the drowning planter," as an old planter put it. When a combination of floods, drought, frosts, and a wider financial panic wiped away the hopes of many Louisiana sugar planters in 1873, Louis Bouchereau unequivocally advised planters to adopt the "share system," which entailed "comparatively small" losses in poor seasons. He claimed that "White tenants" were the most productive, followed by, in descending order, "Negro Share labor" and "Negro gang labor," the worst being those paid in full monthly. Bouchereau's call for a rapid transition to white tenants failed to materialize, but his message resonated in Louisiana. "Negroes are better hands as monthly wages, as sugar plantations are now conducted, than either China-men or whites," Gilmore stated in 1877, "for the Celestials are altogether too slow for this kind of work, while no white man worth having is willing to work as a common monthly laborer, when he can do so much better working on the tenant or share system." Whites on shares were profitable, he insisted, whereas "negroes" lacked the "ambition or forethought" to work independently.[69]

But unable to work their indebted estates on wage labor, desperate planters relied on share arrangements with black workers to survive the financial disaster enveloping the sugar industry. In December 1873, Richard McCall found it impossible to "work my place on the wages system next year, owing to the want of money," and noted that the "share plan" was "generally talked of" in his neighborhood. These "share men," another planter complained, were "preaching to the negroes that however little they make on shares they will do better than to work for $13.00 per month." But it was the elite planters, a shrinking minority with access to capital, who had the upper hand in labor ne-gotiations—with white, black, and Chinese workers. "The scarcity of capital and labor will compel men of small means to work their sugar estates entirely upon the share system," a planter explained in 1877. "Large planters from the lower districts will come up here and bid $4 or $5 more per month than we are able to pay, and in this way they will finally secure all the labor, from the small estates."[70]

Growing divisions among Louisiana's planters and among whites galvanized immigration advocates to plea louder than ever for racial solidarity, pleas that ultimately left a lasting imprint on the racial division of labor. The entire region faced dark days ahead, Dennett maintained, "unless the planters encourage white immigration, and the share o[r] tenant system, with white men to make and take off their crops." After the overthrow of Republican rule in April 1877,

Governor Francis T. Nicholls seemed poised to renew public efforts to encourage white immigration. In June, he appointed new commissioners, including Dennett, to the state Bureau of Immigration, but its mode of operation remained the same. Lacking additional authority or public funds, the agency could only publish and distribute circulars extolling Louisiana and court planter participation in selling or leasing excess lands. Indeed, immigration advocates paid endless tributes to owners of capacious mills and huge tracts of land, casting them as the key to "redemption" in the form of white unity, immigration, and central factories. Some of these planters, Gilmore wrote approvingly, furnished houses and lands to white growers in exchange for lower prices on the cane, a system wanting only "the requisite number of white laborers." In such ways, while the resort to shares with black workers emerged as a mark of shame and destitution, the embrace of white tenant families came to signify the reinvigoration of "progressive" agriculture and white supremacy. By the late 1870s and 1880s, rental and share arrangements became a social privilege ideologically reserved for whites only in the sugar region.[71]

The movement for "redemption" seemingly had cast the coolie—a cultural figure that embodied the contradictions, anxieties, and hopes of the age of emancipation—beyond the pale of the white nation, but the continued struggles of Louisiana's working peoples kept it alive. When reports and rumors of a "negro exodus" to Kansas transfixed the Deep South and the nation in 1879, many planters resuscitated their grand old visions of coolies. In April 1879, a group of planters and merchants organized the Mississippi Valley Immigration Company in New Orleans. "We deprecate the present negro exodus and believe the colored people will soon discover their error and return to their homes, as many are now doing," the organizers proclaimed. In place of the "unsettled" and insufficient labor then on cotton and sugar plantations, they believed "an unlimited supply of good labor suited to our climate, can be had from China at an early day, if our enterprise is met with proper support." Louisiana planters had no choice, a sugar pundit argued, given "the total lack of national sympathy with our Sugar interest, and its active sympathy with its enemies, together with the constrained exodus of negro labor from our plantations." A Mississippi planter subscribed to the company, convinced that "sooner or later we shall be forced to abandon negro labor or rather that negro labor will abandon us."[72] Old racial dreams made immediate realities bearable, apparently changeable.

But Chinese workers, almost exclusively young, mobile men, could find no place within the dominant ideological formations of the "American" family and nation and, indeed, came to embody the greatest threats thereto. In Louisiana's sugar politics, coolies eventually symbolized the local industry's menace rather than its salvation, a foreign problem that warranted federal intervention and protection. It was an argument long identified with the Republican party. All Louisianians interested in reviving the local sugar industry, the *New Orleans Republican* had editorialized in 1868, ought to lobby Congress to abolish slavery in Cuba. "Directly at our doors is Cuba," the official voice of the state party argued, "which, from the character of her labor—the most cruel and abominable among any people in the world calling themselves Christians—enjoys the monopoly of sugar raising." The end of slavery there "would instantly double, if not quadruple, the value of the sugar lands of Louisiana." Coolies fit logically within this old antislavery position. In 1874, Rep. Chester B. Darrall, a Republican planter from St. Mary Parish, proclaimed that "Cuba and India with slave and coolie labor, can produce sugar and rice much cheaper than can be done here, and if the government ceased to exact the two or three cents upon every pound of those articles brought from foreign countries our planting interests would be ruined."[73] A stand against coolies was now a stand for Louisiana, for America.

Louisiana Democrats (or "Conservatives") were not to be outdone in recasting coolies as anathema to American sugar. Shortly before his death, Louis Bouchereau demanded federal protection from "invasions of foreign sugars cultivated by slave and cooley labor." The Louisiana Sugar Planters' Association, reconstituted in 1877, also protested against "the slave or coolie grown sugars of the tropics" and the 1876 reciprocity treaty with Hawai'i which, it argued, undercut "our struggling sugar industry" in Louisiana.[74] Randall Lee Gibson, a Democrat first elected to Congress in 1874, lobbied assiduously in Washington for sugar tariffs. In the spring of 1882, when Congress prohibited the entry of Chinese laborers into the United States, Gibson pleaded for an "equity in this tariff system." "Will you not afford equal protection to the freedmen of Louisiana and freemen of that State against the unpaid labor, the slave labor of Cuba and the gang or cooly labor . . . of the tropics, that is still more exacting?" he asked. Gibson concluded that the federal protection of Louisiana sugar was a matter of "freedom and justice against slavery and injustice, American freedom against Cuban slavery and Hawaiian coolyism." That he himself had employed Chinese workers a decade earlier, and that other Louisiana planters continued to do so, had to be erased, forgotten.[75] The drive to expunge coolies from the United

States not only united Louisiana Republicans and Democrats but also ultimately reunited a nation, a white nation of immigrants.

No one wished to forget coolies more than Edward Gay. In the years following his failed experiment with Chinese workers, he began operating a refinery in New Orleans under the central factory system. In 1884, he became a founding trustee of the Southern and Western Immigration Bureau, a private enterprise involving the New South's commercial and railroad barons as well as longtime advocates of white immigration like J. Y. Gilmore. Gay entered electoral politics the same year, running as a Democrat against the Republican ex-governor William Kellogg for a congressional seat. In a bitter contest marked by accusations of planters' bribing and intimidating the black majority, Kellogg, formerly a federal officer charged with suppressing the coolie trade, tried to attract black voters by condemning his rival's "attempt to substitute Chinese for colored labor" more than a decade earlier. Kellogg recounted how Gay had "turned out . . . free citizens to make room for . . . saffron slaves," whom he "treated so niggardly that even their Chinese blood revolted, and they sued him in open court for breach of contract." But his old Republican stand against slavery could not check Gay's profligate march to "redemption" in the heart of the sugar region.[76] That Kellogg had sided with them in the Terrebonne "war" of 1874 mattered little to Gay and other men of property.

Neither fully remembered nor forgotten, both the demand for and the exclusion of coolies served to reproduce racial and national boundaries in the age of emancipation. By the time the U.S. Supreme Court heard Homer Plessy's challenge to Louisiana's segregation code in 1896, the nation appeared ready to move beyond the slavery issue. In validating Louisiana's 1890 law that mandated separate railway cars for "white" and "colored" races, the Supreme Court justices easily cast aside the Thirteenth Amendment's relevance. It abolished "involuntary servitude," the majority ruled, and encompassed "Mexican peonage" and "the Chinese coolie trade" but not legal distinctions based on race. The legal prohibition of slavery, peonage, and coolieism seemingly sanctified freedom (and race) in the United States. In his dissent, Justice John Marshall Harlan stood fast for "universal civil freedom," declaring that "our Constitution is color-blind, and neither knows nor tolerates classes among citizens." But Harlan's defense of universal inclusion had distinct limits. He objected to the implicit eligibility of the "Chinese race"—who were, "with few exceptions, absolutely excluded from our country"—to travel with "white citizens" when "citizens of the black race in Louisiana, many of whom, perhaps, risked their lives for the preservation of the Union" could not.[77] Whether in justifying black segregation by commending the abolition of coolieism or denouncing black segregation by justifying Chinese exclusion, *Plessy* was but the latest example of the deep ties between slavery and coolieism, segregation and exclusion in American culture. Although excluded from the nation, and thereby defining the nation, Chinese workers struggled on in Louisiana, California, and beyond, on familiar paths traveled by black workers.

Conclusion

The *Hot*tentots stand heat better than Coolies.

—*HARPER'S WEEKLY* (1862)

If the Philippines are annexed, what is to prevent the Chinese, the Negritos and the Malays [from] coming to our country? How can we prevent the Chinese coolies from going to the Philippines and from there swarming into the United States engulfing our people and our civilization?

—SAMUEL GOMPERS (1898)

The emancipation of man is the emancipation of labor and the emancipation of labor is the freeing of that basic majority of workers who are yellow, brown and black.   —W. E. B. DU BOIS (1935)

Seventy years ago, historian W. E. B. Du Bois characterized Reconstruction as a "splendid failure" because "it did not fail where it was expected to fail." To him, the age of emancipation was defined by a violent confrontation between capital and labor, always in articulation with the ideology of white supremacy. Reconstruction's demise in the United States, he argued, was due to an "understanding between the Southern exploiter of labor and the Northern exploiter" and the fatal decision by "poor whites" to seek "redress by demanding unity of white against black, and not unity of poor against rich, or of worker against exploiter." The millions of black workers who essentially effected their own emancipation, however, did not fail and in their "hands and heart[s]" rested "the consciousness of a great and just cause; fighting the battle of all the oppressed and despised humanity of every race and color, against the massed hirelings of Religion, Science, Education, Law, and brute force." Writing in an era defined by racist denunciations of multiracial democracy, Du Bois's bold claim that black workers' struggles for democracy and justice had shaped the course of U.S. history was beyond prescient. It was revolutionary. But his analysis suggested even more. He insisted that U.S. Reconstruction be situated within a global framework and its collapse in relation to the superexploitation of "the dark proletariat" all over the world, what he termed "the real modern labor problem."[1] More than any other work, Du Bois's landmark study has guided my interpretation of the age of emancipation.

Throughout this book, I have tried to show how racial imaginings of coolies disrupted and reestablished a series of overlapping social and cultural dualisms at the heart of American culture—slavery and freedom, black and white, domestic and foreign, alien and citizen, modern and premodern. In the decades before the Civil War, chiefly through reports from the Caribbean and Asia, coolies came to epitomize enslaved labor, a foreign scourge that threatened to undermine both American freedom and American slavery. The close association between slavery and coolieism, in turn, incorporated coolies in the domestic struggle over slavery, with Republicans taking charge of the crusade against the coolie trade during the Civil War. In their desire to protect an "inferior race" of coolies, Republican officials expressed the popular antebellum notion that the transport of Asian laborers marked a reversion to slavery rather than a progression toward freedom. Even as the antislavery rhetoric and logic would lead to the exclusion of Asian workers from the United States beginning with Chinese laborers in 1882, coolies defied singular categorization. In the wake of emancipation, Louisiana planters and merchants—culturally and socially tied to the orbits of sugar, empires, and revolutions of the Greater Caribbean— launched a campaign to import coolies and, in the face of federal intervention, to recast them as voluntary immigrants.

Though reluctantly accorded the legal status of immigrants by federal officials, Asian migrants could never overcome their racialization as coolies to become immigrants in nineteenth-century American culture. The impulse to import and to exclude coolies served to make immigrants European and white during Reconstruction, an era defined by the first concrete steps toward removing racial barriers to citizenship rights. But race remained central in the project of U.S. nationalism after slavery, with the contested status of coolies perhaps posing the greatest challenge to the Radical Republican goal of universalizing free labor and republican citizenship. Were coolies, in fact, slaves or immigrants? Social critics, government officials, plantation owners, and many others grappled for decades with this seemingly simple question that could produce only contradictory and ambiguous answers. In the end, coolies represented something between and beyond slaves and immigrants, an ideal noncitizen, migrant labor force for the age of emancipation, allowed to enter the United States for decades as tenuous "immigrants" and racially excluded from naturalization and then immigration. Indeed, the notion that coolies were slaves, an idea imported to the United States from the Caribbean before the Civil War, displayed incredible resiliency in the postslavery era and was made all the more palpable by the words and actions of Louisiana planters and merchants. The movement to exclude coolies on behalf of former and future immigrants thus temporarily divided whites along class lines but eventually helped to forge a white national identity across regional and class divisions, in the bayous of Louisiana as much as in the halls of Congress.

Asian workers began arriving in Louisiana, and in the Americas in general, at a critical moment in national and global history. Their migrations were facilitated by multiple historical developments, from old dreams of slavery and empire to new aspirations of industrial development and free trade. These diverse forces shaped not only the shifting geographical origins of Chinese workers in postemancipation Louisiana—Cuba, China, Martinique, and then California—but the global shifts in sugar production and consumption. The worldwide demand for cheaper, finer sugar coincided roughly with the social and physical destruction of the Civil War and devastated Louisiana's standing in the domestic and global sugar market. The federal government's declining support for sugar tariffs and its expanding vision of an American empire in the Pacific and the Caribbean exacerbated and accelerated this trend. Republican federal officials' suspicion of coolie schemes, moreover, increased the risks of investing in Asian migrant labor in the South, leaving only a handful of planters willing and able to afford the high costs of recruiting and transporting "cheap" workers. The New South's own imperial ambitions, rooted in its longings for coerced labor and the promises of industrial capitalism, turned out to be much mightier than its imperial reach. Grand expectations of a mass flood of coolies into the South, as in the Caribbean, dwindled into smaller streams and all but dried up by the global depression of the 1870s.

These so-called coolies, however, had an influence far greater than their numbers would suggest in shaping Louisiana's social relations. The capitalization and consolidation of sugar production—made conspicuous by elite planters' consumption of land, machinery, and migrant workers—spawned a countermovement for white immigrants and small farms. If the terror unleashed against blacks united whites politically, coolies exposed deep socioeconomic rifts that seemed capable of mobilizing Louisiana's growing ranks of dispossessed whites against the upward redistribution of property. The march against African Americans encompassed movements for and against coolies, a contradiction that resolved itself through a racial compact that muffled antiplanter criticisms and amplified appeals for central factories and immigration. Renewed agrarian fantasies welcomed capital and immigrants, rejected coolies and blacks, and fueled a "redemption" of white supremacy from multiracial democracy. But the soul of democracy did not die with "redemption." It survived in the consciousness of Louisiana's working peoples, particularly in the struggles of black and Chinese workers. Within the violent world that sugar and slavery had made, they discovered tortuous paths toward freedom which they readily recognized, pursued, and extended. These were the intense struggles, mirroring and reinforcing similar struggles in the Caribbean and beyond, that preserved the true promise of democracy and justice.

In the broadest sense, the creation and regeneration of coolies in American culture proved pivotal in reconstructing race and nation in the second half of the nineteenth century. If coolies confused and collapsed seemingly indissoluble divides, such as slavery and freedom, the never-ending search to locate, define, and outlaw coolies, in turn, made them reappear as fixed, permanent, and natural. The ambiguities surrounding coolies not only reflected the contradictions of emancipation but also became a vital instrument in the reproduction of racial, nationalist, and class provincialisms. The contradictory processes of promoting and rejecting coolies ultimately served to justify racial exclusions in the aftermath of black legal inclusion. The drive to prohibit coolies from the United States, manifesting in the denial of naturalization and immigration rights to Chinese laborers, did not interrupt but invigorated the national and racial celebration of the "land of immigrants." And, as in Louisiana, excluding coolies became the battle cry of organized white labor across the nation, which would coronate Samuel Gompers as the official voice of American labor. Echoing Louisiana sugar's representatives, Gompers's denunciation of coolies as unfair and uncivilized competition for "American" workers and goods formed the basis of his argument against the annexation of the Philippines. In contrast, ever since the 1850s, U.S. government officials had cited the liberation of coolies (and other enslaved workers) as a cause requiring American intervention abroad.[2] The project of outlawing coolies unified U.S. imperialists and anti-imperialists under the banner of white supremacy and freedom.

All in all, the recruitment *and* exclusion of coolies enabled and justified a series of historical transitions—from slave-trade laws to racially coded immigration laws, from a slaveholding nation to a "nation of immigrants," and from a continental empire of "manifest destiny" to a liberating empire across the seas. Racial imaginings of Asian workers were instrumental in the reconstruction of the United States as a "free," "white," and "modern" nation in the age of emancipation, intimately connected but distantly removed from a wider world of coolies and cane. The kind of emancipation and democracy that Du Bois and the dark proletariat envisioned was not possible in that nation, in that world.

Notes

Abbreviations

ASC	Assistant Subassistant Commissioner
BRFAL	Records of the Bureau of Refugees, Freedmen, and Abandoned Lands
DR	*De Bow's Review*
EJGP	Edward J. Gay and Family Papers
HED	House Executive Document
HNOC	Historic New Orleans Collection, New Orleans, Louisiana
LSL	Louisiana Department, Louisiana State Library, Baton Rouge, Louisiana
LSU	Louisiana and Lower Mississippi Valley Collections, Louisiana State University Libraries, Baton Rouge, Louisiana
NA	National Archives, Washington, D.C.
NILSB	*New Iberia Louisiana Sugar-Bowl*
NODP	*New Orleans Daily Picayune*
NYHS	New-York Historical Society, New York, New York
NYT	*New York Times*
RG	Record Group
SED	Senate Executive Document
Tulane	Manuscripts Department, Howard-Tilton Memorial Library, Tulane University, New Orleans, Louisiana
UNC	Southern Historical Collection, University of North Carolina, Chapel Hill, North Carolina
WBRSP	*West Baton Rouge Sugar Planter*

Introduction

1. Reuben Kartick, "O Tye Kim and the Establishment of the Chinese Settlement of Hopetown," *Guyana Historical Journal* 1 (1989): 37; Marlene Kwok Crawford, *Scenes from the History of the Chinese in Guyana* (Georgetown: Author, 1989), 43, 46–47; Walton Look Lai, *Indentured Labor, Caribbean Sugar: Chinese and Indian Migrants to the British West Indies, 1838–1918* (Baltimore: Johns Hopkins University Press, 1993), 199; Lucy M. Cohen, *Chinese in the Post–Civil War South: A People without a History* (Baton Rouge: Louisiana State University Press, 1984), 68. Orr was also known as O Tye Kim and Wu Tai Kam.

2. Look Lai, *Indentured Labor, Caribbean Sugar*, 197–98 (quote); Kartick, "O Tye Kim and the Establishment," 37–38; Crawford, *Scenes from the History of the Chinese*, 48.

Ultimately, 238,909 South Asian (most commonly called East Indian in the Caribbean) and 13,533 Chinese migrants arrived in British Guiana between 1838 and 1917 (Look Lai, *Indentured Labor, Caribbean Sugar*, 19).

3. Kartick, "O Tye Kim and the Establishment," 38–44 (newspaper quotes on 41); Look Lai, *Indentured Labor, Caribbean Sugar*, 198–99; Crawford, *Scenes from the History of the Chinese*, 43–46; Edward Jenkins, *The Coolie: His Rights and Wrongs* (New York: George Routledge and Sons, 1871), 114–16.

4. Kartick, "O Tye Kim and the Establishment," 44–46; Look Lai, *Indentured Labor, Caribbean Sugar*, 199; Crawford, *Scenes from the History of the Chinese*, 43; Etta B. Peabody, "Effort of the South to Import Chinese Coolies, 1865–1870" (M.A. thesis, Baylor University, 1967), 23; *NODP*, November 16, 1867.

5. John H. Brough to Bvt. Capt. H. H. Pierce, General Superintendent of Education, August 31, 1868, vol. 264:102, Letters Sent; District Superintendent's Monthly School Report by John H. Brough, August 31, 1868; District Superintendent's Monthly School Report by Victor Benthien, September 30, 1868; District Superintendents School Reports; Agent and ASC, Donaldsonville, LA, BRFAL, RG 105, NA.

6. Marina E. Espina, *Filipinos in Louisiana* (New Orleans: A. F. Laborde and Sons, 1988), 1–18. These Filipinos had been involved in the galleon trade across the Pacific, between the Philippines and Mexico, which lasted for more than two centuries.

7. I am building on the work of anthropologist Lucy M. Cohen, who argued that southern proponents of Asian labor migration drew their historical lessons most dearly from the Caribbean. See Cohen, *Chinese in the Post–Civil War South;* "Entry of Chinese to the Lower South from 1865 to 1870: Policy Dilemmas," *Southern Studies* 17, no. 1 (Spring 1978): 5–37.

8. See, e.g., Ronald Takaki, *Strangers from a Different Shore: A History of Asian Americans* (Boston: Little, Brown and Co., 1989), 35–36.

9. Historians have tended to interpret southern postbellum movements for Asian migrant laborers and white immigrants as analogous, if not equivalent, in origin and effect. For a recent iteration, see John C. Rodrigue, *Reconstruction in the Cane Fields: From Slavery to Free Labor in Louisiana's Sugar Parishes, 1862–1880* (Baton Rouge: Louisiana State University Press, 2001), 136–38.

10. Edward D. Beechert, "Patterns of Resistance and the Social Relations of Production in Hawaii," in *Plantation Workers: Resistance and Accommodation*, ed. Brij V. Lal et al. (Honolulu: University of Hawaii Press, 1993), 45–46.

11. Gary Y. Okihiro, *Margins and Mainstreams: Asians in American History and Culture* (Seattle: University of Washington Press, 1994), 3–30. See also Lucie Cheng and Edna Bonacich, eds., *Labor Immigration under Capitalism: Asian Workers in the United States before World War II* (Berkeley and Los Angeles: University of California Press, 1984); John Kuo Wei Tchen, *New York before Chinatown: Orientalism and the Shaping of American Culture, 1776–1882* (Baltimore: Johns Hopkins University Press, 1999).

12. Matthew Frye Jacobson, *Whiteness of a Different Color: European Immigrants and the Alchemy of Race* (Cambridge: Harvard University Press, 1998), ix–x.

ONE: Outlawing Coolies

1. *Congressional Record*, 47th Cong., 1st Sess., 1482, 1581, 1932, 1936.

2. *Congressional Record*, 47th Cong., 1st Sess., 1934, 1517.

3. Amy Dru Stanley, *From Bondage to Contract: Wage Labor, Marriage, and the Market in the Age of Slave Emancipation* (Cambridge: Cambridge University Press, 1998), esp. 218–63.

4. *The Oxford English Dictionary*, 2d ed. (Oxford: Clarendon Press, 1989), 891–92; Hugh Tinker, *A New System of Slavery: The Export of Indian Labour Overseas, 1830–1920* (London: Oxford University Press, 1974), 41–43; Robert L. Irick, *Ch'ing Policy toward the Coolie Trade, 1847–1878* (Taipei: Chinese Materials Center, 1982), 2–6; Vijay Prashad, *Everybody Was Kung Fu Fighting: Afro-Asian Connections and the Myth of Cultural Purity* (Boston: Beacon Press, 2001), 71–72.

5. The term *cooly*, defined as an "East Indian porter or carrier," had first appeared in 1842. Noah Webster, *An American Dictionary of the English Language* (New York: White and Sheffield, 1842), 953; Noah Webster and Chauncey A. Goodrich, *An American Dictionary of the English Language* (Springfield: George and Charles Merriam, 1848), 264.

6. Alan H. Adamson, *Sugar without Slaves: The Political Economy of British Guiana, 1838–1904* (New Haven: Yale University Press, 1972), 41–42 (Gladstone quote on 41); Tinker, *A New System of Slavery*, 61–63 (quote on 63).

7. Tinker, *A New System of Slavery*, v (quote), 69–70; Adamson, *Sugar without Slaves*, 42–43; Walton Look Lai, *Indentured Labor, Caribbean Sugar: Chinese and Indian Migrants to the British West Indies, 1838–1918* (Baltimore: Johns Hopkins University Press, 1993), 109, 156–57; Dwarka Nath, *A History of Indians in British Guiana* (London: Thomas Nelson and Sons, Ltd., 1950), 8–21.

8. Walter Rodney, *A History of the Guyanese Working People, 1881–1905* (Baltimore: Johns Hopkins University Press, 1981), 32–33.

9. Look Lai, *Indentured Labor, Caribbean Sugar*, 13–18; K. O. Laurence, *Immigration into the West Indies in the 19th Century* (Mona: Caribbean Universities Press, 1971), 9–18; Thomas C. Holt, *The Problem of Freedom: Race, Labor, and Politics in Jamaica and Britain, 1832–1938* (Baltimore: Johns Hopkins University Press, 1992), 197–200; Monica Schuler, *"Alas, Alas, Kongo": A Social History of Indentured African Immigration into Jamaica, 1841–1865* (Baltimore: Johns Hopkins University Press, 1980), 1–29.

10. See, e.g., Adamson, *Sugar without Slaves*, 44–56, 104–53; Look Lai, *Indentured Labor, Caribbean Sugar*, 16, 50–86, 107–35; Tinker, *A New System of Slavery*, 61–287; Rodney, *A History of the Guyanese Working People*, 33–42.

11. See, e.g., Denise Helly, introduction to *The Cuba Commission Report: A Hidden History of the Chinese in Cuba: The Original English-Language Text of 1876* (Baltimore: Johns Hopkins University Press, 1993), 5–27; Evelyn Hu-DeHart, "Chinese Coolie Labour in Cuba in the Nineteenth Century: Free Labour or Neo-slavery?" *Slavery and Abolition* 14, no. 1 (April 1993): 67–83; Rebecca J. Scott, *Slave Emancipation in Cuba: The Transition to Free Labor, 1860–1899* (Princeton: Princeton University Press, 1985), 29–35, 89–110.

12. Look Lai, *Indentured Labor, Caribbean Sugar*, 19, 37–49, 58–61, 70–75, 87–106; Wally Look Lai, "Chinese Indentured Labor: Migrations to the British West Indies in the Nineteenth Century," *Amerasia Journal* 15, no. 2 (1989): 117–35.

13. "Slavery in Jamaica, W.I.," *Littell's Living Age* 9 (May 30, 1846): 429; "Miscellany: West-India Immigration," *Littell's Living Age* 10 (September 19, 1846): 582; *Liberator*, April 23, 1847.

14. "The Celestials at Home and Abroad," *Littell's Living Age* 34 (August 14, 1852): 289–91, 297–98.

15. P. L. Simmonds, "Sugar—Its Culture and Consumption in the World—No. 2," *DR* 19 (September 1855): 356; "Sugar Culture in Singapore," *DR* 5 (April 1848): 384–85; E. T. Freedley, *Opportunities for Industry and the Safe Investment of Capital; or, A Thousand Chances to Make Money* (Philadelphia: J. B. Lippincott and Co., 1859), 121–25; T. Robinson Warren, *Dust and Foam; or, Three Oceans and Two Continents* (New York: Charles Scribner, 1859), 364–65. On the Chinese in Peru, see Watt Stewart, *Chinese Bondage in Peru: A History of the Chinese Coolie in Peru, 1849–1874* (Durham: Duke University Press, 1951).

16. *NYT*, April 15, May 3, 15, June 14, December 10, 1852; J. Carlyle Sitterson, *Sugar Country: The Cane Sugar Industry in the South, 1753–1950* (Lexington: University of Kentucky Press, 1953), 13.

17. Jules Davids, ed., *American Diplomatic and Public Papers: The United States and China*, ser. 1, vol. 17, *The Treaty System and the Taiping Rebellion, 1842–1860: The Coolie Trade and Chinese Emigration* (Wilmington: Scholarly Resources, Inc., 1973), B13–B15; M. Foster Farley, "The Chinese Coolie Trade, 1845–1875," *Journal of Asian and African Studies* 3, nos. 3–4 (July and October 1968): 262; Humphrey Marshall to Secretary of State, March 8, 1853, 33rd Cong., 1st Sess., HED 123, 78–82.

18. John Kuo Wei Tchen, *New York before Chinatown: Orientalism and the Shaping of American Culture, 1776–1882* (Baltimore: Johns Hopkins University Press, 1999), 3–59.

19. Robert J. Schwendinger, *Ocean of Bitter Dreams: Maritime Relations between China and the United States, 1850–1915* (Tucson: Westernlore Press, 1988), 30–37; Irick, *Ch'ing Policy toward the Coolie Trade*, 32–34; Peter Parker to Secretary of State Daniel Webster, May 21, June 19, 1852, 34th Cong., 1st Sess., HED 105, 94–96, 108–10.

20. Schwendinger, *Ocean of Bitter Dreams*, 29–30; Ching-Hwang Yen, *Coolies and Mandarins: China's Protection of Overseas Chinese during the Late Ch'ing Period (1851–1911)* (Singapore: Singapore University Press, 1985), 41–52.

21. Peter Parker to Commodore [J. H.] Aulick, June 5, 1852; J. H. Aulick to [Peter] Parker, June 19, 1852; Peter Parker to Chinese Commissioners, June 22, 1852; Peter Parker to [Secretary of State Daniel] Webster, July 20, 1852; [Chinese Commissioners' Reports], July 9, August 1, 1852; Peter Parker to Seu and Pih, Commissioners, etc., July 12, August 10, 1852; 34th Cong., 1st Sess., HED 105, 121–22, 127–28, 130–36, 144, 148–49.

22. Schwendinger, *Ocean of Bitter Dreams*, 47–55, 60–61, 195; Wm. H. Robertson to Secretary of State William L. Marcy, August 6, 1855, 34th Cong., 1st Sess., SED 99, 3; Wm. H. Robertson to Secretary of State William L. Marcy, July 27, 1855, 34th Cong., 1st Sess., HED 105, 68.

23. T. Hart Hyatt to William L. Marcy, June 1, 1856 (including log excerpts), in Davids, *American Diplomatic and Public Papers*, ser. 1, 17:356–60; H. N. Palmer to Thomas R. Rootes, February 15, 1856 (including log excerpts), 34th Cong., 1st Sess., SED 99, 8–10; H. N. Palmer to Secretary of State W. L. Marcy, November 9, December 6, 1855, 34th Cong., 1st Sess., HED 105, 71–73.

24. Public Notification, January 10, 1856; Peter Parker to Messrs. Sampson and Tappan, September 8, 1856; Extract from a private letter by Peter Parker, April 6, 1856; Peter Parker to George R. Sampson, May 24, 1856; 35th Cong., 2d Sess., SED 22, 625–26, 773–74, 837–39, 1129–30.

25. Irick, *Ch'ing Policy toward the Coolie Trade*, 53; *Liberator*, April 18, 25, May 9, 16, 1856; Geo[rge] Francis Train, *An American Merchant in Europe, Asia, and Australia: A*

Series of Letters from Java, Singapore, China, Bengal, Egypt, the Holy Land, the Crimea and Its Battle Grounds, England, Melbourne, Sydney, Etc., Etc. (New York: G. P. Putnam and Co., 1857), 76–80, 147–48; *NYT*, April 21, 1856; 34th Cong., 1st Sess., HED 105, 1.

26. William B. Reed to H. Anthon Jr., December 4, 1857; William B. Reed to Secretary of State Lewis Cass, January 13, 1858; 36th Cong., 1st Sess., SED 30, 59–65, 68–69. The 1818 law is quoted in Lucy M. Cohen, *Chinese in the Post–Civil War South: A People without a History* (Baton Rouge: Louisiana State University Press, 1984), 37–38.

27. Public Notification, January 10, 1856, 35th Cong., 2d Sess., SED 22, 625–26; William B. Reed to Secretary of State Lewis Cass, January 13, 1858, 36th Cong., 1st Sess., SED 30, 59–65.

28. William B. Reed to E. Doty, February 15, 1858; Circular letter by S. Wells Williams, Secretary of the U.S. Legation, to U.S. Consuls, February 18, 1858; 36th Cong., 1st Sess., SED 30, 203–6.

29. *Harper's Weekly*, April 24, 1858; Lewis Cass to J. S. Black, April 28, 1858; Domestic Letters of the Department of State (NA Microfilm M40, roll 46); J. S. Black to Lewis Cass, March 11, 1859; Miscellaneous Letters of the Department of State (NA Microfilm M179, roll 168); General Records of the Department of State, RG 59, NA; William B. Reed to Lewis Cass, September 1, 1858, 36th Cong., 1st Sess., SED 30, 422–25.

30. Irick, *Ch'ing Policy toward the Coolie Trade*, 57–60, 67–104, 148–49; Yen, *Coolies and Mandarins*, 84–100.

31. Translations of declarations by Governor General Laú [*sic*] to O. H. Perry, January 2, 1860; Oliver H. Perry to John E. Ward, January 10, 1860; Governor General Laú to John E. Ward, January 8, 17, 1860; John E. Ward to Governor General Laú, January 12, 23, February 3, 1860; John E. Ward to Secretary of State Lewis Cass, January 24, 1860; 36th Cong., 1st Sess., HED 88, 2–3, 8–16, 19–24, 34–35; M. F. Farley, "John E. Ward and the Chinese Coolie Trade," *American Neptune* 20, no. 3 (July 1960): 209.

32. Governor General Laú to John E. Ward, January 30, February 5, 18, 1860; Minutes of an interview between Governor General Laú and U.S. officials, February 1, 1860; John E. Ward to Governor General Laú, February 3, 24, 1860; S. Wells Williams, Secretary of the U.S. Legation, to John E. Ward, February 7, 20, 1860; John E. Ward to Secretary of State Lewis Cass, February 24, 1860; 36th Cong., 1st Sess., HED 88, 29–37, 40–46, 48.

33. "Slaves and Slavery," *The United States Magazine, and Democratic Review* 19 (October 1846): 243–55; "Gov. Hammond's Letters on Slavery—No. 3," *DR* 8 (February 1850): 128–31; Josiah Priest, *Bible Defence of Slavery; and Origin, Fortunes, and History of the Negro Race*, 5th ed. (Glasgow, KY: Rev. W. S. Brown, 1852), 359–60.

34. "The West India Islands," *DR* 5 (May and June 1848): 455–500 (quotes from 487, 488, 492, 493; emphases in original).

35. "The Coolie Trade," *DR* 23 (July 1857): 30–35.

36. "Asiatic Free Colonists in Cuba," *DR* 24 (May 1858): 470–71; "The Coolie Trade; or, The Encomienda System of the Nineteenth Century," *DR* 27 (September 1859): 296–321.

37. "Editorial—Correspondence—Book Notices," *DR* 22 (June 1857): 663–64; J. J. Pettigrew, "Protest Against a Renewal of the Slave-Trade," *DR* 25 (August 1858): 166–85; William Beach Lawrence, *Visitation and Search; or, an Historical Sketch of the British Claim to Exercise a Maritime Police over the Vessels of All Nations, in Peace as Well as in War . . .* (Boston: Little Brown and Co., 1858), 133–69. Those calling for the ameliora-

tion—and against the abolition—of slavery also expressed a desire to reject the Caribbean model. See, e.g., E. J. Stearns, *Notes on "Uncle Tom's Cabin": Being a Logical Answer to Its Allegations and Inferences against Slavery as an Institution* (Philadelphia: Lippincott, Grambo and Co., 1853), 110–11, 287–88; Samuel Nott, *Slavery and the Remedy; or, Principles and Suggestions for a Remedial Code*, 5th ed. (New York: D. Appleton and Co., 1857), esp. 134. De Bow renounced the importation of "coolies" and "free Africans" but reserved the South's legal right to import the latter and remained noncommittal on reopening the African slave trade ("Editorial, Miscellanies, Book Notices, Etc.," *DR* 22 [May 1857]: 554–55; James Paisley Hendrix Jr., "The Efforts to Reopen the African Slave Trade in Louisiana," *Louisiana History* 10, no. 2 [Spring 1969]: 117).

38. D[aniel] Lee, "Agricultural Apprentices and Laborers," *Southern Cultivator* 12, no. 6 (June 1854): 169–70; "The Future of Cotton Culture in the Southern States, No. II," *Southern Cultivator* 16, no. 3 (March 1858): 90–92; "The Future of Cotton Culture in the Southern States," *Southern Cultivator* 16, no. 5 (May 1858): 137–39; "Laborers for the South," *Southern Cultivator* 16, no. 8 (August 1858): 233–36.

39. [George] Fitzhugh, "The Conservative Principle; or, Social Evils and Their Remedies: Part II—Slave Trade," *DR* 22 (May 1857): 449–50, 457; Edward Delony, "The South Demands More Negro Labor," *DR* 25 (November 1858): 491–506. Delony had chaired the committee that reported on a proposal to import African laborers into Louisiana.

40. Thomas L. Clingman, "Coolies—Cuba and Emancipation," *DR* 22 (April 1857): 414–19; "Monthly Record of Current Events," *Harper's New Monthly Magazine* 18 (March 1859): 543–44; "Continental Policy of the United States—The Acquisition of Cuba," *The United States' Democratic Review* 43 (April 1859): 29–30. On the antebellum movement for the annexation of Cuba, see Philip S. Foner, *A History of Cuba and Its Relations with the United States*, vol. 2, *1845–1895: From the Era of Annexationism to the Outbreak of the Second War for Independence* (New York: International Publishers, 1963), 9–124.

41. *Liberator*, May 23, 1856 (quoting *Concord Independent Democrat*); J. Smith Homans and J. Smith Homans Jr., *A Cyclopedia of Commerce and Commercial Navigation*, 2d ed. (New York: Harper and Brothers, 1859), 1726–29; "Present Growth and Future Supply of Cotton," *DR* 22 (February 1857): 197–201 (quoting *New York Herald*); "The Coffee Trade—Its Production and Consumption over the World," *DR* 23 (September 1857): 287; "The Southern Commercial Convention," *DR* 24 (May 1858): 466–67; "Late Southern Convention at Montgomery," *DR* 24 (June 1858): 582; "British Interference with Our Commerce," *United States' Democratic Review* 41 (June 1858): 465–67; "Our Foreign Gossip," *Harper's New Monthly Magazine* 17 (September 1858): 557–58; "Proposed International Committee on the Slave-Trade Treaties," *Littell's Living Age* 56 (March 20, 1858): 753–54; "Where Is the Mistake?" *Littell's Living Age* 58 (July 10, 1858): 113–14; Amelia M. Murray, *Letters from the United States, Cuba and Canada* (1856; reprint, New York: Negro Universities Press, 1969), esp. 175–76, 243–52, 279–80; Rev. Dr. Leyburn, "Cuban Life and Capabilities," *DR* 26 (March 1859): 347–49.

42. *Congressional Globe*, 36th Cong., 1st Sess., 1441, 1492, 1557, 1735; 36th Cong., 1st Sess., Journal of the House of Representatives, 736, 744; *NYT*, April 17, 1860. The *Liberator* acknowledged receipt of the report and published an excerpt on "the horrible coolie traffic" (May 11, 1860).

43. 36th Cong., 1st Sess., House Report 443, 1–5, 24.

44. *NYT*, April 21, 1860; John S. C. Abbott, *South and North: or, Impressions Received during a Trip to Cuba and the South* (1860; reprint, New York: Negro Universities Press, 1969), 47–52, 184, 352. A Creole newspaper in British Guiana, on the other hand, described indentured migration as "the enemy, instead of the auxiliary, of freedom" (Look Lai, *Indentured Labor, Caribbean Sugar*, 180).

45. J. Russell to Lord Lyons, July 11, September 10, 1860; Wm. Henry Trescot to W. Douglas Irvine, August 10, 1860; 36th Cong., 2d Sess., HED 7, 441–43, 446–48, 455–57; Andrew Gyory, *Closing the Gate: Race, Politics, and the Chinese Exclusion Act* (Chapel Hill: University of North Carolina Press, 1998), 213.

46. Foner, *A History of Cuba*, 2:121–22; L. E. Chittenden, *A Report of the Debates and Proceedings in the Secret Sessions of the Conference Convention, for Proposing Amendments to the Constitution of the United States, Held at Washington, D.C., in February, A.D. 1861* (New York: D. Appleton and Co., 1864), 268, 379.

47. 36th Cong., 2d Sess., Journal of the Senate, 373–87 (esp. 382, 386); "Monthly Record of Current Events," *Harper's New Monthly Magazine* 22 (April 1861): 689–90; *Journal of the Congress of the Confederate States of America, 1861–1865*, vol. 1 (Washington: Government Printing Office, 1904), 868.

48. 36th Cong., 1st Sess., HED 88, 1; 37th Cong., 1st Sess., Journal of the House of Representatives, 78; *Congressional Globe*, 37th Cong., 2d Sess., 16; 37th Cong., 2d Sess., HED 16, esp. 1, 3–16, 21–36.

49. *Congressional Globe*, 37th Cong., 2d Sess., 350–52. Burnett might have been referring to the Chinese laborers who worked in Kentucky in the 1850s, mostly at iron-refining factories (Cohen, *Chinese in the Post–Civil War South*, 16–19).

50. *Congressional Globe*, 37th Cong., 2d Sess., 555–56, 581–82, 593, 838, 849, 855, 911; *Harper's Weekly*, February 15, March 1, 1862.

51. The full text of the 1862 law is in Cohen, *Chinese in the Post–Civil War South*, 177–79.

52. *Congressional Globe*, 37th Cong., 2d Sess., 350.

53. The Page Law, named after Rep. Horace F. Page of California, also prohibited the entry of convicted felons. For the full text and a discussion of its passage, see George Anthony Peffer, *If They Don't Bring Their Women Here: Chinese Female Immigration before Exclusion* (Urbana: University of Illinois Press, 1999), 32–37, 115–17.

T W O : Envisioning Freedoms

1. Testimony of Wm. J. Minor before the Smith-Brady Commission, April 25, 1865, in Ira Berlin et al., eds., *Freedom: A Documentary History of Emancipation, 1861–1867*, ser. 1, vol. 3, *The Wartime Genesis of Free Labor: The Lower South* (Cambridge: Cambridge University Press, 1990), 599–607.

2. Ira Berlin, *Many Thousands Gone: The First Two Centuries of Slavery in North America* (Cambridge: Harvard University Press, 1998), 77–90, 193–214; Gwendolyn Midlo Hall, *Africans in Colonial Louisiana: The Development of Afro-Creole Culture in the Eighteenth Century* (Baton Rouge: Louisiana State University Press, 1992); Daniel H. Usner Jr., *Indians, Settlers, and Slaves in a Frontier Exchange Economy: The Lower Mississippi Valley before 1783* (Chapel Hill: University of North Carolina Press, 1992); David Barry Gaspar and David Patrick Geggus, introduction to *A Turbulent Time: The French Revolution and the Greater Caribbean*, ed. Gaspar and Geggus (Bloomington: Indiana University Press,

1997), viii; Sarah Paradise Russell, "Cultural Conflicts and Common Interests: The Making of the Sugar Planter Class in Louisiana, 1795–1853" (Ph.D. diss., University of Maryland, 2000), 19–46. On how sugar and slavery historically defined the Caribbean, see Franklin W. Knight, *The Caribbean: The Genesis of a Fragmented Nationalism*, 2d ed. (New York: Oxford University Press, 1990).

3. Peter Linebaugh and Marcus Rediker, *The Many-Headed Hydra: Sailors, Slaves, Commoners, and the Hidden History of the Revolutionary Atlantic* (Boston: Beacon Press, 2000), 4; Berlin, *Many Thousands Gone*, 326–29; Hall, *Africans in Colonial Louisiana*, 306–7, 317–48; David Patrick Geggus, "Slavery, War, and Revolution in the Greater Caribbean, 1789–1815," in *A Turbulent Time*, ed. Gaspar and Geggus, 1–50. On the Haitian Revolution, see C. L. R. James, *The Black Jacobins: Toussaint L'Ouverture and the San Domingo Revolution*, 2d rev. ed. (1938; reprint, New York: Vintage Books, 1989).

4. Hall, *Africans in Colonial Louisiana*, 344–74 (quotes from 357–58 and 371).

5. Hall, *Africans in Colonial Louisiana*, 378; Robert L. Paquette, "Revolutionary Saint Domingue in the Making of Territorial Louisiana," in *A Turbulent Time*, ed. Gaspar and Geggus, 204–20 (quotes from 209 and 214).

6. J. Carlyle Sitterson, *Sugar Country: The Cane Sugar Industry in the South, 1753–1950* (Lexington: University of Kentucky Press, 1953), 3–11; Richard J. Follett, "The Sugar Masters: Slavery, Economic Development, and Modernization on Louisiana Sugar Plantations, 1820–1860" (Ph.D. diss., Louisiana State University, 1997), 55–78; Franklin W. Knight, *Slave Society in Cuba during the Nineteenth Century* (Madison: University of Wisconsin Press, 1970), 12–13; Knight, *The Caribbean*, 212–13; Thomas Fiehrer, "Saint Domingue/Haiti: Louisiana's Caribbean Connection," *Louisiana History* 30, no. 4 (Fall 1989): 428–32; Paquette, "Revolutionary Saint Domingue," 211–14; Russell, "Cultural Conflicts and Common Interests," 52–55, 89–98. I have borrowed from Knight the term *sugar revolution*, which captures the profound changes wrought by the advent of export-oriented, monocultural plantation agriculture.

7. Russell, "Cultural Conflicts and Common Interests," 70, 94–95 (governor's quote), 106–241; Sitterson, *Sugar Country*, 30. Walter Johnson explores the complex, brutal nature of the New Orleans slave market in *Soul by Soul: Life Inside the Antebellum Slave Market* (Cambridge: Harvard University Press, 1999).

8. Sidney W. Mintz, *Sweetness and Power: The Place of Sugar in Modern History* (New York: Penguin Books, 1985), 50–51; Michael Tadman, *Speculators and Slaves: Masters, Traders, and Slaves in the Old South* (Madison: University of Wisconsin Press, 1989), 22–25, 64–70 (quotes from 66, 67); Follett, "The Sugar Masters," 278–314; Ann Patton Malone, *Sweet Chariot: Slave Family and Household Structure in Nineteenth-Century Louisiana* (Chapel Hill: University of North Carolina Press, 1992), 54–55, 138–65.

9. WPA Ex-Slave Interview with Ceceil George, LSL. George's interview also appears in Ronnie W. Clayton, ed., *Mother Wit: The Ex-Slave Narratives of the Louisiana Writers' Project* (New York: Peter Lang, 1990), 83–84.

10. B. W. Higman, *Slave Populations of the British Caribbean, 1807–1834* (Baltimore: Johns Hopkins University Press, 1984), 58–64, 72–85, 115–21; Knight, *Slave Society in Cuba*, 47–58; Rebecca J. Scott, *Slave Emancipation in Cuba: The Transition to Free Labor, 1860–1899* (Princeton: Princeton University Press, 1985), 92–97.

11. Donald Wood, *Trinidad in Transition: The Years after Slavery* (London: Oxford University Press, 1968), 66–68; Walton Look Lai, *Indentured Labor, Caribbean Sugar:*

Chinese and Indian Migrants to the British West Indies, 1838–1918 (Baltimore: Johns Hopkins University Press, 1993), 14–16; Howell Cobb, Secretary of the Treasury, to F. H. Hatch, Collector of Customs, New Orleans, January 10, 1860, vol. 35:40; Letters Sent to the Customs Collectors at Baltimore, Boston, New Orleans, and Philadelphia ("I" Series), RG 56, NA; Tadman, *Speculators and Slaves;* Johnson, *Soul by Soul.*

12. S. F. Griffin to F. H. Hatch, Collector of Customs, New Orleans, February 18, 1859; F. H. Hatch to Howell Cobb, Secretary of the Treasury, February 18, April 14, 1859; Letters Received from the Customs Collectors at Large Ports ("I" Series) (NA Microfilm M174, roll 194); Howell Cobb to F. H. Hatch, April 26, 1859, vol. 8:433–34, Letters Sent to the Customs Collectors at Baltimore, Boston, New Orleans, and Philadelphia ("I" Series), RG 56, NA; Lucy M. Cohen, "Entry of Chinese to the Lower South from 1865 to 1870: Policy Dilemmas," *Southern Studies* 17, no. 1 (Spring 1978): 10–11; *Chinese in the Post–Civil War South: A People without a History* (Baton Rouge: Louisiana State University Press, 1984), 20.

13. Mintz, *Sweetness and Power*, 148–86. For a perceptive analysis of the contradictions arising from British Guiana's similarly dependent role within the world capitalist economy, see Walter Rodney, *A History of the Guyanese Working People, 1881–1905* (Baltimore: Johns Hopkins University Press, 1981), 1–30.

14. Sitterson, *Sugar Country*, 23–30, 157–84; Joseph George Tregle Jr., "Louisiana and the Tariff, 1816–1846," *Louisiana Historical Quarterly* 25, no. 1 (January 1942): 24–148; John Alfred Heitmann, *The Modernization of the Louisiana Sugar Industry, 1830–1910* (Baton Rouge: Louisiana State University Press, 1987), 57–59.

15. Russell, "Cultural Conflicts and Common Interests," 105–260; Follett, "The Sugar Masters," 81–114; John C. Rodrigue, *Reconstruction in the Cane Fields: From Slavery to Free Labor in Louisiana's Sugar Parishes, 1862–1880* (Baton Rouge: Louisiana State University Press, 2001), 11–12, 20–31; Joseph Karl Menn, *The Large Slaveholders of Louisiana—1860* (New Orleans: Pelican Publishing Co., 1964), 23–31, 112.

16. Walter Prichard, "The Effects of the Civil War on the Louisiana Sugar Industry," *Journal of Southern History* 5, no. 3 (August 1939): 317, 322; for slightly different estimates, see Sitterson, *Sugar Country*, 226.

17. Pre. Soniat to General, December 20, 1862, in Ira Berlin et al., eds., *Freedom: A Documentary History of Emancipation, 1861–1867*, ser. 1, vol. 1, *The Destruction of Slavery* (Cambridge: Cambridge University Press, 1985), 231.

18. Clayton, *Mother Wit*, 106; Barnes Fletcher Lathrop, "The Pugh Plantations, 1860–1865: A Study in the Life of Louisiana" (Ph.D. diss., University of Texas, 1945), 83–84 (planter quote); Charles P. Roland, *Louisiana Sugar Plantations during the American Civil War* (Leiden: E. J. Brill, 1957), 32–34; N. P. S. Hamilton to C. L. Mathews, April 16, 1861, Charles L. Mathews and Family Papers, LSU.

19. W. E. B. Du Bois, *Black Reconstruction in America* (1935; reprint, New York: Atheneum, 1992), 55–83; Testimony of Corporal Octave Johnson before the American Freedmen's Inquiry Commission, February 1864 [date conjectured by the editors], in Berlin et al., *Freedom*, ser. 1, 1:217; Diary entries for June 14, 16, 1862, John A. Dougherty Papers, LSU.

20. Ambert [O. Remington] to "Dear Mother," November 15, 27, 1862, Ambert [O. Remington] to "Dear Father," November 26, 1862, Ambert O. Remington Letters, Tulane; G. L. Fuselier to Henri Roman, September 18, 1862; Célina [Roman] to [Henri Roman], December 29, 1862, January 7, February 25, 1863; Roman Family Papers,

Tulane. My quotations are from the typescript English translations of the original letters in French.

21. Quoted in John D. Winters, *The Civil War in Louisiana* (Baton Rouge: Louisiana State University Press, 1963), 158.

22. Mary [W. Pugh] to [Richard L. Pugh], November 9, 1862, Pugh-Williams-Mayes Papers, LSU.

23. "Dark days[:] A woman['] s record," Josephine N. Pugh Civil War Account, LSU. Drew Gilpin Faust, *Mothers of Invention: Women of the Slaveholding South in the American Civil War* (Chapel Hill: University of North Carolina Press, 1996) discusses the wartime experiences of women among the planter elite.

24. [Ralph Keeler and A. R. Waud], "The 'Heathen Chinee' in the South," *Every Saturday*, July 29, 1871; *Mobile Daily Register*, September 19, 1871 (quoting *New York Journal of Commerce*); Cohen, *Chinese in the Post–Civil War South*, 95–96; excerpts from proceedings of a military commission in the case of George Windberry et al., November 21, 24, 1862, in Berlin et al., *Freedom*, ser. 1, 3:389–93; *NYT*, October 26, 1862; Leon F. Litwack, *Been in the Storm So Long: The Aftermath of Slavery* (New York: Alfred A. Knopf, 1979), 145–46. The *Franklin Planters' Banner* (April 13, 1870) reported the postbellum sale price as $180,000; the 1860 census had valued H. C. Millaudon's real property at $500,000 and personal property at $400,000 (Menn, *The Large Slaveholders of Louisiana*, 257). Chinese laborers' experiences on Millaudon are discussed in later chapters.

25. Peyton McCrary, *Abraham Lincoln and Reconstruction: The Louisiana Experiment* (Princeton: Princeton University Press, 1978), 113–14; Brig. Gen. C. Grover to the Asst. Adjt. Gen., December 29, 1862, in Berlin et al., *Freedom*, ser. 1, 3:400–401; E. E. Mc[Collam] to Andrew [McCollam, Jr.], March 26, 1863, Andrew McCollam Papers, UNC; undated manuscripts in Rosella Kenner Brent Papers and Rosella Kenner Brent Recollections, LSU.

26. [Mary C. Moore] to [John Moore], August 2, 1863, David Weeks and Family Papers, LSU; Clayton, ed., *Mother Wit*, 38, 205–6.

27. John H. Ransdell to [Thomas O. Moore], May 24, June 3, 6, 12, 1863, John H. Ransdell Papers, HNOC.

28. McCrary, *Abraham Lincoln and Reconstruction*, 44–46, 57–65; Ted Tunnell, *Crucible of Reconstruction: War, Radicalism and Race in Louisiana, 1862–1877* (Baton Rouge: Louisiana State University Press, 1984), 10–17.

29. William F. Messner, *Freedmen and the Ideology of Free Labor: Louisiana, 1862–1865* (Lafayette: Center for Louisiana Studies, University of Southwestern Louisiana, 1978), 9–15; Proclamation of Brig. Gen. J. W. Phelps to the Loyal Citizens of the South-West, December 4, 1861 and Brig. Gen. J. W. Phelps to Capt. R. S. Davis, June 16, 1862, in Berlin et al., *Freedom*, ser. 1, 1:199–201, 210–16; Brig. Gen. J. W. Phelps to Captain R. S. Davis, July 30, 1862, in Ira Berlin et al., eds., *Freedom: A Documentary History of Emancipation, 1861–1867*, ser. 2, *The Black Military Experience* (Cambridge: Cambridge University Press, 1982), 62–63. Phelps, like many Republicans of his time, advocated the colonization of freed slaves in Africa to preserve the sanctity of American republicanism for the Anglo-Saxon race and to develop the "underdeveloped riches of Africa."

30. Eric Foner, *Free Soil, Free Labor, Free Men: The Ideology of the Republican Party before the Civil War* (London: Oxford University Press, 1970), 11–72, 266–80, 301–17; *Politics and Ideology in the Age of the Civil War* (New York: Oxford University Press, 1980), 100–103.

31. Maj. Gen. Benj. F. Butler to Hon. Edward [Edwin] M. Stanton, May 25, 1862, in Berlin et al., *Freedom*, ser. 1, 1:203–8.

32. LaWanda Cox, *Lincoln and Black Freedom: A Study in Presidential Leadership* (Columbia: University of South Carolina Press, 1981), 14–15; Messner, *Freedmen and the Ideology of Free Labor*, 15–26; McCrary, *Abraham Lincoln and Reconstruction*, 82–90; Winters, *The Civil War in Louisiana*, 34–35, 144–45.

33. Testimony of Maj. Gen. B. F. Butler before the American Freedmen's Inquiry Commission, May 1, 1863, in Berlin et al., *Freedom*, ser. 1, 3:440–47; ser. 2, 312–15.

34. William A. Green, *British Slave Emancipation: The Sugar Colonies and the Great Experiment, 1830–1865* (Oxford: Clarendon Press, 1976), 116–22.

35. Agreement in Berlin et al., *Freedom*, ser. 1, 3:383–85; Maj. Gen. Benj. F. Butler to Hon. Edwin M. Stanton, November 14, 1862, in Berlin et al., *Freedom*, ser. 1, 3:383; Messner, *Freedmen and the Ideology of Free Labor*, 36–39.

36. Maj. Gen. Benj. F. Butler to the President, November 28, 1862, in Berlin et al., *Freedom*, ser. 1, 3:394–97; Stanley, *From Bondage to Contract*, 1–59; Messner, *Freedmen and the Ideology of Free Labor*, 39–41.

37. *DR*, after the war ser., 2 (October 1866): 416; Prichard, "The Effects of the Civil War," 318–19; Joe Gray Taylor, *Louisiana Reconstructed, 1863–1877* (Baton Rouge: Louisiana State University Press, 1974), 8.

38. Messner, *Freedmen and the Ideology of Free Labor*, 42–53; General Orders No. 116, December 24, 1862, in Berlin et al., *Freedom*, ser. 1, 1:236–38.

39. General Orders No. 12, January 29, 1863, in Berlin et al., *Freedom*, ser. 1, 3:414–15; Circular, Headquarters, Department of the Gulf, Office of the Sequestration Commission, February 6, 1863 and enclosed contract, in Berlin et al., *Freedom*, ser. 1, 3:419–20; Louis S. Gerteis, *From Contraband to Freedman: Federal Policy toward Southern Blacks, 1861–1865* (Westport: Greenwood Press, 1973), 88–98, 105–6; Messner, *Freedmen and the Ideology of Free Labor*, 61–65; Lathrop, "The Pugh Plantations," 257–60; D. Tureaud et al. to Maj. Gen. N. P. Banks, February 1863 [date conjectured by the editors], in Berlin et al., *Freedom*, ser. 1, 3:421–23.

40. George H. Hepworth, *The Whip, Hoe, and Sword: or, The Gulf-Department in '63*, 2d ed. (Boston: Walker, Wise, and Co., 1864), 26, 31, 161–62; *National Anti-Slavery Standard*, April 25, May 2, 1863; Capt. John W. Ela to Brig. Gen. James Bowen, June 11, 1863, in Berlin et al., *Freedom*, ser. 1, 3:454–56; Rodrigue, *Reconstruction in the Cane Fields*, 42–43 (Minor quote).

41. *DR*, after the war ser., 2 (October 1866): 416; McCrary, *Abraham Lincoln and Reconstruction*, 153–55; Tunnell, *Crucible of Reconstruction*, 30, 35; General Orders No. 23, Headquarters, Department of the Gulf, February 3, 1864, in Berlin et al., *Freedom*, ser. 1, 3:512–17.

42. H. Styles, "Report Dick Robinsons Plantation," August 18, 1863, in Berlin et al., *Freedom*, ser. 1, 3:460; C. Peter Ripley, *Slaves and Freedmen in Civil War Louisiana* (Baton Rouge: Louisiana State University Press, 1976), 75–83; Paul K. Eiss, "A Share in the Land: Freedpeople and the Government of Labour in Southern Louisiana, 1862–65," *Slavery and Abolition* 19, no. 1 (April 1998): 46–89.

43. Rodrigue, *Reconstruction in the Cane Fields*, 47–48; Messner, *Freedmen and the Ideology of Free Labor*, 76; Lathrop, "The Pugh Plantations," 344 (quote).

44. General Orders No. 23, Headquarters Department of the Gulf, March 11, 1865, in Berlin et al., *Freedom*, ser. 1, 3:591–94.

45. A. McCollam to B. F. Flanders, November 15, 1864, in Berlin et al., *Freedom*, ser. 1, 3:554–56; Lathrop, "The Pugh Plantations," 408, 412–23; Rodrigue, *Reconstruction in the Cane Fields*, 52–53 (Pugh quote from 53).

46. Prichard, "The Effects of the Civil War," 317, 320–24, 330; *DR*, after the war ser., 2 (October 1866): 416.

47. Mède [L. A. Bringier] to Stel[la Bringier], August 20, 1865, Louis A. Bringier and Family Papers, LSU; John H. Brough to Lieut. L. O. Parker, September, n.d., 1867, vol. 263:82–85, Letters Sent, Agent and ASC, Donaldsonville, LA, BRFAL, RG 105, NA; Testimony of Tobias Gibson before the Smith-Brady Commission, April 25, 1865, in Berlin et al., *Freedom*, ser. 1, 3:607–11.

48. John Mei Liu, "Cultivating Cane: Asian Labor and the Hawaiian Sugar Plantation System within the Capitalist World Economy, 1835–1920" (Ph.D. diss., UCLA, 1985), 67–119; Gary Y. Okihiro, *Cane Fires: The Anti-Japanese Movement in Hawaii, 1865–1945* (Philadelphia: Temple University Press, 1991), 3–11. See also Sally Engle Merry, *Colonizing Hawai'i: The Cultural Power of Law* (Princeton: Princeton University Press, 2000).

49. Heitmann, *The Modernization of the Louisiana Sugar Industry*, 51–59; William T. Gay to Edward J. Gay, February 16, 1865, EJGP, LSU; *New Orleans Times*, January 7, 9, 1867.

50. Mintz, *Sweetness and Power*, 153, 175–76.

51. Lydia Maria Child, *The Right Way the Safe Way* (1860; reprint, New York: Arno Press, 1969), 82; James M. McPherson, "Was West Indian Emancipation a Success? The Abolitionist Argument during the American Civil War," *Caribbean Studies* 4, no. 2 (July 1964): 28–34; Eric Foner, *Nothing but Freedom: Emancipation and Its Legacy* (Baton Rouge: Louisiana State University Press, 1983), 40–43. Child's pamphlet curiously did not address Asian migrants.

52. William G. Sewell, *The Ordeal of Free Labor in the British West Indies*, 2d ed. (1861; reprint, New York: Augustus M. Kelley, 1968), v, 27; McPherson, "Was West Indian Emancipation a Success?" 29–30, 32–33; "Literary Notices," *Harper's New Monthly Magazine* 22 (April 1861): 692–93. *Harper's* devoted about half of its review to "coolie immigration."

53. Sewell, *The Ordeal of Free Labor*, 105–8, 122, 132, 227, 297.

54. Sewell, *The Ordeal of Free Labor*, 290, 253, 183, 127, 134. Sewell at times included the Chinese in the "coolie" category but mostly drew sharp distinctions between "the Indian coolie" and "the Chinaman" (e.g., 126–27, 298).

55. Sewell, *The Ordeal of Free Labor*, 323, 134, 308, 253, 107. Sewell did not consider smaller islands with high population densities suitable for immigration schemes.

56. McPherson, "Was West Indian Emancipation a Success?" 31; Augustin Cochin, *The Results of Emancipation*, trans. Mary L. Booth (Boston: Walker, Wise, and Co., 1863), 221–27, 230. Unlike Sewell, Cochin insisted that immigration would lower wages through competition. I have borrowed the term *romantic racialism* from George M. Fredrickson, *The Black Image in the White Mind: The Debate on Afro-American Character and Destiny, 1817–1914* (New York: Harper and Row, 1971), 101–2.

57. Cochin, *The Results of Emancipation*, 225; "Abolitionism a Curse to the North and a Blessing to the South," *DR* 32 (March and April 1862): 295–96, 304; *The Debates of the Constitutional Convention of the State of Maryland, Assembled at the City of Annapolis, Wednesday, April 27, 1864*, vol. 1 (Annapolis: Richard P. Bayly, 1864), 626.

58. Thomas C. Holt, "'An Empire over the Mind': Emancipation, Race, and Ideology in the British West Indies and the American South," in *Region, Race, and Reconstruction: Essays in Honor of C. Vann Woodward*, ed. J. Morgan Kousser and James M. McPherson (New York: Oxford University Press, 1982), 303.

59. Edgar Holden, "A Chapter on the Coolie Trade," *Harper's New Monthly Magazine* 29 (June 1864): 1–5. Holden's narrative indicated that he had been a member of the crew that sailed from Macao in the late 1850s.

60. Holden, "A Chapter on the Coolie Trade," 5–7.

61. Holden, "A Chapter on the Coolie Trade," 7–10.

62. *NYT*, January 13, 1853; Dr. Wood, "Our Island Neighbors," *DR* 22 (March 1857): 290; Mrs. E. M. Wills Parker, *The Sandwich Islands as They Are, Not as They Should Be* (San Francisco: Burgess, Gilbert and Still, 1852), 17; Rufus Anderson, *The Hawaiian Islands: Their Progress and Condition under Missionary Labors*, 3d ed. (Boston: Gould and Lincoln, 1865), 246–48; "Miscellaneous Summary," *Scientific American*, new ser. 9 (October 3, 1863): 211.

63. "Southern Cotton—Competition of Algeria," *DR* 24 (March 1858): 199; *NYT*, January 26, 1861; "Cotton—Napoleon—Cobden," *Littell's Living Age* 68 (March 9, 1861): 625–26; "Cotton in Algeria," *Scientific American*, new ser. 5 (August 17, 1861): 101; "The Coolie Traffic," *Hunt's Merchants' Magazine and Commercial Review* 45, no. 3 (September 1861): 275; Anthony Trollope, *North America*, vol. 2 (Philadelphia: J. B. Lippincott, 1863), 67; "A Labor Market for Free Negroes," *Littell's Living Age* 74 (July 19, 1862): 135–36; *Harper's Weekly*, February 2, 1861, April 5, June 28, 1862, January 31, 1863; Rev. Wm. Ashmore, "The Chinese Coolie Trade," *Christian Review* 107 (April 1862): 221.

THREE: Demanding Coolies

1. Note by R. Semmes, n.d.; Extracts from the journal of Commander Semmes, May 24, 1861, to April 11, 1862; Lists of vessels captured and overhauled by the C.S.S. *Sumter*, 1861–62; R. Semmes to S. R. Mallory, November 9, 1861, in *Official Records of the Union and Confederate Navies in the War of the Rebellion*, ser. 1, vol. 1, *The Operations of the Cruisers, from January 19, 1861, to December 31, 1862* (Washington: Government Printing Office, 1894), 613, 691–95, 744–45, 635.

2. Extracts from the journal of Commander Semmes, May 24, 1861, to April 11, 1862, in *Official Records of the Union and Confederate Navies*, 709, 699, 720, 704, 706.

3. R. Semmes to S. R. Mallory, November 9, 1861; Extracts from the journal of Commander Semmes, May 24, 1861, to April 11, 1862; Raphael Semmes to J. W. Gefken, August 31, 1861; Raphael Semmes to R. F. Van Lansberge, August 31, 1861; in *Official Records of the Union and Confederate Navies*, 634, 706–7, 627, 635, 699, 703, 720.

4. Raphael Semmes, *Memoirs of Service Afloat during the War between the States* (1869; reprint, Baton Rouge: Louisiana State University Press, 1996), 201–2, 224, 225, 228, 184.

5. Chinese leaders in San Francisco, in response, defended the "poor Chinaman" against the charge of being "a free slave" (*NYT*, June 5, 1852; "The Chinese in California," *Littell's Living Age* 34 [July 3, 1852]: 32–34).

6. Eliza McHatton-Ripley, *From Flag to Flag: A Woman's Adventures and Experiences in the South during the War, in Mexico, and in Cuba* (New York: D. Appleton and Co., 1889), 125–33, 164.

7. *Galveston Daily News*, July 12, August 18, 1865; *New Orleans Bee*, July 19, November 21, 1865; *NODP*, September 19, 23, October 17, 1865; *Mobile Daily Advertiser and Register*, October 24, 1865; Lucy M. Cohen, *Chinese in the Post–Civil War South: A People without a History* (Baton Rouge: Louisiana State University Press, 1984), 46–47; "Entry of Chinese to the Lower South from 1865 to 1870: Policy Dilemmas," *Southern Studies* 17, no. 1 (Spring 1978): 12.

8. Ted Tunnell, *Crucible of Reconstruction: War, Radicalism and Race in Louisiana, 1862–1877* (Baton Rouge: Louisiana State University Press, 1984), 95–101; Joe Gray Taylor, *Louisiana Reconstructed, 1863–1877* (Baton Rouge: Louisiana State University Press, 1974), 58–62, 70–73, 98–103; Theodore Brantner Wilson, *The Black Codes of the South* (University, AL: University of Alabama Press, 1965), 77–80; Donald G. Nieman, *To Set the Law in Motion: The Freedmen's Bureau and the Legal Rights of Blacks, 1865–1868* (Millwood, NY: KTO Press, 1979), 86–88.

9. *New Orleans Times*, July 1, 1865; *Mobile Daily Advertiser and Register*, November 26, 1865; *Opelousas Courier*, December 9, 1865.

10. *NODP*, October 22, November 23, 1865, January 24, 1866; *New Orleans Bee*, November 21, 1865; *Opelousas Courier*, December 16, 23, 1865; Samuel Rainey to [Secretary of State], August 30, 1865; Wm. Hunter and Co. to [Commissioner of Immigration], December 30, 1865; F. Rimmoning [*sic*] and Co. to [Commissioner of Immigration], January 3, 5, 1866; Index to Letters Received, Records of the Office of the Commissioner of Immigration (Commissioner of Immigration), RG 59, NA.

11. H. N. Congar to Samuel Rainey, September 29, 1865, Letters Sent, Commissioner of Immigration, RG 59, NA; 39th Cong., 1st Sess., HED 66, 6.

12. Charlotte Erickson, *American Industry and the European Immigrant, 1860–1885* (Cambridge: Harvard University Press, 1957), 7–8, 13; E. Peshine Smith to F. Rimoning [*sic*] and Co. and to Messrs. Hunter and Co., March 8, 1866, Letters Sent, Commissioner of Immigration, RG 59, NA; Secretary of State William H. Seward to George A. Stewart, April 6, 1866, Domestic Letters of the Department of State (NA Microfilm M40, roll 61), RG 59, NA.

13. *NODP*, October 22, 1865, October 28, 1866; *Galveston Daily News*, October 28, 1865; *Opelousas Courier*, December 9, 1865, February 17, 1866; *DR*, after the war ser., 1 (February 1866): 224; A. Bretton, "West India Emancipation—Its Practical Workings," *DR*, after the war ser., 1 (June 1866): 595–609; "Coolies as a Substitute for Negroes," *DR*, after the war ser., 2 (August 1866): 215–17; "The Cultivation and Manufacture of Sugar," *DR*, after the war ser., 3 (April–May 1867): 460; "Sugar Trade and Prospects," *DR*, after the war ser., 4 (September 1867): 236–40; *Mobile Daily Advertiser and Register*, October 26, 1866; *WBRSP*, December 1, 1866; *New Orleans Crescent*, May 24, 1867; Whitelaw Reid, *After the War: A Tour of the Southern States, 1865–1866*, ed. C. Vann Woodward (1866; reprint, New York: Harper and Row, 1965), 417.

14. Gilles Vandal, *The New Orleans Riot of 1866: Anatomy of a Tragedy* (Lafayette: Center for Louisiana Studies, University of Southwestern Louisiana, 1983), 95–193; Tunnell, *Crucible of Reconstruction*, 101–7; Taylor, *Louisiana Reconstructed*, 103–13; William Edwards to Edward J. Gay, July 31, 1866, EJGP, LSU; Eric Foner, *Reconstruction: America's Unfinished Revolution, 1863–1877* (New York: Harper and Row, 1988), 239–80.

15. 39th Cong., 2d Sess., Journal of the House of Representatives, 169; 39th Cong., 2d Sess., Journal of the Senate, 103; *Congressional Globe*, 39th Cong., 2d Sess., 483;

William H. Seward, "Circular Relative to the Coolie Trade," January 17, 1867, Circulars of the Department of State, RG 59, NA.

16. Thos. Savage to William H. Seward, July 12, 1867, Despatches from U.S. Consuls in Havana, Cuba (NA Microfilm M899, roll 49), RG 59, NA. The name Wyckes also appeared as Wickes, Wicks, or Weeks.

17. William H. Seward to Thomas Savage, July 23, 1867, vol. 46:116–17, Consular Instructions, RG 59, NA; William H. Seward to H. McCulloch, Secretary of the Treasury, July 23, 1867, Domestic Letters of the Department of State (NA Microfilm M40, roll 63), RG 59, NA; Will[iam] H. Seward to Henry Stanbery, Attorney General, July 23, 1867; Letters Received, Department of State; Records of the Attorney General's Office, General Records of the Department of Justice, RG 60, NA.

18. John M. Binckley to Samuel H. Torrey, July 25, 1867; John M. Binckley to W.H. Seward, July 26, 1867; vol. 12:440–42; Letters Sent, General Letter Books, RG 60, NA; H. McCulloch to [William P. Kellogg], July 29, 1867, vol. 36:15, Letters Sent to the Customs Collectors at Baltimore, Boston, New Orleans, and Philadelphia ("I" Series), RG 56, NA; *Harper's Weekly*, August 10, 1867.

19. Sam H. Torrey to John M. Binckley, August 1, 2, December 27, 1867, Letters Received, Louisiana, RG 60, NA; Sam H. Torrey to S. A. Stockdale, August 26, 1867, Letters Received, U.S. Attorney, Records of Customhouses, New Orleans, Records of the United States Customs Service, RG 36, NA; *United States v. American Brig Wm. Robertson &c.*, vol. 4:38, Dockets; "Release Bond," August 12, 1867, vol. 2:146–47, Record of Case Papers and Appointments; General Records of the United States Circuit Court for the Eastern District of Louisiana, New Orleans Division; Records of the District Courts of the United States, RG 21; National Archives-Southwest Region, Fort Worth, Texas (NA-Southwest); *NODP*, August 14, 1867.

20. "Copy of Contract with Coolies" between "a native of China" and J. J. Wyckes, July 2, 1867, enclosed in Sam H. Torrey to John M. Binckley, August 2, 1867, Letters Received, Louisiana, RG 60, NA.

21. Sam H. Torrey to Edwd. Jordan, Solicitor of the Treasury, September 25, 1867 [with the following 2 enclosures]; Thos. Savage to United States Attorney for the Eastern District of Louisiana, September 10, 1867; W.M. Reed to Hugh McCullock [*sic*], September 21, 1867; Letters Received from U.S. District Attorneys, Marshals, and Clerks of Court; Records of the Solicitor of the Treasury, RG 206, NA; Sam H. Torrey to John M. Binckley, December 27, 1867, Letters Received, Louisiana, RG 60, NA; *United States v. American Brig Wm. Robertson &c.*, vol. 4:38, Dockets, General Records of the United States Circuit Court for the Eastern District of Louisiana, New Orleans Division, RG 21, NA–Southwest.

22. *WBRSP*, August 24, 1867; *New Orleans Bee*, October 23, 1867; *New Orleans Crescent*, October 26, 30, 1867; "Coolies," *DR*, after the war ser., 4 (July and August 1867): 151–52; "The Importation of Coolies," *DR*, after the war ser., 4 (October 1867): 363–64 (quoting *Nashville Union and Dispatch*); John M. Binckley to Samuel H. Torrey, December 16, 1867, vol. 12:617, Letters Sent, General Letter Books, RG 60, NA; Sam H. Torrey to John M. Binckley, December 27, 1867, enclosing D. Urban, U.S. Circuit Court Clerk and U.S. Commissioner, to S.H. Torrey, December 27, 1867, Letters Received, Louisiana, RG 60, NA.

23. Cohen, *Chinese in the Post–Civil War South*, 52–55, 150–51; *New Orleans Bee*, January 16, 1867; *New Orleans Times*, January 16, 1867; *Semi-Weekly Natchitoches Times*,

January 30, April 6, 10, 1867; *NODP*, March 1, 1867; *New Orleans Crescent*, March 30, June 14, 1867.

24. "Memorandum of Information received from Ed. T. Wyckes," enclosed in Sam H. Torrey to John M. Binckley, August 2, 1867, Letters Received, Louisiana, RG 60, NA; Thos. Savage to William H. Seward, August 23, 1867, Despatches from U.S. Consuls in Havana, Cuba (NA Microfilm M899, roll 49), RG 59, NA.

25. William H. Seward to Henry Stanbery, September 7, 1867, Letters Received, Department of State, RG 60, NA; H. McCulloch to William P. Kellogg, August 19, 1867, vol. 36:33, Letters Sent to the Customs Collectors at Baltimore, Boston, New Orleans, and Philadelphia ("I" Series), RG 56, NA; S. A. Stockdale to Hugh McCulloch, August 26, 30, 1867, Letters Received from the Customs Collectors at Large Ports ("I" Series) (NA Microfilm M174, roll 214), RG 56, NA; Sam H. Torrey to S. A. Stockdale, August 26, 1867, Letters Received, U.S. Attorney, RG 36, NA.

26. *NYT*, July 26, 1867.

27. *NYT*, April 7, July 26, 1867; *Harper's Weekly*, August 31, 1867.

28. *New Orleans Commercial Bulletin*, October 21, 31, 1867; *New Orleans Crescent*, October 30, 1867; *New Orleans Bee*, October 22, 23, 1867.

29. William Edwards and Co. to Edward J. Gay, September 12, 1867, EJGP, LSU; Joseph Karl Menn, *The Large Slaveholders of Louisiana—1860* (New Orleans: Pelican Publishing Co., 1964), 79, 99.

30. *NODP*, November 16, 1867; *New Orleans Bee*, November 16, 1867; Cohen, *Chinese in the Post–Civil War South*, 61–62.

31. A. C. Ellis to Capt. W. H. Sterling, January 31, February 10, 28, 1867; [A. C. Ellis] to [W. H. Sterling?], n.d.; Letters Sent, Agent and ASC, Napoleonville, LA, BRFAL, RG 105, NA; A. D. McCoy to A. C. Ellis, January 23, 1867; Wm. H. Sterling to A. C. Ellis, February 21, 1867; Letters Received, Agent and ASC, Napoleonville, LA, BRFAL, RG 105, NA; "Memorandum of Information received from Ed. T. Wyckes," enclosed in Sam H. Torrey to John M. Binckley, August 2, 1867, Letters Received, Louisiana, RG 60, NA; *L'Abeille de la Nouvelle Orléans* (quoting *La Sentinelle de Thibodaux*), June 5, 1867; *NODP* (quoting *Thibodaux Sentinel*), June 6, 1867. Torrey referred to Kittredge as "Dr. Goodrich."

32. *New Orleans Crescent*, July 12, 1867; *DR*, after the war ser., 4 (October 1867): 362–63; *NODP* (quoting *[Semi-Weekly] Natchitoches Times*), February 15, 1867; *Semi-Weekly Natchitoches Times*, April 10, 1867; *WBRSP* (quoting *[Semi-Weekly] Natchitoches Times*), May 4, 1867; Cohen, *Chinese in the Post–Civil War South*, 150–51.

33. *WBRSP* (quoting *[Semi-Weekly] Natchitoches Times*), October 19 1867; Cohen, *Chinese in the Post–Civil War South*, 151–52; Etta B. Peabody, "Effort of the South to Import Chinese Coolies, 1865–1870" (M.A. thesis, Baylor University, 1967), 17.

34. *WBRSP*, February 9, 1867; L. Bouchereau, *Statement of the Sugar and Rice Crops, Made in Louisiana, in 1868–69* (New Orleans: Young, Bright and Co., 1869), v, 49–51; *Franklin Planters' Banner*, December 28, 1867.

35. Andrew McCollam [Sr.] to Andrew and Edmund McCollam, March 20, 1867, Andrew McCollam Papers, UNC; P. O. Daigre to Edward J. Gay, March 24, April 15, 1867, EJGP, LSU.

36. Evelyn Hu-DeHart, "Chinese Coolie Labour in Cuba in the Nineteenth Century: Free Labour or Neo-slavery," *Slavery and Abolition* 14, no. 1 (April 1993): 69–76 (population figures from 71); Rebecca J. Scott, *Slave Emancipation in Cuba: The Transition*

to Free Labor, 1860–1899 (Princeton: Princeton University Press, 1985), 29, 35–38; "Memorandum of Information received from Ed. T. Wyckes" and "Copy of Contract with Coolies" between "a native of China" and J. J. Wyckes, July 2, 1867, enclosed in Sam H. Torrey to John M. Binckley, August 2, 1867, Letters Received, Louisiana, RG 60, NA; McHatton-Ripley, *From Flag to Flag*, 166.

37. McHatton-Ripley, *From Flag to Flag*, 170–75.

38. *New Orleans Crescent*, July 12, 1867; Scott, *Slave Emancipation in Cuba*, 99; Hu-DeHart, "Chinese Coolie Labour in Cuba in the Nineteenth Century," 77–78; Duvon Clough Corbitt, *A Study of the Chinese in Cuba, 1847–1947* (Wilmore, KY: Asbury College, 1971), 91.

39. Ada Ferrer, *Insurgent Cuba: Race, Nation, and Revolution, 1868–1898* (Chapel Hill: University of North Carolina Press, 1999), 15–42; Franklin W. Knight, *Slave Society in Cuba during the Nineteenth Century* (Madison: University of Wisconsin Press, 1970), 154–70; Scott, *Slave Emancipation in Cuba*, 45–62; Corbitt, *A Study of the Chinese in Cuba*, 21–22.

40. Scott, *Slave Emancipation in Cuba*, 63–89; Henry C. Hall to J. C. B. Davis, June 8, 16, August 30, 1871, and enclosures, Despatches from U.S. Consuls in Havana, Cuba (NA Microfilm M899, rolls 64 and 65), RG 59, NA; Denise Helly, introduction to *The Cuba Commission Report: A Hidden History of the Chinese in Cuba: The Original English-Language Text of 1876* (Baltimore: Johns Hopkins University Press, 1993), 23–24.

41. Henry C. Hall to J. C. B. Davis, September 14, 1871, and enclosures; Translation of the decree enclosed in A. T. A. Torbert to Wm. Hunter, January 26, 1872, Despatches from U.S. Consuls in Havana, Cuba (NA Microfilm M899, rolls 65 and 66), RG 59, NA; *The Cuba Commission Report*, 78, 127–28; Scott, *Slave Emancipation in Cuba*, 100–101; Hu-DeHart, "Chinese Coolie Labour in Cuba in the Nineteenth Century," 78.

42. Regulations dated September 14, 1872, and May 7, 1873, in *The Cuba Commission Report*, 141–56.

43. McHatton-Ripley, *From Flag to Flag*, 177; *The Cuba Commission Report*, 117.

44. Thos. Biddle to J. C. B. Davis, May 23, 1870; E. Peshine Smith, "Memorandum for Mr. Jasper Smith for Answer to Despatch, No. 125 of Consul General at Havana—Relating to Emigration of Coolies from Cuba to the United States," June 6, 1870; Despatches from U.S. Consuls in Havana, Cuba (NA Microfifilm M899, roll 58), RG 59, NA; J. C. B. Davis to Thomas Biddle, June 8, 1870, vol. 59:134–35, Consular Instructions, RG 59, NA. Discouraging news from Cuba and Washington notwithstanding, parties in New Orleans continued to promote "Chinamen" from Cuba to Louisiana under eight-year contracts as late as July 1871 (*NILSB*, July 13, 1871).

45. Bouchereau, *Statement of the Sugar and Rice Crops . . . 1868–69*, v, vii; Samuel Cranwill to Edward J. Gay, February 19, 1869, EJGP, LSU; *WBRSP*, September 4, 1869; Andrew McCollam Jr. to Edmund McCollam, March 7, 1869, Andrew McCollam Papers, UNC; H. S. Leverich to Messrs. Leverich and Co., February 24, March 3, 8, 1869, Leverich Papers, NYHS; Taylor, *Louisiana Reconstructed*, 343–46; James H. Dobie to Bvt. Lieut. Col. Lucius H. Warren, December 31, 1868, vol. 264:207–12, Letters Sent, Agent and ASC, Donaldsonville, LA, BRFAL, RG 105, NA.

46. See, e.g., Claude F. Oubre, *Forty Acres and a Mule: The Freedmen's Bureau and Black Land Ownership* (Baton Rouge: Louisiana State University Press, 1978); William S. McFeely, *Yankee Stepfather: General O. O. Howard and the Freedmen* (New Haven: Yale

University Press, 1968); Nieman, *To Set the Law in Motion;* Eric Foner, *Politics and Ideology in the Age of the Civil War* (New York: Oxford University Press, 1980), 100–102.

47. Charles E. Merrill to Lucius H. Warren, December 31, 1868, vol. 428:82–84, Letters Sent, Agent and ASC, Plaquemine, LA, BRFAL, RG 105, NA.

48. Taylor, *Louisiana Reconstructed,* 134–73; Tunnell, *Crucible of Reconstruction,* 111–35, 153–59; John C. Rodrigue, *Reconstruction in the Cane Fields: From Slavery to Free Labor in Louisiana's Sugar Parishes, 1862–1880* (Baton Rouge: Louisiana State University Press, 2001), 78–103; John H. Brough to Bvt. Lieut. Col. L. H. Warren, September 11, 1868, vol. 264:119–20, Letters Sent, Agent and ASC, Donaldsonville, LA, BRFAL, RG 105, NA; Allen W. Trelease, *White Terror: The Ku Klux Klan Conspiracy and Southern Reconstruction* (1971; reprint, Baton Rouge: Louisiana State University Press, 1995), 127–36; P. L. de Clouet's diary entry for November 3, 1868, Alexandre E. DeClouet and Family Papers, LSU.

49. *WBRSP,* January 9, 1869; Bouchereau, *Statement of the Sugar and Rice Crops . . . 1868–69,* viii.

50. Eric Hobsbawm, *The Age of Capital, 1848–1875* (New York: Vintage Books, 1975); Robert J. Schwendinger, *Ocean of Bitter Dreams: Maritime Relations between China and the United States, 1850–1915* (Tucson: Westernlore Press, 1988), 73; Heather Cox Richardson, *The Greatest Nation of the Earth: Republican Economic Policies during the Civil War* (Cambridge: Harvard University Press, 1997), 170–208; *Harper's Weekly,* May 30, 1868, May 29, 1869.

51. [Editors], "The Chinese Embassy—Its Value to the South," *DR,* after the war ser., 5 (August 1868): 769; "The Mississippi River," *DR,* after the war ser., 5 (May 1868): 471 (reprinted from *Putnam's Monthly Magazine*); Cohen, *Chinese in the Post–Civil War South,* 133; *NODP,* December 4, 1870.

52. Foner, *Reconstruction,* 412–25; *Memphis Daily Appeal,* July 13, 1869.

53. Ping Chiu, *Chinese Labor in California, 1850–1880: An Economic Study* (Madison: State Historical Society of Wisconsin, 1963), 40–47; Sucheng Chan, *Asian Americans: An Interpretive History* (Boston: Twayne Publishers, 1991), 28–31.

54. *NODP,* September 8, 12, 13, October 28, 1866; *Mobile Daily Advertiser and Register,* September 9, 1866; *New York Tribune,* September 12, 1866; *New Orleans Bee,* September 14, 1866; *DR,* after the war ser., 4 (July–August 1867): 160.

55. G. L. Hall to "My dear niece Libbie," December 28, 1870, David Weeks and Family Papers, LSU; Gunther Barth, *Bitter Strength: A History of the Chinese in the United States, 1850–1870* (Cambridge: Harvard University Press, 1964), 187; *NODP,* February 7, June 5, 1869. On how the Asian American subject erodes the geographical constructs West and East, see Gary Y. Okihiro, *Common Ground: Reimagining American History* (Princeton: Princeton University Press, 2001), 3–27.

56. *NODP,* June 8, July 16 (quoting *Franklin Planters' Banner*), 1869; *WBRSP,* June 19, 1869; *New Orleans Times,* July 3, 1869.

57. *WBRSP,* May 29, June 5, 12, 1869; Cohen, *Chinese in the Post–Civil War South,* 63–64; *Memphis Daily Appeal,* June 22, 27, July 11, 15, 1869. The movement to encourage immigration from Europe is discussed in chapter 5.

58. Trelease, *White Terror,* 3–46, 175–85; *Memphis Daily Appeal,* June 23, 24, 26, 27, 29, 30, July 1, 1869.

59. *Memphis Daily Appeal,* July 1, 1869.

60. *Memphis Daily Appeal,* July 14, 1869.

61. *Memphis Daily Appeal*, July 12, 15, 16, 1869. The allusion to "Lascars and Manillamen" most likely refers to the Filipino sailors who established small villages in southern Louisiana, possibly as early as the 1760s (Marina E. Espina, *Filipinos in Louisiana* [New Orleans: A. F. Laborde and Sons, 1988]).

62. *Memphis Daily Appeal*, July 15, 1869; *NODP*, July 27, 1869.

63. *Memphis Daily Appeal*, July 1, 14, 1869; *NYT*, July 21, 1869; Barth, *Bitter Strength*, 192–93; Cohen, *Chinese in the Post–Civil War South*, 69.

64. *Memphis Daily Appeal*, July 15, 1869; *WBRSP*, December 8, 1866.

65. *Memphis Daily Appeal*, July 15, 16, 1869.

66. *Memphis Daily Appeal*, July 16, 1869.

67. *Memphis Daily Appeal*, July 15, 16, 1869.

68. *Memphis Daily Appeal*, July 14, 15, 16, 1869. Louisiana's delegates evidently received financial assistance from the state government as well.

69. *Memphis Daily Appeal*, July 16, 1869.

70. *Memphis Daily Appeal*, July 16, 1869; Trelease, *White Terror*, 19–20; McFeely, *Yankee Stepfather*, 263–64; Cohen, *Chinese in the Post–Civil War South*, 68.

FOUR: Domesticating Labor

1. Frederick Douglass, "Composite Nation," in Philip S. Foner and Daniel Rosenberg, eds., *Racism, Dissent, and Asian Americans from 1850 to the Present: A Documentary History* (Westport: Greenwood Press, 1993), 215–31.

2. Call and Proceedings of the Colored National Labor Union Convention, in Philip S. Foner and Ronald Lewis, eds., *The Black Worker: A Documentary History from Colonial Times to the Present*, vol. 2, *The Black Worker during the Era of the National Labor Union* (Philadelphia: Temple University Press, 1978), 3, 36, 44–45, 54.

3. *NODP*, July 11, 13, 14, August 29, 1869; *New Orleans Times*, August 6, 10, September 5, 1869; *Franklin Planters' Banner*, August 11, 1869; *Memphis Daily Appeal*, July 16, 17, 18, 20, 22, 25, 1869; B. F. Nourse, "The Future Production of Cotton," *Hunt's Merchants' Magazine and Commercial Review* 61 (August 1869): 85–90; n.a., "The Coming Chinese," *Hunt's Merchants' Magazine and Commercial Review* 61 (August 1869): 123–26; n.a., "The Chinese Again," *Hunt's Merchants' Magazine and Commercial Review* 61 (September 1869): 214–17; *Opelousas Courier*, August 21, 1869; *WBRSP*, August 21, October 9, 1869.

4. *Harper's Weekly*, August 14, 1869; *New York Evening Post*, July 20, 1869; Etta B. Peabody, "Effort of the South to Import Chinese Coolies, 1865–1870" (M.A. thesis, Baylor University, 1967), 46–48.

5. R. B. Van Valkenburgh to William H. Seward, May 29, 1868, and enclosures; William H. Seward to Robert B. Van Valkenburgh, July 15, 1868; William H. Seward to President [Andrew Johnson], July 15, 1868; Andrew Johnson to the Congress of the United States, July 15, 1868; 40th Cong., 2d Sess., SED 80, 1–4; Noah Webster, Chauncey A. Goodrich, and Noah Porter, *An American Dictionary of the English Language* (Springfield: G. and C. Merriam, 1866), 291; Lyman Abbott, "Pictures of the Japanese," *Harper's New Monthly Magazine* 39 (August 1869): 305–22.

6. William Creevy to James F. Casey, June 26, 1869, in *NODP*, July 30, 1869; *New Orleans Times*, July 30, 1869; *Memphis Daily Appeal*, August 8, 1869; [James F. Casey] to Geo. S. Boutwell, June 25, 1869, Letters Sent to the Treasury Department, Records of Customhouses, New Orleans, RG 36, NA; Geo. S. Boutwell to [James F. Casey], July 23,

1869, vol. 37:112–13, Letters Sent to the Customs Collectors at Baltimore, Boston, New Orleans, and Philadelphia ("I" Series), RG 56, NA. The Burlingame Treaty (1868) legalized the "voluntary emigration" of U.S. citizens and Chinese subjects between the two countries "for the purpose of curiosity or trade or as permanent residents." At the same time, it prohibited the entry of contract laborers, criminals, and persons likely to become wards of the state (George Anthony Peffer, *If They Don't Bring Their Women Here: Chinese Female Immigration before Exclusion* [Urbana: University of Illinois Press, 1999], 8, 32).

7. Geo. S. Boutwell to [James F. Casey], July 23, 1869, vol. 37:112–13, Letters Sent to the Customs Collectors at Baltimore, Boston, New Orleans, and Philadelphia ("I" Series), RG 56, NA; *Memphis Daily Appeal*, July 14, August 8, 29 (quoting *New Orleans Times*), September 1 (quoting *Vicksburg Daily Times*), 1869; *New Orleans Times*, August 26, September 5 (quoting *Vicksburg [Daily] Times*), 1869.

8. Eric Foner, *Reconstruction: America's Unfinished Revolution, 1863–1877* (New York: Harper and Row, 1988), 445–48; Ellen Carol DuBois, "Outgrowing the Compact of the Fathers: Equal Rights, Woman Suffrage, and the United States Constitution, 1820–1878," *Journal of American History* 74, no. 3 (December 1987): 844–52; Alexander Saxton, *The Indispensable Enemy: Labor and the Anti-Chinese Movement in California* (Berkeley and Los Angeles: University of California Press, 1971), 67–105; Andrew Gyory, *Closing the Gate: Race, Politics, and the Chinese Exclusion Act* (Chapel Hill: University of North Carolina Press, 1998), 28–37; John Kuo Wei Tchen, *New York before Chinatown: Orientalism and the Shaping of American Culture, 1776–1882* (Baltimore: Johns Hopkins University Press, 1999), 167–95.

9. *National Anti-Slavery Standard*, July 17, 1869. Boutwell investigated possible violations of slave and coolie trade prohibitions in San Francisco after writing his letter on New Orleans (*NODP*, August 3, 1869).

10. *NYT*, July 21, 1869; *Memphis Daily Appeal* (quoting *New York Herald*), July 26, 1869.

11. *Memphis Daily Appeal*, July 14, 25, 29, 31, August 4, 5, 6, 8, 15, 28, 1869.

12. *NODP*, July 30, August 6, 1869; *New Orleans Times*, July 30, 1869.

13. *New Orleans Times*, August 6, 1869; *NODP*, July 7 (including a quote from the *Jeffersonian*), 28, 1869.

14. *Memphis Daily Appeal*, August 14, 18, 1869; A. P. Merrill, "Southern Labor," *DR*, after the war ser., 7 (July 1869): 586–92. On the 1790 law's origins, see Matthew Frye Jacobson, *Whiteness of a Different Color: European Immigrants and the Alchemy of Race* (Cambridge: Harvard University Press, 1998), 22–31.

15. Francis Newton Thorpe, ed., *The Federal and State Constitutions, Colonial Charters, and Other Organic Laws of the States, Territories, and Colonies Now or Heretofore Forming the United States of America* (Washington: Government Printing Office, 1909), 6:3593; *New Orleans Times*, September 29, 1869.

16. *Memphis Daily Appeal*, July 21, 27, August 1, 4, 5, 15, November 24, 28, 1869; Lucy M. Cohen, *Chinese in the Post–Civil War South: A People without a History* (Baton Rouge: Louisiana State University Press, 1984), 72.

17. *New Orleans Times*, October 3, 14, 1869; *NODP*, October 14, 1869.

18. *NYT*, July 26, 1867; *Memphis Daily Appeal*, July 15, 16, 1869; Clarke, Bayne, and Renshaw to John Williams, August 23, 1869, in *NODP*, August 29, 1869. The 1867 article identified the man simply as "Mr. Williams."

19. George W. Gift to [Ellen Shackelford Gift], January 12, 1870, George Washington Gift Papers, UNC; Editorial, *DR*, after the war ser., 7 (July 1869): 630; *NODP*, August 3, September 1, 1869; *WBRSP*, August 14, September 4, 1869; *Franklin Planters' Banner*, September 8 (quoting *Thibodaux Sentinel*), November 10, 1869.

20. *Memphis Daily Appeal*, July 20, 1869; George [W. Gift] to [Ellen Shackelford Gift], September 17, 1866, George Washington Gift Papers, UNC; George W. Gift to Editors *Southern Cultivator*, October 7, 1867, *Southern Cultivator* 25, no. 12 (December 1867): 374–75; George W. Gift to Editors *Southern Cultivator*, February 15, 1868, *Southern Cultivator* 26, no. 3 (March 1868): 93–94.

21. *Memphis Daily Appeal*, July 20, 23, 27, 1869; George W. Gift to [Ellen Shackelford Gift], July 24, 1869, January 12, 1870, George Washington Gift Papers, UNC; Cohen, *Chinese in the Post–Civil War South*, 74–75 (including last Gift quote); *NODP*, October 15, 1869.

22. George W. Gift to [Ellen Shackelford Gift], December 18, 1869, January 12, 1870, George Washington Gift Papers, UNC.

23. C. N. Goulding to Hamilton Fish, November 19, 1869, Despatches from U.S. Consuls in Hong Kong (NA Microfilm M108, roll 6), RG 59, NA.

24. J. C. B. Davis to C. N. Goulding, January 20, 1870, vol. 56:340–43; J. C. B. Davis to Thomas Biddle, June 8, 1870, vol. 59:134–35; Consular Instructions, RG 59, NA; Thos. Biddle to J. C. B. Davis, May 23, 1870; E. Peshine Smith, "Memorandum for Mr. Jasper Smith for Answer to Despatch, No. 125 of Consul General at Havana—Relating to Emigration of Coolies from Cuba to the United States," June 6, 1870; Despatches from U.S. Consuls in Havana, Cuba (NA Microfilm M899, roll 58), RG 59, NA.

25. C. N. Goulding to Hamilton Fish, February 9, 1870, Despatches from U.S. Consuls in Hong Kong (NA Microfilm M108, roll 7), RG 59, NA; *New Orleans Republican*, July 29, 1870; Cohen, *Chinese in the Post–Civil War South*, 76–77; George W. Gift to [Ellen Shackelford Gift], January 12, February 11, 1870, George Washington Gift Papers, UNC.

26. *New Orleans Times*, June 3, 1870; Cohen, *Chinese in the Post–Civil War South*, 77–78; *Franklin Planters' Banner*, June 8, 1870. A medical examiner reported slightly different figures: 167 of the 187 adult males who had left Hong Kong arrived in New Orleans after a 110–day trip.

27. George [W. Gift] to [Ellen Shackelford Gift], June 4, 1870, George Washington Gift Papers, UNC; Cohen, *Chinese in the Post–Civil War South*, 76–77.

28. Geo[rge] W. Gift to [Ellen Shackelford Gift], February 11, 1870, George Washington Gift Papers, UNC; C. N. Goulding to Secretary of State Hamilton Fish, April 9, 1870, 41st Cong., 2d Sess., SED 116, 4; *NILSB*, November 24, 1870; *NODP*, October 8, 1870.

29. George W. Gift to [Ellen Shackelford Gift], January 12, February 11, June 4, 1870, George Washington Gift Papers, UNC; *NILSB*, November 24, 1870; *New Orleans Times*, June 3, 10, 1870; *NODP*, October 9, 1870.

30. Capt. Sam[ue]l W. Cozzens to Col. S. B. Holabird, May 15, 1863, in Ira Berlin et al., eds., *Freedom: A Documentary History of Emancipation, 1861–1867*, ser. 1, vol. 3, *The Wartime Genesis of Free Labor: The Lower South* (Cambridge: Cambridge University Press, 1990), 447–53; Geo. E. Payne to Charly [Leverich], December 8, 1865, Leverich Papers, NYHS; *NODP*, January 24, 1866; L. Bouchereau, *Statement of the Sugar and Rice Crops, Made in Louisiana, in 1868–69* (New Orleans: Young, Bright and Co., 1869), 17;

John C. Rodrigue, *Reconstruction in the Cane Fields: From Slavery to Free Labor in Louisiana's Sugar Parishes, 1862–1880* (Baton Rouge: Louisiana State University Press, 2001), 108–9.

31. Chs. E. Leverich to Messrs. Leverich and Co., New York, October 22, 1869; "Estate of James Porter to Leverich & Co., New York," January 3, 1871; Geo. E. Payne to Messrs. Leverich and Co., New York, July 4, November 11, 1870; Geo. E. Payne to [Ed Leverich], January 12, 1871; Leverich Papers, NYHS.

32. *NODP*, January 8, 10, 1871; H. S. Leverich to Messrs. Leverich and Co., January 9, February 15, 1869; Wm. E. Leverich to Messrs. Leverich and Co., January 18, 1871; H. S. L[everich] to Edward [Leverich], March 11, 18, 1871; Leverich and Co., New York, to Edward [Leverich], March 20, 1871; Leverich Papers, NYHS.

33. William Edwards and Co. to Edward J. Gay, September 12, 1867, EJGP, LSU; *Franklin Planters' Banner*, September 8, 1869; "Contract with Geo. E. Payne for Chinamen," February 4, 1871, James Amédée Gaudet Papers, UNC; H. S. L[everich] to Edward [Leverich], March 22, 1871; Geo. E. Payne to Ed Leverich, February 1, 5, 1871; Wm. E. Leverich to Messrs. Leverich and Co., May 31, 1871; Leverich Papers, NYHS; *NILSB*, June 8, July 6, 1871.

34. Wm. E. Leverich to Messrs. Leverich and Co., July 27, August 1, September 2, 27, October 2, 5, 1871; H. S. L[everich] to Edward [Leverich], May 10, August 4, 1871; Thos. J. Foster to Messrs. Leverich and Co., September 16, 29, 1871; Geo. E. Payne to Leverich and Co., November 16, 1871; Geo. E. Payne to [Edward Leverich], January 2, 21, February 27, 1872; Geo. E. Payne to A. A. Low and Brothers, February 8, 1872; Leverich Papers, NYHS.

35. *NILSB*, July 6, 1871; Persia Crawford Campbell, *Chinese Coolie Emigration to Countries within the British Empire* (London: P. S. King and Son, Ltd., 1923), 150–52; Cohen, *Chinese in the Post–Civil War South*, 114–15; Geo. E. Payne to [Edward Leverich], February 1, May 5, June 13, 1872, Leverich Papers, NYHS. Payne, who blamed Treasury Secretary Boutwell for denying his claims, would pursue his case for more than a decade.

36. Samuel Cranwill to Edward J. Gay, March 20, 1871, EJGP, LSU; *NILSB*, June 8, 1871; [Ralph Keeler and A. R. Waud], "The 'Heathen Chinee' in the South," *Every Saturday*, July 29, 1871; Cohen, *Chinese in the Post–Civil War South*, 114.

37. In reference to the British West Indies, see Walter Rodney, *A History of the Guyanese Working People, 1881–1905* (Baltimore: Johns Hopkins University Press, 1981), 151–60; Brinsley Samaroo, "Two Abolitions: African Slavery and East Indian Indentureship," in *India in the Caribbean*, ed. David Dabydeen and Brinsley Samaroo (London: Hansib Publishing, 1987), 25–41.

38. Leverich and Co., New York, to Edward [Leverich], March 20, 1871; Advertisement for the sale of Oaklawn and Dogberry (in *Chicago Times*), December 28, 1870; Wm. E. Leverich to Messrs. Leverich and Co., January 18, 28, 1871; H. S. [Leverich] to Edward [Leverich], March 20, 21, 1871; Annie Porter to Messrs. Leverich and Co., May 24, 1871; Thos. J. Foster to Messrs. Leverich and Co., September 16, 29, October 2, 1871; Leverich Papers, NYHS.

39. Thos. J. Foster to Messrs. Leverich and Co., May 22, August 1, 27, September 16, October 30, November 27, December 6, 1871; Wm. E. Leverich to Messrs. Leverich and Co., October 5, November 8, 21, 25, 1871; Sam'l Levy to Wm. E. Leverich, November 21, 1871; Leverich Papers, NYHS.

40. Gavin Wright, *Old South, New South: Revolutions in the Southern Economy since the Civil War* (1986; reprint, Baton Rouge: Louisiana State University Press, 1996), 3–80; Thos. J. Foster to Messrs. Leverich and Co., January 21, February 7, 1872, Leverich Papers, NYHS.

41. Michael Tadman, *Speculators and Slaves: Masters, Traders, and Slaves in the Old South* (Madison: University of Wisconsin Press, 1989), 5–7, 22–25, 57–70, 79–81; A. A. Taylor, "The Movement of Negroes from the East to the Gulf States from 1830 to 1850," *Journal of Negro History* 8, no. 4 (October 1923): 379; William Cohen, *At Freedom's Edge: Black Mobility and the Southern White Conquest for Racial Control, 1861–1915* (Baton Rouge: Louisiana State University Press, 1991), 44–77, 114 (Howard's quotes from 57, 58).

42. William S. McFeely, *Yankee Stepfather: General O. O. Howard and the Freedmen* (New Haven: Yale University Press, 1968), 215–16; *New Orleans Times*, October 20, 1866; *NODP*, October 28, 1866.

43. William H. Seward to Maj. Gen. O. O. Howard, October 3, 1866; Memorandum by A. P. Ketchum by order of Maj. Gen. O. O. Howard, October 9, 1866; Unregistered Letters Received, Agent, Donaldsonville, LA, BRFAL, RG 105, NA.

44. *New Orleans Bee*, December 4, 7, 1865; *WBRSP*, February 2, 1867; Andrew H. Gay to Edward J. Gay, February 1867, EJGP, LSU.

45. Roman Daigre to Edward J. Gay, December 19, 1867, January 15, 25, February 16, 1868; agreement between Edward J. Gay and Roman Daigre, January 16, 1868, EJGP, LSU.

46. Roman Daigre to Edward J. Gay, February 16, 18, 1868; Thos. S. Garrett to Edward J. Gay, February 19, 24, March 12, April 25, 1868, EJGP, LSU.

47. J. T. Rogers to Edward J. Gay, February 4, 1867; [Roman] Daigre to Edward J. Gay, February 1, 1867; N. G. Pierson to William Edwards and Co. (telegrams), February 7, 9, 1867; N. G. Pierson to Edward J. Gay, February 15, 1867; Andrew H. Gay to Edward J. Gay, March 7, 1867; U.S. Order for Transportation, March 1, 1867; Account with N. G. Pearson [*sic*] for February 2–March 24, 1867, as written on O. Lejeune to Edward J. Gay, March 16, 1867; William Edwards (and Co.) to Edward J. Gay, March 30, 1867, EJGP, LSU.

48. COSMOPOLITAN, "The Question of Labor," *Southern Cultivator* 26, no. 1 (January 1868): 12–13; H. C. Worsham to John Moore, March 18, 1867, David Weeks and Family Papers, LSU; Andrew H. Gay to Edward J. Gay, March 7, 1867, EJGP, LSU; V. F. Allain to [Sarah Turnbull Allain], January 23, 1869, Turnbull-Allain Family Papers, LSU; *Franklin Planters' Banner*, February 13 (quoting *Baton Rouge Advocate*), June 9, 1869.

49. *Franklin Planters' Banner*, March 27, July 21, 1869.

50. *WBRSP*, October 23, 1869 (including a reprinted article from the *New Orleans [Commercial] Bulletin*), January 22, 1870; *Franklin Planters' Banner*, December 22, 1869, January 19, 1870; "Virginia Laborers," *DR*, after the war ser., 7 (October 1869): 903 (quoting *Planters' Banner*).

51. L. Bouchereau, *Statement of the Sugar and Rice Crops, Made in Louisiana, in 1869–70* (New Orleans: Young, Bright and Co., 1870), v, ix–x; *WBRSP*, December 4, 1869, January 1, 1870; *Franklin Planters' Banner*, December 22, 29, 1869.

52. Diary entries for January 1–5, 10, 29, 30, 1870, and the employee list before the diary entries, Alexandre E. DeClouet and Family Papers, LSU; *WBRSP*, November 13,

1869; *Franklin Planters' Banner*, January 19, February 9 (quoting *Virginia Herald*), March 23, 30, 1870.

53. William T. Gay to Edward J. Gay, December 31, 1869, January 8, 14, 19, February 7, 1870; Joe Munn to Ed. J. Gay and Co., January 6, 1870; Lavinia Gay to [John H. Gay, Jr.], January 2, 1870; Thos. S. Garrett to Edward J. Gay, January 2, 1870; Roman Daigre to Edward J. Gay, January 3, 1870; W. F. J. Davis to Edward J. Gay, January 8, 1870; Samuel Cranwill to Edward J. Gay, January 11, 14, 25, 1870; Thos. S. Garrett to E. J. Gay and Co., January 24, 30, 1870; O. Robicheau to Edward J. Gay, January 26, 1870; Daigre and Garrett to E. J. Gay and Co., January 31, 1870, EJGP, LSU.

54. William T. Gay to Edward J. Gay, February 7 and n.d., 1870; T. S. Garrett to E. J. Gay and Co., January 30, 1870; S. Cranwill to Edward J. Gay, February 3, 5, 1870; Chas. H. Dickinson to Edward J. Gay, February 4, 1870; Thos. S. Garrett to Edward J. Gay, February 9, 14, 21, 1870; R. Daigre to Edward J. Gay, February 9, 1870, EJGP, LSU.

55. Thos. S. Garrett to Edward J. Gay, March 28, May 2 (note attached to a wage list), 8, 12, 25, 1870; William T. Gay to Edward J. Gay, February 7 and n.d., 1870, EJGP, LSU; Diary entries for February 8, March 8, 1870, and the employee list before the diary entries, Alexandre E. DeClouet and Family Papers, LSU; Entries for March 18, 20, 23, June 6, 7, 1870, Frank Webb Plantation Diary, UNC.

56. *New Orleans Times*, July 16, 1870; T. Gibson to McKinley [Gibson], August 25, 31, 1870, David Weeks and Family Papers, LSU.

57. *Congressional Globe*, 41st Cong., 2d Sess., 4268, 4266, 4275–79; Najia Aarim-Heriot, *Chinese Immigrants, African Americans, and Racial Anxiety in the United States, 1848–82* (Urbana: University of Illinois Press, 2003), 140.

58. *Congressional Globe*, 41st Cong., 2d Sess., 4271–75, 4282, 4368.

59. *Congressional Globe*, 41st Cong., 2d Sess., 4834–36, 5115, 5118, 4838, 5123.

60. *Congressional Globe*, 41st Cong., 2d Sess., 5121, 5122–23, 5124, 5161–62, 5175–77, 5154, 5159–60, 5166, 5172–73. Wilson, who had formerly collaborated with the Know-Nothing party and recently introduced a bill to outlaw the importation of Chinese contract laborers, was also likely hoping to attract white laborers' votes back home (Dale Baum, "Woman Suffrage and the 'Chinese Question': The Limits of Radical Republicanism in Massachusetts, 1865–1876," *New England Quarterly* 56, no. 1 [March 1983]: 74–76; Aarim-Heriot, *Chinese Immigrants, African Americans*, 130–31, 136–37, 145, 151).

61. *Congressional Globe*, 41st Cong., 2d Sess., 5121, 5123–25.

62. *Congressional Globe*, 41st Cong., 2d Sess., 5173, 5124–25, 5150, 5155, 5125, 5152. Stewart, indeed, had recently advocated the extension of equal legal protections to noncitizens in the United States, pointing to the Chinese in particular (Charles J. McClain, *In Search of Equality: The Chinese Struggle against Discrimination in Nineteenth-Century America* [Berkeley: University of California Press, 1994], 37–40; Gyory, *Closing the Gate*, 52–56).

63. *Congressional Globe*, 41st Cong., 2d Sess., 5164, 5168–69, 5172, 5176, 5151, 5125, 5152, 5173. Just a month earlier, Stewart had introduced a bill to prohibit "contracts for servile labor," with the Chinese in mind (*Harper's Weekly*, June 25, 1870).

64. *Congressional Globe*, 41st Cong., 2d Sess., 5163, 5158, 5151, 5155, 5162. On how the Chinese came to represent pernicious threats to nineteenth-century gender and sexual norms, see Robert G. Lee, *Orientals: Asian Americans in Popular Culture* (Philadelphia:

Temple University, 1999), 51–105; Nayan Shah, *Contagious Divides: Epidemics and Race in San Francisco's Chinatown* (Berkeley and Los Angeles: University of California Press, 2001), 77–104; and Karen J. Leong, "'A Distinct and Antagonistic Race': Constructions of Chinese Manhood in the Exclusionist Debates, 1869–1878," in *Across the Great Divide: Cultures of Manhood in the American West,* ed. Matthew Basso et al. (New York: Routledge, 2001), 131–48.

65. *Congressional Globe,* 41st Cong., 2d Sess., 5123, 5173, 5154–55, 5175.

66. *Congressional Globe,* 41st Cong., 2d Sess., 5160–61, 5154, 5164–65, 5168–69.

67. *Congressional Globe,* 41st Cong., 2d Sess., 5160, 5155–57. Williams was willing to modify his amendment to include Europeans born in the Chinese empire, as long as all Chinese were barred from naturalization (5158).

68. *Congressional Globe,* 41st Cong., 2d Sess., 5159, 5161–62, 5168, 5173, 5176–77.

69. *Congressional Globe,* 41st Cong., 2d Sess., 4277–78, 4276, 5157, 5162. On the antebellum meanings of "wage slavery," see David R. Roediger, *The Wages of Whiteness: Race and the Making of the American Working Class* (London: Verso, 1991), 65–87.

70. William Speer, *The Oldest and the Newest Empire: China and the United States* (Hartford: S. S. Scranton and Co., 1870), 473.

FIVE: Redeeming White Supremacy

1. Hinton Rowan Helper, *The Impending Crisis of the South: How to Meet It* (New York: Burdick Brothers, 1857), 299; *The Land of Gold: Reality Versus Fiction* (Baltimore: Henry Taylor, 1855), 96.

2. Excerpts from J. McKaye, "The Emancipated Slave face to face with his old Master: Valley of the Lower Mississippi," April 1864, in Ira Berlin et al., eds., *Freedom: A Documentary History of Emancipation, 1861–1867,* ser. 1, vol. 3, *The Wartime Genesis of Free Labor: The Lower South* (Cambridge: Cambridge University Press, 1990), 529–34; Roger W. Shugg, *Origins of Class Struggle in Louisiana: A Social History of White Farmers and Laborers during Slavery and after, 1840–1875* (Baton Rouge: Louisiana State University Press, 1939), 197–211 (quotes from 203, 205). For more information on Helper, see George M. Fredrickson, *The Arrogance of Race: Historical Perspectives on Slavery, Racism, and Social Inequality* (Middletown: Wesleyan University Press, 1988), 28–53.

3. Gavin Wright, *Old South, New South: Revolutions in the Southern Economy since the Civil War* (1986; reprint, Baton Rouge: Louisiana State University Press, 1996), 17–33; George H. Hepworth, *The Whip, Hoe, and Sword: or, The Gulf-Department in '63,* 2d ed. (Boston: Walker, Wise, and Co., 1864), 92; W. H. Ballard to [Lewis] Thompson, October 17, 1866, Lewis Thompson Papers, UNC; "The Sugar Interests of Louisiana," *DR,* after the war ser., 3 (March 1867): 308.

4. Jas. Flower to [Harriet Mathews], April 27, 1868, Charles L. Mathews and Family Papers, LSU; Wm. W. Pugh to Thos. B Pugh, January 8, 1872, Colonel W. W. Pugh and Family Papers, LSU; E. J. Gay Jr. to "Dear Cousin Will," November 25, 1872, EJGP, LSU; Nellie to Alex McCollam, December 30, 1872, Andrew McCollam Papers, UNC.

5. John C. Rodrigue, *Reconstruction in the Cane Fields: From Slavery to Free Labor in Louisiana's Sugar Parishes, 1862–1880* (Baton Rouge: Louisiana State University Press, 2001), 108–11; Joe Gray Taylor, *Louisiana Reconstructed, 1863–1877* (Baton Rouge: Louisiana State University Press, 1974), 366–67; Shugg, *Origins of Class Struggle in*

Louisiana, 234–73; William E. Highsmith, "Louisiana Landholding during War and Reconstruction." *Louisiana Historical Quarterly* 38, no. 1 (January 1955): 50–54.

6. *NODP,* February 12, 1870; *Memphis Daily Appeal,* February 23, 1870; *Franklin Planters' Banner,* May 4, 1870; John Alfred Heitmann, *The Modernization of the Louisiana Sugar Industry, 1830–1910* (Baton Rouge: Louisiana State University Press, 1987), 74.

7. Roulhac B. Toledano, "Louisiana's Golden Age: Valcour Aime in St. James Parish," *Louisiana History* 10, no. 3 (Summer 1969): 217, 223–24; S. Cranwill to Edward J. Gay, February 3, 1870, EJGP, LSU; J. Carlyle Sitterson, *Sugar Country: The Cane Sugar Industry in the South, 1753–1950* (Lexington: University of Kentucky Press, 1953), 291–94.

8. Entries for January 29, February 9, 1867, September 6, 1868, Isaac Erwin Diary (typescript), LSL; Edward J. Gay to [L. L. Butler], July 26, 1869; Wm. Edwards to Edward J. Gay, April 13, 29, 1868; Wm. Edwards to G. Bredow, July 24, 1868, EJGP, LSU.

9. Samuel Cranwill to Edward J. Gay, October 23, November 13, 14, 18, 1871; A. Ferry to Edward J. Gay, November 24, 1871, November 16, 1872, January 20, 1873, EJGP, LSU; Heitmann, *The Modernization of the Louisiana Sugar Industry,* 18–25, 33, 59.

10. Florent Fortier to Edward J. Gay and Co., January 6, 1873; E. J. Gay Jr. to Edward J. Gay, January 11, 1873; W. C. Murray to Edward J. Gay and Co., January 17, 1873; A. Ferry to Edward J. Gay, January 20, 23, December 27, 1873, January 23, 1874; Samuel Cranwill to Edward J. Gay, January 18, 19, 28, December 6, 9, 1873, January 26, 1874, EJGP, LSU.

11. A. Ferry to Edward J. Gay, March 31, September 12, 1872, December 9, 26, 1874; A. Ferry to Edward J. Gay and Co., May 4, 1872; Alfd. Roman to Edward J. Gay, July 7, 1872, EJGP, LSU.

12. Samuel Cranwill to Edward J. Gay, June 28, October 9, 1872, EJGP, LSU.

13. Mary A. Gay to "Dear Mother," October 29, 1870, Andrew Hynes Gay and Family Papers, LSU; Lavinia Gay to John H. Gay Jr., November 15, 1870; "White Labor Account," October 27, 1870, EJGP, LSU.

14. *WBRSP,* November 20, 1869; *Franklin Planters' Banner,* January 19, 1870; William T. Gay to Edward J. Gay, October 3, 1870, EJGP, LSU; 41st Cong., 2d Sess., Journal of the Senate, 1013; Hamilton Fish to President [U. S. Grant], July 14, 1870, 41st Cong., 2d Sess., SED 116, 1–2; Lucy M. Cohen, *Chinese in the Post–Civil War South: A People without a History* (Baton Rouge: Louisiana State University Press, 1984), 90–91.

15. John G. Walker to *New Orleans [Daily] Picayune, Memphis Daily Appeal,* February 20, 1870; *NODP,* January 8, 9, 1870; *Harper's Weekly,* January 22, 1870; *New Orleans Times,* April 28, July 16, August 5, 1870; Sitterson, *Sugar Country,* 238; *NILSB,* September 14, 1871.

16. *New Orleans Times,* July 8, 1870; T. J. S[haffer] to *Louisiana Sugar-Bowl,* June 14, 1871, in *NILSB,* July 6, 1871.

17. *NODP,* August 3, 8, 1869, January 8, 10, 1871; *New Orleans Times,* October 14, 1869, June 26, August 12, 1870, February 7, June 3, 28, October 10, December 18, 1871; *Memphis Daily Appeal,* September 2, 1869, July 29, 1870; *New Orleans Bee,* September 14, 1866; *NILSB,* June 1, October 19, November 16, 1871, May 23, 1872; Cohen, *Chinese in the Post–Civil War South,* 133–36.

18. L. Bouchereau, *Statement of the Sugar and Rice Crops Made in Louisiana, 1870–71* (New Orleans: Bronze Pen Steam Book and Job Office, 1871), vii; Samuel Cranwill to Edward J. Gay, June 21, August 25, 1870; L. L. Butler to Edward J. Gay, November 22, 1873, EJGP, LSU.

19. Joseph Karl Menn, *The Large Slaveholders of Louisiana—1860* (New Orleans: Pelican Publishing Co., 1964), 99, 114; Sitterson, *Sugar Country*, 45–47; *Donaldsonville Chief,* March 13, 1875 (quoting *New Orleans Times*); Agreement between J. Burnside and J. M. Hixson and Co., New Orleans, August 5, 1870, James Amédée Gaudet Papers, UNC.

20. [Ralph Keeler and A. R. Waud], "The 'Heathen Chinee' in the South," *Every Saturday*, July 29, 1871; *Mobile Daily Register*, September 19, 1871 (quoting *New York Journal of Commerce*); *New Orleans Times*, July 8, 1870. The number of Chinese laborers on Millaudon ranged up to 224 (*Springfield Daily Republican*, October 8, 1870) and their recruitment costs up to $12,000 (*New Iberia Planters' Banner*, September 20, 1871). At a minimum, Merrill and his partners paid $8,960 for the delivery of 140 workers.

21. Andrew H. Gay to Edward J. Gay, August 13, 1870; L. L. Butler to Edward J. Gay, August 14, 20, 1870; Samuel Cranwill to Edward J. Gay, September 3, 7, 9, 1870; A. Kissam to Edward J. Gay, September 8, 1870, EJGP, LSU.

22. L. L. Butler to Edward J. Gay, July 10, 17, 31, August 7, 10, 14, 1870; Edward J. Gay and Co. [Samuel Cranwill] to L. L. Butler, July 27 (and enclosed contract), 30, August 6, 1870; Samuel Cranwill to Edward J. Gay, July 22, 23, September 12, 1870; Jno. W. Austin to Edward J. Gay, September 4, 1870, EJGP, LSU.

23. Edward J. Gay and Co. [Samuel Cranwill] to L. L. Butler, September 9, 1870; William T. Gay to Edward J. Gay, September 15, 1870, EJGP, LSU.

· 24. William T. Gay to Edward J. Gay, September 18, 20, 21, 26, October 3, 1870, EJGP, LSU.

25. William T. Gay to Edward J. Gay, October 3, 6, 7, 1870; Samuel Cranwill to Edward J. Gay, September 29, 30, October 10, 1870; A. Kissam to [Samuel] Cranwill, September 29, 1870, EJGP, LSU.

26. L. L. Butler to Edward J. Gay, September 18, 1870; J. T. Nolan to Edward J. Gay, October 6, 10, 18, 1870, EJGP, LSU.

27. J. Blom to Edward J. Gay, April 11, November 5, December 14, 1869; Samuel Cranwill to Edward J. Gay, November 15, 1869, April 23, July 27, August 16, 1870; Lavinia Gay to John H. Gay Jr., November 26, 1869, January 25, May 9, 1870; L. L. Butler to Edward J. Gay, August 20, 1870, EJGP, LSU.

28. L. L. Butler to Edward J. Gay, October 10, 15, 19, 1870; Lavinia Gay to John H. Gay Jr., October 17, 1870; Samuel Cranwill to Edward J. Gay, October 19, 20, 1870; Memorandum by L. L. Butler, October 19, 1870; L. L. Butler to Messrs. Johnson and Peterson, October 19, 1870; "White Labor Account," October 27, 1870; Gay and Hanenkamp to Edward J. Gay, October 19, 1870; Lavinia Gay to Edward J. Gay, October 22, 1870; Settlement memorandum with agent Kroom [Croom] of Koopmanschap and Co., October 28, 1870, EJGP, LSU. All European laborers in excess of thirty-five were to cost Gay a five-dollar commission fee.

29. Agreement between Chinese laborers and Koopmanschap and Co. as agents of Edward J. Gay and William T. Gay, October 8, 1870, Iberville Parish District Court Records, Office of the Clerk of Court, Iberville Parish Courthouse, Plaquemine, LA; Settlement memorandum with agent Kroom [Croom] of Koopmanschap and Co., October 28, 1870; Samuel Cranwill to Edward J. Gay, October 31, 1870, EJGP, LSU. Cranwill and Croom, Koopmanschap's agent, became embroiled in a dispute over the amount actually advanced to the laborers in California and Gay's refusal to pay $65 for the "one man sickly delivered," which ended in a compromise. Cranwill ultimately gave Croom a check for $4,788.10 and paid a 0.5 percent premium of $23.94.

30. L. L. Butler to Edward J. Gay, October 15, 1870; Memorandum by L. L. Butler, October 19, 1870; "White Labor Account," October 27, 1870, EJGP, LSU.

31. Samuel Cranwill to Edward J. Gay, October 26, December 12, 1870; T. B. Stevens to E. J. Gay, November 27, 1870, EJGP, LSU; Cohen, *Chinese in the Post–Civil War South,* 125; *NILSB,* June 8, 1871; John C. Rodrigue, "Raising Cane: From Slavery to Free Labor in Louisiana's Sugar Parishes, 1862–1880" (Ph.D. diss., Emory University, 1993), 418.

32. *New Orleans Times,* June 27, 1865.

33. J. D. B. De Bow, "The Future of the South," *DR,* after the war ser., 1 (January 1866): 6–16; "Editorial Notes and Miscellanies," *DR,* after the war ser., 1 (February 1866): 224; "Coolies as a Substitute for Negroes," *DR,* after the war ser., 2 (August 1866): 215–17.

34. George M. Fredrickson, *The Black Image in the White Mind: The Debate on Afro-American Character and Destiny, 1817–1914* (New York: Harper and Row, 1971), 56–82; J. C. Nott, "Climates of the South in Their Relation to White Labor," *DR,* after the war ser., 1 (February 1866): 166–73; J. C. Nott, "The Problem of the Black Races," *DR,* after the war ser., 1 (March 1866): 266–83; Geo. Fitzhugh, "The Freedmen," *DR,* after the war ser., 2 (November 1866): 489–93; Geo. Fitzhugh, "Exodus from the South," *DR,* after the war ser., 3 (April–May 1867): 352–56.

35. [Editors], "Political Economy and Its Professors," *DR,* after the war ser., 5 (June 1868): 541; "Mechanical Aids to Labor," *DR,* after the war ser., 6 (June 1869): 505, 526; "The Cooley-ite Controversy," *DR,* after the war ser., 7 (August 1869): 716, 720.

36. [Editors], "The Cooley-ite Controversy," 710, 722, 724; William M. Burwell, "Science and the Mechanic Arts against Coolies," *DR,* after the war ser., 7 (July 1869): 560–62, 570–71.

37. *New Orleans Times,* October 3, 13, 14, 15, 17, 20, 1869; *WBRSP,* October 23, 1869; *Memphis Daily Appeal,* July 26, 1869. Despite some convergences, the two conventions represented different constituencies and objectives.

38. *Galveston Daily News,* August 1, 1866 (quoting *Richmond Enquirer*); *New Orleans Times,* October 20, 1866; *NODP,* October 22, 1865; *New Orleans Crescent,* July 12, 1867; *WBRSP,* November 7, 1868.

39. Editors, *Southern Cultivator* 27, no. 8 (August 1869): 239; "Selling Lands to Immigrants," *DR,* after the war ser., 4 (July and August 1867): 150–51 (quoting *NODP*).

40. *WBRSP,* January 27, December 1, 1866, January 16, 1869; *Franklin Planters' Banner,* May 26, 1869.

41. *WBRSP,* January 27, 1866, May 4, 25, 1867; *New Orleans Commercial Bulletin* (quoting *Franklin Planters' Banner*), January 16, 1867; *New Orleans Crescent,* July 12, 1867 (quoting *Franklin Planters' Banner*).

42. *Franklin Planters' Banner,* September 5, 1868, June 9, 1869; Taylor, *Louisiana Reconstructed,* 169. Andrew Johnson had appointed Dennett the collector of customs for the Teche District (*WBRSP,* December 14, 1867).

43. *WBRSP,* December 5, 1868, June 12, 1869; *Franklin Planters' Banner,* May 26, 1869.

44. *Franklin Planters' Banner,* June 23, July 21, September 8, 15, 1869; *NODP,* July 16, 1869 (quoting *Franklin Planters' Banner*).

45. *WBRSP,* July 17, October 30, 1869, January 15, 1870; *Franklin Planters' Banner,* July 21, 1869, February 22, 1871; "Gen. Lee on Chinese Immigration," *DR,* after the war ser., 8 (May–June 1870): 498–99.

46. *WBRSP*, July 17, November 20 (quoting *Franklin Planters' Banner*), 1869; *Franklin Planters' Banner*, January 19, April 13, 1870.

47. *Franklin Planters' Banner*, December 22, 1869, January 19, February 9, March 9, April 13, May 4, June 8, July 27, September 21, October 5, November 9, 16, 1870; *New Iberia Planters' Banner and Times*, April 5, 1871; *New Iberia Planters' Banner*, August 9, September 20, 1871. Dennett moved his paper to New Iberia in March 1871, merging it with that town's *Times* for a short period.

48. *New Orleans Times*, July 3, 1869; *Memphis Daily Appeal*, July 1, 1869; *NILSB*, April 27, June 8, 15, 1871.

49. Alexander Saxton, *The Rise and Fall of the White Republic: Class Politics and Mass Culture in Nineteenth-Century America* (London: Verso, 1990), 250; Heather Cox Richardson, *The Greatest Nation of the Earth: Republican Economic Policies during the Civil War* (Cambridge: Harvard University Press, 1997), 139–49, 160–68 (newspaper quote from 167); Charlotte Erickson, *American Industry and the European Immigrant, 1860–1885* (Cambridge: Harvard University Press, 1957), 3–31.

50. Governor of Louisiana to [Commissioner of Immigration], October 13, 1865; J. D. B. De Bow to [Commissioner of Immigration], October 4, 13, 16, 1865; Index to Letters Received, Commissioner of Immigration; RG 59, NA; Bert James Loewenberg, "Efforts of the South to Encourage Immigration, 1865–1900," *South Atlantic Quarterly* 33, no. 4 (October 1934): 369–72; Rowland T. Berthoff, "Southern Attitudes toward Immigration, 1865–1914," *Journal of Southern History* 17, no. 3 (August 1951): 336–38.

51. "An Act to Organize a Bureau of Immigration" in J. C. Kathman, *Information for Immigrants into the State of Louisiana* (New Orleans: Republican Office, 1868), iii; Saxton, *The Rise and Fall of the White Republic*, 256; E. P. Jacobson to H. F. Stickney, December 8, 1865, Letters Sent, Commissioner of Immigration, RG 59, NA.

52. 39th Cong., 1st Sess., HED 66, 6; *NYT*, March 22, 1867; *WBRSP*, May 4, 1867.

53. James O. Noyes, *Report of the Bureau of Immigration to the General Assembly of Louisiana* (New Orleans: A. L. Lee, State Printer, 1869), 28–29; E. Russ Williams Jr., "Louisiana's Public and Private Immigration Endeavors: 1866–1893," *Louisiana History* 15, no. 2 (Spring 1974): 156–58; *Franklin Planters' Banner*, May 4, 1870; *NODP*, June 6, 1869, February 15, 1870; *NILSB*, November 28, 1872.

54. Noyes, *Report of the Bureau of Immigration*, 5, 10–12, 18–19; Burwell, "Science and the Mechanic Arts against Coolies," 570; Cohen, *Chinese in the Post–Civil War South*, 63.

55. W. E. B. Du Bois, *Black Reconstruction in America* (1935; reprint, New York: Atheneum, 1992), 183. On the ideological crisis in the North which eventually manifested in the great railroad strikes of 1877, see Eric Foner, *Politics and Ideology in the Age of the Civil War* (New York: Oxford University Press, 1980), 125–27.

56. *New Orleans Crescent*, October 26, 1867; Kathman, *Information for Immigrants*, 28, 41–54; Noyes, *Report of the Bureau of Immigration*, 10; advertisement for Free Labor Exchange and Land Registry in, e.g., *New Orleans Times*, October 14, 1869.

57. "Sugar Trade and Prospects," *DR*, after the war ser., 4 (September 1867): 238 (excerpting *New Orleans Price-Current*); L. Bouchereau, *Statement of the Sugar and Rice Crops, Made in Louisiana, in 1869–70* (New Orleans: Young, Bright and Co., 1870), xi.

58. *Franklin Planters' Banner*, December 5, 1868, June 23, 1869, March 30, 1870 (quoting *New Orleans Times*); *New Iberia Planters' Banner and Times*, March 29, April 5, 1871; Daniel Dennett, *Louisiana as It Is* (New Orleans: Eureka Press, 1876), 119–20.

59. [Editors], "The Cooley-ite Controversy," 723; [Editors], "Editorial—The Labor Question," *DR*, after the war ser., 8 (April–May 1870): 420–23; *Franklin Planters' Banner*, November 10 (quoting *New Iberia Times*), December 29, 1869, February 9, 1870; Bouchereau, *Statement of the Sugar and Rice Crops . . . 1870–71*, xviii–xx; L. Bouchereau, *The Louisiana Sugar Report, 1871–72* (New Orleans: Pelican Book and Job Printing Office, 1872), ix; "Agency for Immigrants in New York," *DR*, after the war ser., 4 (December 1867): 579–80; P. Bonfort to Editor, *DR*, after the war ser., 5 (January 1868): 111.

60. *Franklin Planters' Banner*, December 29, 1869, November 16, 23, 1870, March 8, 1871; Geo. E. Payne to Messrs. Leverich and Co., New York, November 11, 1870, Leverich Papers, NYHS; *NODP*, January 5, 1870; *New Orleans Times*, February 7, 1871; *NILSB*, November 24, 1870, March 2, July 13, 1871.

61. E. J. Gay Jr. to Edward J. Gay, September 14, 16, 21, October 4, 23, 28, 1871; Samuel Cranwill to Edward J. Gay, December 14, 16, 1869, September 21, 1870, November 3, 1871; J. K. Skov and Co. to Edward J. Gay, October 2, 1871; P. A. Crow to Edward J. Gay, October 2, 1871; Labor Agreement, October 16, 1871; E. J. Gay Jr. to Edward J. Gay and Co., October 21, 1871; Gay and Hanenkamp to Edward J. Gay and Co., October 19, 1871; R. P. Hanenkamp to Edward J. Gay, October 20, 1871; S[ue] G[ay] B[utler] to John H. Gay Jr., November 2, 1871; C. C. Neally to Edward J. Gay, October 2, 1871; Chas. Roback to Andrew Gay, July 21, 1872; E. J. Gay Jr. to L. L. Butler, August 8, 1872; L. L. Butler to Edward J. Gay, October 18, 20, November 10, 1873, EJGP, LSU; Jean Ann Scarpaci, *Italian Immigrants in Louisiana's Sugar Parishes: Recruitment, Labor Conditions, and Community Relations, 1880–1910* (New York: Arno Press, 1980), 21; *New Orleans Times*, May 3, 1870, November 8, 1871; *Franklin Planters' Banner*, July 13, 1870; *NILSB*, March 2, April 13, September 28, 1871, July 17, 1873.

62. *Franklin Planters' Banner*, September 15, 1869, August 17, November 16, December 7, 1870, February 1, 1871; J. C. Delavigne, "The Labor Question," *DR*, after the war ser., 8 (February 1870): 169.

63. L. Bouchereau, *Statement of the Sugar and Rice Crops Made in Louisiana in 1873–74* (New Orleans: Pelican Book and Job Printing Office, 1874), x–xii; *NILSB*, April 6, 27, August 3, 10, 17, 1871, January 4, 1872, June 19, July 17, September 11, 18, 1873; D. F. Kenner to [J. L.] Brent, August 18, 1873, Duncan Kenner Materials and Ashland Materials, Hermitage Foundation Papers, HNOC. Portable mills reached their height of popularity in 1871 and declined precipitously afterwards (L. Bouchereau, *Statement of the Sugar and Rice Crops, Made in Louisiana, in 1868–69* [New Orleans: Young, Bright and Co., 1869], 53; *Statement . . . 1869–70*, 87; *Statement . . . 1870–71*, 66, 74; *The Louisiana Sugar Report, 1871–72*, 65, 73; *Statement of the Sugar and Rice Crops Made in Louisiana in 1872–73* [New Orleans: Pelican Book and Job Printing Office, 1873], 80).

64. Louisiana Immigration and Homestead Company, *Address to the People of Louisiana* (New Orleans: A. W. Hyatt, 1873), 1, 3, 6, 8–11; *NILSB*, February 27, June 12, July 3, September 11, October 30, 1873.

65. *NILSB*, December 18, 1873, January 15, May 14, July 30, October 1, 1874, July 22, 1875; William Ivy Hair, *Bourbonism and Agrarian Protest: Louisiana Politics, 1877–1900* (Baton Rouge: Louisiana State University Press, 1969), 67; Du Bois, *Black Reconstruction in America*, 241.

SIX: Resisting Coolies

1. *NILSB,* January 8, 1874; Gilbert A. Daigre to Edward J. Gay, January 11, 1874, EJGP, LSU; John C. Rodrigue, "'The Great Law of Demand and Supply': The Contest over Wages in Louisiana's Sugar Region, 1870–1880," *Agricultural History* 72, no. 2 (Spring 1998): 164–65; *Donaldsonville Chief,* January 3, 1874.

2. *NILSB* and *Le Sucrier de la Louisiane,* January 15, 1874; *Donaldsonville Chief,* January 17, 1874; *NODP,* January 10, 15, 20, 1874, in Philip S. Foner and Ronald Lewis, eds., *The Black Worker: A Documentary History from Colonial Times to the Present,* vol. 2, *The Black Worker during the Era of the National Labor Union* (Philadelphia: Temple University Press, 1978), 152–59.

3. *NODP,* January 14, 15, 16, 20, 21, 1874, in Foner and Lewis, *The Black Worker,* 2:153–60; *NILSB,* January 22, 29, February 5, 1874; *Donaldsonville Chief,* January 24, 1874; Joe Gray Taylor, *Louisiana Reconstructed, 1863–1877* (Baton Rouge: Louisiana State University Press, 1974), 177–78.

4. D. Caffery to "My dear Wife," June 9, 18, 1874, August 17, 1877, Letter File Book #3, 50–51, 63, Donelson Caffery and Family Papers, LSU; Taylor, *Louisiana Reconstructed,* 282.

5. *Donaldsonville Chief,* January 17, March 14, May 2, 1874.

6. Lucy M. Cohen, *Chinese in the Post–Civil War South: A People without a History* (Baton Rouge: Louisiana State University Press, 1984), 152; [Ralph Keeler and A. R. Waud], "The 'Heathen Chinee' in the South," *Every Saturday,* July 29, 1871; *Springfield Daily Republican,* September 14, 1871; *Mobile Daily Register,* September 19, 1871.

7. Dennett's report quoted in [Editors], "Mechanical Aids to Labor," *DR,* after the war ser., 6 (June 1869): 525; Rev. Edward Fontaine, "Missionary Labor on the Lower Coast of Louisiana among the Creoles, Negroes & Chinese," 2–4, 9, 14–15, Miscellaneous Manuscripts, NYHS. I am grateful to Mary Lui for bringing Fontaine's journal to my attention.

8. *NILSB,* November 24, 1870, June 8, August 31, 1871; D. A. Long to C. C. Gould, March 17, 1871, in *NILSB,* April 27, 1871; T. J. S[haffer] to *Louisiana Sugar-Bowl,* June 14, 1871, in *NILSB,* July 6, 1871; *Harper's Weekly,* August 26, 1871.

9. *New Orleans Republican,* July 24, 26, 1870; *New Orleans Times,* July 26, 1870.

10. *New Orleans Republican,* July 26, 1870; *New Orleans Times,* July 26, 1870.

11. [Keeler and Waud], "The 'Heathen Chinee' in the South," *Every Saturday,* July 29, 1871; *New Iberia Planters' Banner,* September 20, 1871.

12. *New Orleans Republican,* July 26, 1870; *New Orleans Times,* August 5, 1870, April 13, 1871; *NYT,* April 22, 1871.

13. *NILSB,* July 27, September 14, 1871; *NODP* (quoting *Thibodaux Sentinel*), September 28, 1871.

14. *NILSB,* August 31, October 5, 1871.

15. California's Supreme Court, for example, had prohibited the Chinese from testifying against whites in 1854 (Charles J. McClain, *In Search of Equality: The Chinese Struggle against Discrimination in Nineteenth-Century America* [Berkeley: University of California Press, 1994], 20–23).

16. *NILSB,* October 12, 1871; Cohen, *Chinese in the Post–Civil War South,* 112–13.

17. *NILSB,* July 13, 20, 1871.

18. L. L. Butler to Edward J. Gay, October 15, 19, 1870; Memorandum by L. L. Butler, October 19, 1870; Payrolls for "Front Place" and "Back Place," October 1870,

Manuscript vol. 81:68–73, EJGP, LSU; Agreement between Chinese laborers and Koopmanschap and Co. as agents of Edward J. Gay and William T. Gay, October 8, 1870, Iberville Parish District Court Records, Office of the Clerk of Court, Iberville Parish Courthouse, Plaquemine, LA; Gerald David Jaynes, *Branches without Roots: Genesis of the Black Working Class in the American South, 1862–1882* (New York: Oxford University Press, 1986), 228–36; John C. Rodrigue, *Reconstruction in the Cane Fields: From Slavery to Free Labor in Louisiana's Sugar Parishes, 1862–1880* (Baton Rouge: Louisiana State University Press, 2001), 90–91.

19. Lavinia Gay to John H. Gay Jr., November 15, 1870; Accounts and Wages with White Laborers, St. Louis Plantation, Manuscript vol. 81:110–11; Sue Gay [Butler] to John H. Gay Jr., December 4, 1870, EJGP, LSU.

20. Settlement memorandum with agent Kroom [Croom] of Koopmanschap and Co., October 28, 1870; Samuel Cranwill to Edward J. Gay, October 31, 1870; "Chineese [*sic*]-Settlement No. 1," Manuscript vol. 82:174–75, EJGP, LSU.

21. Agreement between Chinese laborers and Koopmanschap and Co., October 8, 1870, Iberville Parish Courthouse; "Chineese-Settlement No. 1," Manuscript vol. 82:174–75, EJGP, LSU.

22. Lavinia Gay to John H. Gay Jr., January 15, February 10, 1871; L. L. Butler to Edward J. Gay, January 19, 1871; "Chineese-Settlement No. 2," Manuscript vol. 82:177, EJGP, LSU.

23. Agreement between Chinese laborers and Koopmanschap and Co., October 8, 1870, Iberville Parish Courthouse; "Chineese-Settlement No. 2," "26 Day Settlements with Chinese," Manuscript vol. 82:177, 179–81, EJGP, LSU. Among the original twenty-six recruits was Ah Hook, who did not begin work until January 1871. His name ceased to appear after February 1.

24. "26 Day Settlements with Chinese," Manuscript vol. 82:180–81; William T. Gay to [Edward J. Gay], March 20, 21, 22, 1871, EJGP, LSU.

25. William T. Gay to [Edward J. Gay], March 22, April 19, May 1, 3, 8, 1871; "26 Day Settlements with Chinese," Manuscript vol. 82:180–81, EJGP, LSU; Agreement between Chinese laborers and Koopmanschap and Co., October 8, 1870, Iberville Parish Courthouse.

26. *Edward J. Gay v. Yu Kid* (Docket No. 188, Citation No. 1363); *Edward J. Gay v. Yook Chow* (Docket No. 190, Citation No. 1365); *Edward J. Gay v. Yu loong* (Docket No. 189, Citation No. 1364); *Edward J. Gay v. Lee Tai* (Docket No. 191, Citation No. 1366); *Edward J. Gay v. Yu wa hing* (Docket No. 192, Citation No. 1367); *Edward J. Gay v. Yu Sum* (Docket No. 193, Citation No. 1368); *Edward J. Gay v. Lee Gee* (Docket No. 194, Citation No. 1369); *Edward J. Gay v. Yu He* (Docket No. 195, Citation No. 1370); *Edward J. Gay v. Tam You* (Docket No. 196, Citation No. 1371); *Edward J. Gay v. Yu Choi* (Docket No. 197, Citation No. 1373); Iberville Parish Courthouse; "26 Day Settlements with Chinese," Manuscript vol. 82:180–81, EJGP, LSU.

27. "26 Day Settlements with Chinese," Manuscript vol. 82:180–81; William T. Gay to Edward J. Gay, May 20, 1871, EJGP, LSU.

28. *Mobile Daily Register* (quoting *New York Journal of Commerce*), September 19, 1871; [Keeler and Waud], "The 'Heathen Chinee' in the South," *Every Saturday*, July 29, 1871; *New Iberia Planters' Banner*, September 20, 1871. These figures are from *New Iberia Planters' Banner*, which differed slightly from the other reports.

29. *Mobile Daily Register* (quoting *New York Journal of Commerce*), September 19, 1871; [Keeler and Waud], "The 'Heathen Chinee' in the South," *Every Saturday*, July 29, 1871; *New Iberia Planters' Banner*, September 20, 1871; *NILSB*, August 29, 1872.

30. Cohen, *Chinese in the Post–Civil War South*, 89–91; A. B. Moore, "Railroad Building in Alabama during the Reconstruction Period," *Journal of Southern History* 1, no. 4 (November 1935): 427–31; *NODP*, December 10, 1870; Robert Somers, *The Southern States since the War, 1870–71* (1871; reprint, University: University of Alabama Press, 1965), 163–64.

31. "MORE ANON." to editors, in *Memphis Daily Appeal*, March 21, 1871; "HOWE." to editors, in *Memphis Daily Appeal*, March 29, 1871; *Mobile Daily Register*, June 16, 21, July 20, 21, September 19, 26, 1871; Cohen, *Chinese in the Post–Civil War South*, 93–95; Gunther Barth, *Bitter Strength: A History of the Chinese in the United States, 1850–1870* (Cambridge: Harvard University Press, 1964), 195. In May 1872, Koopmanschap filed for bankruptcy, a fitting denouement to his speculation in the New South.

32. John H. Brough to Lieut. G. A. H. Clements, December 21, 1867, vol. 263:168–69, Letters Sent, Agent and ASC, Donaldsonville, LA, BRFAL, RG 105, NA; *New Orleans Bee*, December 5, 1871; *New Orleans Times*, November 8, 1871.

33. Diary entry for January 3, 1868, Alexandre E. DeClouet and Family Papers, LSU; P. O. Daigre to Edward J. Gay, January 5, 1868, EJGP, LSU; Jno. M. Avery to Judge D. D. Avery, July 14, 1868, Avery Family Papers, UNC. On black migrant labor, see chapters 4 and 5.

34. Cohen, *Chinese in the Post–Civil War South*, 89; *New Orleans Times*, November 2, 1870; *Report of the State Registrar of Voters to the General Assembly of Louisiana* (New Orleans: n.p., 1876). The state census listed three racial categories: "White," "Colored," and "[American] Indian and Chinese." To put some perspective on these figures, New York state officials counted 157 Chinese residents in New York City in 1875, less than in Ascension Parish alone (Henry Tom, "Colonia Incognita: The Formation of Chinatown, New York City, 1850–1890" [M.A. thesis, University of Maryland, 1975], 61). Historian Louis Ferleger estimates 40,090 laborers in Louisiana's sugar parishes in 1870 ("Productivity Change in the Post-Bellum Louisiana Sugar Industry," in *Time Series Analysis: Proceedings of the International Conference Held at Houston, Texas, August 1980*, ed. O. D. Anderson and M. Ray Perryman [Amsterdam: North-Holland Publishing Company, 1981], 157).

35. *NILSB*, July 13, November 23, 1871; Samuel Cranwill to [Edward J. Gay], February 22, 1871, EJGP, LSU; "Statement of Disbursements for Blithewood by M. L. Randolph," June 20, 1871, John H. Randolph Papers, LSU; *Donaldsonville Chief*, February 24, 1872. Randolph reportedly hired twenty-five Chinese laborers, listed as "Importation of Chinese" in the statement. John Williams also secured forty laborers from Alabama.

36. *Mobile Daily Register* (quoting *New York Journal of Commerce*), September 19, 1871; Cohen, *Chinese in the Post–Civil War South*, 93–94; *New Orleans Times*, July 8, 1870; *NODP*, June 30, 1871; *New Iberia Planters' Banner*, September 20, 1871; *NILSB*, August 31, 1871. Kissam supplied many of the laborers from Alabama.

37. Samuel Cranwill to Edward J. Gay, n.d., 1871, EJGP, LSU. Kissam immediately offered these laborers to Edward Gay. Burnside's agreements with Hixson and Payne are discussed in chapters 4 and 5.

38. Agreement between twenty-nine "Chinamen" and one foreman and J. Burnside per Colton, October 10, 187[1], James Amédée Gaudet Papers, UNC; Thos. S. Garrett to Edward J. Gay, October 10, 20, 27, 1871; Roman Daigre to Edward J. Gay, November 26, 1871, EJGP, LSU.

39. D. W. McDonald to Jno. Burnside, January 30, 1872; W. M. McDonald to J. Burnside, March 21, 1872; Agreement between twenty-nine "Chinamen" and one foreman and J. Burnside per Colton, October 10, 187[1]; Agreement between A. Yune and J. Burnside per C. O. Colton, February 5, 1872, James Amédée Gaudet Papers, UNC.

40. Agreement with Richard Bard, November 8, 1872, James Amédée Gaudet Papers, UNC; Cohen, *Chinese in the Post–Civil War South*, 134–36; *New Orleans Bee*, November 5, 1871; *Donaldsonville Chief*, October 26, 1872.

41. Agreement between Too Jam and J. Burnside per Colton, September 7, 1872 [retroactive from July 1, 1872], James Amédée Gaudet Papers, UNC. Too Jam and his workers began working for Burnside in July but did not formalize a one-year contract until September. Burnside probably insisted on a written contract in preparation for the grinding season. Too Jam was paid $35 per month and his workers $26.

42. I. H. Van Antwerp to Bvt. Maj. B. T. Hutchins, October 10, 1868, vol. 472:129–31, Letters Sent, Agent and ASC, Thibodaux, LA, BRFAL, RG 105, NA; "Shem." to Editor, *Franklin Planters' Banner*, June 23, 1869; *Donaldsonville Chief*, January 13, 1872.

43. W. F. J. Davis to Edward J. Gay, May 6, 1869, EJGP, LSU; *Mobile Daily Register* (quoting *New York Journal of Commerce*), September 19, 1871.

44. George [W. Gift] to [Ellen Shackelford Gift], June 4, 1870, George Washington Gift Papers, UNC; *Memphis Daily Appeal*, July 17, 1869; *New Orleans Times*, August 6, 1869; *NILSB*, March 30 (quoting *Baton Rouge Advocate*), August 31, 1871.

45. *NYT*, October 28, 1867; *NILSB*, April 27, 1871.

46. *New Orleans Republican*, July 24, 1870; *New Iberia Planters' Banner*, September 20, 1871; [Keeler and Waud], "The 'Heathen Chinee' in the South," *Every Saturday*, July 29, 1871; *Mobile Daily Register* (quoting *New York Journal of Commerce*), September 19, 1871; *Donaldsonville Chief*, October 19, 1872. I borrow the phrase "splendid failure" from W. E. B. Du Bois, *Black Reconstruction in America* (1935; reprint, New York: Atheneum, 1992), 708.

47. *Donaldsonville Chief*, November 18, December 9, 16, 1871, May 18, 25, October 19, 1872, January 18, 1873, January 30, July 17, 24, 1875.

48. *NILSB*, June 8, 1871; T. J. S[haffer] to *Louisiana Sugar-Bowl*, June 14, 1871, in *NILSB*, July 6, 1871; [Keeler and Waud], "The 'Heathen Chinee' in the South," *Every Saturday*, July 29, 1871.

49. Walter Rodney, *A History of the Guyanese Working People, 1881–1905* (Baltimore: Johns Hopkins University Press, 1981), 42–59, 179; Evelyn Hu-DeHart, "Chinese Coolie Labour in Cuba in the Nineteenth Century: Free Labour or Neo-slavery?" *Slavery and Abolition* 14, no. 1 (April 1993): 76–78, 81; Rebecca J. Scott, "Defining the Boundaries of Freedom in the World of Cane: Cuba, Brazil, and Louisiana after Emancipation," *American Historical Review* 99, no. 1 (February 1994): 90, 96–99; William Cohen, *At Freedom's Edge: Black Mobility and the Southern White Conquest for Racial Control, 1861–1915* (Baton Rouge: Louisiana State University Press, 1991), 127–37; Rodrigue, *Reconstruction in the Cane Fields*, 124–31; *NILSB*, July 26, 1877.

50. Gavin Wright, "Postbellum Southern Labor Markets," in *Quantity and Quiddity: Essays in U.S. Economic History*, ed. Peter Kilby (Middletown: Wesleyan University Press,

1987), 98–134; Gavin Wright, *Old South, New South: Revolutions in the Southern Economy since the Civil War* (1986; reprint, Baton Rouge: Louisiana State University Press, 1996), 90–98; Ronnie W. Clayton, ed., *Mother Wit: The Ex-Slave Narratives of the Louisiana Writers' Project* (New York: Peter Lang, 1990), 173–74 (bracketed word added by Clayton); *Harper's Weekly*, October 30, 1875.

51. Unless noted otherwise, all information on the Tureaud plantations is based on the following sources from the Benjamin Tureaud Papers, LSU: "Wages Paid Labourers on Houmas Plantation 1871," Manuscript vol. 79:1–51 (Houmas and Brulé without distinction); "Wages Paid Labourers on Houmas Plantation," February 3, March 2 and 30, May 4, June 1 and 29, October 5, December 15, 1872 (Houmas and Brulé on distinct lists); "Time-Book of Benj. Tureaud and Co. Houmas Ption: commenced 1873," Manuscript vol. 82 (Houmas only, January 1873–July 1, 1876); "Wages Paid Laborers on Brulé up to Nov[ember] 30th, 1874"; "Wages Paid Laborers on Brulé," February 27, April 3, May 1, June 4, July 3 and 31, September 3, October 2 and 30, November 30, 1875, January 3, 1876; "Time-book of Benj. Tureaud and Co: Houmas Plantation Ascension La., Commenced July, 1876," Manuscript vol. 83 (Houmas only, July 8, 1876–May 4, 1878).

52. "26 Day Settlements with Chineese," Manuscript vol. 82:180–81; Ah. Lee to Edward J. Gay, June 8, 1872, EJGP, LSU; Rodrigue, "The Great Law of Demand and Supply," 173–74. Planters' payrolls generally did not record Chinese laborers' full names, often simply noting "Ah" (a common Cantonese diminutive form) and the person's first name. Because Ah Lee and two other individuals (Ah Loy and Ah How) appeared together on two separate plantations in adjoining parishes—Ah Lee played a leading role on Gay's plantation as well, receiving the payment of a discharged laborer—I inferred that the Tureauds and Gay employed the same Ah Lee. On December 24 the Tureauds paid Ah Lee a lump sum payment of $120, almost certainly his commission fees.

53. Because of lapses in the extant payrolls, the figure on Houmas and Brulé plantations represents only the minimum numbers of Chinese laborers at particular points in time (i.e., numbers from existing documents). The "0" for July and August 1872, for example, reflects the unavailability of records for those months rather than the actual number of Chinese on the plantations.

54. Ah Lee received $82 for "Bonus &c." and $10.20 later for the transport of workers ("Extra Expenses on Houmas," January 1872; "Wages Paid Labourers on Houmas," February 3, 1872, Benjamin Tureaud Papers, LSU).

55. The low transportation cost ($2.50 for seven laborers to Houmas) suggested that they had been recruited locally ("Wages Paid Labourers on Houmas," May 4, 1872, Benjamin Tureaud Papers, LSU).

56. Waybills from the steamer *Henry Tete*, January 8, 13, 1873, Benjamin Tureaud Papers, LSU. On work patterns in Louisiana's sugar parishes, see Rodrigue, *Reconstruction in the Cane Fields*, 124–26.

57. Thos. J. Foster to Messrs. Leverich and Co., February 7, March 2, May 15, June 8, July 21, August 27, 1872, August 20, 1873; Wm. E. Leverich to Messrs. Leverich and Co., May 30, June 11, August 12, 1873; Messrs. Leverich and Co., New York, account with Wm. E. Leverich, Agent New Orleans, September 1, 1873; Leverich Papers, NYHS; Eric Hobsbawm, *The Age of Capital, 1848–1875* (New York: Vintage Books, 1975), 46, 303–8. Foster continued to employ six "Chinamen" among a force of forty-five laborers on a neighboring plantation he also managed (*NILSB*, September 11, 1873).

58. C. D. Leverich to Messrs. Leverich and Co., New York, December 23, 1873, Leverich Papers, NYHS; "Rates on Houmas Plantn. 1874," Benjamin Tureaud Papers, LSU.

59. *Donaldsonville Chief*, January 17, 1874; Edward J. M. Rhoads, "Asian Pioneers in the Eastern United States: Chinese Cutlery Workers in Beaver Falls, Pennsylvania, in the 1870s," *Journal of Asian American Studies* 2, no. 2 (June 1999): 122–23, 132–33.

60. *Donaldsonville Chief*, March 14, May 2, 9, 1874.

61. Night watch lists from November 12, 1874 to January 5, 1875 (Benjamin Tureaud Papers, LSU) indicated the integration of these Chinese laborers into the grinding season routine.

62. Benjamin Tureaud Jr.'s time book listed a *P* next to these "day" laborers, whereas other laborers had twenty-six workdays counted on a rolling basis.

63. "Wages Paid Labourers on Houmas," April 3, May 8, June 19, 1875, Benjamin Tureaud Papers, LSU.

64. Waybills for steamer *Wm. S. Pike*, January 20, 27, 31, 1875; Benjamin Tureaud to Benjamin Tureaud Jr., August 28, 1875; D. F. Kenner to Ben Tureaud Jr., July 16, 1875; Alf. Lindsy to [J. Ephege] Leblanc [*sic*], September 15, 1875; Waybills for steamer *Wm. S. Pike*, April 19, October 10, 17, 18, 21, 24, 25, 27, November 7, 1875; P. O. Daigre to Ben Tureau[d] Jr., May 12, 1875; L. A. Johnson to Benjamin Tureaud Jr., October 3, 1875; J. Ephege LeBlanc to Benjamin Tureaud Jr., December 21, 1875, Benjamin Tureaud Papers, LSU.

65. B[enjamin] T[ureaud] to [Benjamin Tureaud Jr.], January 18, 1876; Ben Tureaud per A. Lindsy to the steamer *Governor Allen*, January 7, 1876, Benjamin Tureaud Papers, LSU; *NILSB*, January 13, 1876, July 13, 27, 1871; Barbara Jeanne Fields, *Slavery and Freedom on the Middle Ground: Maryland during the Nineteenth Century* (New Haven: Yale University Press, 1985), 192–93.

66. C. M. Gillis to Edward J. Gay, January 14, 1874; Roman Daigre to Edward J. Gay, January 1, 14, 1874, EJGP, LSU; *Donaldsonville Chief*, January 27, March 3 (quoting *New Orleans Price-Current*), 10 (quoting *WBRSP*), September 8, October 20, 27, 1877; *Lucy Le Meschacébé*, September 1, 1877.

67. L. Bouchereau, *Statement of the Sugar and Rice Crops Made in Louisiana in 1874–75* (New Orleans: Pelican and Job Printing Office, 1875), vi; [Alexandre DeClouet], "Address to the White Citizens of St. Martin," [1874], Alexandre E. DeClouet and Family Papers, LSU; *NILSB*, July 16, August 6, August 27 (quoting Franklin *Enterprise*), 1874; *Lucy Le Meschacébé*, May 8, 1875.

68. *NILSB*, July 31, 1873, August 6, 1874; Louisiana Immigration and Homestead Company, *Address to the People of Louisiana* (New Orleans: A. W. Hyatt, 1873), 10.

69. Rodrigue, *Reconstruction in the Cane Fields*, 74–76; "Salt River" to Editor, *NILSB*, December 24, 1874; L. Bouchereau, *Statement of the Sugar and Rice Crops Made in Louisiana in 1873–74* (New Orleans: Pelican Book and Job Printing Office, 1874), x–xi; *NILSB*, June 28, 1877. On the complex transition to family-based sharecropping in the cotton South, see Jaynes, *Branches without Roots*, 224–49.

70. R. McCall to Edward J. Gay, December 28, 1873; Roman Daigre to Edward J. Gay, January 14, 1874, EJGP, LSU; *NILSB*, April 5, 1877.

71. *NILSB*, May 17, July 26, November 1, 1877; *Donaldsonville Chief*, June 23 (quoting *New Orleans Times*), 30, July 7 (quoting *Attakapas Register*), October 20, 1877; *Lucy*

Le Meschacébé, August 25, 1877; Wm. Bogel, President La. Board of Immigration, and W. P. Freret, Secretary, to the People of Louisiana, July 20, 1877, Colonel W. W. Pugh and Family Papers, LSU; J. Carlyle Sitterson, *Sugar Country: The Cane Sugar Industry in the South, 1753–1950* (Lexington: University of Kentucky Press, 1953), 258–62; Mark Schmitz, "The Transformation of the Southern Cane Sugar Sector, 1860–1930," *Agricultural History* 53, no. 1 (January 1979): 275–80; Scott, "Defining the Boundaries of Freedom," 77–78.

72. Nell Irvin Painter, *Exodusters: Black Migration to Kansas after Reconstruction* (New York: Alfred A. Knopf, 1977); *NILSB*, May 15, 1879; A. Bouchereau, *Statement of the Sugar and Rice Crops, Made in Louisiana, in 1878–79* (New Orleans: Pelican Steam Book and Job Printing Office, 1879), xvi; R. E. Conner to L. P. Conner, July 1, 29, 1879, Lemuel P. Conner Family Papers, LSU.

73. "A Great Opportunity," *DR*, after the war ser., 5 (April 1868): 420–23 (excerpting *New Orleans Republican*); *Donaldsonville Chief*, October 17, 1874.

74. A. Bouchereau, *Statement of the Sugar and Rice Crops, Made in Louisiana, in 1877–78* (New Orleans: Pelican Book and Job Printing Office, 1878), xx; A. Bouchereau, *Statement of the Sugar and Rice Crops Made in Louisiana in 1881–82* (New Orleans: L. Graham and Son, 1882), xlviii–xlix. On the reorganization of the LSPA, see John Alfred Heitmann, *The Modernization of the Louisiana Sugar Industry, 1830–1910* (Baton Rouge: Louisiana State University Press, 1987), 71–97.

75. *Donaldsonville Chief*, May 27, 1882; *NILSB*, July 13, 27, 1871, January 30, 1879. The Tureauds, for example, continued to employ Chinese laborers into the 1880s ("Brûlé Time Book, 1880–1881," Manuscript vol. 87; "Pay Roll Book, 1881–1882," Benjamin Tureaud Papers, LSU). There were enough Chinese in or near Donaldsonville to support a "little eating-house" as late as 1884 (*Donaldsonville Chief*, November 15, 1884).

76. *Donaldsonville Chief*, December 15, 1877, October 25, November 1, 8, 22, December 27, 1884.

77. *Plessy v. Ferguson*, 163 U.S. 537 (1896).

Conclusion

1. W. E. B. Du Bois, *Black Reconstruction in America* (1935; reprint, New York: Atheneum, 1992), 708, 240, 130, 16 (including the epigraph). The other epigraphs are from *Harper's Weekly*, October 25, 1862; "An Address at the Chicago Peace Jubilee," October 18, 1898, in Stuart B. Kaufman et al., eds., *The Samuel Gompers Papers*, vol. 5, *An Expanding Movement at the Turn of the Century, 1898–1902* (Urbana: University of Illinois Press, 1996), 28.

2. Michael Salman, *The Embarrassment of Slavery: Controversies over Bondage and Nationalism in the American Colonial Philippines* (Berkeley and Los Angeles: University of California Press, 2001).

A Note on Primary Sources

This brief essay may help direct researchers to the richest primary sources used in researching this book. Most sources I examined held fragmentary references to coolies; piecing them together in relation to their surrounding materials cumulatively shaped my interpretations, even if all too many stories failed to make it into the final product. I make no attempt to list all of these sources here but restrict my discussion to those that yielded the greatest results. Readers seeking a more comprehensive listing of primary and secondary sources should consult the endnotes and the preliminary and much longer version of this study ("'Coolies' and Cane: Race, Labor, and Sugar Production in Louisiana, 1852–1877," Ph.D. diss., Cornell University, 2000).

The published and unpublished records of the federal government led me to probe the depths to which coolies permeated and influenced U.S. political discourse in the nineteenth century. The incorporation of the coolie trade in the antislavery campaign is chronicled in a series of reports mandated by the Senate and the House of Representatives, as in President Franklin Pierce's 1856 submission "in regard to the Slave and Coolie Trade" (34th Congress, 1st Session, House Executive Document 105). The diplomatic correspondence copiously included in these reports (see chap. 1 notes for specific citations) proved crucial in tracing how U.S. politics imported notions of coolies. Letters by U.S. consuls in China and Cuba and by federal officials in Washington, D.C., and Louisiana (Record Groups 36, 56, 59, and 60, National Archives) convey their frustrating attempts to define and outlaw coolies. Congressional debates over naturalization and Chinese exclusion (*Congressional Globe*, *Congressional Record*) do the same and highlight the need to interpret both within the context of Reconstruction, something few scholars have done to date. Though largely absent from this book's final narrative and notes, I learned much about the social landscape that Chinese workers entered through the Records of the Bureau of Refugees, Freedmen, and Abandoned Lands (Record Group 105, National Archives). Fortunately, the *Freedom* documentary volumes produced by the Freedmen and Southern Society Project, University of Maryland, College Park, and published by Cambridge University Press provide smart and easy access to many of these documents.

I spent more time poring through microfilmed newspapers and periodicals than I care to remember, but those hours delivered some of the most exciting discoveries. Coolies appeared in almost every antebellum periodical concerned with slavery, abolition, or Asia; the range and intensity of articles and editorials in *De Bow's Review*, *Harper's Weekly*, the *Liberator*, *Littell's Living Age*, the *New York Times*, and the *Southern Cultivator* are especially informative. The *New Orleans Daily Picayune* and the *New Orleans Times* devoted considerable attention to the movement for coolies after the Civil War, as did the *Memphis Daily Appeal* in 1869 and several rural Louisiana newspapers in the 1860s and 1870s. Henry J. Hyams's *West Baton Rouge Sugar Planter* and Daniel Dennett's *Franklin Planters'*

Banner (published as the *New Iberia Planters' Banner and Times* and the *New Iberia Planters' Banner* in 1871–72) came to share a passion for white immigrants and small farms that led them to rant against coolies and large planters who would employ them. Similar opinions can be found in the postbellum issues of *De Bow's Review*. The *New Iberia Louisiana Sugar-Bowl's* extensive surveys of the sugar-producing region leave no doubt that Louisiana planters employed many working peoples under multiple labor arrangements, even as its editor, J. Y. Gilmore, championed white immigrants and "redemption" as fervently as Dennett and Hyams. The coverage of local Chinese workers, sugar production, and political battles in the *Louisiana Sugar-Bowl* and the *Donaldsonville Chief*, a Republican newspaper, proved extremely useful in explaining why so many planters became disenchanted with coolies and how Republican rule came to an end in a region with a black majority.

Contemporary books and pamphlets also addressed coolies in myriad ways. Among the many eyewitness accounts of coolie labor in the Caribbean (and around the world), Edward Jenkins, *The Coolie: His Rights and Wrongs* (New York: George Routledge and Sons, 1871) and William G. Sewell, *The Ordeal of Free Labor in the British West Indies*, 2d ed. (1861; reprint, New York: Augustus M. Kelley, 1968) clearly reflect the contradictory views of liberal reformers. Eliza McHatton-Ripley, *From Flag to Flag: A Woman's Adventures and Experiences in the South during the War, in Mexico, and in Cuba* (New York: D. Appleton and Company, 1889), and *The Cuba Commission Report: A Hidden History of the Chinese in Cuba: The Original English-Language Text of 1876* (Baltimore: Johns Hopkins University Press, 1993) offer intriguing introductions to developments in Cuba, the former by a Confederate exile from Louisiana and the latter by Chinese workers. Louis Bouchereau's annual statements on Louisiana's sugar and rice crops (see the notes for full citations) contain records of individual plantations and commentary on sugar production and consumption, and race and labor. In addition to Bouchereau, the contrasting and overlapping logics behind white immigration can be found in: J. C. Kathman, *Information for Immigrants into the State of Louisiana* (New Orleans: Republican Office, 1868); James O. Noyes, *Report of the Bureau of Immigration to the General Assembly of Louisiana* (New Orleans: A. L. Lee, State Printer, 1869); Louisiana Immigration and Homestead Company, *Address to the People of Louisiana* (New Orleans: A. W. Hyatt, 1873); and Daniel Dennett, *Louisiana as It Is* (New Orleans: Eureka Press, 1876).

Among the almost one hundred manuscript collections I researched over the years, I found a handful indispensable in understanding the roots and effects of planters' demands for coolies. Though intimidating in their sheer scope and volume, the Edward J. Gay and Family Papers at Louisiana State University capture in vivid detail the intense struggles between and among planters, merchants, and workers (black, white, and Chinese). Gay, it seems, kept almost every document he received, leaving behind unparalleled sources on the changing dynamics of sugar production in Louisiana. Personal letters and payroll records of his family's efforts to recruit new sets of migrant workers in the 1860s and 1870s—from the Upper South, the Midwest, and California—are particularly instructive in deciphering their convergent and divergent origins and objectives. In contrast to Chinese workers' brief stay on the Gay plantations, the wage lists and time books in the Benjamin Tureaud Papers (also at LSU) document the persistent and evolving Chinese presence on Louisiana's plantations. In addition to these collections, the intricacies of recruiting and employing Chinese workers are revealed readily in the James Amédée Gaudet Papers and the George Washington Gift Papers at the University of North Carolina, Chapel Hill, and the Leverich Papers at the New-York Historical Society.

Index

Page numbers followed by f refer to figures; page numbers followed by m refer to maps.